Gakken

TOEICテスト 600点攻略 リーディング 5回模試

TOEIC is a registered trademark of Educational Testing Service(ETS).
This publication is not endorsed or approved by ETS.

はじめに

TOEIC テストの『模試本』選び，皆さんは間違っていませんか。

　ある程度のスコアがあれば『公式問題集』にトライするのがベターです。ですが，スコア 600 を目指そうという場合，『公式問題集』は少々難しいですし，市販の『模試本』は論外。難問・奇問が多く，ハイレベルが前提となっているからです。ならば，『公式問題集』より先にトライする，はじめての『模試本』があってもいいはずです。

　本書は，そのような要望を受けて作られた TOEIC テスト『模試本』です。はじめて模試にトライする読者を想定し，標準的な良問のみで問題を構成しました。ここにはネイティブも間違う難問や，TOEIC のハイスコアホルダーをうならせる奇問は存在しません。取りこぼし厳禁の頻出問題に触れて，「解く」感覚を養い，「解ける」喜びを体感して下さい。きっと，スコアがアップするはずです。この『模試本』をクリアして，次は『公式問題集』！すると，どれが難問かはっきりと見えてくるはずです。

　まずは，本書をトライして下さい。5回の模試はすべて同じレベルの良問です。そして「テクニック解説」を復習すれば，スコアが急上昇するはずです。スコア 600 超えを目指して，最初の一歩ですね。

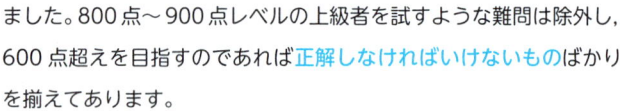
塚田　幸光

　実際の TOEIC テストには難易度の低い問題から高い問題までが混在しています。1問，1問難しさが違うのです。TOEIC 受験者がよく犯す間違いに，難問ばかりに気を取られ，易しいレベルの問題をポロポロ落としてしまう点があげられます。これは絶対やってはいけない致命的なミスです。このミスを繰り返す限り安定的にスコアは上がっていきません。易しめの問題を取りこぼさず確実に正解していく。これこそがスコアアップへの最短距離です。

　そこで，本書では近年の傾向を反映した 400 点〜 700 点レベルまでの比較的難易度の低い良問ばかりを厳選し，リスニング・リーディングそれぞれを別冊で5セットにまとめあげ

ました。800 点〜 900 点レベルの上級者を試すような難問は除外し，600 点超えを目指すのであれば正解しなければいけないものばかりを揃えてあります。

　まずはこの模試を使って，難易度の低い問題がちゃんと正解できているかどうか確認してください。できない問題を洗い出し，間違えないようになってから，他の模試に進むと効果的です。

　本書を『公式問題集』や市販の模試をやる前の最初の一冊として利用していただければ嬉しく思います。

高橋　基治

もくじ　READING TEST

本冊 解答と解説

はじめに……………………………………………… 2
本書について………………………………………… 4
本書の使い方………………………………………… 6
無料ダウンロードの音声について………………… 8
TOEIC® テストとは ………………………………… 9
スコア換算表………………………………………… 10

模試1 解答と解説 ………………………………… 11

模試2 解答と解説 ………………………………… 67

模試3 解答と解説 ………………………………… 119

模試4 解答と解説 ………………………………… 173

模試5 解答と解説 ………………………………… 229

解答一覧……………………………………………… 282

巻末ふろく

押さえておきたい！ TOEIC頻出　単語&フレーズ ……… 285

別冊 テスト

模試1 …………………………………………………… 2
模試2 …………………………………………………… 34
模試3 …………………………………………………… 66
模試4 …………………………………………………… 98
模試5 …………………………………………………… 130

アンサーシート……………………………………… 163

本書について

■ TOEIC スコア 600 点は,「使える英語の入り口」です!

　多くの企業が,新入社員に期待するスコアは 600 点前後といわれています。就職・転職時に英語力をアピールするために,頑張って獲得しておきたいスコアの目安が 600 点なのです。したがって TOEIC テストを受験する人の多くが,最初のスタートとして目指すスコアが 600 点なのでしょう。

■ いきなり「本番レベルの模試」で挫折する人が続出!

　TOEIC テストは時間との勝負です。スコアアップするには,模試を使ってテスト形式に慣れ,本番と同じように時間を計って勉強することが有効なのは言うまでもありません。

　しかし,TOEIC のスコアが現在 600 点に到達していない方が,いきなり本番と同じレベルの模試を解いてもよい効果は得られません。目標のスコアに到達できないばかりか,どこから手をつければよいかわからず,「TOEIC は難しすぎる…」と勉強自体をあきらめてしまう方も多くいます。

■ 簡単な問題を確実に解けば, 600 点を取れる!

　TOEIC テストは英検のように 1 級,準 1 級,2 級,準 2 級…などとレベルに合わせて試験が分かれていません。そのため TOEIC では,受験者のレベルを計るために 1 回のテストの中で様々な難易度の問題が出題されています。

　以下のように難易度をレベル A,B,C と 3 つに分けると,出題される問題の約 60% はレベル C（400 ～ 600 点レベル）で構成されています。

TOEIC テスト ｛ レベル A　難易度の高い問題　　（800 ～ 900 点以上のレベル）　約 30%
　　　　　　　　レベル B　難易度中程度の問題　（600 ～ 700 点レベル）　　　　　約 10%
　　　　　　　　レベル C　難易度の低い問題　　（400 ～ 600 点レベル）　　　　　約 60%

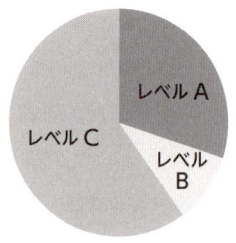

　もし,あなたが TOEIC テストで 600 点を目指すのなら,難易度の高いレベル A の問題をすべて間違えても構いません。確実にレベル C の問題を正解しさえすればよいのです。レベル C の問題に的を絞って,集中的に基礎的な問題を学習することが,スコアアップするための近道なのです。

600点を目指しているあなたがレベルAの問題に時間をかけすぎてしまうと，レベルB，Cの問題を解く実力がつかないまま本番を迎え，残念な結果を迎えることになりかねません。繰り返しますが，TOEICで多く出題されるのは，レベルCの問題です！　ここをまずしっかり解けるようにしてから，次のステップに進みましょう。

　まずやるべきことはあなたのレベルと目標にあわせた問題を使って勉強すること。そうした方が，圧倒的に効率よくスコアが上がります。これが，本番と同じレベルの模試をいきなり解かない方がよい理由です。

■ 難問を排除した模試こそがスコアアップの近道

　しかし，世間に出回っている模試の多くは，本番と同じレベルか，本番よりも高いレベルで作られています。そういった模試本で勉強しては600点（〜700点）を目指す人たちがなかなか目標を達成できない…，この現状をなんとかしたい！　そんな想いで，本書は企画されました。

　本書には，レベルB,C（400点〜700点レベル）の良問ばかりを厳選した模試を掲載しています。

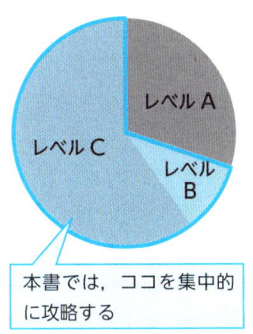

　出題パターンも本番にあわせて作成しているので，この「600点攻略模試」を繰り返し解いて正解できるようになれば，あなたが目標とする600点（〜700点）を超えることができるでしょう。

　この「600点攻略模試」は，TOEICを長年にわたって研究されてきた高橋基治先生と塚田幸光先生に最新のTOEICテストの傾向を加味して精査，加筆していただきました。編集部でも何度も何度も修正を加え，TOEICテストに頻出のレベルB，Cの問題ばかりを徹底的に絞り込んで制作しました。難問を排除した5セット＝500問の600点攻略模試を解いていく中で，出題パターンが自然に身につき，あなたの必要とする実力がつくように設計されています。ぜひ全問正解を目指して取り組んでみてください。

　　さあ，600点攻略の第一歩です！　本書を使って学習を始めましょう。

本書の使い方

　本書は，TOEICテストのリーディングセクションと同形式で，スコア600点を目標とした問題のみで構成したリーディング模試5回分500問と，付録の「押さえておきたい！TOEIC頻出　単語＆フレーズ」から成っています。模試（テスト問題）は別冊に，解答と解説，訳，そして付録は本冊に含まれています。

　　本冊　　解答と解説・訳
　　　　　　付録の「押さえておきたい！　TOEIC頻出　単語＆フレーズ」
　　別冊　　模試1〜模試5
　　　　　　アンサーシート

　本書は，別冊にリーディングセクションの模試5回分を収録しています。模試を使った学習の最大の目的は，テストの形式に慣れることです。実際のリーディングテストと同じように約75分間で取り組んでください。アンサーシートは，別冊の巻末にありますので，本番さながらにマークをしていきましょう。

別冊　模試の内容

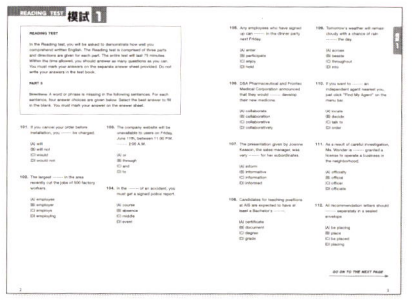 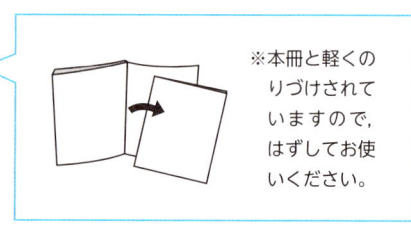

※本冊と軽くのりづけされていますので，はずしてお使いください。

　TOEICテストのリーディングセクションと同じに，100問の模試が5セット，別冊の冊子に掲載されています。
　解答用紙（アンサーシート）は，別冊の巻末にあります。切り離してお使いください。

本冊 解答と解説の内容

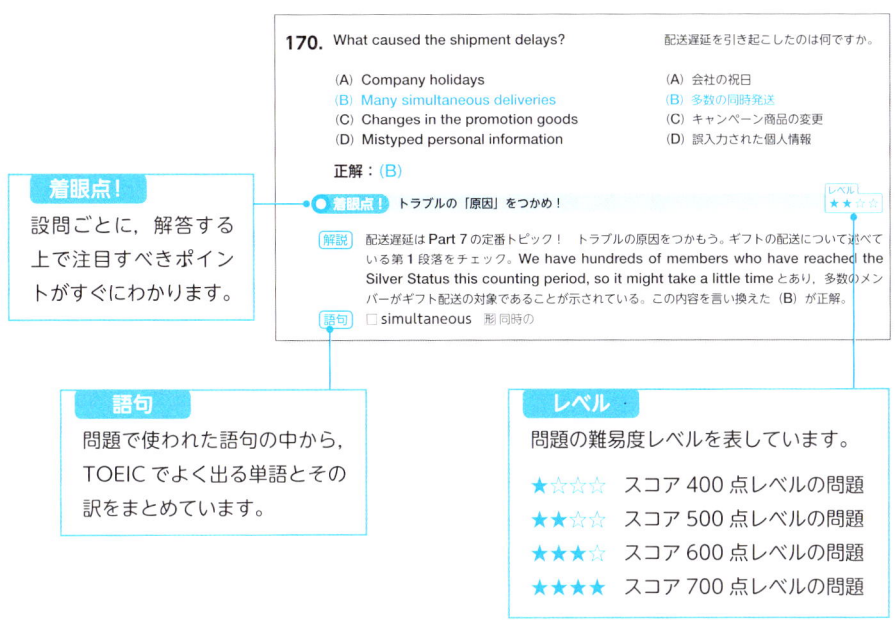

模試を解き終わったら，本冊の解答・解説で答え合わせをしましょう。解説には，問題を解く攻略法や，基本的な文法解説，正答にたどりつく根拠となる部分はもちろん，誤答を避けるために学習しておきたい項目も含まれています。

本書の模試は，4ページ「本書について」で説明をした通り，レベルB, C（400点〜700点レベル）の問題に的を絞って作成しています。それぞれの問題には「難易度マーク」がついています。★マークで表している難易度レベルを参考にして学習を進めてください（この難易度レベルは目安です）。

600点攻略をするには，★1つ〜★3つの問題を間違えないようにすることを目標にしましょう。間違えた場合は，必ず解説を読み込んで理解できるようにするのが大切です。理解できたら，解説部分をかくして，自分の言葉で問題を解説できるようにしてください。自分の言葉で説明ができるようになれば，同じような問題に出会ったときには必ず正解が出せるようになります。

無料ダウンロードの音声について

　リーディングパートでも，音声を確認しながら学習することができるように，「TOEIC テスト　600点攻略　リーディング　5回模試」の模試1〜模試5のPART 5の音声ファイルをご用意しています。

　下記のURLにアクセスすると，本書のPART 5をアメリカ発音の音声で録音しているMP3形式のファイルを無料でダウンロードすることができます。

http://webgk.gakken.jp/toeic/

　これらの音声は，MP3プレーヤーや，MP3再生ソフトがインストールされたパソコンで再生してお聞きください。

　模試ごとのPART 5の音声が，ひとかたまりでMP3音源の音声ファイルになっています。リーディング力と同時にリスニング力にもお役立ていただけます。

　　　　　　　　　　　※お客様のインターネット環境によってダウンロードができない場合，当社では責任を負いかねます。ご理解ご了承いただきますよう，お願いいたします。

PART 5の音声ファイルの聞き方

　パソコンの音楽再生ソフトに取り込みます。音声ソフトには，iTunes (Mac／Windows)，Windows Media Player (Windows) などがあります。

　この音声は，パソコンの音楽再生ソフトを使用して，再生し音声をお聞きください。

　また，パソコンを使って音声を聞く以外にも，音楽ファイル(MP3)を携帯音楽プレイヤーに取り込んで再生し，音声を聞くことができます（各携帯音楽プレイヤーへの音声ファイルの取り込み方は，その機器の説明書などでご確認ください）。

TOEIC® テストとは

概　略

　TOEIC（Test of English for International Communication）とは，英語のコミュニケーション能力を評価するための世界共通のテストです。TOEIC テストを開発した ETS(Educational Testing Service) は，世界最大の教育機関で，米国における公共テストの大半を開発・製作し，実施しています。日本における TOEIC テストの実施・運営は一般財団法人国際ビジネスコミュニケーション協会 TOEIC 運営委員会が行っています。

試験内容

　TOEIC は，リスニングとリーディングの 2 つのセクションに分かれており，問題構成は以下のようになっています。

リスニングセクション	100 問　45 分
Part 1　写真描写問題	10 問
Part 2　応答問題	30 問
Part 3　会話問題	30 問
Part 4　説明文問題	30 問

リーディングセクション	100 問　75 分
Part 5　短文穴埋め問題	40 問
Part 6　長文穴埋め問題	12 問
Part 7　読解問題（1 つの文書）	28 問
読解問題（2 つの文書）	20 問

公開テスト実施時期

　公開テストは，原則として年 10 回（1 月，3 月，4 月，5 月，6 月，7 月，9 月，10 月，11 月，12 月）実施されています（受験地ごとに実施時期が異なる場合があるので，事前に確認が必要です）。

受験料

　受験料は，5,725 円（税込み）です（2014 年 12 月現在）。

成績とスコア

　評価は合否ではなく，スコアで算出されます。正答数を，リスニングセクション 5 ～ 495 点，リーディングセクション 5 ～ 495 点に換算し，トータルの最低点は 10 点，最高点は 990 点となり，5 点刻みで表示されます。

テスト結果の通知

　受験者には試験終了後 30 日以内に，自分のテスト結果が，Official Score Certificate（公式認定証）として送られます。

申し込み方法

　TOEIC 公開テストは，インターネット，コンビニエンスストアの店頭などで申し込むことができます。20 歳未満の方は，保護者の同意が必要となります。より詳しい説明や最新情報などは，TOEIC テスト公式ホームページでご確認ください。

　URL：http://www.toeic.or.jp

スコア換算表

　模試の正解数から，実際の TOEIC テストの参考スコアを予測します。各模試の採点を行い，正解した問題数を数えます。下の参考スコア換算表で，正解した問題数の右に書かれている予想スコアを確認しましょう。

※このスコア換算表は，600 点攻略を目指した本模試のために作成されたものです。実際の TOEIC 公開テストのスコア算出法とは異なるため，予想スコアは目安としてお考えください。

READING TEST

正解した問題数	予想スコア
96 〜 100	380 点以上
91 〜 95	350 〜 380
86 〜 90	330 〜 360
81 〜 85	300 〜 350
76 〜 80	280 〜 325
71 〜 75	250 〜 300
66 〜 70	225 〜 260
61 〜 65	200 〜 230
56 〜 60	170 〜 210
51 〜 55	150 〜 180
46 〜 50	125 〜 160
41 〜 45	100 〜 150
36 〜 40	70 〜 100
31 〜 35	50 〜 75
26 〜 30	40 〜 60
21 〜 25	30 〜 50
11 〜 20	20 〜 35
1 〜 10	5 〜 20

READING TEST
模試 1
解答と解説

- 問題は，別冊の 2 ～ 33 ページに掲載されています。

模試 1 解答と解説

PART 5

101. If you cancel your order before installation, you ------- be charged.
(A) will
(B) will not
(C) would
(D) would not

インストール前に注文を取り消す場合には、料金はかかりません。

正解：(B)

● 着眼点！ 主語と時制に着目せよ！

解説　if で始まる通常の条件文なので、主節の時制は現在形または will/will not となる。「インストール前の取り消しなら」という条件で、後ろに続く動詞が be charged「課金される、料金がかかる」なので、文意から (B) will not が適切である。

語句　□ installation 名 インストール、据え付け

---

102. The largest ------- in the area recently cut the jobs of 500 factory workers.
(A) employee
(B) employer
(C) employs
(D) employing

その地域で最大の雇用主が、最近、500人の工場労働者の職を削減しました。

正解：(B)

● 着眼点！ 空所の前後から品詞を決定せよ！

解説　形容詞の最上級 The largest と in the area に挟まれているので、空所に入るのは名詞。cut the jobs が動詞なので、主語になるのは (A)「従業員」ではなく (B)「雇用主」。

語句　□ cut 動 ～を縮小する、切り詰める

---

103. The company website will be unavailable to users on Friday, June 11th, between 11:00 P.M. ------- 2:00 A.M.
(A) or
(B) through
(C) and
(D) to

会社のウェブサイトは、6月11日金曜日の午後11時から午前2時までの間、ユーザーが利用できなくなります。

正解：(C)

● 着眼点！ 時間帯を表す表現を整理せよ！

解説　時間帯を表す between A and B「AとBの間に」が適切。よって、(C) が正解。他にも、from A to B, from A through B「AからBまで」という表現も、時間帯を表す場合があるので押さえておこう。(A) 接続詞「～または～」、(B) 前置詞「～を通り抜けて」、(C) 接続詞「～および～」、(D) 前置詞「～の方へ」の意味。

---

104. In the ------- of an accident, you must get a signed police report.
(A) course
(B) absence
(C) middle
(D) event

事故の場合には、署名のある警察の報告書を入手しなければなりません。

正解：(D)

| 着眼点！| イディオムに精通せよ！

| 解説 | 選択肢に並ぶ名詞はいずれも in the +名詞+ of という形で使われるもの。それぞれのイディオムの意味をきちんと理解していることが正解を導くカギ。(A) in the course of ~「~の過程で」, (B) in the absence of ~「~がない（いない）場合には」, (C) in the middle of ~「~の真ん中に, ~の途中で」, (D) in the event of ~「~の場合には」。したがって, ここでは (D) が適切。

| 語句 | □ sign 動 ~に署名する

105. Any employees who have signed up can ------- in the dinner party next Friday.
　(A) enter　　　　　(B) participate
　(C) enjoy　　　　　(D) hold

申し込みをした従業員はだれでも, 次の金曜日の晩餐会に参加できます。

正解：(B)

| 着眼点！| イディオムの知識でしっかり得点せよ！

| 解説 | 動詞を選択する問題。空所直後の in に注目。participate in ~「~に参加する」という意味を表す語句がポイント。(B) が適切。イディオムを素早く見つけて判断しよう。(B) 以外の選択肢はすべて他動詞である点もポイント。(A)「~に入る」, (B)「参加する」, (C)「~を楽しむ」, (D)「~を催す」の意味。

106. DSA Pharmaceutical and Frontec Medical Corporation announced that they would ------- develop their new medicine.
　(A) collaborate　　　(B) collaboration
　(C) collaborative　　(D) collaboratively

DSA Pharmaceutical 社と Frontec Medical 社は, 新薬を協力して開発することを発表しました。

正解：(D)

| 着眼点！| 品詞問題はまず空所前後を確認せよ！

| 解説 | 空所の直前にある would から, (A) を選択するのは間違い。空所の直後に動詞 develop があることに気をつける。助動詞の後ろ, 動詞の前に位置するのは (D) の副詞 collaboratively が適切である。(A) 動詞「協力する」, (B) 名詞「協力」, (C) 形容詞「協同の」, (D) 副詞「協力して」。

| 語句 | □ pharmaceutical 形 製薬の, 薬学の

107. The presentation given by Joanne Keason, the sales manager, was very ------- for her subordinates.
　(A) inform　　　　　(B) informative
　(C) information　　　(D) informed

営業部長の Joanne Keason が行ったプレゼンテーションは, 彼女の部下にとって非常にためになりました。

正解：(B)

| 着眼点！| 消去法で考えよ！

| 解説 | 品詞を選ぶ問題。この文の補語に当たる語が空所になって問われている。補語には形容詞か名詞が入るので, 消去法で考えよう。選択肢 (A) は動詞なので除外。次に, 文全体に注目する。プレゼンテーションが彼女の部下にとって「どうだったか」を表す語が, 空所に入る。(B) と (D) が形容詞だが, この中では, (B) informative が適切。(A) 動詞「~に知らせる」, (B) 形容詞「知識を提供する, 有益な」, (C) 名詞「情報」, (D) 形容詞「情報に通じている」。

| 語句 | □ subordinate 名 部下

108. Candidates for teaching positions at AIS are expected to have at least a Bachelor's -------.
 (A) certificate (B) document
 (C) degree (D) grade

AISの教職志望者は，少なくとも学士号を取得していることが期待されています。

正解：(C)

● 着眼点！ 頻出語彙を押さえておこう！

解説 Bachelor's degree「学士号」という言葉を知っているかどうかがポイント。正解の (C) degree は「学位」という意味。履歴書などでは頻出単語。Master's degree「修士号」，Doctor's degree「博士号」もあわせて確認しておこう。degree にはこの他に，「程度，度合い，（温度計・経度・緯度などの）度」という意味もある。(D) の grade にも「度合い」の意味があるので，混同しないよう注意。選択肢はすべて名詞で，(A)「証明書」，(B)「書類」，(D)「等級，度合い」の意味。

語句 □ candidate 名 志願者，候補者　□ position 名 職，勤め口

109. Tomorrow's weather will remain cloudy with a chance of rain ------- the day.
 (A) across (B) beside
 (C) throughout (D) into

明日の天気はくもりのまま，一日中雨が降る恐れがあります。

正解：(C)

● 着眼点！ 相性のよい前置詞を選べ！

解説 空所前後をまず確認。空所は後ろの the day と結びつくと判断し，適切な前置詞を選ぶ。正解は (C) throughout。(A)「～を横切って」，(B)「～のそばに」，(C)「～中ずっと」，(D)「～の中へ」。基本となる前置詞の意味を確認しておこう。

語句 □ a chance of ～　～の可能性

110. If you want to ------- an independent agent nearest you, just click "Find My Agent" on the menu bar.
 (A) locate (B) decide
 (C) talk to (D) order

あなたのお住まいに最も近い独立代理店をお探しでしたら，メニューバーの「Find My Agent」をクリックしてください。

正解：(A)

● 着眼点！ 用例とあわせて単語を覚えよ！

解説 適切な動詞を選ぶ問題。文の後半でメニューバーをクリックするよう指示しているので，この部分に適切につながるように空所の動詞を選びたい。正解は (A)。locate は受動態 be located の形などで「位置する」の意味で使われるほか，「～を捜し出す」の意味でもよく用いられる。このことを知っていると解答がよりすばやくできる。用例とあわせて覚えよう。(A)「位置する，（場所などを）見つける」，(B)「決心する」，(C)「～に話しかける」，(D)「～に命令する，～を注文する」。

語句 □ independent 形 独立した　□ agent 名 代理人，代理店

111. As a result of careful investigation, Ms. Wonder is ------- granted a license to operate a business in the neighborhood.
 (A) officially (B) official
 (C) officer (D) officiate

慎重な調査の結果，その近隣でビジネスを行うためのライセンスが Wonder さんへ公式に与えられました。

正解：(A)

- 着眼点！ 空所に入る語の品詞を特定せよ！
- 解説　派生語の中から適切な品詞を選ぶ問題。空所に単語がないままでも文意が通るため、空所には副詞が入ることがわかる。選択肢の中では、(A) officially のみが副詞である。よって、(A) が正解。(A) 副詞「公式に」、(B) 形容詞「公の」、(C) 名詞「役人，士官」、(D) 動詞「役を務める」。
- 語句　□ grant 動 〜を与える　□ operate 動 〜を経営する

112. All recommendation letters should ------- separately in a sealed envelope.
(A) be placing　　(B) place
(C) be placed　　(D) placing

推薦状はすべて，必ず封印をした封筒に別々に入っているようにしなければなりません。

正解：(C)

- 着眼点！ 受動態を見抜け！
- 解説　動詞の形を問う問題。空所のあとには目的語がない。should の主語は letters なので，「する側」ではなく「される側」である。よって，ここでは受動態の (C) が適切。
- 語句　□ recommendation letter 推薦状　□ seal 動 〜を封印する
□ envelope 名 封筒

113. The typhoon affected ------- 2 million people in China, with about 900,000 of them evacuated from their homes.
(A) as much　　(B) mostly
(C) more than　　(D) better than

中国では，台風が 200 万人あまりの人々に影響を及ぼし，このうちおよそ 90 万人が自宅を離れて避難しました。

正解：(C)

- 着眼点！ 適切な比較級を選べ！
- 解説　適切な比較表現を選ぶ問題。空所後の 2 million people を適切に修飾するのは (C)。(A) as much「ちょうどそれだけ，等しく」は，最後にもうひとつ as を加えて，as much as 〜「〜と同程度の，〜だけの」とすれば，正解になりうる。
- 語句　□ typhoon 名 台風　□ affect 動 〜に影響を及ぼす，作用する
□ evacuate 動 避難する

114. ------- Ms. Chen's performance was indisputably excellent, she didn't get promoted.
(A) However　　(B) Although
(C) With　　(D) Nonetheless

Chen さんの業績は議論の余地なしに素晴らしかったにもかかわらず，彼女は昇進しませんでした。

正解：(B)

- 着眼点！ カンマの前後の文脈を見よ！
- 解説　空所には文と文を結びつけるための接続詞が入る。(C) With は前置詞で，(D) Nonetheless は副詞。(A) However は接続詞として使われることがあるが，カンマの前後の文脈を見て「A だけれども B」という流れを読みとり，(B) Although が正解だと判断する。indisputably は「議論の余地のなく，明白に」という意味の副詞。
- 語句　□ performance 名 業績，実績

115. Because of ------- association with an international banking scandal, Senator Bruno was questioned by concerned authorities.
(A) he (B) him
(C) he's (D) his

国際的な金融スキャンダルと自らの関連性により、Bruno 上院議員は関係当局から事情聴取を受けました。

正解：(D)

着眼点！ 空所の直後の語に注目せよ！

解説 空所の直後に名詞が続くので、それを修飾する語としては、代名詞の所有格の (D) his が適切。文自体は長いが、空所の前後だけで解ける。concerned authorities は「関係当局」という意味。

語句 □ association 名 つながり、関連性　□ scandal 名 スキャンダル、不祥事

116. This new personnel evaluation method may help you assess ------- aspects of your employees' abilities.
(A) divert (B) diversion
(C) diversity (D) diverse

この新しい人事評価方法は、貴社従業員の能力の様々な側面を評価するのに役立つかもしれません。

正解：(D)

着眼点！ 品詞をピンポイントで捉えよ！

解説 正しい品詞の単語を選択する問題。空所が名詞 aspects「側面」を修飾していることをつかめば、形容詞 (D) が入るとわかる。よって、diverse が正解。(B) と (C) はともに名詞であるが、意味の違いに注意。(A) 動詞「～をそらす、転換する」、(B) 名詞「転換」、(C) 名詞「多様性」、(D) 形容詞「多様性な、異なった」。

語句 □ personnel evaluation 人事評価　□ assess 動 ～を評価する

117. ------- you have any questions or comments about our products, please feel free to contact us anytime.
(A) Should (B) Will
(C) May (D) Must

当社の製品についてご質問やご意見がございましたら、いつでもお気軽に私どもまでご連絡ください。

正解：(A)

着眼点！ 定型表現をマスターせよ！

解説 適切な助動詞を選ぶ問題。正解の (A) Should は、Should A do ..., の形で「もし～でしたら」の意味を表す。if が省略された倒置文と考えられる。Should you have any questions or comments ... は、メールなどの応答でよく用いられる表現なのでこのまま覚えておこう。

118. A group of volunteers founded an NPO to support the unemployed and provide them with the ------- to live.
(A) income (B) means
(C) wage (D) talent

有志のグループが失業者を支援し、彼らに生活手段を提供するための NPO を設立しました。

正解：(B)

● **着眼点！** 表現の貯金が多いほどスピードアップ！ レベル ★★★☆

解説 空所は，provide A with B「AにBを提供する」という定型表現のBに相当する。選択肢は一見，どれも生活の何かを提供するために必要なもののように見えるが，to live と結びついて意味をなす語を見極めるのがポイント。means to live で「生活手段」の意味。よって，正解は (B)。(A)「所得」，(B)「手段，方法」，(C)「賃金」，(D)「才能，人材」。

語句
☐ volunteer 名 有志，ボランティア
☐ NPO 非営利団体（= nonprofit organization）

---

119. The Service Center is ------- for dealing with all inquiries and complaints from our customers.
(A) responsive　　(B) responsibility
(C) response　　(D) responsible

サービスセンターは，当社のお客様からのすべての照会や苦情に対応する責任を負っています。

正解：(D)

● **着眼点！** イディオムを攻略せよ！ レベル ★☆☆☆

解説 よく似た単語とそれぞれの派生語から選択する問題。ここは be responsible for ～「～について責任がある」にすばやく気づくと解答が早い。(D) が正解。(A) 形容詞「すぐに反応する，反応のよい」，(B) 名詞「責任，責務」，(C) 名詞「返答，応答，反応」，(D) 形容詞「責任のある」。

語句
☐ deal with ～　～を処理する，～に対応する　☐ inquiry 名 照会
☐ complaint 名 苦情　☐ customer 名 顧客

---

120. Because of an accident in the factory, TM Imports will not ------- new orders until further notice.
(A) processed　　(B) be processing
(C) be processed　　(D) processing

工場での事故が原因で，TM Imports 社は追って通知があるまでは新たな注文を処理できないことになるでしょう。

正解：(B)

● **着眼点！** 全体を読むな！ レベル ★☆☆☆

解説 動詞の形を選ぶ問題なので，文全体を読まず，空所前後の限られた範囲だけを見て解く。空所には，前にある助動詞 will + not に続くものが入る。よって，正解は (B) か (C) に絞り込まれる。次に，process という動詞と new orders という名詞句の関係を考えると，new orders は process の目的語だと考えられるので，受動態の (C) ではなく，目的語をすぐ後ろに取れる未来進行形の (B) が正解。

語句
☐ process orders　注文を処理する
☐ until further notice　追って通知があるまで

121. ------- to the success of their new line of office supplies, Abelco & Cain, Inc. shareholders enjoyed increased third-quarter profits.
(A) In addition　　(B) Such
(C) According　　(D) Due

事務用品の新製品の成功のおかげで，Abelco & Cain 社の株主は第 3 四半期の利益増を享受しました。

正解：(D)

着眼点！ 主文からヒントをつかめ！

解説 空所のあとに to があるので，to を取れない (B) は形の上から不可。カンマ以下の主文から利益増との内容をつかみ，新製品の成功と，利益増との関係を表す語を選ぶ。「～のために」を意味する (D) が正解。(A) in addition to ～で「～に加えてさらに」，(B)「そのような」，(C) according to ～で「～によると」，(D) due to ～ で「～のために」。

語句 □ office supply 事務用品　□ shareholder 名 株主
□ third-quarter 名 第 3 四半期

---

122. Mr. Raymond P. Barlow is best known for his financial ------- to geophysical society.
(A) contribute　　(B) contributed
(C) contribution　　(D) contributing

Raymond P. Barlow さんは，地球物理学会への財政的貢献で最もよく知られています。

正解：(C)

着眼点！ 品詞は前後から決定せよ！

解説 空所の直前が形容詞 financial なので，空所には名詞が入ることがわかる。よって，(C) の名詞 contribution「貢献」が正解。is best known for ～ は「～で最もよく知られている」の意味。

語句 □ financial 形 財政の，財務の，金銭上の　□ geophysical 形 地球物理学の

---

123. I would appreciate your ------- me an updated copy of my account statement.
(A) send　　(B) sending
(C) sold　　(D) being sold

私の口座明細書の最新版を送っていただければ幸いです。

正解：(B)

着眼点！ 所有格のあとは「名詞」か「動名詞」！

解説 send の適切な形を選ぶ問題。直前の語が所有格 your なので，これに続くのは名詞か動名詞。よって，(B) の sending が適切。appreciate は thank のフォーマルな表現で「～を感謝する，ありがたく思う」の意味。

語句 □ update 動 ～を更新する　□ account statement 口座明細書

---

124. The chairman repeatedly emphasized the ------- of market trends in his speech.
(A) signify　　(B) significance
(C) significantly　　(D) significant

会長は講演で，市場動向の重要性について繰り返し強調しました。

正解：(B)

着眼点！ 平易な問題は瞬時に解け！

解説 冠詞 the と前置詞 of の間にくるのは名詞。"the ------- of" の形を見たら，時間をかけずに解答を選択したい。(B) が適切。(A) 動詞「～を意味する，表す」，(B) 名詞「重要性，意味」，(C) 副詞「かなり，著しく，意味ありげに」，(D) 形容詞「重要な，意義深い，意味のある」。

語句 □ emphasize 動 ～を強調する　□ trend 名 傾向，トレンド

125. A world financial leader, Japan relies on oil-rich nations ------- Qatar for petroleum.
(A) even though (B) such as
(C) already (D) still

世界の財政のリーダーである日本は、石油をカタールといった産油国に頼っています。

正解：(B)

レベル ★★☆

● 着眼点！ 単語とイディオムの力は解答時間短縮→高得点へのポイント！

解説　Qatar は oil-rich nations の 1 つの例。したがって、「例えば～など」という意味を表すイディオム（B）such as が適切。oil-rich や petroleum などの時事問題の常連単語がわかっていれば、解答時間を短縮できる。(A)「たとえ～でも」、(B)「例えば～など」、(C)「すでに」、(D)「いまだに」。

語句　□ rely on ～　～に頼る　□ petroleum　名 石油

---

126. The president's speech focused on the fragile state of the economy, and he urged everyone to be ------- to make some sacrifices.
(A) prepared (B) prepare
(C) preparation (D) prepares

大統領の演説は不安定な経済状況に焦点を当てたもので、彼は皆に対し何らかの犠牲を払う覚悟をしておくようにと促しました。

正解：(A)

レベル ★★☆

● 着眼点！ イディオムは一瞬で解く！

解説　動詞の be が直前にあるので、空所には形容詞か名詞がくることがわかる。後ろにも to 不定詞の形があるので、形容詞の（A）prepared が正解。be prepared to ～ で「～する準備ができている、覚悟している」という意味。よく使われるイディオムを素早く解答できれば、ハイスコアへの近道となる。

語句　□ fragile　形 壊れやすい、脆弱な　□ urge　動 ～に促す　□ sacrifice　名 犠牲

---

127. All members should actively take part in the discussion ------- we can improve our proposal before we take it to the competition.
(A) as if (B) even so
(C) through (D) so that

コンペティションにかける前に提案を改善できるよう、全メンバーは議論に積極的に参加しなければなりません。

正解：(D)

レベル ★★★

● 着眼点！ 全文を読んで文意をつかむ！

解説　つなぎの詞句が並んでいる選択肢を見たら、まず全文を読んで文意を理解しよう。空所の前後は、それぞれ文として成立しているので、文をつなぐ語句が入るとわかる。ここから、(B) と (C) は除外できる。文意から（D）が正解。(A)「あたかも～かのように」、(B)「それでも」、(C)「～を通して」、(D)「～するために」。

語句　□ take part in ～　～に参加する　□ competition　名 コンペティション、競技会

128. Tony Eagleton and Juan Dormirado, both high school students in Denmark, were honored last night for their volunteer work ------- behalf of the homeless.
(A) in
(B) on
(C) to
(D) for

どちらもデンマークの高校生である Tony Eagleton と Juan Dormirado は，昨夜，ホームレスの人々のためのボランティア活動で表彰されました。

正解：(B)

● 着眼点！ 頻出イディオム on behalf of は即答せよ！

解説 volunteer work と the homeless をつなぐ意味を持っているのは (B)。on behalf of ～で「～のために」という TOEIC 頻出イディオム。

---

129. In an effort to reduce expenses, Whitman Film Co. has decided to halve its production ------- for the upcoming year.
(A) refunds
(B) costs
(C) rewards
(D) values

経費を減らす試みの一つとして，Whitman Film 社は来るべき年の生産費用を半減させることを決定しました。

正解：(B)

● 着眼点！ 文意から空所の意味を特定せよ！

解説 紛らわしい選択肢が並んでいるときは，文意から空所の意味を特定しよう。ヒントは，文の最初にある「経費を減らす試みのひとつとして」という部分。選択肢の中で (B) だけが文意に適している。わからない単語があっても，諦めずに空所前後から意味を判断しよう。

語句 □ halve 動 ～を半減させる

---

130. Instead of hiring an accountant, Ms. Iwata did her company's bookkeeping all by -------.
(A) her own
(B) her
(C) herself
(D) hers

Iwata さんは会計士を雇わずに，会社の帳簿を自分ひとりでつけました。

正解：(C)

● 着眼点！ 表現の貯金が多いほどスピードアップ！

解説 代名詞を含むイディオムの問題。all by oneself で「自分だけで，独力で」の意味なので，正解は (C)。それ以外に all by ------- で意味が通る語は，選択肢の中にはない。

語句 □ accountant 名 会計士　□ do bookkeeping 帳簿をつける
□ all by oneself 自分だけで，独力で

---

131. Any expenditure ------- budget allotment should be reported to your supervisor immediately.
(A) toward
(B) beyond
(C) against
(D) within

予算配分を超える支出はすべて，ただちに上司に報告すべきです。

正解：(B)

● 着眼点！ 頻出単語をチェックせよ！

解説 適切な前置詞を選択する問題。直前の expenditure「支出」と直後の budget allotment「予算配分」をつなぐ前置詞として適切なのは，(B) beyond のみ。その他の選択肢では意味が通らない。expenditure, budget allotment, supervisor などビジネス関連語は TOEIC でも頻出。覚えておこう。

語句 □ supervisor 名 管理者，監督者，上司　□ immediately 副 ただちに

132. The new air conditioner released last month has a special sensor that adjusts the room temperature and air volume -------.

(A) automatic
(B) automatically
(C) automate
(D) automation

先月発売された新型エアコンは，室温と風量を自動的に調節する特殊なセンサーを備えています。

正解：(B)

● 着眼点！ 空所周辺だけでも解ける！

解説 空所が文末に位置している。空所がなくても文が完結するので，ここには副詞が入ることがわかる。よって，(B) が正解。that 節内の動詞 adjusts を修飾している。品詞の問題は部分を見ただけで即答できることも多いので，解答時間短縮→高得点につながる。(A) 形容詞「自動（式）の」，(B) 副詞「自動的に」，(C) 動詞「〜を自動化する」，(D) 名詞「自動操作」。

133. Both the costs and the benefits should be considered ------- assess the effectiveness of the new inventory control system.

(A) as well as
(B) because of
(C) in order to
(D) as for

新しい在庫管理システムの有効性を評価するためには，費用と利益双方を考慮するべきです。

正解：(C)

● 着眼点！ 空所後の動詞に注目せよ！

解説 空所後 assess は動詞。すぐ後ろに動詞を取ることのできる選択肢は (C) のみである。in order to assess「評価するために」で，目的を表す。(A)「〜と同様に」，(B)「〜のせいで，〜のために」，(D)「〜に関しては」は，いずれも後ろに動詞の原形は取れない。

語句 □ benefit 名 利益 □ consider 動 〜を考慮する □ inventory 名 在庫

134. Environmentally friendly products are on the increase in many markets around the world, most -------, the U.S. and Japan.

(A) casually
(B) affordably
(C) notably
(D) worthy

環境に優しい製品は世界中の多くの市場で上昇傾向にあり，アメリカと日本において最も顕著です。

正解：(C)

● 着眼点！ 頻出表現を押さえてスピードアップせよ！

解説 many markets around the world のあとに，the U.S. and Japan と例を挙げた形になっているので，空所にはその例に対する意味の語が入る。正解は (C)。(A)「何げなく」，(B)「手頃に」，(C)「とりわけ，顕著に」，(D)「〜に値する」。いずれも TOEIC でよく出題される単語なので覚えておこう。

語句 □ environmentally friendly 環境に優しい □ on the increase 上昇中で

135. The glasswork I received from Simon Jewellers Inc. was damaged, so I asked them to send me -------.

(A) the other　　　(B) one
(C) each other　　(D) another

Simon Jewellers 社から受け取ったガラス細工は破損していたので，私はもう1つ送るように依頼しました。

正解：(D)

● 着眼点！　文を整理しよう！

レベル ★★☆☆

解説　長く複雑な文は整理して考えよう。カンマの前は「受け取ったものが破損していた」という内容。それに続いて，「～を送るように依頼した」という内容が書かれている。ここから，破損したものに代わる品を表す語が，空所に入ることがわかる。よって，(D) が正解。

---

136. James Consulting Services Inc. offers ------- benefits programs to full-time workers, including dental coverage.

(A) attraction　　(B) attract
(C) attracted　　 (D) attractive

James コンサルティングサービス社は常勤の労働者に対して，歯科保険を含む魅力的な福利厚生制度を提供しています。

正解：(D)

● 着眼点！　前後を確認して品詞を特定せよ！

レベル ★☆☆☆

解説　まずは選択肢を見て品詞問題であることを把握しよう。意味を考えなくても形から解こう。空所あとには benefits programs という名詞句があるので，ここには形容詞が入るとわかる。よって，(D) が正解。空所に名詞が入って複合名詞となる可能性も考えられるが，attraction benefits programs という複合名詞はないので (A) は不適切。

語句　□ offer 動 ～を提供する　□ benefits program 福利厚生制度
□ coverage 名 保険適用（範囲）

---

137. These days, Magno Electronics has taken the ------ in dealing with the issue of a downturn in domestic demand.

(A) effective　　(B) initiative
(C) incentive　　(D) objective

最近，Magno Electronics 社は国内需要が落ち込んでいる問題への取り組みを率先して行っています。

正解：(B)

● 着眼点！　よく使われる単語の組み合わせに注意！

レベル ★★★☆

解説　イディオムを問う問題。take the initiative で「率先して行う，主導権を取る」という意味になる。その他にも，deal with → 「～に取り組む」や，domestic demand 「国内需要」という語句もポイント。取り組むべき「問題」は problem でなく issue が使われることも覚えておこう。選択肢はそれぞれ，(A) 形容詞「効果的な」，(B) 名詞「自発性，主導権」，(C) 名詞「刺激，励みとなるもの」，(D) 名詞「目標，目的」。

---

138. The conference room ------- the panel discussion will be held is equipped with the latest computer technology.

(A) which　　(B) where
(C) how　　 (D) when

パネルディスカッションが開催される会議室は，最新のコンピューター技術の設備が整っています。

正解：(B)

22

● **着眼点!** 関係詞は空所前に注目せよ！

解説 選択肢はすべて関係詞。空所前の先行詞が何を表しているのかを確認する。the conference room と場所を表す語句なので、迷わずに（B）を選ぼう。（A）which だと、場所を表す前置詞が必要となるので×。

語句 □ be equipped with ～　～の設備がある

---

139. Four earthquakes were ------- in the Greater Los Angeles Area last week and all occurred on Tuesday.
(A) happened　　(B) given
(C) shaken　　　(D) felt

先週ロサンゼルス大都市圏で4回の地震が感じられ、すべて火曜日に発生しました。

正解：(D)

● **着眼点!** 英語の語感を鍛えよ！

解説 空所と選択肢から受け身形だとわかる。happen「発生する」は受け身にできない動詞。were given「与えられた」も were shaken「揺すられた」も主語と相容れない。were felt「感じられた」が最適。earthquake には feel という動詞と相性がいいことを知ることは、自然な英文を書くためにも重要。

語句 □ the Greater Los Angeles Area　ロサンゼルス大都市圏（ロサンゼルス市を中心とする複合都市圏）

---

140. Catering to the rich, ------- of luxury resort hotels in Europe and the Caribbean has been on the rise.
(A) construct　　　(B) constructive
(C) construction　 (D) constructor

富裕層に応えるため、ヨーロッパとカリブ海では、ぜいたくなリゾートホテルの建設が増えつつあります。

正解：(C)

● **着眼点!** 「品詞」から解こう！

解説 動詞 has been の主語は空所から Caribbean までの部分。名詞あるいは名詞相当句が入る。また空所のあとに前置詞 of があることからも、空所に入るのは名詞と判断できる。選択肢のうち名詞は（C）と（D）で、on the rise という文脈からこの文に合っているのは（C）。（A）動詞「～を建設する」、（B）形容詞「建設的な」、（C）名詞「建設」、（D）名詞「建設者、建設会社」。

語句 □ cater to ～　～に応じる　□ the rich　金持ちの人々　□ luxury　形 ぜいたくな
□ on the rise　上昇中で

PART 6

Questions 141-143 refer to the following memo.
問題 141-143 は次のメモに関するものです。

To: All Branch Employees
Re: Annual Training Seminar

Due to the rising costs of fuel, we are arranging for branch staff transportation to the Annual Training Seminar several months ⎡ 141 ⎦ than usual. Someone in personnel at each branch has been designated as the contact person. If you don't know who it is, contact the ⎡ 142 ⎦ of personnel at your branch to find out. Training is required for all management level staff and ⎡ 143 ⎦ for other full time employees. Part time employees may only participate with special written permission from their supervisor. If there are any questions about eligibility, please speak with your immediate supervisor before contacting headquarters.

宛先：支店の全社員へ
件名：返信　年次研修セミナー

燃料価格高騰のため，支店スタッフの年次研修セミナーへの移動手段をいつも<u>より</u>数か月<u>早く</u>から準備しています。各支店の人事課には担当者が任命されています。もし，担当者がだれかわからない場合には，支店の人事<u>課長</u>に連絡を取って聞いてください。
研修は管理職職員に関しては必須とし，他の正社員は<u>自由参加</u>です。パートタイマー社員は，管理者の特別な書面による許可がある場合のみ参加可能です。参加資格について質問がありましたら，本部に連絡する前に直属の上司とお話しください。

語句
- fuel 名 燃料
- arrange for ～　～の準備をする
- transportation 名 移動，輸送
- annual 形 年次の，毎年の
- personnel 名 人事課
- designate 動 ～を指名する
- eligibility 名 参加資格
- immediate 形 直接の，直属の

141.
(A) early
(B) earlier
(C) earliest
(D) earliness

正解：(B)

● 着眼点！　基本文法をマスターせよ！

解説　early の派生語から選択する問題。空所のあとに than があるので，空所に入るのは比較級であるとわかる。(B) が正解。(A) 形容詞「早い」の原級，(B) 比較級，(C) 最上級，(D) 名詞「早いこと」。

142.
(A) lead
(B) charge
(C) front
(D) head

正解：(D)

● 着眼点！　文脈からアタリをつけよ！

解説　動詞 contact の目的語で，後ろに of personnel「人事課の」とあるので，空所には人事課の中の「人」か「役職名」が入ると考えられる。選択肢の中で，その意味を持つのは (D) の head「部長，課長」のみ。(A)「先頭」，(B)「責任」，(C)「前方」，(D)「長」。

143.
(A) rational
(B) reasonable
(C) optional
(D) opposite

正解：(C)

● 着眼点！　文の構造をまず把握せよ！

解説　空所のあとに for があるので，その前の required for all management level staff と ------- for other full time employees とが並列されていると考えられる。required「必須の」と対比できるのは，選択肢の中では (C) optional「任意の，自由意志の」のみで，これが正解となる。(A)「分別のある」，(B)「道理にかなった」，(D)「反対の」。

Questions 144-146 refer to the following article.
問題 144-146 は次の記事に関するものです。

Do you ⬜144 your lack of accomplishment on your habit of procrastinating? Do not feel bad, says an article by popular blogger Marvin Mansfield. In his latest entry, Mr. Mansfield writes that many of the most successful and productive people deal with the urge to whine about and avoid work projects every day. The difference between the chronic procrastinator and ⬜145 who get to work is that the latter have figured out concrete tricks to get past TV watching, unneeded web surfing and daydreaming. One recommended method is to work on a task for ten minutes uninterrupted and take a two minute break (don't skip the break even if you feel like continuing). Do this five times and you'll ⬜146 close to an hour of productive work.

仕事が終わらないのは，ぐずぐず先送りにする自分の習慣のせいだと思っていませんか。人気ブロガーである Marvin Mansfield の記事では，それを悪いことだと思わないようにと書かれています。Mansfield さんは最近の投稿で，最も成功して成果を上げている人々の多くは，泣き言を言ったり，作業計画を避けたりしたいという衝動を毎日抑えているのだと書いています。常習的に仕事を先送りにする人々と，仕事にしっかり取り掛かれる人々との違いは，後者はテレビを見たり，不必要なウェブサーフィンをしたり，ぼんやり考え事をしたりしないようしっかりとした技を持っているということです。お勧めの方法の一つは，一つの仕事に 10 分中断せずに取り組み，2 分の休憩をとる（続けたいと思っても休憩をとる）ことです。これを 5 回行うと，生産性のある仕事を 1 時間近くしたことになります。

語句
- ☐ accomplishment 名 達成，完了
- ☐ procrastinate 動 ～をぐずぐず先送りにする
- ☐ blogger 名 ブロガー，ブログを書く人
- ☐ urge 名 衝動
- ☐ whine 動 泣き言を言う，弱音を吐く
- ☐ chronic 形 常習的な
- ☐ procrastinator 名 仕事を先送りにする人
- ☐ figure out ～ ～を理解する，～がわかる
- ☐ concrete 形 しっかりとした
- ☐ trick 名 こつ，秘訣
- ☐ get past ～ ～を克服する，～を通りぬける
- ☐ daydream 動 ぼんやりする
- ☐ uninterrupted 形 連続した

144. (A) blame
 (B) abuse
 (C) praise
 (D) attain

正解：(A)

● 着眼点！ 言い換えにも注目せよ！

解説　accomplishment のあとの on がポイント。blame A on B で「A を B のせいにする」という意味。次の文で「自分で自分を責めること」を feel bad と言い換えていることに注目しよう。正解は (A)。各選択肢の意味は，(A)「～を責める」，(B)「～を虐待する」，(C)「～をほめる」，(D)「～を達成する」。

---

145. (A) them
 (B) those
 (C) one
 (D) ones

正解：(B)

● 着眼点！ 動詞の活用形に注目せよ！

解説　空所のあとに who があり，文脈から「～する人」という意味だとわかるので，(B) those か (C) one に絞ることができる。次に who 以下の動詞の活用形を確認すると, get になっているので (B) が正解。those who ～ で「～する人々」という意味の TOEIC 頻出フレーズ。他の選択肢は，(A) they の目的格，(C)「一つ，人」，(D) one の複数形。

---

146. (A) be
 (B) have done
 (C) have been doing
 (D) have been done

正解：(B)

● 着眼点！ 完了形の型をマスターせよ！

解説　未来における完了の意味を表すのは未来完了形「～したことになる」。〈will have ＋過去分詞〉の形になる (B) が正解。(A) 動詞 be の原形，(B) 動詞 do の現在完了形，(C) 現在完了進行形，(D) 受動態の現在完了形。

Questions 147-149 refer to the following advertisement.
問題 147-149 は次の広告に関するものです。

GRAND OPENING - NEIL'S BEACHFRONT NAIL SALON
4225 Ocean Avenue
Suite #12
Laguna Beach, California

Welcome to the Grand Opening of Neil's Beachfront Nail Salon! This week only, we offer you ⬚147⬚ on all nail art designs, as well as several prizes.
For those of you who like Bubble Bunny, Captain Cod, and Ratman, we think you will be especially happy to hear our news. Believe it or not, all cartoon character nails will be at half price, ⬚148⬚ for finger and toe nails.
Also, the first one hundred men to come to the salon ⬚149⬚ a free nail art design of their choice. We offer a variety of colors and sparkling rhinestones for men.

グランド・オープニング ― Neil's Beachfront ネイルサロン
4225 Ocean Avenue
Suite #12
Laguna Beach, California

Neil's Beachfront ネイルサロンのグランド・オープニングにようこそ！　今週に限り，全デザインのネイルアートを割り引きし，いくつかの景品も差し上げています。
Bubble Bunny や Captain Cod, Ratman がお好きな方にとっては特にいい知らせだと思います。なんと，手の指も足の指のネイルも，アニメキャラクターのネイルはすべて半額になります。
また，サロンにお越しの先着 100 名の男性の方には，お好きなデザインのネイルアートが無料になります。当店では男性用にさまざまな色とキラキラ光るラインストーンを用意しています。

[語句]
- ☐ prize　名 賞品，景品
- ☐ cartoon　名 マンガ，アニメ
- ☐ sparkling　形 キラキラ光る
- ☐ rhinestone　名 ラインストーン

147. (A) discount
(B) discounts
(C) to discount
(D) discounted

正解：(B)

●着眼点！ 基本文型を見抜け！

[解説] we offer you ------- までは第4文型 SVO（間接目的語）O（直接目的語）の文となる。直接目的語には名詞である（A）discount か（B）discounts が考えられるが，discount は可算名詞なので，a discount か discounts と複数形で使う。したがって，（A）は冠詞を伴っていないので×。（B）が正解。offer discounts on ~ は「～の値引きをする」という広告表現の常套句であることも押さえておこう。その他の選択肢はそれぞれ，（C）動詞 discount「～を割引する」の to 不定詞，（D）動詞の過去形・過去分詞。

---

148. (A) both
(B) none
(C) which
(D) either

正解：(A)

●着眼点！ 並列接続詞は即答せよ！

[解説] both A and B「AとBの両方」が見つけられれば，容易に解答できる問題。空所のあとに finger and toe nails と違うものが2つ並んでいるので，その「両方」という意味だと判断できる。（D）either「どちらか一方の」という場合には，finger or toe nails と or が入る。（B）代名詞「どれも～でない」，（C）関係代名詞「～するところの」，（D）形容詞「どちらか一方の」。

---

149. (A) received
(B) will receive
(C) receive
(D) were received

正解：(B)

●着眼点！ 時制をチェックせよ！

[解説] この文の主語は the first one hundred men to come to the salon。to come to the salon は men「男性」という名詞を修飾していて，〈to + do〉は「これからすること」を含意する。主語の直後にくる動詞としては，これからのことを表す（B）の未来形が適切。（A）動詞 receive「～を受け取る」の過去形・過去分詞，（C）原形，（D）受動態の過去形。

Questions 150-152 refer to the following letter.
問題 150-152 は次の手紙に関するものです。

Hummer Flax Inc.
18 Maple Ave.
Georgetown, VA
January 12

Dear Ms. Lund,
I received your request to transfer to our marketing division in Arizona. We are grateful for your ambition and enthusiasm to take on a challenge in a new environment.
Unfortunately, however, we have put a temporary freeze on hiring at the division, ⬚150 our marketing department in Arizona is large in size and we usually recruit most staff there. Our company is going ⬚151 restructuring and consolidation of its organization due to a recent merger, and it hasn't been decided which position will be available yet. The availability of all positions will be ⬚152 within 3 months, so I would appreciate it if you could wait until then.
Thank you for your patience and interest in staying with the company.
Sincerely,
Bill Framer, Human Resources Manager

Hummer Flax 社
18 Maple Ave.
Georgetown, Virginia
1月12日

Lund 様
アリゾナの営業部への転任願を受け取りました。新しい環境で挑戦することに対するあなたの志と熱意を嬉しく思います。
しかしながら、残念なことに、アリゾナの営業部は規模が大きく、通常は最も多くの職員を採用しますが、一時的に雇用をストップしています。最近行われた合併のため、当社は組織の再編と統合の最中であり、どの職が空くか、まだ決まっていません。職の空き状況は3か月以内にすべて確定しますので、それまでお待ちくださいますようお願いいたします。
当社で勤務を続けていただくことへのご辛抱とご関心に感謝いたします。
敬具
人事部長
Bill Framer

語句
- transfer 動 転勤する
- ambition 名 大志, 意欲
- enthusiasm 名 熱意
- freeze 名 凍結
- consolidation 名 統合
- merger 名 合併

150. (A) if
(B) although
(C) in spite of
(D) since

正解：(B)

● 着眼点！ カンマ前後の関係をつかめ！

[解説] we have put a temporary freeze on hiring と we usually recruit most staff there とを結ぶ接続詞を選ぶ。接続詞を選ぶ問題では，空所でつながれた文の前後の関係をつかむことが大切。2文の意味を考えると，この2文は相対立する内容なので，「～ではあるが」と逆接の意味を表す (B) が適切。(A)「もし～ならば」，(C)「～にもかかわらず」，(D)「～なので」。

151. (A) through
(B) under
(C) with
(D) over

正解：(A)

● 着眼点！ 前置詞を攻略せよ！

[解説] 基本動詞は伴う前置詞で全く異なる意味を持つようになるので，意識して覚えよう。最近合併があったというのだから，現在組織の再編と統合を迎えていることがわかる。go through ～ で「～を経験する」という意味になるので，(A) が文脈に合う。他の選択肢では文脈に合わない。(B) go under「(事業などが) 失敗する」，(C) go with ～ で「～と一緒に行く」，(D) go over ～ で「～を越えて行く」。

152. (A) fixing
(B) fix
(C) to fix
(D) fixed

正解：(D)

● 着眼点！ 動詞の形を問う問題。

[解説] 〈助動詞＋be動詞＋過去分詞〉の受動態だとすぐに判断しよう。(D) の過去分詞が適切。ここでは助動詞の will が使われているので，受動態の未来形である。(A) 動詞 fix「～を明確に確定する」の ing 形，(B) 原形，(C) to 不定詞。

PART 7

問題 153-154 は次のお知らせに関するものです。

BIAD
相談セミナー

日時：2月2日（月）
場所：Midway アートセンター，大ホール

ボストン芸術デザイン専門学校（BIAD）は，ウェブデザイナーとしてのキャリアに興味を持つ方々のために相談セミナーを主催いたします。

当日は，以下のような質問にお答えします。
● デザイナーになるための教育はどこで受けることができるのか。
● 政府からはどのような経済的援助が受けられるのか。
● 教育を終了したあとは，どのようにキャリアを積んでいくことになるのか。

ワークショップ終了後に，短時間の個別相談も可能です。

語句
- □ host　動 〜を主催する
- □ consultation　名 相談
- □ advance one's career　キャリアを積む

153. What is being announced?　　　　　　何のお知らせですか。

(A) A training opportunity for school consultants
(B) A workshop for experienced physicians
(C) An advice session for prospective designers
(D) A mandatory seminar for sports instructors

(A) 学校コンサルタントに対する訓練の機会
(B) 熟練医師のためのワークショップ
(C) 将来のデザイナーのための助言のための集会
(D) スポーツインストラクターのための必修セミナー

正解：(C)

● 着眼点！ 冒頭から主題を見抜け！

解説　メールや手紙，お知らせや広告などの文章の大半は，冒頭から主題を推測できる。ここでは，冒頭でウェブデザイナー志望者のためのセミナーを開くとあるので，正解は (C)。即答して次に行こう。

---

154. What information is NOT available at the event?　イベントで得られない情報は何ですか。

(A) Government support
(B) Job vacancies
(C) Training providers
(D) Career development

(A) 政府の援助
(B) 求人
(C) 教育の提供者
(D) キャリア開発

正解：(B)

● 着眼点！ 「並列箇所」にヒント！

解説　NOT 問題は，本文と選択肢の比較が必要。難問だが，ヒントは割と単純。項目の「並列」箇所にヒントがある。ここでは中盤の，the following questions will be answered の下に注目しよう。この3つの項目と選択肢を比較すれば OK。(B) を消去法で選べる。

問題 155-156 は次の記事に関するものです。

読者レビュー：Fox Mountain

Fox Mountain Trail は初心者にも熟練ハイカーにもお勧めです。許可があれば，夜間ハイクも可能です。野の花が咲く草原やコケむした森がたくさんあり，秋には紅葉が美しいですが，冬季は降雪が厳しい地域です。**Whitehill** 湖は通常 **11** 月までは雪と氷に覆われ，ハイカーは知らないうちに湖の上にいるという危険にさらされます。**North Peak** から西尾根に下る登山道は険しく，深い雪に覆われるため，ピッケルは必需品であるということも冬季のハイカーは念頭においてください。

語句
- □ review　名 レビュー，批評
- □ trail　名 山道，跡
- □ novice　名 初心者
- □ meadow　名 草地，草原
- □ moss-ridden　形 コケむした
- □ foliage　名 木の葉
- □ descend　動 下る，降りる
- □ ridge　名 尾根
- □ steep　形 険しい
- □ ice axe　ピッケル
- □ must　名 必需品

155. Where does the article most likely appear?

この記事はどこに載っていると考えられますか。

(A) In a road map
(B) In a company newsletter
(C) In an outdoor magazine
(D) In a scientific journal

(A) 道路地図
(B) 社内報
(C) アウトドア向けの雑誌
(D) 科学雑誌

正解：(C)

● 着眼点！ 選択肢の「タテ読み」を活用しよう！

解説 選択肢を「タテ読み」してキーワードをつかもう。road, company, outdoor, scientific とあるうち、本文の内容と最も合うのは outdoor で、正解は（C）となる。もちろん、本文では見出しと冒頭に集中しよう！

---

156. What is NOT mentioned in the article?

記事に述べられていないことは何ですか。

(A) Overnight facilities
(B) Trail scenery
(C) Snow coverage
(D) Necessary equipment

(A) 宿泊施設
(B) 山道の景色
(C) 積雪
(D) 必要な装備

正解：(A)

● 着眼点！ NOT 問題は選択肢からチェック！

解説 NOT 問題では、選択肢を先に見ておこう。本文と選択肢の比較は、あくまで上から。本文で宿泊に関しては何も述べられていないので、いきなり（A）が正解とわかる。他の選択肢（B），（C），（D）について確認していくと、（B）「景色」は 3 文目、（C）「積雪」は 4 文目以降に書かれている。（D）の equipment「装備」は最後の文の ice axe「ピッケル」の言い換え。

問題 157-159 は次のメモに関するものです。

社内連絡メモ

宛先：**Dream Build** 社全従業員
発信者：**Peter Channing** 最高業務執行責任者
件名：社内報
日付：1月21日

従業員の皆さんより社内報発行の要請を多く受けてきました。ここに隔月での社内報の発行を開始することをお知らせでき、うれしい限りです。決まっている内容のリストは以下の通りです。

トップストーリー：	ビジネスニュース，会社情報，報道発表
従業員ニュース：	昇格，新入社員，求人
新製品：	イノベーション，製品に対する従業員のアイデア
広告：	売ります，買います
注目記事：	従業員のニュースと紹介
お知らせ，健康と安全：	方針の変更，健康と安全の秘訣

従業員全員の寄稿を奨励します。そうすれば同僚にもあなたの情報が大いに役立つのです。研究によれば，社内報を発行することは職員の士気を全般的に上げ，職場への関心を呼び起こすということです。半年ごとに最もよい寄稿を決めるコンペを行うつもりです。優勝者には町の **Turin** レストランより招待クーポンが贈られます。

最後になりますが，パートタイムの編集者も選任したいと思っています。したがって，この業務に興味を持つ方を紹介していただけると非常に助かります。この業務にふさわしい方をご存じの場合は，人事部の **Pamela Smith** までEメール（smith-P@dream-build.com），または内線 175 へご連絡をお願いします。

[語句]
- □ issue 動 ～を発行する
- □ contribute 動 寄稿する，投稿する
- □ morale 名 士気
- □ submission 名 投稿，提出

157. How often will the company newsletter be published?

社内報の発行される頻度はどのくらいですか。

(A) Every January
(B) Every month
(C) Every 2 months
(D) Every 6 months

(A) 毎年1月
(B) 毎月
(C) 2か月に1回
(D) 6か月に1回

正解：(C)

●着眼点！ 数字の「言い換え」に注意しよう！

| 解説 | 社内報の発行頻度が問われている。メモの本文の2文目を見ると，we will begin to issue a newsletter every other month とある。every other month は「隔月」で，選択肢の中では，every 2 months「2か月に1回」と同じ意味になる。よって，正解は（C）。

---

158. Where will personnel transfers most likely appear?

人事異動はどのコーナーに載ると考えられますか。

(A) Top Stories
(B) New Products
(C) Classifieds
(D) Employee News

(A) トップストーリー
(B) 新製品
(C) 広告
(D) 従業員ニュース

正解：(D)

● 着眼点！ キーワードに注目！

レベル ★★☆☆

| 解説 | 選択肢が，社内報の regular contents と気づけば簡単。キーワード personnel transfers は「人事異動」。これに関係しているコーナーは，Employee News に記載の各項目。よって，正解は（D）。

---

159. What does the company encourage employees to do?

会社は従業員に何をするよう奨励していますか。

(A) E-mail Pamela Smith
(B) Develop editing expertise
(C) Get coupons from a restaurant
(D) Write an article for a newsletter

(A) Pamela Smith にEメールを送る。
(B) 編集技術を開発する。
(C) レストランからクーポンを入手する。
(D) 社内報の記事を書く。

正解：(D)

● 着眼点！ 「お願い」表現をサーチ！

レベル ★★☆☆

| 解説 | 設問の encourage に注目し，本文中の「お願い」表現をサーチしよう。第2段落の We urge all employees to contribute がポイント。encourage → urge「促す」の言い換えがわかればOK。正解は（D）。

問題 160-162 は次のプレスリリースに関するものです。

大手半導体メーカーが新しい高速プロセッサを発表

Harry Jonson 記
8月10日

オレゴン州ポートランド － Intelligent Chip 社は，全く新しい技術を用いた最新の高速プロセッサの発売を発表したところだ。この最先端プロセッサのノートパソコン主要メーカー全社への流通は今週開始される。Intelligent Chip 社のスポークスマン，Iain Foster は，この真新しい技術は開発に数年を要したが，ベンチマークテストでは現在のプロセッサの 100 倍の速度の性能を証明したと述べた。

Intelligent Chip 社について。Intelligent Chip 社は現在の最高経営責任者である Dave Stern により創設され，29 年間事業を行っており，世界中で使用される全プロセッサの約 20% をコンピューター業界に供給している。新しい超高速半導体の発売により，当社は市場シェアが伸びることを期待している。来年，同じチップの小型版が続くことになっている。それは急速に変化を続けるモバイル機器市場に向けて特別に開発されたものである。

この技術革新の詳細については以下までお問い合わせください。
Bill Murphy,　メディア対応広報窓口
1568　NW,　Sandy 大通り, 300A 号室
事務所：(503) 555-5309
ファクス：(503) 555-5609
murphyb@intelligentchip.com

語句
- □ cutting-edge　形 最先端の
- □ notebook　名 ノートパソコン
- □ benchmark test　ベンチマーク（基準）テスト
- □ found　動 ～を創設する
- □ approximately　副 約，およそ
- □ miniature　形 小型の
- □ media relations　メディアへの広報窓口

160. What is NOT mentioned about the new product?

(A) Release time
(B) Sales price
(C) Development period
(D) Performance

新製品について述べられていないことは何ですか。

(A) 発売時期
(B) 販売価格
(C) 開発期間
(D) 性能

正解：(B)

● 着眼点！　新製品名を目印にせよ！

レベル
★★☆☆

解説　新製品の説明は，まとめて述べられていることが多い。ここでは第 1 段落に注目！ Intelligent Chip が目印になる。2 文目に Distribution of ... will begin this week とあるので，(A) は

OK。同じく最後の文に new technology has taken several years to develop and that the benchmark test has proven it performs at up to 100 times faster than the current processors とあり，(C) については数年，(D) については従来の 100 倍の速度という記述があり，消去法で残りの (B) が正解とわかる。

161.

What is true about Intelligent Chip Ltd.?

Intelligent Chip 社について当てはまることは何ですか。

(A) Its founder has already retired.
(B) It makes a secret of its future plans.
(C) It anticipates an increase in the market share.
(D) It has recently entered the IT industry.

(A) 創設者はすでに引退している。
(B) 将来の計画については秘密にしている。
(C) 市場シェア拡大を見込んでいる。
(D) 最近 IT 業界に参入した。

正解：(C)

●着眼点！ 難問 What is true ～？ に注意せよ！

レベル ★★★☆

解説 What is true ～？ は，本文と選択肢の比較が必要な難問。キーワード Intelligent Chip Ltd. を目印に，第 2 段落を見よう。1 文目に founded by the current CEO とあるので，創設者は現在の CEO であり引退はしておらず (A) は不適切。同じく has been in business for 29 years 「29 年間事業を行っている」とあるので，(D) も誤り。3 文目に A miniature version of the same chip will follow next year. とあり，来年の計画を明らかにしているので，(B) も×。2 文目の The company expects that ... they will gain a larger share of the market. が (C) と一致するので，これが正解。

162.

Who can provide more information about the new processor?

新しいプロセッサについての詳細を提供できるのはだれですか。

(A) Iain Foster
(B) Dave Stern
(C) Bill Murphy
(D) Harry Jonson

(A) Iain Foster
(B) Dave Stern
(C) Bill Murphy
(D) Harry Jonson

正解：(C)

●着眼点！ 人物の役割を把握しよう！

レベル ★☆☆☆

解説 選択肢の順番に固有名詞をチェックしてもよいが，設問と関係する箇所を探す方が早い。最後の段落の To learn more about this innovation, please contact 「この技術革新の詳細については以下までお問い合わせください」の this innovation とは the new processor を指している。その担当者が Bill Murphy なので，(C) が正解。

問題 163-165 は次のスケジュールに関するものです。

Morgana 大学 Shreya Sen 博士のスケジュール
8月1日 − 4日

8月1日 (日)
17:30　　デンバー国際空港到着，St. Paul ホテルへ移動

8月2日 (月)
11:00　　Griffin 大学教授陣との会合
14:00　　大学院生による森林再生提案のプレゼンテーション

8月3日 (火)
9:00　　 Sanders へ移動
11:30　　Sanders 森林協会理事長の Robert Kwon とランチミーティング
13:30　　土壌再生作業途中の Redham 森林地帯の現地調査

8月4日 (水)
9:30 − 14:00　Blueridge 製紙工場訪問。Juan José 工場長による Blueridge 社の持続可能な森林管理計画の概要説明と工場見学
15:30　　デンバー国際空港へ移動

[語句]
- faculty　名 教授陣
- reforestation　名 森林再生
- graduate student　大学院生
- soil　名 土壌
- reconstruction　名 再生，改造
- paper mill　製紙工場
- overview　名 概要
- sustainable　形 持続可能な
- scheme　名 計画

163. Who most likely is Dr. Sen?　　Sen 博士とはだれだと考えられますか。

(A) A grounds keeper　　　　　(A) グラウンドの整備員
(B) A factory manager　　　　 (B) 工場長
(C) A marine biologist　　　　 (C) 海洋生物学者
(D) A scientist　　　　　　　　(D) 科学者

正解：(D)

● 着眼点！　「職種」をつかめ！

[解説] Who 設問なので，「職種」を見抜こう。タイトル中の Dr. の称号や大学名から，医者または博士号を持つ大学関係者だとわかる。訪問先やプレゼンテーションのテーマから (C) marine biologist ではなく，(D) が正解。

164. On which day will Dr. Sen take a factory tour?　　何日に Sen 博士は工場見学をする予定ですか。

(A) August 1
(B) August 2
(C) August 3
(D) August 4

(A) 8月1日
(B) 8月2日
(C) 8月3日
(D) 8月4日

正解：(D)

● 着眼点！ 言い換えに反応せよ！

解説　factory tour「工場見学」がキーワード。tour をサーチすると August 4 で，give a tour of the mill が目につく。ここでの the mill とは paper mill「製紙工場」のこと。つまり，a tour of the mill とは「(製紙) 工場見学」のことなので，(D) が正解となる。

---

165. What is suggested in the schedule?　　スケジュールで何がわかりますか。

(A) Juan José will pick Dr. Sen up at the St. Paul Hotel.
(B) Robert Kwon will visit Blueridge paper mill.
(C) Dr. Sen will meet other university professors.
(D) Graduate students will hear Dr. Sen's special lecture.

(A) Juan José は Sen 博士を St. Paul ホテルに迎えに行く。
(B) Robert Kwon は Blueridge 製紙工場を訪問する。
(C) Sen 博士は他の大学教授らと会う。
(D) 大学院生は Sen 博士の特別講義を聴講する。

正解：(C)

● 着眼点！ 選択肢のキーワードをサーチ！

解説　suggest 問題では，本文と選択肢の比較が必要。選択肢の固有名詞やキーワードを本文の中から探したら，その前後を読んで選択肢を検証し，素早く正解を見つけよう。(A) の Juan José は 8月4日の paper mill の工場長なので，St. Paul ホテルとは関係がないので誤り。(B) の Robert Kwon は 8月3日の登場人物で paper mill とは関係がないのでこれも誤り。(C) は 8月2日に Griffin 大学の faculty「教授陣」と会う予定なので正解。(D) Graduate students は 8月2日にプレゼンを行うが，「特別講義を聴講する」とは述べられていないので誤り。

問題 166-168 は次の広告に関するものです。

Wimhaven テニスクラブ 100 周年記念
英国の国民的テニススターになることを夢見たことはありませんか？

Wimhaven テニスクラブは国際トーナメント試合に施設を提供し，創設 100 年になります。

我々は，イギリス諸島内のクラブに所属するすべての年代のテニスプレーヤーのための国内トーナメントを開催してこの年を祝うつもりでいます。シード権を持つ当クラブのトッププレーヤーやそのコーチ陣の何人かが出席して，トーナメント開催中に指導や練習会をする予定です。

加えて，国立テニス協会は上位 4 名のプレーヤーに対し，ここロンドンの我々のトップクオリティの施設を利用して当クラブのプロのコーチ陣によって行われている指導プログラムを 1 年間提供します。

Wimhaven テニスクラブの自慢は，試合用と練習用の名高い芝生コートです。

トーナメントの参加は，あなたの所属するテニスクラブを通じて当方までご連絡ください。

Alexander Jones
Wimhaven テニスクラブ
Wimhaven 通り
London W15
020 555 4647

語句
- provide 動 ～を提供する
- facility 名 施設
- on hand 出席して，待機して
- ongoing 形 現在行われている，進行中の
- boast 動 ～を持つ，自慢は～である
- renowned 形 名高い

166. For whom is the advertisement intended?

(A) Young students wanting to be athletes
(B) Current Wimhaven Tennis Club Members
(C) Tournament officials
(D) Ordinary tennis club players

この広告はだれに向けたものですか。

(A) スポーツ選手になりたい若い学生
(B) Wimhaven テニスクラブの現メンバー
(C) トーナメントの関係者
(D) 一般のテニスクラブのテニスプレーヤー

正解：(D)

● **着眼点！** 広告の「対象」を見抜け！

解説 広告の「対象」は「見出し」と冒頭から推測できる。見出しがテニスクラブに関するものであり，その下で，Have you ever dreamed of becoming a UK national tennis star? とあるので，一般のテニスプレーヤーが対象だとわかる。よって，正解は (D)。

167. Who will offer tennis instructions during the competition?

(A) First-class professionals
(B) Retired star players
(C) Tournament winners
(D) Olympic medalists

競技会の間，だれがテニスの指導を行いますか。

(A) 一流のプロ
(B) 引退したスター選手
(C) トーナメントの入賞者
(D) オリンピックのメダリスト

正解：(A)

● 着眼点！　キーワードの言い換えを意識せよ！

解説　設問のキーワード offer tennis instructions を本文中でサーチしよう。第 2 段落・2 文目の Some of our top seeded players and their coaches will be on hand to offer guidance and training during the tournament. から，トーナメント中はシード選手とコーチが指導・トレーニングをすることがわかる。これを言い換えた表現（A）first-class professionals「一流のプロ」が正解。(B) と (D) は本文中に記述がなく×。(C) は，トーナメント後にトレーニングを受けられる人たちであるため誤り。

---

168. How can people apply for the tournament?

(A) By sending an enrollment fee by post
(B) By asking their own club
(C) By becoming a Wimhaven club member
(D) By making a phone call to Mr. Jones

人々はどうやってトーナメントに申し込むことができますか。

(A) 郵便で登録料を送る。
(B) 所属クラブに頼む。
(C) Wimhaven の会員になる。
(D) Jones さんに電話をする。

正解：(B)

● 着眼点！　「申し込み方法」は出る！

解説　「申し込み方法」は定番の設問。本文の最後に注目しよう。最後の段落の To participate in the tournament, contact us through your own local tennis club. から，申し込むには地元の所属クラブを通じて連絡をすることがわかる。よって，正解は（B）。

問題 169-171 は次の E メールに関するものです。

送信者：customerservice@ortmart.com
宛先：Jennifer Lowe<jlowe@yus.com>
件名：Silver Status ギフト
日付：6月24日

会員の皆様

Silver Status ギフトの発送を開始しましたことをご連絡申し上げます！ 数多くの会員様が，今回の集計期間で Silver Status に到達され，少しお時間がかかるかと思われます。ご近所の方やご友人と同時にご注文の品がお手元に届かない場合は，ご容赦ください！ お品物の配送日につきましては，改めて E メールにてご連絡差し上げます。7月10日までにギフトはすべて配送される予定です。

今回の集計期間中，Silver Status に到達されなかった方にも朗報です。7月1日に次の集計期間が始まります！ 7月1日から11月31日までの間に当店でのお買い物を通じて 10,000 ポイント以上獲得された場合，次の Silver Status ギフトの応募資格がある Silver Status を獲得できます。

近々のご来店をお待ちしております！

Vijay Khan
ORT Mart 店長

[語句]
□ reward 名 報酬，報い
□ entitle ~ to ... ~に…する資格を与える

169. What is the purpose of this e-mail?

(A) To inform that an item has been shipped
(B) To notify that a campaign term has changed
(C) To apologize for a change in the delivery date
(D) To congratulate a winner of a competition

この E メールの目的は何ですか。

(A) 品物が配送されたことを知らせること。
(B) キャンペーン期間の変更を通知すること。
(C) 配達日時の変更を謝罪すること。
(D) コンテストの受賞者を祝うこと。

正解：(A)

● 着眼点！ セオリーを忘れるな！

レベル ★★☆☆

[解説] メールの主題は冒頭にある。最初の数行に集中して，アウトラインをつかもう。ここでは，we have begun shipping the Silver Status Gifts! とあるように，ギフトが順次発送されていることがわかる。よって，(A) が正解。

170. What caused the shipment delays?

(A) Company holidays
(B) Many simultaneous deliveries
(C) Changes in the promotion goods
(D) Mistyped personal information

配送遅延を引き起こしたのは何ですか。

(A) 会社の祝日
(B) 多数の同時発送
(C) キャンペーン商品の変更
(D) 誤入力された個人情報

正解：(B)

● 着眼点！ トラブルの「原因」をつかめ！

レベル ★★☆☆

[解説] 配送遅延は Part 7 の定番トピック！ トラブルの原因をつかもう。ギフトの配送について述べている第 1 段落をチェック。We have hundreds of members who have reached the Silver Status this counting period, so it might take a little time とあり，多数のメンバーがギフト配送の対象であることが示されている。この内容を言い換えた (B) が正解。

[語句] □ simultaneous 形 同時の

---

171. How can members reach Silver Status?

(A) By recruiting new members
(B) By contributing to the Web site
(C) By making large purchases
(D) By collecting stamps

会員はどうすると Silver Status に達成できますか。

(A) 新しい会員を勧誘する。
(B) ウェブサイトに寄稿する。
(C) 多量の購入をする。
(D) 切手を集める。

正解：(C)

● 着眼点！ 会員「特典」を見抜け！

レベル ★★☆☆

[解説] Silver Status がキーワード。これが会員のステータスだとわかれば OK。Part 7 では会員の加入方法や特典がよく出る。ここでは，第 2 段落の，By earning over 10,000 points ..., you can earn a Silver Status がポイント。この内容を言い換えた (C) が正解。

[語句] □ contribute ... to 〜 〜に…を寄稿する，寄付する

問題 **172-175** は次の覚え書きに関するものです。

11月30日
宛先：**J. Wyatt** 様
　　　人事部部長
　　　Power Net 社
送信者：**Paul Green**
　　　　Peters & Lloyd 社

Wyatt 様

現在進行中の御社 e コマース部門の担当役員の適任者を探す調査の最新の状況をご報告いたします。
現在，御社のご要望に沿うと思われる候補者が **2** 人おります。以下は，各人の簡単な概要報告です。

1. Brian French さん，42 歳
　- 現在，通信販売会社のマーケティング部門部長
　- Orange County に在住
　- Stapleton College of Commerce で経営学修士号を取得
　- 自社を業界第 1 位の通信販売会社にするための事業拡大に貢献
　- 同僚たちからの人望が厚い模様

2. Peter Matthews さん，36 歳
　- 現在，オンラインストアの副社長
　- State County に在住
　- Metropolitan University で経営学修士号を取得
　- ティーンエイジャーに最も人気のあるブランドの 1 つである **Bright** ブランドを開発，発展させた
　- ハードワーカーとして知られる；現在の地位につくまで地道に働いてきた

これはあくまで予備的情報です。どちらかの候補者に関心がおありでしたら，**Wyatt** 様の承認をいただいて，さらなる情報を得るべく候補者に直接接触してみます。現在，**Peter Matthews** が新しい職を探しているという内部情報を得ております。彼は勤務するオンラインストアでも高く評価されている幹部ですが，現在の会社にほぼ 10 年いるので，新しいことにチャレンジしたいのかもしれません。
引き続き適切な候補者を探してまいりますが，御社の基準を満たすこの地域に住んでいる企業幹部はあまり多くはいません。**French** と **Matthews** はどちらも素晴らしい経歴と経験を兼ね備えたプロフェッショナルです。
これらの候補者たちについてのご意見と，また本件をどのように進めたいとお考えかを，お知らせください。

語句
□ preliminary　形 準備の，予備的な
□ approval　名 承認
□ criteria（criterion の複数形）　名 基準

172. What kind of firm is Peters & Lloyd?

(A) Accounting house
(B) A head hunter
(C) A consulting firm
(D) An Internet service provider

Peters & Lloyd社はどんな会社ですか。

(A) 会計事務所
(B) （幹部級）人材スカウト会社
(C) コンサルティング会社
(D) インターネットサービスのプロバイダー

正解：(B)

● 着眼点！ 会社のジャンルを見抜け！

レベル ★☆☆

解説　会社の「業種」が問われている。冒頭から判断しよう。冒頭，This is to update you on our ongoing search for someone to fill the position of director of your e-commerce department. とあり，有能な管理職を探して企業のヘッドハンティングをサポートする会社（A head hunter）であることがわかる。よって，正解は（B）。選択肢の先読みが大切。

---

173. What is NOT true about Mr. French?

(A) He earned a graduate degree in management.
(B) He is running a shop-by-mail service company.
(C) He lives in Orange County.
(D) He has a likable personality.

Frenchさんについて当てはまらないものはどれですか。

(A) 経営学の大学院学位を取得した。
(B) 通販会社を経営している。
(C) Orange Countyに住んでいる。
(D) 人柄がいい。

正解：(B)

● 着眼点！ 項目の「並列」をチェック！

レベル ★☆☆

解説　NOT問題は，What is true ～ ？問題の逆バージョン。本文と選択肢を対応させ，Frenchさんについて書かれていないものを効率よく見つけよう。ここでは，Frenchさんの下に並んでいる項目をチェックしよう。(A) MBA, (C) residing in Orange County, (D) be well liked among colleagues は文書内にあるので，残る（B）が正解となる。

---

174. What is suggested about Mr. Green?

(A) He has worked with Peters & Lloyd over ten years.
(B) He has already contacted some other candidates.
(C) He highly values the two candidates.
(D) He is thoroughly acquainted with Mr. Matthews.

Greenさんについてどんなことが推測されますか。

(A) 10年以上Peters & Lloyd社に勤めている。
(B) すでに他の候補者何人かと接触を取っている。
(C) 2人の候補者を高く評価している。
(D) Matthewsさんをよく知っている。

正解：(C)

● 着眼点！ suggest 問題は，まとめの文をねらいうて！

[解説] suggest 問題では，選択肢の名詞をキーワードに本文を読もう。基本的に全体をまとめている選択肢が正解になりやすい。最後から2番目の段落の最終文，Both French and Matthews are professionals with excellent backgrounds and business experience. と書かれているので，2人の候補者に対する Green さんの評価は高いとわかる。よって，正解は（C）。

---

175. What will Mr. Wyatt most probably do next? Wyatt さんは，次に何をすると思われますか。

(A) He will lower the minimum hiring standards.
(B) He will raise the incentive for the position.
(C) He will interview the candidates.
(D) He will write Mr. Green back.

(A) 最低雇用基準を緩和する。
(B) その役職の報酬を上げる。
(C) 2人の候補者を面接する。
(D) Green さんに返信をする。

正解：(D)

● 着眼点！ do next 問題では，次の展開を見抜け！

[解説] do next 問題では文末に注目。最終文で Green さんが，Please let me know your thoughts on these candidates and how you want to proceed with this matter. と考えを知らせてほしいと頼んでいる。Wyatt さんが write back「返信する」だろうと想像でき，(D) が正解だとわかる。

問題 **176-180** は次の手紙に関するものです。

Copy and Print 社

5月10日
James Bryant 様
Flower Design 社
515 Crest St.

Bryant 様

お客様の高速カラーコピー機（**ID: CPS2000-5I4D**）の保守契約が **6月30日** をもって終了することをご報告いたします。今後もコピー機を快適にお使いいただくために，ご契約を更新されるようご案内申し上げます。つきましては，同封いたしました保守契約更新申込書（**RFMC**）を郵送，ファクス，または **E** メールにて当方までご返送ください。

書類：
1. 申込書の契約者様情報（会社名，住所，連絡担当者様名）は，すでにご登録いただいている情報に基づき記入されています。もし書かれていることに変更がありましたら詳細を更新してください。
2. 保守サービス契約は原則 **1** 年です。複数年契約を希望される方はチェックボックスにチェックを入れ，年数を記載してください。
3. 「サービスの詳細」欄には，今現在お申込みいただいているプランが記載されています。グレードアップを希望される場合は追加で希望されるサービスのチェックボックスにチェックを入れてください。

支払い方法：
料金の支払い方法は今年から月賦または，従来の一括前払いにてお支払いいただけるようになりました。しかしながら，前払いで一括払いのお客様には **10%** の割引を適用させていただきます。申込書を受領後，請求書をお送りしますので，そちらにしたがって，銀行にてお支払いください。

注意事項：
保守契約の期間延長は契約終了後にもしていただけますが，その場合は『保守契約申込書』の記入が必要になりますので，ご了承ください。

敬具
Heather Thomas
保守管理部
Copy & Print 社

| 語句 | □ **expire** 動 有効期限が切れる，（契約などが）満了する，終了する |
| | □ **renew** 動 （契約などを）更新する，延長する |

176. What is indicated about the maintenance contract?

(A) It is automatically extended.
(B) It allows for applications by phone.
(C) It is annually renewed in most cases.
(D) It provides customer support 7 days a week.

保守契約について何が述べられていますか。

(A) 自動更新である。
(B) 電話での申し込みを受け付けている。
(C) 原則1年更新である。
(D) 年中無休のサポート体制である。

正解：(C)

● 着眼点！　キーワードをサーチせよ！

レベル ★★★☆

解説　キーワード maintenance contract をサーチしよう。第1段落の最後に見つかるはず。さらに次の段落を見ると，Documentation の2. に Our maintenance service is mainly provided on a yearly basis.「保守サービス契約は原則1年です」とある。これを is annually renewed で言い換えている (C) が正解。(A) automatically extended「自動更新される」とはどこにも書かれていない。

---

177. The word "expire" in paragraph 1, line 2, is closest in meaning to

(A) conclude
(B) fulfill
(C) end
(D) term

第1段落・2行目の expire に最も近い意味の語は

(A) （契約などを）締結する，～を完結する
(B) ～を成就する
(C) 終わる
(D) 期間

正解：(C)

● 着眼点！　「語彙」問題は，文脈を見抜け！

レベル ★★☆☆

解説　Part 7 の語彙問題は文脈から解くのが基本。ここでは，expire「期限が失効する，満期になる」の意味がわかれば，(C) end「終わる」を選べる。(A) conclude the contract で「契約を成立させる」という意味になる。

---

178. Which detail is mentioned as contractor information?

(A) The name of the sales representative
(B) The contact details of the person in charge
(C) The product ID under coverage
(D) The duration of the maintenance contract

契約者情報として書かれている詳細はどれですか。

(A) 販売担当者の氏名
(B) 担当者の連絡先
(C) 保守対象製品の ID
(D) 保守契約の期間

正解：(B)

● 着眼点！　コロン（：）のあとをチェック！

レベル ★★★☆

解説　セオリー通り，キーワード contractor information をサーチしよう。Documentation の

1. に見つけたら，内容をチェック！ The contractor information on the form is filled out ... : company name, address, and the information on contact personnel. とあり，コロン「すなわち」のあとが contractor information となる。contact personnel は「連絡担当者」。the person in charge が言い換えとなっている（B）が正解。

---

179. What is true about the methods of payment?

支払いに関して当てはまるのは何ですか。

(A) The outsourcing of collecting payment begins.
(B) The installment is deducted from one's bank account.
(C) The yearly sum is charged on one's bill.
(D) Documents will be sent before payment.

(A) 集金の業務委託が始まる。
(B) 分割払込金が銀行口座から引き落とされる。
(C) 年額を一括請求される。
(D) 支払い前に書類が送られてくる。

正解：(D)

●着眼点！ 選択肢と本文をクロスチェックしよう！

レベル ★★★★

[解説] What is true ～？なので，本文と選択肢を比較しよう。キーワード **payment** は本文の **Methods of Payment** にあるので，その下を見る。(A)，(B) に関して記述はないので×。(C) は一括払いのことを言っているが，今年から installment plan「分割払い」が始まったと言っていることから，これも不正解。残った (D) が正解。**Methods of Payment** の最後，**you will be sent the bill and asked to make payment at your bank** は「請求書をもらってから銀行で支払ってください」という意味。

---

180. What will Copy & Print, Inc. do with late applications?

締め切りを過ぎた申し込みに対して Copy & Print 社は何をしますか。

(A) Ask the customer to fill out another form
(B) Charge handling fees for late applications
(C) Send a bill stating additional rates
(D) Confirm it with a person in charge

(A) 別の書類に記入をするよう頼む。
(B) 遅延手数料を請求する。
(C) 割増料金を明記した請求書を送付する。
(D) 担当者に確認の連絡をする。

正解：(A)

●着眼点！ 「注意事項」を見落とすな！

レベル ★★★☆

[解説] 「注意事項」は，たいてい文書の最後に書かれている。**Attention**「注意事項」を見ると，**current one has expired**「現在のものが失効する」場合について，**you are encouraged to sign the Form of Maintenance Contract** とある。契約を続けるためには，新たな契約を締結する必要があることがわかる。ここから，**fill out another form**「別の書類に記入をする」とある (A) が正解。

問題 181-185 は次の 2 つの E メールに関するものです。

差出人：ratner@worldcheese.co.jp
宛先：j.vandermeer@vonkagkaas.nl
件名：訪問希望
日付：10 月 31 日（金）

ご担当者様

私どもは日本のチーズ卸売業者でございます。東京エリアのレストランを中心に販売しており，ヨーロッパ製品の取り扱いを拡大することに関心を寄せています。現在オランダの酪農家を何人かお招きし，フランス産とイタリア産のものですでに充実している当社の商品ラインナップに，その商品を加えたいと思っております。独占契約にのみ興味があります。

本日，東京でのフードフェアに参加いたしました。そちらで貴社のチーズを当社取扱商品に加えるという私の考えを貴社の方々に手短にお伝えしました。来月末までにミーティングを行うために，お電話をいただけないでしょうか。当社マーケティング担当者 Andrew Nonaka と販売部部長 Louis Gasset が，最初のミーティングとプレゼンテーションに参加させていただければと思います。

お返事お待ちしております。

敬具

J Ratner
World Cheese 社 最高経営責任者
電話：030 5555 8787　　携帯：080 5555 4008
メール：ratner@worldcheese.co.jp

差出人：j.vandermeer@vonkagkaas.nl
宛先：ratner@worldcheese.co.jp
件名：Re: 訪問希望
日付：11 月 3 日（月）

Ratner 様

当社の手作り乳製品にご興味を示してくださり，ありがとうございます。

喜んでご訪問させていただきます。より詳しいお話をするために，当社製造ラインや優れた商品についてプレゼンテーションをさせていただきます。実のところ，お会いする際に当社チーズをご試食していただこうと思っております。

今週末に日本を発つため，今週木曜日か遅くとも金曜日午前中で，貴社の方々の都合のいい時間で，ミーティングをご提案いたします。ご都合が悪ければ，アムステルダムまで皆様をお招きしたく思います。いただいたメールに誠意をもってお答えするために，ご都合のよろしい時間帯をお伺いしたく，お電話を差し上げます。何かお急ぎのご質問があれば，私の携帯 070 5555 4221 までお電話ください。

敬具

Johan Van der Meer
営業販売責任者
Vonk AG Kaas 社 国際貿易部
030 5555 2411

語句
- □ wholesaler 名 卸売業者
- □ homemade 形 (食品が) 手作りの
- □ dairy product 乳製品

---

181. What does Mr. Ratner indicate about World Cheese?

(A) It aims to diversify sales regions in Japan.
(B) It does not have an extensive list of French cheeses.
(C) It has participated in a trade show in Italy.
(D) It plans to trade Dutch foods.

Ratner さんは World Cheese 社についてどんなことを述べていますか。

(A) 日本での販売地域の多角化を図っている。
(B) フランス産チーズの大規模な取り扱いはない。
(C) イタリアの貿易展に参加していた。
(D) オランダ食品の貿易を計画している。

正解：(D)

着眼点！ メールの冒頭に集中！

レベル ★★☆☆

解説 1つ目のメールで Ratner さんが World Cheese 社を紹介している冒頭に注目しよう。2 文目の We are currently inviting several Dutch dairy farmers という箇所から (D) が正解。第 1 段落を読むと、(A) は多角化しようとしているのはヨーロッパ産商品の取り扱いであり販売地域ではない。また (B) も本文の内容と反対である。(C) は第 2 段落・1 文目から同社が参加したのは東京でのフードフェアであるため誤り。

語句
- □ diversify 動 〜を多様化する、多角的にする

---

182. Why did Mr. Ratner send an e-mail to Mr. Van der Meer?

(A) To set up negotiations
(B) To offer promotion goods
(C) To increase market shares
(D) To head-hunt personnel

Ratner さんはなぜ Van der Meer さんに E メールを送ったのですか。

(A) 商談を取り付けるため。
(B) 販売促進グッズを提供するため。
(C) 市場シェアを伸ばすため。
(D) 人材を引き抜くため。

正解：(A)

着眼点！ 「メールの目的」の応用編！

レベル ★★☆☆

解説 メールの目的は基本的に冒頭に書かれているが、1つ目のメールでは最初に自己紹介をしているので、それに続く箇所を見よう。問い合わせや依頼などの場合、メール送信者が聞きたい内容はクエスチョンマークで終わる文に記されていることが多い。第 2 段落・2 文目 Could you please call to arrange a meeting before the end of next month? に注目して，Ratner さんが商談の場を設けたいと考えていることをつかもう。正解は（A）。

---

183. What does Mr. Van der Meer propose to show at the meeting?

(A) A guided tour to the company's farmstead
(B) A release of the company's quality control process
(C) A variety of sample merchandise
(D) An official dinner at a restaurant

Van der Meer さんは商談の場で何を見せると申し出ていますか。

(A) 会社の農場への案内ツアー
(B) 会社の品質管理工程の公開
(C) 各種サンプル商品
(D) レストランでの公式な会食

正解：(C)

●着眼点！ やり取りの流れをつかめ！

レベル ★★★☆

[解説] Mr. Van der Meer とあるので，2つ目のメールを見よう。2つ目のメールには，Ratner さんからの依頼への返事が書かれていると予想しながら読み進めよう。第2段落・3文目に we would like to invite you to taste a range of our cheeses とあり，Van der Meer さんは Ratner さんに，さまざまなチーズの試食を申し出ているのがわかる。これを「各種サンプル商品」と言い換えた（C）が正解。やり取りの流れをつかむことが重要。

[語句] □ farmstead 名 農場
□ merchandise 名 商品，関連グッズ

---

184. What is suggested about Vonk AG Kaas?

(A) They mass-produce several products.
(B) They conducted a marketing survey.
(C) They work with local restaurants.
(D) They made a short visit to an event.

Vonk AG Kaas 社について何がわかりますか。

(A) いくつかの製品を大量生産する。
(B) マーケティング調査を行った。
(C) 地元レストランと共に働いている。
(D) イベントに短期訪問した。

正解：(D)

●着眼点！ クロスリファレンスのコツをつかめ！

レベル ★★★☆

[解説] クロスリファレンス問題。Vonk AG Kaas 社に関わることをサーチする。まず1つ目のメールの第2段落・1行目から，Ratner さんが東京でのフードフェアで同社の人と話をしたと述べられている。それ以上はわからないため，2つ目のメールを読むと，第3段落・1文目から，Vonk AG Kaas 社の人たちは週末には日本を去ることがわかる。ここから（D）が正解だと判断する。設問中のキーワードに注目して本文を読み，わかった事実を整理していこう。

[語句] □ conduct 動 ～を行う，導く

185. Why will Mr. Van der Meer make a phone call to Mr. Ratner?

(A) To fix the time of an appointment
(B) To explain about the production lines
(C) To ask questions about the Japanese market
(D) To catch up on a trading event

なぜ Van der Meer さんは Ratner さんに電話をするのですか。

(A) 約束の時間を確定するため。
(B) 生産ラインについて説明するため。
(C) 日本市場について質問するため。
(D) 貿易イベントについての最新事情を聞くため。

正解：(A)

着眼点！ 見るべき箇所を特定せよ！

レベル ★★☆☆

[解説] 電話の目的についての問題。Van der Meer さんから Ratner さんへの電話について書かれているのは2つ目のメールの第4段落で，1文目に I will of course follow up on your mail with a telephone call to you to confirm a suitable time. とあり，商談の時間を決めるために電話をするつもりであることがわかる。つまり（A）が正解。

[語句] □ catch up on ～　～を理解する，遅れを取り戻す

問題 186-190 は次の E メールと文書に関するものです。

宛先： Ms. Sheila Barnett, 人事部長
送信者： William Brown, アジア営業部長, ソウル
送信日： 3月11日（月）
件名： Re: 上海支社人事についての推薦

Barnett 様

打診いただいております上海支社の人事部での勤務に意欲のある若手社員を紹介する件で回答します。慎重に検討した結果，Dorothy Scott さんを推薦したいと思います。彼女の業績評価表を添付しています。Scott さんは 3 年前に入社して，アジア営業部で私の下で働いています。優秀で，チームプレーヤーとして実力を発揮しています。彼女は営業以外の仕事の経験はありませんが，新しい環境に適応する能力を持ち合わせており，問題なく新しいポストに従事できることを私が保証します。
中国語も堪能でさらに条件を満たしています。Shanghai College of Commerce で 2 年間の留学経験があり，中国標準語を流暢に話せます。上海語の習得にも意欲を持っており，基本的なビジネス会話と文章は理解できます。
もちろん Scott さんは当部の貴重な人材です。この異動について十分に考えましたが，彼女自身のキャリア形成だけでなく，わが社の上海での事業に必ず貢献するものと信じております。
前向きにご検討のほど，よろしくお願いします。

敬具

William Brown

業績評価表

氏名：Scott Dorothy さん
職位：営業担当
職員番号：F8000987

評価実施日：3月9日

(該当箇所にチェック)

業績	評価				スコア
	A	B	C	D	
正確に業務を遂行する	✓				10
時間を守って業務を遂行する	✓				10
自主性をもってプロジェクトに取り組む		✓			8
総合評価	✓				10

評価（スコア 1-10）
　A＝優秀　（9-10）
　B＝優良　（7-8）
　C＝可　　（4-6）
　D＝不十分（1-3）

コメント：
Scott さんは業務を正確かつ時間通りに遂行します。彼女はまた顧客との問題の対処に適任です。よい顧客関係を築くと同時に，全体として彼女には潜在能力が備わっています。しかしながら，研修や経験を通じてより一層指導力を向上させることが必要でしょう。もし彼女が自信をもって自己主張をすることが可能になれば，この分野でさらに伸びると思われます。

評価者：**William R. Brown**
職位：国際営業事業部アジア営業部長

[語句]
- **competent** 形 有能な
- **command** 名 駆使能力，自由に使える能力
- **dialect** 名 方言
- **be qualified for** ～ ～に適任の，～の能力のある
- **clientele** 名 常連客
- **potential** 名 潜在能力，将来性
- **assert oneself** 自己主張する

186. What is the purpose of this e-mail?　　このEメールの目的は何ですか。

(A) To recommend an employee for a position　　(A) あるポストに従業員を推薦すること。
(B) To request feedback on sales figures　　(B) 売上高についての意見を求めること。
(C) To evaluate a new worker from Shanghai　　(C) 上海からの新しい社員の評価をすること。
(D) To inquire about an evaluation record　　(D) 評価記録について問い合わせること。

正解：(A)

● 着眼点！ Eメールでは，まず To，From，Subject をチェック！

[解説] Eメールの目的が問われている。Eメールの問題では，最初に To（受信者）と From（送信者）と Subject（件名）をチェックしよう。ここでも Subject の Recommendation for Personnel in Shanghai Office がヒントとなる。第1段落の This is a response to your request to introduce a motivated junior employee「意欲のある若手社員の紹介の依頼に回答」，I would like to recommend「～を推薦したいと思う」という部分から (A) が正解ということがわかる。(B) feedback on sales figures「売上高に対する意見」，(D) inquire about ～「～について問い合わせる」，そして (C) もEメールの内容とは合っていない。

187. Where does Mr. Brown work?　　Brown さんはどこで働いていますか。

(A) Human Resources　　(A) 人事部
(B) Corporate Planning　　(B) 経営企画部
(C) Asian Sales　　(C) アジア営業部
(D) General Affairs　　(D) 総務部

正解：(C)

● 着眼点！ E メールの送信者の欄を見よ！

解説　E メールの From（送信者）の欄に注目。William Brown, Division Manager, Asian Sales Division とある。ここを見れば（C）を選ぶのは簡単。

---

188. In the evaluation form, the word "initiative" in line 7, is closest in meaning to

(A) collaborative
(B) readiness
(C) administrative
(D) politeness

評価表の 7 行目の initiative に最も近い意味の語は

(A) 協力的な
(B) 喜んですること
(C) 経営上の，管理上の
(D) 礼儀正しさ

正解：(B)

● 着眼点！ 単語の見た目に惑わされるな！

解説　Part 7 定番の語彙の問題なので，文脈を見て素早く解けるようにしよう。on one's initiative は「率先して」という意味。ここでは名詞として使われているので，「自発性，率先」ということになる。(A)，(C) は語尾が tive で外見上 initiative と似ているが，いずれも形容詞なので不正解。単語の形に惑わされてはダメ！ (D) は polite「礼儀正しい」の名詞形だが，意味が全く違う。正解は (B) の readiness「喜んですること」となる。readiness はやや難しい単語だが，選択肢の消去法からも正解を導き出せるだろう。

---

189. What is implied about the evaluation record?

(A) It showed the best marks on all the performance criteria.
(B) It referred to Ms. Scott's recent promotion.
(C) It was submitted shortly before the e-mail was sent.
(D) It suggested conducting an interview to set a higher goal.

評価表について何がわかりますか。

(A) すべての業績基準に最高の評価がついていた。
(B) Scott さんの最近の昇進を反映していた。
(C) E メールが送られる直前に提出された。
(D) より高い目標を定めるための面接の実施を示していた。

正解：(C)

● 着眼点！ imply →「推測」が必要！

解説　imply 問題は推測が必要な問題。だが選択肢を見て本文を読めば，大半は解ける。(A) は「自主性」に関する項目は B 評価であることから誤り。(B) の Scott さんの昇進および，(D) の Brown さんと Scott さんの面談については，記載がないので×。E メールの送信日と評価表の日付に注目して，(C) の解答を導こう。

190. What is NOT suggested about Ms. Scott?　　Scott さんについて示されていないことは何ですか。

(A) She has cooperated with coworkers.　　(A) 同僚と協力している。
(B) She has gone through leadership training.　　(B) 指導力養成トレーニングを受けている。
(C) She has worked in Asian Sales.　　(C) アジア営業部で働いている。
(D) She has studied abroad for years.　　(D) 数年間外国で勉強している。

正解：(B)

● 着眼点！　サーチ読みのススメ！　　レベル ★★★☆

[解説] Scott さんについて，示されていないことが問われている。選択肢のキーワードを軸に E メールをサーチ読みしよう。(A) E メールの第 2 段落・2 文目に has proven herself to be a team player とあり，これは cooperated with coworkers の言い換え。(C) は E メールの第 2 段落・1 文目に has worked for me in the Asian Sales Division とあるので本文と一致する。(D) は E メールの第 3 段落・2 文目に Having studied for two years at Shanghai College「2 年の上海留学の経験がある」とあり，これも本文と一致。評価表のコメントに needs to gain more leadership skills「指導能力が必要」とあるが，そのトレーニングを受けたかどうかは何も記されていないので，(B) が正解とわかる。

問題 191-195 は次の記事と手紙に関するものです。

Town Weekly コラム
新 Cinestar 劇場の映画に行きたくなる魔法　Brendan Hawk

Cinestar シネマコンプレックスが，先週大きな期待と興奮の中でオープンした。Cinestar は期待を裏切らないだろう。Wonder Movies の 9 つに次ぎ，Cinestar が持つ市内で 2 番目に多い 8 つの大スクリーンにはすべて最新技術のサラウンドサウンドシステムが備わっている。

由緒ある Plaza 劇場が昨年春に閉館してから，地域の人々は価値のあるものが代わりに建つのを待っていた。そのとき，Walter 投資会社が劇場を救済する決定をした。投資会社は Walker Brothers の当時のチーフプロデューサーであった Tracy Hepburn を新劇場の監督に任命した。

劇場マネージャーの Tracy Hepburn が一番自慢にしているのは，美しくデザインされた Cinestar のロビーだ。彼女は，ソファーやカウンターを含むすべてがレトロな外観だと指摘している。例えば，壁は 50 年代のハリウッド映画のポスターで覆われている。

チケット売り場も売店もカウンターが 5 つあり，チケットや軽食は長い間待たずに買えるだろう。コンピューターゲーム機や映画の予告編スクリーンがあちこちにあり，映画が始まるのを待つ間，だれもがリラックスできるようなレトロなソファーがたくさんある。劇場内の座席はゆったりしていて，豪華でちょうど座り心地よく傾いているが，すぐに眠ってしまうほどは傾いていない。

Brendan Hawk 様

Cinestar についての好意的な評価をありがとうございます。最高の映画鑑賞体験を提供するのが私たちの目標であり，その目標の達成過程にいるということがわかり嬉しいです。あなたの評論は正確かつ丁寧でしたが，いくつかご指摘したいことがあります。

スクリーンの数ですが，正しくは 10 です。元々は 8 の計画でしたが，10 に増えましたので，混乱が起きたのでしょう。スクリーンの 2 つは特大で，それぞれにカップルと家族用のソファーが 4 つずつあります。すべてのスクリーンに，車椅子の席が何列もあります。

また，毎月第 1 日曜日は，18 歳以下の方の鑑賞料金が半額になりますこともお伝えしておきます。4 歳以下の子どもとシニアの方は，常に割引料金が適用されます。

重ね重ね好意的な記事に対してお礼を申し上げます。いつでも当方にお越しください。

敬具
Tracy Hepburn
Cinestar シネマコンプレックス

語句
- □ anticipation 名 期待　□ state-of-the-art 形 最新技術の
- □ venerable 形 伝統的な　□ bail out ～ ～を救済する
- □ then- 当時の　□ concession 名 売店
- □ plush 形 豪華な　□ thorough 形 丁寧な，完璧な
- □ oversized 形 特大の，大きすぎる

191. What is the purpose of the article?

(A) To introduce a movie star
(B) To publicize a magic show
(C) To review a new cultural institution
(D) To announce a construction plan

この記事の目的は何ですか。

(A) 映画スターを紹介すること。
(B) マジックショーを宣伝すること。
(C) 新しい文化施設を評論すること。
(D) 建築計画を発表すること。

正解：(C)

● 着眼点！ 記事の冒頭に集中！

レベル ★★★★

解説 セオリー通り，「記事」の見出しと冒頭を見よう。見出しの下には，Movie Going Magic at the New Cinestar とあり，冒頭ではシネコンの内容が紹介されているので，正解は (C)。

---

192. In the article, the word "state-of-the-art" in paragraph 1, line 6, is closest in meaning to

(A) newest
(B) vintage
(C) expensive
(D) imported

記事の第1段落・6行目の state-of-the-art に最も近い意味の語は

(A) 最新の
(B) 年代物の
(C) 高価な
(D) 輸入された

正解：(A)

● 着眼点！ 頻出形容詞をチェックせよ！

レベル ★★★☆

解説 state-of-the-art は TOEIC 大好物の形容詞。「最先端の」の意味。ここでは，「プラス」の文脈で使われているので，(A) を選ぶことは難しくないはずだ。

---

193. Who is Ms. Hepburn?

(A) An architect
(B) An investor
(C) A facility director
(D) An interior designer

Hepburn さんとはだれですか。

(A) 建築家
(B) 出資者
(C) 施設長
(D) 内装デザイナー

正解：(C)

● 着眼点！ 人名サーチをして，周辺を見よ！

レベル ★★★☆

解説 Ms. Hepburn をサーチしてその周辺を読めば OK。記事の第2段落に，The company appointed Tracy Hepburn, ... as the director of the new complex. と彼女の立場を表す記述がある。劇場の支配人，監督ということがわかり，facility director「施設長」と言い換えている (C) が正解となる。appoint A as B 「A を B に任命する」を覚えよう。

194. What is the main purpose of the e-mail?

(A) To sell a brand-new event plan
(B) To order the refurbishment of theatrical facilities
(C) To announce a thank-you party
(D) To highlight the inaccurate points in the article

Eメールの主な目的は何ですか。

(A) 新しいイベント企画を売り込むこと。
(B) 劇場施設の改修を依頼すること。
(C) 謝恩パーティーを告知すること。
(D) 記事の内容について不正確な点を明らかにすること。

正解：(D)

● 着眼点！ メールの「ひねり」に反応せよ！

レベル ★★☆☆

解説　メールの冒頭ではお礼が述べられているが，第1段落の最後，there are a few things we'd like to point out に注目。このあとに主張がくるというサインである。本題は第1段落・3文目の Although 以下と，その内容を詳しく説明した第2段落・1文目，The correct number of screens is ten. と書かれているところで，記事中のスクリーン数が間違っていたことを指摘している。よって，(D) が正解。inaccurate は「不正確な，誤った」という意味。(A)，(B)，(C) についての記述はどこにもない。(B) の refurbishment は「改装，改修」という意味。

---

195. What is true about Cinestar Movie Complex?

(A) It prohibits bringing in any food and drink.
(B) It offers discounts on Tuesdays.
(C) It has the most screens in the municipality.
(D) It screens the latest Hollywood movies.

Cinestar Movie Complex について当てはまるのはどれですか。

(A) 飲食物の持ち込みを禁じている。
(B) 毎週火曜日に割引きしている。
(C) 市内最多のスクリーン数を持つ。
(D) 最新のハリウッド映画を上映する。

正解：(C)

● 着眼点！ 選択肢のキーワードをサーチ！

レベル ★★★☆

解説　定番の true 問題。選択肢のキーワードを本文でサーチしよう。(A) food and drink, (B) Tuesdays, (C) the most screens, (D) latest Hollywood movies。(A)「持ち込み禁止」の記述はどこにもない。(B) Eメールの第3段落・1文目に half off the ticket price (discounts の言い換え) とあるが，それは every first Sunday「第1日曜日」。(D) についての記述も特にない。(C) Eメールでスクリーン数は10が正しいと言っているので，最多スクリーンの映画館となり，これが正解。

問題 **196-200** は次のチラシとアンケートに関するものです。

Bottles on the Shore
Caesal Palace Hotel 1 階
6 月 1 日に 1 か月ぶりの新装開店!!

Bottles on the Shore は世界的に有名なシェフの **Nichola Fàbregas** が料理長を務めるオーシャンフロントのシーフードレストランです。先月の改装工事を経て，新装開店の運びとなりました。どうぞ皆様のお越しをお待ちしております。

オープニングはトップレストランとしての私たちの開店 30 周年を祝うものです。私たちは過去 30 年にわたり，またこれからも，ずっと同じ場所で営業していくつもりでおります。また変わることなく，皆様にご好評いただいている季節の料理を提供いたします。改装により店舗に大きな変化がもたらされました。テラス席では夏の間，素晴らしいオーシャンビューをお楽しみいただけます。ただしテラス席は数に限りがありますので，事前のご予約が必要となります。

再オープンより 2 週間，次のような特典をご用意しております。
- 30 年の歴史のあるオリジナルレシピにのっとったフルコースディナー，70 ドル
- 毎日先着順でテラス席のお客様 50 名に特別プレゼント
- 現金でお支払いのお客様には飲食代から 10％割引（クレジットカード払いは割引がございません）

当店での夕食，誠にありがとうございます。**Bottles on the Shore** での食事に対するご意見をいただければと思います。下の表で当レストランを評価し，下にはコメントをお願いいたします。真摯な気持ちですべてのご意見を尊重させていただく所存でございます。

スコア（5 ＝非常によい，1 ＝非常に悪い）

項目	5	4	3	2	1
景色	5	✓	3	2	1
価格	5	4	✓	2	1
料理	✓	4	3	2	1
サービス	5	✓	3	2	1

コメント
　友人夫妻にここのシーフードを勧められたので会社の同僚と初めてここで食事をとることにしました。オーシャンフロントのテラス席からの景色は期待を上回りました。友人はフルコースのディナーを楽しんだということなので，私たちも同じものをいただきました。プレゼントをもらえなかったのはとても残念でした。正直に言って，値段を見ただけのときは料理の味はどうなのかなと思っていました。ほんの 10％ の割引はそれほどということもないと思いましたが，料理は最高でした。丁寧なサービスにも満足しております。これからまた違う季節にも，ここでの素晴らしい食事を見逃せないと思っています。

かさねて，ご来店誠にありがとうございました。

語句
- refurbishment　名 改装
- commemorate　動 ～を祝う，記念する
- decade　名 10 年
- with greatest sincerity　真摯な気持ちで

196. What does the flyer indicate about the restaurant?

(A) It has welcomed a new head chef.
(B) It has been in the same place.
(C) It never accepts credit cards.
(D) It will reopen in two weeks' time.

レストランについてチラシの中でどんなことが述べられていますか。

(A) 新しい料理長を迎えた。
(B) 所在地はずっと同じである。
(C) クレジットカードは使用不可。
(D) 2週間後に再オープンの予定である。

正解：(B)

● 着眼点！　まず，レストランの紹介文を見よう！

レベル ★☆☆☆

解説　レストランの新装開店のチラシ。冒頭をチェックしよう。チラシの第 2 段落・2 文目，We have been in the same location for the past three decades と書かれている箇所がヒント。同じ場所で営業しているとわかる。よって，正解は (B)。選択肢の消去法で導き出すより，スピーディに判断できる問題。

---

197. In the flyer, the word "revitalized" in paragraph 1, line 2, is closest in meaning to

(A) refreshment
(B) regenerated
(C) renown
(D) replicated

チラシの第 1 段落・2 行目の revitalized に最も近い意味の語は

(A) 元気回復
(B) 生まれ変わった
(C) 名声
(D) 複製の

正解：(B)

● 着眼点！　単語を分解してみよう！

レベル ★★★☆

解説　レストランのリニューアルオープンのチラシであり，refurbishment「改装工事」のあとrevitalized されたということなので，この言葉の意味が，「再生された，活性化された」という意味だと推測できる。よって，正解は (B)。revitalized の中に vital「命の，元気な」を見つけられれば意味を推測するのは簡単。

---

198. What is being suggested about the $70 full course?

(A) It is available only in June.
(B) It is served to those who bring the flyer.
(C) It is limited to the first 50 groups.
(D) It is cooked only for three people or more.

70 ドルのフルコースについてどんなことがわかりますか。

(A) 6月中のみである。
(B) チラシを持参する人に提供される。
(C) 先着 50 組に限られる。
(D) 3 人以上の場合にのみ調理される。

正解：(A)

● 着眼点！　キーワードを素早くサーチ！

レベル ★★☆☆

解説　設問キーワード $70 full course をサーチしよう。チラシの終盤, special deals「特典」の 1 つ目に見つかるはず。その直前，For the first two weeks after reopening とあり，チラシ

の見出し，On June 1st, REOPENS を見れば，特典の有効期間は明白。ここから（A）を選ぶ。

---

199. According to the review, which of the following is the guest satisfied the most with?

アンケートによると，客は次のうちのどれに最も満足をしていますか。

(A) Sight from the seats
(B) Range in price
(C) Quality of dishes served
(D) Quality of services

(A) 席からのながめ
(B) 価格帯
(C) 提供された料理の質
(D) サービスの質

正解：(C)

● 着眼点！ アンケート結果は出る！

レベル ★★☆☆

解説　アンケートにはスコアやコメントが書かれているが，非常によい（＝5）のスコアを選択しているのは FOOD「食事」のみであることに注目しよう。またコメント欄を読んでみても，5文目に yet our food was exceptional とあることから食事に満足していることがわかる。正解はこの内容を言い換えた（C）。アンケートの結果は必ず設問とからむので注意しよう。

---

200. According to the review, what is true about the guest?

アンケートによると，客について当てはまることは何ですか。

(A) She dined with her husband.
(B) She made a reservation in advance.
(C) She wanted to come back alone.
(D) She paid with a credit card.

(A) 夫と共に夕食を食べた。
(B) 前もって予約をした。
(C) 一人でまた来店したいと望んだ。
(D) クレジットカードで支払いをした。

正解：(B)

● 着眼点！ クロス問題に対応せよ！

レベル ★★★☆

解説　クロスリファレンス問題。「アンケートによると」あるが，チラシも参照しないと解けない。選択肢のキーワードを素早くサーチして解こう。アンケートのコメント欄の1文目を見ると，同僚と来店しているので，(A) は×。同じく2文目に，The view from the oceanfront patio was better than expected. とあり，またチラシには第2段落・5文目に due to limited availability, we would like you to make a reservation for these seats in advance. とあることから，予約なしでは座れないテラス席に座ったということになる。したがって，正解は (B)。(C) については「一人で」とは書かれていない。(D) は 10％ の割引を受けており，チラシの内容から現金で支払っていることがわかる。

READING TEST

模試 2
解答と解説

- 問題は，別冊の 34 〜 65 ページに掲載されています。

模試 2 解答と解説

PART 5

101. Much of Jane's free time has been devoted to ------- care of her sick father.
 (A) take　　　　　　　(B) took
 (C) taking　　　　　　(D) taken

Jane の自由な時間の大部分は、病気の父親を看病することに捧げられてきました。

正解：(C)

● 着眼点！　イディオムで即決せよ！

レベル ★★☆☆

解説　devoted to のあとに続く，take の正しい形を選ぶ。ここでの to は不定詞の to ではないことに注意。devote A to B で「A を B に捧げる」という意味で，前置詞 to のあとの B には名詞か動名詞が来る。したがって，(C) の taking が正解。

語句　□ take care of ～　～の世話をする，看病をする

---

102. Our new computer system, installed this morning, allows ------- to keep track of all orders.
 (A) our　　　　　　　(B) us
 (C) we　　　　　　　(D) ours

今朝インストールされた当社の新しいコンピューターシステムによって、私たちはすべての注文を記録することができます。

正解：(B)

● 着眼点！　空所周辺だけで考える！

レベル ★☆☆☆

解説　人称代名詞の格を選ぶ問題なので，空所周辺の限られた範囲だけを見て，形から解いていこう。空所の前に動詞 allows，空所の後ろに to 不定詞があるので，空所に入る可能性があるのは目的格の (B) のみ。allow someone to do で「人が～することを許す，人が～できるようにする」という意味。

語句　□ install　動 ～をインストールする　□ keep track of ～　～を記録する

---

103. We would like to inform you that new voting laws have ------- since the last election.
 (A) to introduce　　　(B) introduced
 (C) been introduced　(D) introduce

前回の選挙から新たな投票法が導入されたことをお知らせいたします。

正解：(C)

● 着眼点！　動詞の形はふさわしい態と時制で決まる！

レベル ★☆☆☆

解説　選択肢を見て動詞の形を選ぶ問題。なるべく狭い範囲だけを読んで解いていこう。空所の前には have，空所の後ろには since があるので，〈have ＋過去分詞〉で現在完了形になると考えられる。ここで，正解は (B) か (C) に絞られる。他動詞 introduce の目的語がないので，受動態だとわかる。したがって，正解は (C)。

語句　□ voting　名 投票，形 投票の　□ election　名 選挙　□ introduce　動 ～を導入する

---

104. Please present your invitation card to the receptionist as ------- as you reach the venue.
 (A) long　　　　　　(B) far
 (C) soon　　　　　　(D) much

会場にご到着されたらすぐに招待状を受付にご提示ください。

正解：(C)

68

- **着眼点！** 基本表現は確実に押さえよ！

[解説] 正解は（C）。as soon as ～「～するとすぐに」という表現がポイントとなる問題。残りの選択肢では、次の意味になり文意が通らない。(A) as long as ～「～の間，～する間は」，(B) as far as ～「～まで，～の及ぶ限りは」，(D) as much as ～「～と同量の，～ほども多く」。どれも基本表現なので確実に覚えておこう。

[語句] □ venue 名 会場

---

105. MOSCOW PETROL decided to lower its ------- quota from 25 million to 24.5 million barrels per day.
(A) production　　(B) produce
(C) producing　　(D) produced

MOSCOW PETROL社は，原油生産枠を1日当たり2500万バレルから2450万バレルに引き下げることを決定しました。

正解：(A)

- **着眼点！** 2ステップで選べ！

[解説] 正しい語形を選ぶ問題。所有格 its の直後にくるので，空所は名詞あるいは名詞句だとわかる。(B) produce は名詞としても使えるが，「農作物」という意味になる。ここでは (A) の名詞 production が適切。(A) 名詞「生産」，(B) 動詞「～を生産する」，(C) 動詞のing形，(D) 動詞の過去形・過去分詞。

[語句] □ lower 動 ～を低くする，下げる，減じる　□ quota 名 割り当て量，ノルマ

---

106. If the project -------, Mr. Jenkins would have informed us immediately.
(A) is going to be cancelled
(B) had been cancelled
(C) has cancelled
(D) was cancelled

もしプロジェクトがキャンセルされていたのなら，Jenkinsさんがただちに私たちに連絡してくれていたはずです。

正解：(B)

- **着眼点！** 従属節の時制は主節から導け！

[解説] 正しい時制を選ぶ問題。If で始まっていることと主節の述部 would have informed より，仮定法過去完了の文とわかる。よって，if 節の時制は過去完了になるので，(B) が正解。

[語句] □ immediately 副 ただちに

---

107. I ------- passed the employment examination and was hired as a secretary at the Raywood Next Corporation.
(A) success　　(B) successful
(C) successfully　　(D) succeed

私は首尾よく採用試験に合格し，Raywood Next社に秘書として雇われました。

正解：(C)

- **着眼点！** 空所の品詞を特定せよ！

[解説] 選択肢は (A) から順に，名詞，形容詞，副詞，動詞である。空所には語句が入らなくても，文自体は成り立っている。したがって，副詞が入るとわかる。また，一般動詞の前に位置し，文全体を修飾できることからも副詞だと判断できる。よって，(C) が適切。

[語句] □ pass an examination 試験に合格する

108. At yesterday's meeting, the sales team of APS Holdings ------- surprised to find that the sales figures were far better than expected.
(A) were
(B) was
(C) have been
(D) will be

昨日の会議において，売上高が予想より好結果だったことを知り，APS Holdings 社の営業チームは驚きました。

正解：(B)

レベル ★★☆☆

● 着眼点！ 空所の前後を確認せよ！

解説　be 動詞の時制や人称が問われている問題。空所前後を見て即答しよう。文頭 At yesterday's meeting から，過去の時制であることがわかる。ここから，正解は (A) か (B) に絞られる。さらに主語は the sales team と team が単数なので，(B) was が正解。

語句　□ sales figures　売上高

---

109. All of the new workers are requested to take a medical checkup ------- to their first day at work.
(A) prior
(B) preceding
(C) advance
(D) before

新入社員は全員，入社日より前に健康診断を受けるように要請されました。

正解：(A)

レベル ★★☆☆

● 着眼点！ 単語の選択はまず前後から！

解説　空所のあとの to に注目しよう。(B) と (D) は to を続けることができないので除外。(C) には，in advance という表現があるが，to を伴って「～より」という期間を限定することはないので不適切。正解は (A)。prior to ～で「～より前に」の意。(B) 形容詞「先行する」，(C) 名詞「前進，昇進」，(D) 前置詞「～の前に」。

語句　□ medical checkup　健康診断

---

110. The new vice president for advertising wants to put the focus on ------- a younger set of customers.
(A) attract
(B) attracts
(C) attracting
(D) attraction

広告担当の新しい副社長は，もっと若い顧客集団を引きつけることに焦点を当てたいと考えています。

正解：(C)

レベル ★☆☆☆

● 着眼点！ 空所の前後を確認して品詞を見抜け！

解説　空所は前置詞 on の目的語になるので，名詞が入る。また，後ろには名詞句 a younger set of customers があるので，目的語をとる動名詞の (C) が正解。

---

111. Opening hours at the Brokfeld Museum will be extended ------- the holiday season.
(A) while
(B) during
(C) because
(D) yet

Brokfeld Museum の開館時間は，休暇シーズンの間には延長されます。

正解：(B)

レベル ★☆☆☆

● 着眼点！ 前置詞の特徴をつかめ！

解説　空所後に名詞句が続いていることから，前置詞が入ることがわかる。よって，接続詞である (A)，(C)，(D) は不適切。正解は (B)。前置詞と接続詞の区別とその働きの違いを確認しておこう。(A) 接続詞「～している間に」，(B) 前置詞「～の間に」，(C) 接続詞「～なので」，(D) 接続詞「けれども」。

112. The application form should be filled out with the ------- information and turned in to the human resources department.
 (A) necessity   (B) necessary
 (C) necessitate   (D) necessarily

出願書類には必要な情報をご記入の上，人事部にご提出ください。

正解：(B)

● 着眼点！ 品詞問題のヒントは次の語にあり！

レベル ★☆☆☆

[解説] この問題では，選択肢の品詞が問われている。直後に名詞 information があるので，空所には形容詞が入る。適切なのは (B)。また，information が数えられない不可算名詞だということにも注意。an information や informations にはならない。(A) 名詞「必需品」，(B) 形容詞「必要な」，(C) 動詞「〜を必要とする」，(D) 副詞「必ず」。

---

113. Please be aware that ------- handling fees may be required for international mail orders.
 (A) legal   (B) additional
 (C) original   (D) current

海外向けの通信販売には追加の取扱手数料が必要となる場合がありますのでご留意ください。

正解：(B)

● 着眼点！ 文意から適する語を判断せよ！

レベル ★★★☆

[解説] 語彙問題なので，文意をしっかりと読み取っていこう。that 以下を見ると，handling fees「取り扱い手数料」が may be required「必要になるかもしれない」，for international mail orders「海外向けの通信販売には」，という意味である。この文意で「取り扱い手数料」を修飾するのにふさわしい形容詞は，(B) の additional「追加の」のみ。(A)「法律上の」，(C)「最初の，独創的な」，(D)「現在の，最新の」。

[語句]
□ Please be aware that 〜. 〜にご留意ください。
□ handling fee 取り扱い手数料   □ require 動 〜を必要とする
□ mail order 通信販売

---

114. Traveling slowly by boat, the visitors are given a lesson on identifying the wildlife that resides ------- the river.
 (A) among   (B) about
 (C) along   (D) with

ボートでゆっくり旅をしながら，観光客は川沿いに生息している野生動物の見分け方を教わります。

正解：(C)

● 着眼点！ 前置詞は相性のよい名詞を選べ！

レベル ★★☆☆

[解説] the river の前に入る前置詞を選ぶ。当てはまるのは (C) along。川に「沿って」の意味になる。(A)「〜の間に」，(B)「〜について」，(D)「〜とともに」。

[語句] □ identify 動 〜を見分ける，確認する   □ wildlife 名 野生動物

115. National leaders are asking local governments to take the lead in developing and implementing ------- protection initiatives.
- (A) environment
- (B) environmental
- (C) environmentally
- (D) environmentalism

国の指導者たちは地方政府に対して，率先して環境保護計画の第一歩を踏み出し，遂行するよう要求しています。

正解：(B)

● 着眼点！ 派生語の品詞選びは前後から判断せよ！

レベル ★★☆☆

解説　空所は，名詞句 protection initiatives の前にある。ここから形容詞だとわかれば，(B) environmental が正解だと容易に判断できる。(A) 名詞「環境」，(B) 形容詞「環境の」，(C) 副詞「環境の点で」，(D) 名詞「環境保護主義」。

語句　□ take the lead 先導する，率先する　□ implement 動 ～を遂行する，履行する
□ protection 名 保護　□ initiative 名 計画，構想

---

116. We regret to inform you that the tickets for the reception party have been -------.
- (A) up to par
- (B) laid off
- (C) out of stock
- (D) sold out

残念ながら，レセプションパーティーのチケットは完売したことをお知らせいたします。

正解：(D)

● 着眼点！ 文意から判断せよ！

レベル ★★☆☆

解説　語彙問題なので，文の意味を捉える必要がある。that 以下を見ると，「チケットが～した」とあり，tickets という単語から連想される (D) sold out「完売している」を選ぶことができる。that の前が「残念ながら～をお知らせします」という意味であることからも，(D) が適切。(A)「普段の調子で」，(B) lay off ～で「～を一時解雇する」，(C)「品切れの」。

語句　□ We regret to inform you that ～. 残念ながら～をお知らせいたします。
□ reception 名 歓迎会，披露宴

---

117. Please note that our production line in Myanmar will be ------- shut down this summer for repairs.
- (A) rarely
- (B) frequently
- (C) simply
- (D) temporarily

ミャンマーにある当社の生産ラインは，修理のために今夏一時的に閉鎖されるということにご留意ください。

正解：(D)

● 着眼点！ 文意から判断せよ！

レベル ★★☆☆

解説　全文から文意をつかもう。「生産ラインが修理のため今夏閉鎖される」という内容から，(D) temporarily が適切だとわかる。(A)「まれに」，(B)「頻繁に」，(C)「簡単に」，(D)「一時的に」。

---

118. ------- the exception of the Sapporo branch, we had trouble getting in touch with our domestic offices by phone.
- (A) As
- (B) For
- (C) In
- (D) With

札幌支社を除いて，国内のオフィスと電話で連絡を取るのが困難でした。

正解：(D)

- **着眼点！** イディオムの知識がカギ！
- **解説** 選択肢には前置詞が並んでいるので，空所のあとの語句と自然につながるものを選ぼう。with the exception of ～で「～を例外として，除いて」という意味になる（D）が正解。
- **語句** □ exception 名例外　□ get in touch with ～　～と連絡を取る
  □ domestic 形国内の

---

119. Better public speaking skills help you convey messages on any occasion, at formal gatherings in -------.
(A) particular
(B) specific
(C) example
(D) emphasis

人前で上手に話すスキルは，どんな場面でもメッセージを伝えるのに役立ちますが, 特にフォーマルな集まりでは有効です。

正解：(A)

- **着眼点！** イディオムでスピードアップ！
- **解説** 似たような意味の語から適切なものを選ぶ問題。in particular「とりわけ」という語句を知っていれば解ける。正解は（A）。(A) 形容詞「特にこの」，(B) 形容詞「明確な」，(C) 名詞「例，模範」，(D) 名詞「強調」。また，convey は message との相性がいい。
- **語句** □ convey 動～を伝える　□ occasion 名出来事，機会
  □ gathering 名集会，集まり

---

120. In order to keep your application up-to-date, we recommend checking and installing the latest version -------.
(A) allegedly
(B) equally
(C) occasionally
(D) periodically

アプリケーションを最新のものにしておくために, 定期的に最新バージョンを確認してインストールするように勧めています。

正解：(D)

- **着眼点！** 空所のヒントを文中から見つけよ！
- **解説** 文末の空所に当てはまる副詞を選択する問題。前半部分 In order to keep your application up-to-date をヒントに空所の副詞の意味を推測しよう。文意に当てはまるのは，(D) periodically。選択肢はすべて副詞で，(A)「伝えられるところでは」，(B)「平等に」，(C)「時折」，(D)「定期的に」の意味。
- **語句** □ up-to-date 形最新の

121. The new computer model produced by the Electro Best Company marked the best sales this season, ------- the active sales promotion of its competitors.
(A) although
(B) despite
(C) but
(D) because of

他社の精力的な宣伝活動にもかかわらず、Electro Best 社製の新コンピューターのモデルが今期一番の売り上げを記録しました。

正解：(B)

● 着眼点！ 前置詞か接続詞かは、空所後の文構造が決め手！

解説 空所よりあとの部分に注意。動詞がないので、この部分は節ではない。前置詞（句）がくるとわかる。したがって、(A)、(C) は接続詞なので不適切。また、(D) だと、「他社の精力的な宣伝活動のおかげで」と文意が通らなくなってしまう。よって、(B) が適切。

---

122. Now, we would like to proudly introduce this new model which is far superior ------- any other competing product.
(A) with
(B) than
(C) above
(D) to

それでは、他のいかなる競合製品よりもはるかに優れたこの新モデルを、自信を持ってご紹介したいと思います。

正解：(D)

● 着眼点！ 仲間とペアで覚えよ！

解説 be superior to ～「～よりも優れた」がわかればすぐに解ける問題。正解は (D)。間違えやすいが、(B) than を選ばないよう注意。be inferior to ～「～よりも劣った」とペアで確実に覚えておこう。

語句 □ proudly 副 自信を持って □ competing 形 競合する

---

123. Through its globally linked network, the Hutchison Group ------- a comprehensive range of financial services.
(A) receives
(B) provides
(C) explains
(D) includes

Hutchison Group 社は世界中につながったネットワークを通じて、包括的な金融サービスを提供しています。

正解：(B)

● 着眼点！ コロケーションを攻略せよ！

解説 いずれの動詞も空所以下を目的語として取ることは可能であるが、文意に合致するのは (B) のみ。また、動詞 provide と名詞 service というコロケーションでよく用いられることを知っていれば、すぐに解くことが出来る。動詞と名詞の相性に注目しよう。(A)「～を受ける、受け取る」、(B)「～を提供する」、(C)「～を説明する」、(D)「～を含める」。

語句 □ link 動 ～を結びつける、リンクする □ comprehensive 形 包括的な

---

124. Due to the inclement weather, we had to take an ------- route to the destination.
(A) alternative
(B) alternation
(C) alternating
(D) alternately

悪天候により、目的地まで他のルートを通らなければなりませんでした。

正解：(A)

- **着眼点！** 派生語問題はまず品詞の特定から！

- **解説** 派生語の中から適切なものを選ぶ問題。空所の後ろには **route to the destination** という名詞句がくることから，形容詞が入ると判断。選択肢のうち形容詞は，(A)「代わりの」と (C)「交互の」。文意から，(A) が適切。その他の選択肢は，(B) 名詞「交互，交替」，(D) 副詞「かわるがわる，交互に」の意味。

- **語句** □ inclement 形 (天候などが) 荒れ模様の, 底冷えのする　□ destination 名 目的地

---

125. The recent ------- of digital broadcast systems and networks has been explosive.

(A) evolution　　(B) impression
(C) foundation　(D) pollution

デジタル放送システムおよびネットワークの最近の発展は爆発的です。

正解：(A)

- **着眼点！** 名詞選択では述部に注目せよ！

- **解説** 文全体の主語となる名詞を選択する。述部の has been explosive「爆発的である」に呼応する名詞は (A) のみで，他の選択肢はいずれも不適切である。(A)「進化，展開，発展」，(B)「印象，気持ち」，(C)「土台，基礎」，(D)「公害，汚染」。

- **語句** □ recent 形 最近の　□ digital broadcast デジタル放送
□ explosive 形 爆発的な, 爆発の

---

126. The survey shows that 45 percent of adults disapprove of President Wilson's ------- on making tax cuts permanent.

(A) position　　(B) positioning
(C) positioned　(D) positional

その調査によると, 成人の45％が減税措置の永続化に関する Wilson 大統領の見解に反対しています。

正解：(A)

- **着眼点！** 前後に注目して正解を導け！

- **解説** 品詞を選ぶ問題。空所の直前が所有格 President Wilson's であることから, 空所は名詞だとわかる。また, 空所のあと, on making tax cuts permanent「減税を永続させることについての」から, (B) positioning を除外。正解は (A) である。(A) 名詞「位置, 見解」, (B) 動詞 position「～を置く」の ing 形, (C) 動詞の過去形・過去分詞, (D) 形容詞「位置の」。

- **語句** □ survey 名 調査　□ disapprove of ～ ～を不可とする, ～に反対である
□ permanent 形 永続的な, 常設の

---

127. It has been ------- announced that PAS Bank and Pacific ML Bank will merge into a new bank, which will be the largest in the country.

(A) formalize　(B) formality
(C) formal　　(D) formally

PAS 銀行と Pacific ML 銀行が合併し, 国内最大の新銀行になることが正式に発表されました。

正解：(D)

- **着眼点！** 品詞選択はまず前後をチェック！

- **解説** 適切な品詞を選ぶ問題。空所がなくても文が完結するので, 副詞が入る。よって (D) formally が正解。このように〈be ＋過去分詞〉の間が空所の場合は副詞という型を覚えておこう。(A) 動詞「～を正式なものとする」, (B) 名詞「形式ばった行為」, (C) 形容詞「形式的な」, (D) 副詞「正式に」。

- **語句** □ merge 動 合併する

128. The nutritionist told me that the higher the temperature that food is cooked at, ------- it stays in the gut.
(A) much longer
(B) the longest
(C) as long as
(D) the longer

栄養士は，食物の調理される温度が高ければ高いほど，腸内にとどまる時間が長くなると，私に教えてくれました。

正解：(D)

レベル ★★☆☆

着眼点！ 定型表現を見落とすな！

解説 that 節が始まる部分の the higher the temperature に着目。the ＋比較級 A, the ＋比較級 B で「A なほど，B だ」という定型表現となるので，the higher に呼応させて，空所には (D) the longer が入る。

語句 □ nutritionist 名 栄養士　□ temperature 名 温度　□ gut 名 腸

---

129. The project team will have to ------- extensive research before settling on a final plan.
(A) address
(B) accept
(C) conduct
(D) improve

プロジェクトチームは，最終案を決定する前に広範な調査を実施する必要があるでしょう。

正解：(C)

レベル ★★☆☆

着眼点！ 語彙力で即答せよ！

解説 動詞の語彙問題。空所のあとの extensive research は，「広範な調査，研究」という意味。これを目的語とするのにふさわしい動詞は (C)。conduct research で，「調査，研究を実施する」という意味。動詞と名詞の相性に関する問題でもある。

語句 □ extensive 形 広範囲の　□ settle on ～　～を決定する

---

130. The company's expansion includes creating a 10,000-square-foot production facility, ------ will create close to a hundred new jobs.
(A) that
(B) almost
(C) which
(D) so

会社の増設工事には1万平方フィートの生産施設の設置が含まれており，100人ほどの新規雇用が生み出されるでしょう。

正解：(C)

レベル ★★☆☆

着眼点！ カンマに注意して，文の構造を把握せよ！

解説 カンマの後ろの文に主語がないことから，空所には関係代名詞（主格）が入ることがわかる。ここから (A) と (C) のいずれかが正解となる。さらに，空所前にカンマがあることに注意しよう。カンマの後ろに関係詞がある継続用法には，that は基本的に用いられない。したがって，カンマの前の文全体を先行詞とすることができる (C) which が正解。

語句 □ expansion 名 拡大，拡張　□ square feet 平方フィート
□ production facility 生産施設，生産設備

131. With their growing production, gas and oil industries ------- the city's expansion and economic prosperity over many decades.
(A) have accelerated
(B) accelerating
(C) have been accelerated
(D) accelerate

ガス・石油産業は，増加する生産量で，その都市の拡大と経済的繁栄を何十年にもわたり，加速させ続けてきました。

正解：(A)

● 着眼点！ 時制選択問題は，時を示す語から見抜け！

レベル ★★★☆

解説　動詞 accelerate の適切な形を選ぶ問題。まず，空所は gas and oil industries という主語に続く動詞部分だとわかる。次に，目的語に相当する the city's ... decades があるため，受動態である (C) は除外できる。ここで，文末にある over many decades「何十年にもわたって」という語句がヒントになり，継続を表す現在完了形 (A) が正解と判断できる。(A) 動詞 accelerate「〜を加速させる」の現在完了形，(B) ing 形，(C) 現在完了形の受動態，(D) 原形。

語句　□ prosperity 名 繁栄，成功

132. Keeping up with the latest information technology will provide a ------- advantage for future employment.
(A) substance
(B) substantiate
(C) substantially
(D) substantial

最新の情報技術に遅れずに対応することは，将来の雇用において相当な強みとなります。

正解：(D)

● 着眼点！ 品詞問題は前後から攻略せよ！

レベル ★★☆☆

解説　品詞を問う問題。冠詞 a と名詞 advantage の間にあるので，空所には形容詞が入るとわかる。形容詞は (D) のみなので，品詞がわかれば即座に正解を導くことができる。品詞問題は時間をかけず，空所の前後から瞬時に見極めよう。(A) 名詞「物質」，(B) 動詞「〜を実証する」，(C) 副詞「実質的に，大いに」，(D) 形容詞「実質的な，かなり，多大な」。

語句　□ latest 形 最新の　□ advantage 名 利点，強み

133. In preparation for the banquet, Mr. Lopez visited some supermarkets that have ------- preferred beverage in stock.
(A) his
(B) them
(C) him
(D) their

Lopez さんは宴会の準備として，彼の好む飲み物の在庫があるスーパーマーケットを何軒か訪ねました。

正解：(A)

● 着眼点！ 空所前後から代名詞を選べ！

レベル ★★☆☆

解説　代名詞の選択問題。まず，空所前後を確認して，代名詞の指す人（もの）などを特定しよう。空所前から，文の主語が Mr. Lopez と三人称単数（男性）だとわかる。また，空所後には名詞句 preferred beverage in stock が続いている。よって，所有格の (A) his が適切。

語句　□ in preparation for 〜　〜の準備として　□ stock 名 在庫品，備蓄

134. A ------- approach to reducing CO2 emissions was presented by the environmental agency.
(A) chronic
(B) rational
(C) intimate
(D) mental

二酸化炭素排出量削減のための合理的なアプローチが，環境局により提示されました。

正解：(B)

● 着眼点！ 形容詞の選択は文意をつかめ！

解説　選択肢はいずれも形容詞。どれを選ぶかは，空所に続く approach to reducing CO2 emissions「二酸化炭素排出量を削減するためのアプローチ」という部分がカギとなる。この場合，approach を適切に修飾するのは (B) rational。(A)「慢性の」，(B)「合理的な」，(C)「親密な」，(D)「精神的な」。

---

135. ------- in the late 80s, Mikee Dragon Co. currently has more than 200 stores in the States.
(A) Been established
(B) Establishing
(C) Having established
(D) Established

80年代末に設立された Mikee Dragon 社は，現在ではアメリカ国内に 200 以上の店舗を展開しています。

正解：(D)

● 着眼点！ 省略を見抜け！

解説　分詞構文の時制と態の問題。(A) は文法的に不適なのでまず除外する。次に，主語は Mikee Dragon Co.。会社は「設立される」ものなので，受動態を選ぶ。(D) Established が正解。これは受動態の分詞構文の Having been established の Having been が省略された形である。

語句　□ establish 動 ～を設立する，確立する

---

136. The new residential development will adjoin our existing ones, ------- the plan is approved.
(A) although
(B) provided
(C) unless
(D) because of

もし計画が承認されれば，新たな住宅開発は私たちの既存の住宅に隣接することになります。

正解：(B)

● 着眼点！ カンマ前後の関係を見よ！

解説　正解は，「もし～ならば」という意味の (B) provided。選択肢から適切なものを選ぶためには，カンマの前の部分と後ろの部分の関係を押さえよう。カンマの前は「新たな住宅開発は私たちの既存の住宅に隣接することになる」，カンマの後ろは「計画が承認される」という内容。つまり，「計画が承認される」という条件を満たせば，「隣接することになる」のだとわかる。provided に if と同じ意味があることを知っておこう。

語句　□ residential development 住宅開発（地）　□ adjoin 動 ～に隣接する

---

137. Even though the project was ------- but easy to achieve, the enthusiasm of the whole planning department led it to great success.
(A) something
(B) nothing
(C) everything
(D) anything

プロジェクトは容易には達成できそうにありませんでしたが，企画部全体の情熱が大いなる成功に導きました。

正解：(D)

● 着眼点！ 紛らわしい語句は確実にして差をつけよ！　レベル ★★★★

[解説]　(D) anything が正解。anything but ～ で「少しも～でない」という意味を表す。nothing but ～ は「～に過ぎない」の意味。紛らわしい語句は確実に覚えて，文意を正しく読み取る。きちんと整理して覚えよう。

[語句]　□ enthusiasm　图 熱狂，情熱

138. While most candidates ------- opportunities to meet voters, they rarely venture beyond the safety of their own communities.
(A) trust　　　　　(B) seek
(C) submit　　　　(D) comply

大多数の候補者は有権者と会う機会を求めますが，有権者が自らの社会という安全地帯からあえて踏み出すことはめったにありません。

正解：(B)

● 着眼点！ コロケーションを攻略せよ！　レベル ★★★☆

[解説]　選択肢はすべて動詞の原形。正解は (B)。seek opportunities で「機会を求める」という意味になる。単語と単語の相性であるコロケーションを身につけることは，Part 5, 6 攻略につながるので常に意識しよう。(A)「～を信用する」，(B)「～を求める，捜し求める」，(C)「～を提出する」，(D)「従う，応じる」。

[語句]　□ candidate　图 候補者　□ voter　图 有権者
□ rarely　副 めったに～しない，まれに　□ venture　動 危険を冒して～に行く

139. CyNet Inc. plans to open a new plant in Oregon that will employ 500 people ------- five years to handle their advertising business.
(A) within　　　　(B) about
(C) at　　　　　　(D) during

CyNet 社はオレゴン州に新工場を開設し，5 年以内に広告事業担当者 500 人を雇用する計画です。

正解：(A)

● 着眼点！ 時の前置詞の意味の違いに注目せよ！　レベル ★★☆☆

[解説]　選択肢はいずれも時間に関連する語とともに使われる前置詞である。このうち，ある時点を表すのではなく，一定の期間を表すものは (A) within と (D) during であるが，文意から「ある時間内」という意味が適切。よって (A) が正解となる。

[語句]　□ employ　動 ～を雇う　□ handle　動 ～を処理する，対処する
□ advertising　图 広告，宣伝

140. Mr. Berkley has the ------- to decide what is classified and what is not, so please get approval from him.
(A) assignment　　(B) aspect
(C) audience　　　(D) authority

Berkley さんは何が機密かそうでないかを決める権限をお持ちなので，彼からの承認を得てください。

正解：(D)

● 着眼点！ 名詞の選択は文意から！　レベル ★★★★

[解説]　Berkley さんが to decide 以下をするための「何」を持っているのかに適切な語を探す。接続詞 so の後ろの文意を読み取ることがポイント。so please get approval from him「だから，彼から承認を得てください」とあるので，(D) authority が適切。選択肢はすべて名詞で，(A)「割り当てられた仕事」，(B)「形勢」，(C)「聴衆」，(D)「権限」の意味。

[語句]　□ classified　形 機密の　□ approval　图 承認，賛成

PART 6

Questions 141-143 refer to the following notice.
問題 141-143 は次のお知らせに関するものです。

Park Notices and Park Activities

In recent weeks, there has been an issue with pet waste being found on lawns through the park. It is possible that stray dogs are coming into the park. In order to keep Trudeau Park dog friendly, the lawns need [141] clean. We encourage dog owners to clean up their dog's waste and to be sure to dispose of [142] else they happen to see on the grass.
April 24 - there will be field trials conducted by the Kennel Club of Vancouver. Only registered dogs can participate, but spectators are [143] welcome.
May 10 - the Evening in the Park concert and performance series begins its season. All events are free. For further information, call us at 604-555-1347.

公園内の注意とイベントについて

ここ数週間，園内全域の芝生の上にペットのフンが見つかる問題が生じております。野良犬が公園に入ってきている可能性もあります。**Trudeau Park** を犬に優しい環境にしておくため，芝生はきれいにしておく必要があります。犬の飼い主は自分の犬のフンの後始末をし，偶然，草の上で見つけた何か他のものも必ず捨ててください。
4月24日－バンクーバーの **Kennel Club** が主催するフィールドトライアルがあります。参加できるのは登録した犬だけですが，観覧の方も歓迎します。
5月10日－「公園の夕べ」のコンサートとパフォーマンスシリーズが始まります。イベントはすべて無料です。詳しくは，604-555-1347 までお電話ください。

[語句]
- □ waste 名 排泄物，フン
- □ stray dog 野良犬
- □ encourage 動 ～を促す
- □ dispose of ～ ～を処分する
- □ field trial フィールドトライアル（猟犬などが野外に出て訓練の成果を競うもの）
- □ spectator 名 観客，見物人

141. (A) remain
(B) to remain
(C) remaining
(D) will remain

正解：(B)

● 着眼点！　空所前後から判断せよ！

[解説] In order to からカンマまでの「公園を犬に優しい状態に保つため」から，空所を含むカンマ以下の文は「芝生はきれいである必要がある」という意味だと判断できる。need のあとに続くのは，目的語になる to 不定詞。need to 〜 で「〜する必要がある」という意味。正解は (B)。なお need 〜ing でも「〜される必要がある」という意味になる。しかし，この場合は自動詞 remain は受け身にして意味を表せないため不適。(A) 動詞 remain「〜のままである」の原形，(C) ing 形，(D) 未来形。

---

142. (A) anything
(B) anymore
(C) something
(D) some more

正解：(A)

● 着眼点！　2 ステップで正解を導け！

[解説] 空所周辺と文脈のヒントを使って，答えを導こう。まず，空所に入るのは of の目的語となるものなので，代名詞である (A) か (C)。次に，文脈から，「何か」を拾いなさいということではなく，「あるものは何でも」という意味だと判断できるので，(A) anything が適切。(B)「これ以上（〜ない）」，(C)「何か」，(D)「もう少し」。

---

143. (A) then
(B) also
(C) for
(D) along

正解：(B)

● 着眼点！　接続詞に注目せよ！

[解説] 空所に続く welcome は形容詞なので，これを修飾するのは副詞。Only registered dogs can participate, but … とあるので，but より前の内容とは対照的な意味を成す。文脈に合うのは「観客も歓迎される」という意味になる (B)。

Questions 144-146 refer to the following letter.
問題 144-146 は次の手紙に関するものです。

KIRK PATRICK & LAING, ARCHITECTS
2001 Brownley Circle
Suite 903
Toronto, Ontario

Dear Sir or Madam,
I am writing to apply for a position at your firm. I am ⬚144 a graduate student in architecture at Western Ontario University, and plan to graduate next month.
My primary ⬚145 is in design. My master's project involves designing a residential block of single-family homes.
I have two years of part-time experience at the architecture offices of Parker & Soto, and am ⬚146 in a number of design programs including Vectorworks.
I would greatly appreciate it if you could kindly send me an application form for a position at your firm.

Sincerely,

Stephanie Sjobowicz

KIRK PATRICK & LAING, 設計事務所
2001 Brownley Circle
Suite 903
Toronto, Ontario

拝啓
貴事務所に応募したく，お手紙を差し上げます。私は現在 Western Ontario 大学建築学部の大学院生で，来月卒業を予定しています。
私は主に設計に興味を持っています。私の修士研究は，居住に適した戸建て住宅区画の設計に関することです。
私は Parker & Soto 建築事務所において 2 年間パートタイムで働いた経験があり，Vectorworks を含む数多くの設計プログラムに熟達しています。
貴社の応募用紙をお送りいただければ幸いです。

敬具

Stephanie Sjobowicz

[語句]
- □ graduate student　大学院生
- □ architecture　[名]建築
- □ design　[動]〜を設計する
- □ single-family home　戸建て住宅

144. (A) eagerly
(B) actively
(C) currently
(D) correctly

正解：(C)

● 着眼点！ 自己紹介文の定型表現をマスターせよ！

[解説] 「私は大学の大学院生である」と，自分のことを述べている文に挿入される語としては，「現在」の意味の (C) currently が最もふさわしい。(A)「熱心に」，(B)「活発に」，(D)「正確に」。

---

145. (A) interesting
(B) interested
(C) to interest
(D) interest

正解：(D)

● 着眼点！ 派生語選びは前後から！

[解説] 派生語が問われている場合，空所の前後をまず確認しよう。空所前には形容詞の primary があるので，空所には名詞が入ることがわかる。ここから，「興味，関心」を意味する名詞の (D) が最も適切。(A) 形容詞「興味を引く，おもしろい」，(B) 形容詞「興味を持った」，(C) 動詞「〜に興味を持たせる」の to 不定詞。

---

146. (A) proud
(B) significant
(C) proficient
(D) outstanding

正解：(C)

● 着眼点！ イディオムで即決！

[解説] 空所を含む文は経歴や技能について述べている部分。選択肢はどれもポジティブな意味合いを持つ形容詞だが，空所の後ろに in があることに注目。be proficient in 〜 で「〜に熟練した，堪能な」の意味になる。(C) が適切。(A)「自慢の」，(B)「重要な」，(D)「目立つ」。

Questions 147-149 refer to the following advertisement.
問題 **147-149** は次の広告に関するものです。

We believe in the saying, "The pen really is mightier than the sword."
The Mighty Pen by the Write Company proves it. This revolutionary writing device has a titanium body that is literally strong enough to resist a strike by a sword. Yet, that's not all that makes it mighty.
The Mighty Pen writes well even ⬚147⬚ extreme conditions such as 50 degrees Celsius. Moreover, the pen is not only extremely strong, ⬚148⬚ also extremely kind to the writer. The contoured shape ⬚149⬚ to fit naturally in your hand and reduce strain.
The Mighty Pen is $99.99 with free shipping. There is no doubt that the Mighty Pen is worth every penny as it is the best to write down your thoughts with.

私たちは「ペンは本当に剣よりも強い」ということわざを信じています。
Write Company 社の **Mighty Pen** はそれを証明しています。この革命的な筆記用具は本体がチタンで，文字通り剣の一撃にも耐えられる強さです。けれども，それだけの理由でこれが強いというわけではありません。
Mighty Pen は，例えば摂氏 50 度といった極限状態<u>でも</u>よく書けるのです。さらに，このペンは非常に強いだけ<u>ではなく</u>，書き手に非常に優しくもあるのです。曲線形<u>にデザインされた</u>形はあなたの手に自然になじみ，負担を軽減します。
Mighty Pen は送料無料で 99 ドル 99 セントです。**Mighty Pen** はあなたの考えを書きとめるのには最適で，値段に見合った価値があることは疑いありません。

語句
- ☐ mighty　形 強い
- ☐ device　名 道具
- ☐ titanium　名 チタン
- ☐ literally　副 文字通り
- ☐ resist　動 〜に耐える，〜に抵抗する
- ☐ Celsius　名 摂氏
- ☐ extreme　形 極端な，極限的な
- ☐ contoured　形 曲線形に作られた
- ☐ reduce　動 〜を減らす
- ☐ strain　名 負担
- ☐ free shipping　送料無料

147. (A) over
(B) on
(C) with
(D) under

正解：(D)

● 着眼点！ 「条件下」は日本語の語感と同じ！

レベル ★★☆☆

解説　空所のあとに **extreme conditions** とあるのに着目。under ~ conditions で「~の条件下で」というセットフレーズ。ビジネスの場面では頻繁に使われる表現なので，確実に覚えておこう。（D）が正解。

---

148. (A) although
(B) so
(C) but
(D) for

正解：(C)

● 着眼点！ 定型表現を見つけてスピードアップ！

レベル ★★☆☆

解説　空所を含む文のカンマの前に **not only** とあり，空所のあとには **also** が続くので，not only A but (also) B で「A だけでなく B も」という意味の定型表現だと気がつけば，全体を読まなくても解答できる。（C）**but** が正解。「丈夫なだけでなく優しくもある」という意味。

---

149. (A) designs
(B) is designing
(C) is designed
(D) will design

正解：(C)

● 着眼点！ 主語から態を読み取れ！

レベル ★☆☆☆

解説　The contoured shape が文の主語なので，to 以下の目的のために「デザインされた」という受け身を表す文だとわかる。〈be 動詞＋過去分詞〉で受け身形を表すので，（C）**is designed** が正解。（A）動詞 design の三人称・単数・現在形で，名詞 shape が design するのはおかしいので不正解。（B）現在進行形，（D）未来形も不適切である。

Questions 150-152 refer to the following letter.
問題 150-152 は次の手紙に関するものです。

Dear Calvin,

I hope you are well. Thank you for the invitation to Nathan's graduation party. I am [150] to hear that Nathan is going to be a doctor soon!
At first, I thought Grace and I would be able to make it to Los Angeles that weekend. Checking my schedule, however, I found out that it [151] with a conference in Seattle.
In ordinary circumstances, I would have just canceled my plans, as I've known Nathan since the days we all used to call him "Little Nate." However, as I am appointed as the featured speaker at this conference, I am unable to cancel this time.
Grace and I are so disappointed to find the party and my conference scheduled [152] the same time.
Thank you anyway and hope we can get together sometime soon.

Best,

Mike

Calvin へ

お元気ですか。**Nathan** の卒業パーティーにご招待いただきありがとう。**Nathan** がもうすぐ医者になると聞いて，とても*嬉しく*思います。
当初は，私は **Grace** と共にその週末にロサンゼルスへ行くことができると思っていました。しかし，スケジュールを確認すると，シアトルでの会議と*かち合う*ことがわかりました。
Nathan のことは私たちが皆彼のことを「小さなネイト」と呼んでいたころから知っているので，通常ならば，私は予定をキャンセルしたでしょう。しかし，この会議で私はメイン講演者に指名されていて，今回はキャンセルできそうにありません。
パーティーと私の会議が同じ時間*に*予定されているということがわかり，**Grace** と私はとてもがっかりしています。
ともあれ，ご招待ありがとう，そしてぜひとも近いうちにご一緒しましょう。

では。

Mike

語句
- circumstance 名 状況
- featured speaker メインの講演者

150.
(A) cooperative
(B) delighted
(C) positive
(D) graceful

正解：(B)

● 着眼点！ 文脈から予測せよ！

レベル ★★☆☆

[解説] 選択肢はすべて形容詞。to 以下から「Nathan が医者になると聞いて」私がどういう状態かを表す形容詞を選ぶ。文脈に合うのは (B) delighted「嬉しい」。(A)「協力的な」、(C)「明確な」、(D)「優雅な」。

151.
(A) conflict
(B) conflicting
(C) conflicted
(D) was conflicted

正解：(C)

● 着眼点！ 主節の時制に注目せよ！

レベル ★★☆☆

[解説] conflict の正しい時制と態を選択する問題。動詞 conflict は計画・予定などが「かち合う」という意味。「かち合う」のは今後のことではあるが、主節の動詞が found と過去形になっているので、that 以下の時制を found に一致させる。(C) conflicted が正解。(D) は受動態なので不適切。(A) 原形、(B) ing 形、(D) 過去形の受動態。

152.
(A) at
(B) on
(C) in
(D) of

正解：(A)

● 着眼点！ 熟語をマスターせよ！

レベル ★☆☆☆

[解説] 正解は (A)。ある瞬間の「時」を表すには at を用いる。at the same time で「同時に」という意味の熟語。

PART 7

問題 **153-154** は次の広告に関するものです。

John's プロフェッショナルガーデニング
カリフォルニア州 **Termer** で設立
作業はすべて保証します！

現在はネバダ州の **Claremont** 郡および **Northern Bucks** 郡全域に対応
庭と芝生のメンテナンス
平均サイズの芝生（20 フィート x 10 フィート）：週 20 ドル
小さい庭や大きい庭の価格はサイズに応じて調整，月 1 回もしくは 2 回のサービスも提供します。

初めてご利用の方は，**878-555-4592** までお電話ください。プランを無料でお見積もりいたします。
10 パーセントの割引がもらえますのでコード番号 **245542** をお忘れなく。特別料金は，コード番号をお伝えいただければ，どなたでもご利用いただけます。
・造園
　芝，花，地被植物および樹木の植え付け
　スプリンクラーの修理
　庭園の設計
・植物および芝の施肥
・樹木サービス
　せん定
　刈り込み
　除去

語句
- □ adjust　動 〜を調整する
- □ semimonthly　形 月 2 回の，半月ごとの
- □ estimate　名 見積もり
- □ landscaping　名 造園
- □ fertilize　動 〜に施肥をする
- □ prune　動 〜を刈り込む

153. What is the purpose of the advertisement?　　この広告の目的は何ですか。

(A) To explain a tree service　　(A) 樹木のサービスを説明すること。
(B) To show an estimate　　(B) 見積もりを示すこと。
(C) To attract new customers　　(C) 新しい顧客を呼び込むこと。
(D) To give prices　　(D) 値段を示すこと。

正解：(C)

● 着眼点！　見出しから主題を見抜け！

解説　「広告」の見出しは重要。すべての情報がつまっているので，まずチェックしよう。ガーデニング関係の広告とわかる。広告の基本は，顧客を集めること。これを意識していれば，自然と（C）が選べるはず。

---

154. Who is eligible for discounts?　　割引を受けられるのはだれですか。

(A) Newly signed up clients　　(A) 新たに申し込んだ顧客
(B) Residents in California and Nevada　　(B) カリフォルニア州とネバダ州の住民
(C) Initial 10 people making a call　　(C) 電話をかけてきた最初の10人の人
(D) Whoever mentions the promotional numbers　　(D) 販売促進番号を伝えた人すべて

正解：(D)

● 着眼点！　キーワードをサーチせよ！

解説　設問のキーワード discount をサーチしよう。Please do not forget to refer to the following code, 245542, for a 10 % discount. とあるので，コード番号245542を伝えた人が10パーセント割引を受けられるとわかる。さらに，続く The special rate is ... の文から，この割引はコード番号を伝えさえすればだれでもOKなので，正解は（D）。

問題 **155-157** は次のウェブサイトに関するものです。

Web Books
学習書専門店
(250) 555-9812 までお電話ください。

Web Books
学習書専門店

<u>ホーム</u>　製品　サービス　ショップ　会員　当店について

あらゆる分野の学習書に関してとっておきのウェブサイトにようこそ。あらゆる分野の本を，どなたにとってもお手頃な価格で探すことができます。新刊と中古本を扱っています。

最大のオンライン書店として知られ，学生のみならず一般の方々にご好評いただいています。

当サイトメンバーの方には，以前に読んだ本を転売する機会も提供しております。当店が開発したシンプルなシステムに，お売りになりたい本の **ISBN** 番号を入力していただきますと，自動的に当店の本のデータベースと一致照合します。必要項目欄を入力するだけで，数千ものオンラインバイヤーに販売できます。

このシンプルでとても環境に優しいシステムを，本日よりお試しください。

こちらをクリックしていただくと，中古ソフトウェアのサイトもご覧いただけます。

語句
- premier 形 最高の，第1位の
- field 名 分野，(データの) 記入欄
- resell 動 ～を転売する，再販する

155. For whom is the web site intended?

(A) Customers buying books
(B) Workers advertising a book fair
(C) Sales staff selling books
(D) Engineers providing software

このウェブサイトはだれに向けられたものですか。

(A) 本を買う顧客
(B) ブックフェアを宣伝する労働者
(C) 本を売る販売員
(D) ソフトウェアを提供するエンジニア

正解：(A)

●**着眼点！** ウェブサイトの「対象」を見抜け！

レベル ★☆☆

解説 ウェブの「対象」が問われている。冒頭にヒントがあるので，見逃してはダメ。You have found the premier website for all fields of study books. とあるので，本を求める顧客向けとわかる。よって，正解は (A)。

156. What is suggested about Web Books?　Web Books についてどんなことが述べられていますか。

(A) It specializes in environment related books.
(B) It has many branch shops around the country.
(C) It has created a system to trade used books.
(D) It is the second-biggest shop of web-books.

(A) 環境関連の本に特化している。
(B) 国内に支店がたくさんある。
(C) 中古本を取り扱うシステムを開発した。
(D) 業界第 2 位のオンライン書店である。

正解：(C)

● 着眼点！　suggest 問題に気をつけろ！

レベル ★★☆

解説　suggest 問題は本文と選択肢の比較が必要な難問。時間をかければ解けることが多いので，(A) から順にトライ。(A) は第 1 段落・1 文目 all fields of study books から，あらゆる分野の学習書を取り扱っているので×。(B) は Web Books がオンライン書店であるので誤り。(C) は，データベース検索システムを使って中古本を取り引きできるという第 3 段落の内容と一致するので，正解。(D) は，第 2 段落の the largest「最大の」に反するので誤り。

語句　□ branch 名 支店

---

157. What is NOT mentioned on the web site?　ウェブサイトで述べられていないことは何ですか。

(A) Web Books has established maximum prices.
(B) Registration is required to sell books.
(C) The procedure for selling books is easy.
(D) The books might be sold to many buyers.

(A) Web Books は最高価格を設定した。
(B) 本の販売には登録が必要である。
(C) 本を売る手続きは簡単である。
(D) 本は多くの買い手に売られるだろう。

正解：(A)

● 着眼点！　消去法を上手に使え！

レベル ★★☆

解説　NOT 問題も本文と選択肢の比較が必要。選択肢のキーワードをサーチして，消去法で解いていこう。(B) は第 3 段落・1 文目の We also offer our site members … の記述と合っている。(C) は同じく第 3 段落・2 文目と，(D) は 4 文目の you will have the opportunity to sell your books to thousands of online buyers と合致する。残った (A) については記載がなく，これが正解。

語句　□ registration 名 登録
　　　□ procedure 名 手続き，手順

問題 158-159 は次の記事に関するものです。

石油価格の高騰と手詰まりな経済を理由に，Advantage Airlines 社（以下 AAL 社）は最近，航空券の価格に燃料代を加えると発表した。AAL 社は，5 大航空会社の中でこうした料金を設けた最後の 1 社だ。Delphi 社や Oracle Air 社などの大手航空会社と違い，AAL 社は 500 マイルを超えるフライトにのみ追加料金をかける*。500 マイルに満たないフライトには燃料代はつかない。同社 CEO の Donald Lee は，厳しい市場で競争力を保つために，燃料代は必要だと述べている。国内線の燃料代 200 ドル（国際線は 300 ドル）は 9 月 15 日から実施される。さらに同社は報道発表で，9 月 1 日から 20 キロ（国際線は 40 キロ）の制限を越える荷物すべてに 100 ドルを請求することを明らかにした。また AAL 社は，燃料代のマイナス影響を打ち消すために考えられた宣伝で，全便での無料軽食サービスも発表した。Gremlin 食品会社と提携しているおかげで，AAL 社の乗客はプレッツェルやキャンディーと同様，ソフトドリンクを飲み放題で楽しめるようになる。

*スカイクラブ・プラチナメンバーは免除される。

語句
- flounder 動 手詰まりになる，もがく
- institute 動 〜を設ける
- domestic 形 国内の
- come into effect 実施される
- press release 報道発表
- complimentary 形 無料の
- exempt 名 免除の対象者

158. What is stated about Advantage Airlines?　Advantage Airlines 社についてどんなことが述べられていますか。

(A) It plans to merge with a food company.　(A) 食品会社との合併を予定している。
(B) It owns and runs a hotel chain.　(B) ホテルチェーンを所有し経営している。
(C) It is a leading airline company.　(C) 大手の航空会社である。
(D) It started new domestic and international routes.　(D) 新しい国内線と国際線のルートを開設した。

正解：(C)

● 着眼点！　あせらず「比較」せよ！　レベル ★★★☆

解説　What is stated ～？なので，本文と選択肢を比較検討しよう。セオリー通り，選択肢のキーワードをサーチすればよい。2文目に **AAL is the last of the five major carriers** とあり，大手の航空会社のうちの1社であることがわかるので，(C) が正解。(A) の食品会社も話に出てはくるが，「提携している」という内容であり，合併するとは書かれていない。

---

159. According to the article, what type of advantage will Skyclub Platinum members receive?　記事によると，スカイクラブ・プラチナメンバーにはどのような特典がありますか。

(A) Bonus points　(A) ボーナスポイント
(B) Fuel charge exemption　(B) 燃料代の免除
(C) Extra pieces of baggage　(C) 追加の荷物
(D) Free light meals　(D) 無料の軽食

正解：(B)

● 着眼点！　「欄外」は要注意！　レベル ★★☆☆

解説　スカイクラブ・プラチナメンバーの「特典（利点）」が問われている。特典は「欄外」に書かれていることが多いので，まずは欄外に目を向けよう。**Skyclub Platinum Members are exempt.** とある。exempt は「免除される」という意味。アスタリスクがついている本文を見ると，**AAL will charge only for flights over 500 miles.** と書かれている。つまり，500マイルを超えるフライトへの追加料金をかけるが，スカイクラブ・プラチナメンバーはそれが免除されるということ。この追加料金とは，「燃料代」のこと。よって，正解は (B)。

問題 **160-162** は次の手紙に関するものです。

9月10日

Zak Rojas 様
TTY 社
New Haven 市 Rich Street 18 番
郵便番号 3665　Victoria 州

Rojas 様

10月8日から12日の間，**Backwater Plaza** で開催される **Autumn Toy Fair** に，謹んでご招待させていただきます。おもちゃ業界の上位 **300** 社以上のメーカーが，古典的なおもちゃから双方向エンターテイメントにいたる良質な製品を展示します。

オンラインまたは当日会場で登録していただけます。業者専門のフェアであり，一般には公開されません。18歳未満は入場をお断りしております。

Autumn Toy Fair は，前回同様に成功を収め，国中のバイヤーの皆さんにとても貴重なビジネスチャンスをご提供するものと思われます。最も満足のいく調達先が見つかりますように！

Leonie Yung
Leonie Yung（署名）
National Toy Foundation

語句
- □ delighted　形 喜んでいる
- □ manufacturer　名 製造業者，メーカー
- □ range from ... to ～　…から～にわたる，及ぶ
- □ interactive　形 双方向の，共同しあう
- □ sourcing trip　供給元をつきとめる旅

160. Why was the letter sent?

(A) To get some researchers together
(B) To inform buyers of toy festival
(C) To raise money for charity
(D) To develop a new product

正解：(B)

手紙はなぜ送られましたか。

(A) 何人かの研究者を集めるため。
(B) トイフェスティバルについてバイヤーに知らせるため。
(C) チャリティーのためにお金を集めるため。
(D) 新製品を開発するため。

レベル ★☆☆☆

●着眼点！　フェアの「案内」を見抜け！

解説　手紙形式のフェア案内文である。冒頭，We are delighted to invite you to the Autumn Toy Fair がヒント。この you は，本文中で traders や buyers と言い換えられている点も重要。「案内文」なので，正解は (B)。

語句　□ raise ... for ～　～のために…を集める

94

161. What is true about registration?　　登録について当てはまることは何ですか。

(A) It is exclusively for business people.　　(A) ビジネスパーソン限定である。
(B) It cannot be done over the Internet.　　(B) インターネット上ではできない。
(C) It must be completed in September.　　(C) 9月に完了していなければならない。
(D) It will be open to small children.　　(D) 小さい子どもに開放されている。

正解：(A)

● 着眼点！　選択肢と本文を比較検討せよ！　　レベル ★★☆☆

[解説] What is true about ～？の問題では，本文の内容と一致している選択肢が正解となる。キーワード registration をサーチしよう。Registration can be done online or at the door. Please note that the fair is for traders only and is not open to the public. とあり，一般非公開の業者限定のフェアであることがわかる。よって，(A) が正解。(B)，(D) はそれぞれ第2段落・1文目，3文目の内容に反し，(C) については触れられていない。

[語句] □ exclusively for ～　～限定で

---

162. What is indicated about the Autumn Toy Fair?　　Autumn Toy Fair について何が述べられていますか。

(A) It will last over a week.　　(A) 1週間以上続く。
(B) It has been held before.　　(B) 以前にも開催されたことがある。
(C) It is the largest in the country.　　(C) 国内最大である。
(D) It is an exhibition of vintage toys.　　(D) 年代物のおもちゃの展示会である。

正解：(B)

● 着眼点！　キーワードでサーチせよ！　　レベル ★★★★

[解説] 設問のキーワード the Autumn Toy Fair を本文中でサーチしよう。第3段落・1文目 The Autumn Toy Fair is expected to repeat its previous success から，このイベントが初めてではなく，以前にも行われたことがわかる。よって (B) が正解。(A)，(D) はそれぞれ第1段落・1文目，2文目の内容に反しており，(C) の「イベントの規模」についての記載は本文にない。

[語句] □ vintage　形 年代物の，最盛期の

問題 163-165 は次の E メールに関するものです。

宛先： Light Fixtures 社 顧客サービス係
送信者： May Preston
件名： 蛍光灯の最低注文単位
日付： 12月5日

担当者の方へ

昼白色の 34 ワット直管蛍光灯を探しており，幸運にも，御社のオンラインショッピングサイトで見つけることができました。製品番号 L-5442-GE5 の製品です。私はこの製品をとても気に入っており，自然な照明が，私の部屋の雰囲気にぴったり合っているのです。先日，私の町の電気屋が販売をやめてしまい，他の場所ではどこにも見つけられずにいたので，御社のウェブサイトで見つけることができて喜んでいました。けれども，注文をする前に，この製品はケース（30本入り）単位でしか購入できないことに気がつきました。
蛍光灯は自宅用なので，それほど数は必要ありません。種類によっては，ばら売りされている蛍光灯もあることに気がつきました。上記の製品についても，同じような扱いにしていただくことは可能でしょうか。必要なのは 3 本で，特別取り扱い手数料は，喜んでお支払いいたします。

できるだけ早くご返信いただければ幸いです。

May Preston
123 Washington 大通り
Jacksonville, CT 55555
電話 123-555-4567

語句
□ look for 〜　〜を探す
□ fluorescent light bulb　蛍光灯

163. What is the main purpose of this e-mail?　この E メールの主な目的は何ですか。

(A) To request international shipping　(A) 国際配送を依頼すること。
(B) To order a fewer number of items　(B) 品物の数を少なめに注文すること。
(C) To change the color of products　(C) 商品の色を変えること。
(D) To ask for storing items　(D) 品物を保管するように頼むこと。

正解：(B)

着眼点！ まず subject を見よう！

解説　メールの subject に Minimum order for light bulbs とあるのに注目しよう。さらに，本文冒頭で，I had been looking for a 34-watt linear fluorescent light bulb とあり，蛍光灯を探していると確認できる。ここからでも (B) が選べるが，本文で「ケース単位（30本入り）でしか注文できない」ということに対し，第 3 段落で The light bulb is for my home and there are only so many that I need. とある。メールの送信者は，そんなにたくさん必要ないので少なめにほしい，と思っていることがわかる。

語句 □ store 動 ～を保管する，蓄える

---

164. What is indicated about L-5442-GE5?　L-5442-GE5 についてどんなことが示されていますか。

(A) It is no longer available.　(A) それはもう入手できない。
(B) It is durable.　(B) それは耐久性がある。
(C) It is for business use.　(C) それはビジネス用である。
(D) It is not widely available.　(D) それは広く入手可能ではない。

正解：(D)

● 着眼点！　製品の特徴を押さえよ！　レベル ★★☆☆

解説　キーワード L-5442-GE5 について書かれている箇所を探そう。第1段落・3文目に，Since an electronic shop in my town stopped selling it the other day and I couldn't find it at any other place … とあるので，それは入手しにくい商品だとわかる。正解は (D)。

語句 □ durable 形 耐久性がある

---

165. What is written in the e-mail?　Eメールに書かれていることは何ですか。

(A) Contact information　(A) 連絡先の情報
(B) Payment methods　(B) 支払方法
(C) Delivery period　(C) 希望配達時間
(D) Order numbers　(D) 注文番号

正解：(A)

● 着眼点！　問い合わせのメールには Contact Information が必須！　レベル ★★☆☆

解説　住所や電話番号が書かれているので，(A) の Contact information が正解。「余分な取り扱い手数料が発生する場合には，喜んでお支払いいたします」とあるが，支払いの方法について述べてはいないので (B) は不適切。(D) の Order numbers は紛らわしいが，Eメールの中には Product number「商品番号」しか書かれていないので不正解。

問題 **166-168** は次の用紙に関するものです。

MarketPlace2020
5009 Peachtree 大通り, Atlanta,
GA 55903
電話 1-800-555-3230
ファクス 1-800-555-3240

注文納品書兼請求書

MarketPlace2020 でのお買い上げ，誠にありがとうございます。ご注文いただいた商品の納品書兼請求書でございます。

注文日：1月20日
発送日：1月21日
支払期日：2月17日

注文番号：17-F9NC-540
注文者：
　名前：Ellen Dumont 様
　住所：1973 Rosewood Drive
　市／州／郵便番号：Frankfort, IN 47948
　電話／ファクス：765-555-2975

カタログページ	商品番号	色	数量	商品名	価格	合計
46	24920	NA	2	ポップオーバーの焼型	14.99	29.98
25	24020	青	1	パイ皿	19.99	19.99

商品合計　　$49.97
送料・手数料　$ 4.50
消費税　　　$ 2.08
合計　　　　$56.55

お支払い方法
商品が届いたことをご確認いただきましたら，2月17日までに銀行振り込みでお支払いください。当社口座情報はカタログにございます。そちらにて金融機関名や口座番号をご確認ください。現金での支払いは受け付けておりません。

注文された商品に関して，何かお困りのことがありましたら，電話でお問い合わせください。

カタログからのご注文，ありがとうございました。
MarketPlace2020.com からオンライン注文もできます。

語句　□ popover 名 ポップオーバー（中が空洞になったマフィンに似た形のパン）
　　　□ merchandise 名 商品　□ shipping 名 配送　□ handling 名 取り扱い
　　　□ sales tax 消費税　□ bank transfer 銀行振り込み

166. What is NOT mentioned in the form?　　　この用紙の中で述べられていないものは何ですか。

(A) Names of ordered products　　　　　(A) 注文した商品の名前
(B) Customer's personal information　　(B) 顧客の個人情報
(C) Store e-mail address　　　　　　　　(C) 店舗の E メールアドレス
(D) Detailed statement　　　　　　　　　(D) 内訳明細

正解：(C)

● 着眼点！ 対応関係をチェック！　　　　　　　　　　　　　　レベル ★☆☆☆

解説　NOT mentioned 問題なので，当てはまらないものを探そう。選択肢を「タテ読み」して本文をサーチ。対応関係を見抜こう。店舗の E メールアドレスの記載はないので，(C) が正解。請求書の一番下に書かれている MarketPlace2020.com は，メールアドレスではなくウェブサイトの URL であることに注意。

---

167. What is suggested about the order?　　　注文についてどんなことがわかりますか。

(A) No commodity tax is charged.　　　(A) 物品税がかかっていない。
(B) Discounts have been applied.　　　(B) 割引が適用されている。
(C) Payment is made after delivery.　 (C) 後払いで支払われる。
(D) The order was placed online.　　　(D) インターネット経由で注文された。

正解：(C)

● 着眼点！ suggest 問題は慌てずに！　　　　　　　　　　　　レベル ★☆☆☆

解説　難問の suggest 問題。選択肢の名詞をキーワードにしてサーチしよう。(A) commodity tax はナシ。(B) discounts もナシ。(C) の payment の項目はある。(D) online は最後の文にあるが，その前の文に Thank you for your catalog order. とあるので，誤り。慌てずに順に対処するのがコツだ。

---

168. What is true about the MarketPlace2020's payment?　　MarketPlace2020 の支払いについて正しいものはどれですか。

(A) They return the service charges.　　　　　　(A) 手数料をあとで返却する。
(B) They accept payment within one month.　　　(B) 1 か月以内の支払いを受け付ける。
(C) They take only cash payment.　　　　　　　　(C) 現金払いのみを受け付ける。
(D) They hold a number of bank accounts.　　　 (D) 複数の銀行口座を持っている。

正解：(B)

● 着眼点！ 「日付」は曲者！　　　　　　　　　　　　　　　　レベル ★★★★

解説　payment をキーワード・サーチ！ 終盤の PAYMENT の箇所を見よう。ここでは現金ではなく銀行振り込みに言及しているが，まだヒントは不十分。本文の冒頭にも PAYMENT DUE「支払期日」がある点に注目。注文日が 1 月 20 日，発送日が 1 月 21 日，支払期日が 2 月 17 日なので，注文や発送から 1 か月以内に支払いの期限があることがわかる。よって，正解は (B)。

問題 169-171 は次の書評に関するものです。

Jack Parker 著
The Damaged River
Erin Marks 記

もう何年も，こんなに興味をかき立てられる本を読んでいない。これに抗うことはだれもできないだろう。謎はこの物語の奥深くに潜み，途中で本を置くのは難しい。これは愛と裏切りについての，わくわくするような本だ。この著者によって書かれていなければ，このテーマ自体はいくぶん平凡で普通なものに思えただろう。10 年前にもかかわらず，Jack Parker の *Behind the Door* による衝撃的なデビューは，いまだに鮮明に覚えられている。彼は新作 *The Damaged River* の中で，改めて愛がいかに重要な役割を担うのかを描いている。彼が言うところによれば，あらゆるページで情事がピクチャレスクに描かれている。風景と登場人物のコントラストは，故意にパズルの中へと織り込まれていく。

もしあなたが，前作を引き継いでいる物語が好きならば，この本をより楽しむだろう。今回，彼は前作の登場人物の物語を継続している。例えば **Ann Roberts** はさまざまな失恋のあと，ついに本当の恋を見つける。

物語がよりスリリングになるので，ここからあなたはページをめくるのを止められないだろう。疑う余地なく，この本はとてもお薦めだ。

語句
- intriguing 形 興味をそそる
- riveting 形 注意をひきつける
- mediocre 形 普通の
- commonplace 形 平凡な
- sensational 形 衝撃的な
- picturesque 形 写実的な
- fashion 名 方法
- contrast 名 対比
- deliberately 副 ゆっくり
- weave 動 縫うように進む
- undoubtedly 副 疑いもなく

169. What is implied about *The Damaged River*?

The Damaged River について何がわかりますか。

(A) It is the first romance from the author.
(B) It is filled with many illustrations.
(C) It is an exciting mystery.
(D) It is unique to this genre.

(A) 著者の初めての恋愛小説である。
(B) 挿絵が豊富にある。
(C) 面白い推理小説である。
(D) このジャンルでは独特である。

正解：(C)

● 着眼点！ 本の情報を集めよ！

レベル ★★★★

解説　書評なので，まずは本の情報を冒頭から集めよう。第1段落・1文目に I have not read a book this intriguing in years. とあり，3文目に The mystery is deep in this story とある。こから (C) を選ぶ。他の選択肢をチェックすると時間がかかるので，冒頭から判断しよう。

170. Who is Ann Roberts?　　　　　　　　Ann Roberts とはだれですか。

(A) A character in the book　　　　　　(A) 本の中の人物
(B) An author　　　　　　　　　　　　(B) 著者
(C) A book reviewer　　　　　　　　　(C) 書評家
(D) An actress　　　　　　　　　　　　(D) 女優

正解：(A)

● 着眼点！ Ann Roberts を探せ！

解説　(B)「著者」，(C)「書評家」でないことは，本文の初めの部分でわかる。Ann Roberts という名前を文中にサーチしよう。中ほどに出てくる Ann Roberts という人名が含まれる文は，物語の内容を説明したものなので，物語の登場人物であることがわかる。よって，(A) が正解。

---

171. What is suggested about Jack Parker?　　Jack Parker についてどんなことがわかりますか。

(A) His writing style is plain.　　　　　(A) 文体が平易である。
(B) He is a professional painter.　　　(B) プロの画家である。
(C) He has been in the field for ten years.　(C) 彼はその分野に 10 年間いる。
(D) He directs films based on his novels.　(D) 自分の小説をもとにした映画を監督している。

正解：(C)

● 着眼点！ 消去法を活用せよ！

解説　Jack Parker は本の著者。(B), (D) は本文を一読すれば除外できる。第 1 段落・6 文目に Yet, Jack Parker's sensational debut ... even though it was a decade ago. とあることから (C) が正解。a decade が ten years と言い換えられていることに注意。(A)「文体」については，「平易」とは書いていないので誤り。

語句　□ direct　～を監督する

問題 172-175 は次の広告に関するものです。

水のことは *AQUALEN* 社におまかせ！

Aqualen 社は Sydney, Brisbane と Melbourne で企業向けに浄水冷却器を提供している最大手の会社です。

Aqualen 製品はどうやって動くの？
市の水道管に直結した浄水冷却機器が貴社のオフィスに設置されます。これによりペットボトルの水や水の宅配サービスはもう必要なくなります。ボトルを移動したり，なくなったときに買いに行くのに時間を費やさずにすむので，貴社の従業員は助かるでしょう。何ガロンものペットボトルの水を保管する必要がないので，スペースも節約できます。もちろん，より費用がかからないのが最もよい点です。

だれが *Aualen* 製品を使っているの？
Biznow 誌の「オーストラリアのトップ企業 100」にランク入りした 30 社が Aqualen 製品を利用しています。水を購入するのに，単により賢い方法なのです。

加えて，今年の 6 月から営業地域にあるご家庭にも水に関するソリューションをご提供させていただきます！ これにより，オフィス同様にご家庭でも清潔で安全なお水をご利用いただけます。

無料のお見積もりやご注文を希望される方は，営業所までお越しいただくか，555-8978（携帯電話からご利用の場合は 555-9928）までお電話にて，あるいは customerservice@aqualen.com まで E メールにてご連絡ください。
＊現在ウェブサイトを鋭意更新中です。オンライン上にお問い合わせフォームが復旧するまで，上記の連絡方法をご利用ください。

[語句]
□ provider 名 供給者，プロバイダー　□ install 動 〜を設置する，インストールする
□ bottled water ペットボトル（瓶）入りの水　□ store 動 〜を保管する，蓄える
□ gallon 名 ガロン（1 ガロンは，アメリカでは約 3.8 リットル）
□ quote 名 見積もり額，引用文　□ contact method 連絡方法

172. What is indicated about Aqualen Inc.?

(A) It is ranked among 100 top national companies.
(B) It has a broad range of filtered water cooler products.
(C) It is a local leading provider of filtered water coolers.
(D) It has invented a new filtration technology.

Aqualen 社についてどんなことが述べられていますか。

(A) 国のトップ 100 企業にランク入りしている。
(B) 幅広く浄水冷却器の商品を扱っている。
(C) 地元で第一位の浄水冷却器の供給業者である。
(D) 新しいろ過技術を開発した。

正解：(C)

● 着眼点！　会社説明は冒頭をチェック！

レベル ★★☆☆

[解説] セオリー通り，キーワード Aqualen Inc. をサーチしよう。会社名のサーチなので簡単。冒頭，Aqualen Inc. is the number one provider of filtered water coolers to businesses とあるので，業界トップとわかる。ここから (C) を選ぶ。

173. What will customers NOT save on by choosing Aqualen Inc.'s products?　　Aqualen 社の製品を選ぶことで, 顧客が節約できないのは何ですか。

(A) Delivery charges
(B) Storage space
(C) Water fees
(D) Time and trouble

(A) デリバリー代金
(B) 収納場所
(C) 水道料金
(D) 時間と労力

正解：(C)

● 着眼点！ 製品の「利点」を見抜け！

解説　逆発想で解こう。「何が save できるか」→「製品の利点」と考えれば, サーチしやすい。利点は第 2 段落。2 文目の no bottled water or water delivery service is needed と (A), 3 文目の not having to waste their time moving bottles or going out to get more と (D), 4 文目の It also saves space … と (B) がそれぞれ一致する。消去法で (C) が正解。

---

174. According to the advertisement, what will happen this year?　　広告によると, 今年は何が起こるでしょうか。

(A) A new branch office will open.
(B) The customer base will be expanded.
(C) Water prices will be lowered.
(D) User manuals will be distributed.

(A) 新しい支店が開店する。
(B) 顧客層が広がる。
(C) 水道料金が下がる。
(D) ユーザーマニュアルが配られる。

正解：(B)

● 着眼点！ キーワードをサーチ！

解説　設問のキーワード this year をサーチしよう。第 4 段落・1 文目 from June this year, we are also bringing water solutions to households in the service areas がポイント。企業向けのサービスに加え, 一般家庭向けにもサービスが拡大することがわかる。これを「顧客層が広がる」と言い換えた (B) が正解。

---

175. What is the contact method currently unavailable for customers?　　顧客が現在利用不可能な連絡方法は何でしょうか。

(A) Calling to a representative
(B) E-mailing to customer services
(C) Visiting an office
(D) Inquiring online

(A) 担当者への電話
(B) カスタマーサービスへのメール
(C) オフィスへの訪問
(D) オンライン上での問い合わせ

正解：(D)

● 着眼点！ ＊（アスタリスク）に注目！

解説　利用不可能な「連絡手段」について問われている。広告やメールなどの連絡先情報は, 終盤に書かれるのが定番。最終段落を見ると, ウェブサイトの更新をしているため, オンラインでの問い合わせ以外の連絡手段を利用するように勧めている。＊（アスタリスク）の文章がポイント。したがって, (D) が正解。

問題 **176-180** は次の記事に関するものです。

Chef Paul's, シドニーで最高のレストランに選出

Restaurant Guide の実施した調査によると，Chef Paul's がシドニーで最高のレストランに選出された。回答者の 40％以上が，Chef Paul's が大好きだと答えている。

オーナーシェフ Paul Durand の経営する Chef Paul's は，シドニー湾を見おろし，独創的なフレンチ・チャイニーズのフュージョン料理を提供している。中華の素材が，伝統的なフレンチコースにはない東洋の味わいを添えている。それぞれ上品に喜びを与えるような料理は，見た目にも美しい。Durand 自身が中国の隅々まで旅をして見つけてきたテーブルウェアが，いまでは Chef Paul's の現代的なアジア風のスタイルを特徴づけている。

しかし，料理を上回るのは，多くの人々が「超一流」と絶賛する Chef Paul's の申し分のないサービスだ。ウエーターはみな礼儀正しいが気取ったところはなく，どのテーブルでも完璧なタイミングでサービスを受けることができる。むろん，湾の夜景も一役買っている。

フランス人である Paul Durand は，父親が外交官として赴任していた香港で生まれ育った。彼の中国人と中国の食文化への理解は，この時期に培われたという。

シドニーで最高のレストランに選ばれたことを聞かされた時，彼は控えめにこう言った。「私たちは，ただ自分たちに求められていること，つまり，おいしい料理を，心地よい雰囲気の中でお出しすることを実行しているだけなのです」と。

語句
- □ overlook 動 ～を見おろす　□ cuisine 名 料理　□ ingredient 名 材料
- □ tastefully 副 上品に　□ delightful 形 喜びを与える
- □ impeccable 形 非の打ちどころのない　□ pretentious 形 もったいぶった
- □ diplomat 名 外交官　□ modestly 副 控えめに

176. Where is Chef Paul's located?　　Chef Paul's はどこにありますか。

(A) Downtown　　(B) In the business district　　(A) 繁華街
(C) In the bay area　　(D) In the airport　　(B) ビジネス地区
　　　　　　　　　　　　　　　　　　　　　　　(C) 湾の近く
正解：(C)　　　　　　　　　　　　　　　　　　(D) 空港の中

着眼点！ 選択肢を「タテ読み」！　　レベル ★★☆☆

解説 選択肢をザッと「タテ読み」して，イメージをつかもう。次にキーワード Chef Paul's をサーチ。第2段落の冒頭の Overlooking the Sydney Harbor がヒント。第3段落の最後の the view of the harbor at night helps からも推測できる。ここから正解は (C)。

---

177. Where did Paul Durand buy the dishware used at the restaurant?　　Paul Durand はレストランで使う食器をどこで買いましたか。

(A) In Japan　　(B) In Australia　　(A) 日本
(C) In China　　(D) In France　　　(B) オーストラリア
　　　　　　　　　　　　　　　　　　(C) 中国
正解：(C)　　　　　　　　　　　　　(D) フランス

着眼点！ 人名キーワードをサーチ！　　レベル ★☆☆☆

解説 セオリー通り，キーワード Paul Durand をサーチ。第2段落の最後の文に，Durand has personally traveled to every corner in China looking for tableware とある。every

104

corner in ~ は「~の隅々まで, ~中（じゅう）を」。設問の **dishware** は本文の **tableware** の言い換えになっている。ここから（C）が正解。

---

178. What is mentioned about Paul Durand's family?　Paul Durand の家族について何が述べられていますか。

(A) They run a small restaurant.　　　　　　　　(A) 小さなレストランを経営している。
(B) They enjoy making a voyage.　　　　　　　　(B) 長旅を楽しんでいる。
(C) They financially supported the opening of　(C) 彼がレストランを開くことに財政的
　　his restaurant.　　　　　　　　　　　　　　　　に援助した。
(D) They experienced living abroad.　　　　　　(D) 海外に住んだ経験がある。

正解：(D)

●着眼点！ 人物紹介のパートを探せ！

解説　キーワード Paul Durand をサーチすると、第4段落の最初の文に, Paul Durand, ... , was born and raised in Hong Kong とある。香港に住んでいたことがわかり, 正解は（D）。

---

179. When did Durand cultivate his understanding of　Durand が中国料理に対する理解を
　　 Chinese food?　　　　　　　　　　　　　　　　　培ったのはいつですか。

(A) During his childhood　　　　　　　　　　　　(A) 子ども時代
(B) During his apprenticeship　　　　　　　　　(B) 見習い時代
(C) During his travels　　　　　　　　　　　　　(C) 旅行中
(D) During his work as assistant chef　　　　　(D) アシスタントシェフとして働いていた時代

正解：(A)

●着眼点！ 名詞以外もサーチしてみよう！

解説　設問の **cultivate** に注目して本文をサーチ。第4段落, Durand の生い立ちを紹介する文に続いて, His understanding of the Chinese and their food culture is said to have been cultivated at this time. とある。香港での経験が重要だったとわかる。よって, 正解は（A）。

語句　☐ apprenticeship 名 見習い

---

180. The word "courteous" in paragraph 3, line 4, is　第3段落・4行目の courteous に最も
　　 closest in meaning to　　　　　　　　　　　　　　近い意味の語は

(A) polite　　　　　　(B) sympathetic　　　　　(A) 礼儀正しい
(C) excellent　　　　 (D) anxious　　　　　　　(B) 思いやりのある
　　　　　　　　　　　　　　　　　　　　　　　　(C) 素晴らしい
正解：(A)　　　　　　　　　　　　　　　　　　(D) 不安な

●着眼点！ 語彙問題は即答！

解説　courteous = polite がわかる時は即答しよう。文脈から解くのがセオリーだが,（A）,（B）,（C）ともにプラスイメージのワード。文脈だけだと判断しづらい。**without being pretentious** とのつながりから（A）を選ぶ。

問題 181-185 は次の広告と E メールに関するものです。

SHORTMAN DEPOT
移転セール！　全品売り尽くし!!!
10月17日　土曜日　午前8時－午後9時
テキサス州，SHORTMAN，ステート・フェア会場，セクション G21 ～ G24

セクション
G21　トレーディングルーム
G22　机
G23　椅子とソファ
G24　電化製品

オフィスの家具をお探しですか？　全品低価格で国内屈指のオフィス家具がございます。

デスク：大きい机や小さい机，テーブルは金属，硬材，自然木仕上げの複合材で，さまざまなスタイルを取
　　　り揃えています。220ドルから。
椅子とソファ：Shortman はテキサス州で最大の革のオフィスチェア，マッサージチェアやソファの販売
　　　会社です。お買い得品もたくさんございます。革のオフィスチェア4脚のご注文で，5脚目が無料になり
　　　ます！　お値段は1脚150ドルから。
電化製品：冷蔵庫，電子レンジ，フラットスクリーンのテレビやステレオをお探しですか？　Shortman
　　　にはすべてあります。中古冷蔵庫は580ドルから。中古フラットスクリーンテレビの国内最大の在庫が
　　　あります。それらは780ドルから。注文制作のステレオシステムもぜひ来店してご覧ください！　皆様
　　　の事務所，ご家庭，車用にオリジナルデザインにすることができます。

このイベントに参加するには，受付で登録をしていただきます。その際に，入場料15ドルをお支払いくだ
さい。

宛先：Jeff Peterson, Shortman Depot
送信元：Michael Grandyman
件名：移転セール事前注文
日付：10月15日

先週はありがとうございました。よい取り引きを期待できるので，あなたのトレーディングルームの案はと
てもよいと思います。
電話でお話した通り，私はそちらのセールで売り出される品物に興味を持っているバイヤー数人の地域代表
をしています。したがって，彼らを代表して，イベントに先立ち，あといくつか質問したいことがあります。
まず，フラットスクリーンテレビは液晶，プラズマどちらでしょうか。あるいは両方お持ちでしょうか。
次に，中古冷蔵庫はどんなサイズのものがありますか。このことについて知りたいのは，オフィスのスペー
スに入る大きさであれば，中古冷蔵庫を何台か買うのに興味があるバイヤーがいるためです。そこで，商品
の詳細を何枚かの写真と一緒に送っていただけますでしょうか。
3番目に，革のオフィスチェアの在庫は何脚ありますでしょうか。15脚以下しかない場合は，他の種類の
お勧めを教えていただけますか。250ドルより安価の椅子を購入できたらと思っています。
なるべく早いお返事をお待ちしています。

語句　☐ composite　形 複合の　☐ inventory　名 在庫品　☐ custom-made　形 特注の
　　　☐ on one's behalf　～を代表して，～の代わりに

181. In the advertisement, what area of business is being advertised?

(A) An interior designer
(B) An office supplies store
(C) An appliance repair service
(D) A homemade furniture shop

広告では，どんな業種が宣伝されていますか。

(A) インテリアデザイナー
(B) オフィス用品店
(C) 電化製品修理業者
(D) 手作り家具店

正解：(B)

● 着眼点！ 広告のジャンルを見抜け！　レベル ★★☆☆

解説　広告のジャンルが問われている。広告の最初にLooking to furnish your office? We've got some of the finest office furniture in the country, とあるので，「オフィス家具」の広告だとわかる。したがって(B)が正解。冒頭からジャンルをつかもう。

---

182. What product does Shortman Depot stock the most of in the United States?

(A) Office chairs
(B) Used-flat-screen TVs
(C) Hardwood desks
(D) Used refrigerators

Shortman Depot が全米で一番多くの在庫を持っている製品は何ですか。

(A) オフィスチェア
(B) 中古フラットスクリーンテレビ
(C) 硬材使用の机
(D) 中古冷蔵庫

正解：(B)

● 着眼点！ 最上級をサーチ！　レベル ★☆☆☆

解説　在庫数ナンバー1の製品が問われているので，本文中の「最上級」表現を探す。Appliances「電化製品」のセクションに，We have the biggest inventory of used flat-screen TVs in the country とある。inventory も stock も「在庫品」のこと。したがって，(B)が正解。

---

183. Why is Michael Grandyman writing this e-mail?

(A) To arrange for delivery of goods to his customers
(B) To ask about goods for his clients
(C) To complain about several goods he purchased
(D) To sell desks, couches and refrigerators

Michael Grandyman はなぜこのメールを書いているのですか。

(A) 彼の顧客に品物を配達してもらう手配をするため。
(B) 彼の顧客のために商品について尋ねるため。
(C) 彼が購入したいくつかの商品について苦情を言うため。
(D) 机，ソファ，冷蔵庫を売るため。

正解：(B)

● 着眼点！ ビジネスメールの目的は冒頭を見よ！　レベル ★★☆☆

解説　Michael Grandyman は，メール冒頭で自分の身分を明らかにしている。I am representing several buyers in the area から，顧客を代表していることがわかる。そのあとに I have a few more questions to ask prior to the event. と続き，顧客のために質問をしているとわかる。正解は（**B**）。

---

184. What does Michael ask about the TV sets? | Michael はテレビについて何を聞いていますか。

(A) Production areas
(B) Years of manufacture
(C) Sizes of TV screens
(D) Types of TV displays

(A) 製造場所
(B) 製造年
(C) テレビ画面のサイズ
(D) テレビのディスプレイの種類

正解：（D）

● 着眼点！ 「TV」を素早くサーチ！ レベル ★☆☆☆

解説 Michael Grandyman のメールには多くの質問が含まれている。「TV」に関しては第 3 段落，First, which flat screen TVs do you offer, LCD or plasma? とあり，TV の種類を聞いている。よって，正解は（**D**）。

---

185. Which section will Grandyman NOT likely enter? | Grandyman はどこのセクションには入らないと思われますか。

(A) G21
(B) G22
(C) G23
(D) G24

(A) G21
(B) G22
(C) G23
(D) G24

正解：（B）

● 着眼点！ クロス・サーチしよう！ レベル ★☆☆☆

解説 広告とメールの両方を見て解く。フェア会場のセクション割り当ては G21 トレーディングルーム，G22 机，G23 椅子とソファ，G24 電化製品。Grandyman の関心はメールから判断。第 1 段落に I like your idea of the trading room as I can expect another good deal to be signed. とあるので，G21 のトレーディングルームは OK。第 5 段落に how many leather office chairs do you have in stock? とあるので，G23 の椅子とソファのセクションにも入るだろう。第 3，第 4 段落でテレビと冷蔵庫に関して質問しているので，G24 の電化製品のセクションにも入る。G22 机については言及なし。よって，（**B**）が正解。

問題 186-190 は次の手紙とチラシに関するものです。

11月5日
Chris Taylor 様
Taylor's Deli

Taylor 様

毎年恒例の第3回ホリデー・ビンゴイベントに惜しみなくご寄付いただき，誠にありがとうございました。ご寄付いただいた 50 ドルのギフト券は，結局，Taylor 様のお店でよくお買い物をされる女性が当選されました！
私たちが初めてこのイベントを開催してから，今回で3回目を迎えます。この地域の皆様からの寛大なご寄付のおかげで，今回集まった金額は 230,987 ドルにのぼりました（去年から 30％の増加です）。
ホリデー・ビンゴイベントというアイデアが最初に生まれたのは，祝日休暇の過ごし方について，何人かで話し合っているときでした。この話し合いは最終的に，世界には，基本的な生活にも窮している恵まれない人々がどれほどいるかということ，そしてこのような人々に力を貸すために私たちにできることは何なのか，ということに発展しました。
収益は毎年，異なる慈善団体に贈られます。今回は，アフリカの難民キャンプに住んでいる人々，特に子どもたちに対して，食料と医薬品を提供している慈善団体を寄贈先に選びました。
First Bank Center で開催される写真展のチラシと開催の前日の招待券2枚を同封しています。写真は世界の子どもたちを取り上げています。どの写真も愛らしく心をひきつけられますが，胸が張り裂けるような痛ましいものもあります。だからこそ，私たちは慈善事業を続けるのです。
引き続き私たちの活動をご支援いただければ幸いです。
最後に，寛大なご行為に対し，改めてお礼申し上げます。

敬具
Patricia Walker
運営委員長
（同封物あり）

写真展
世界の子どもたち

開催期間：11月25日～12月3日
会場：　First Bank Center，1階
入場料：
　大人 10 ドル
　子ども（12～18歳）3 ドル
　　　（12歳未満）無料
母親に抱きしめられる子ども。
自分のからだの2倍もある食べ物を運ぶアリをじっと見つめる子ども。
愛らしく，それでいて胸が張り裂けるような写真が，子どもには愛情と安全と保護が必要であるということを，私たちに思い出させてくれます。
3人の写真家がこれらの写真を撮影するために世界中を旅して周りました。彼らは貧しい子どもたちのために使うお金を集めるためにこの展覧会を企画しました。

> 語句
> □ generous 形 寛大な　□ voucher 名 商品券　□ thanks to ～　～のおかげで
> □ eventually 副 最終的に　□ proceeds 名 収益　□ medication 名 医薬品
> □ especially 副 特に　□ refugee 名 難民　□ enclose 動 ～を同封する
> □ exhibition 名 展覧会　□ endearing 形 人に愛される

186. What did Mr. Taylor contribute to the bingo event?

(A) $50 in cash
(B) Items from his shop
(C) A gift certificate for his shop
(D) A gift basket

Taylor 氏がビンゴイベントに寄付したものは何ですか。

(A) 現金 50 ドル
(B) 自分の店の商品
(C) 自分の店で使えるギフト券
(D) ギフトセット

正解：(C)

● 着眼点！　言い換えに反応せよ！　レベル ★★★☆

解説　Patricia Walker からの手紙の冒頭で，まず Taylor 氏に，寄付に対するお礼の言葉を述べている。そして，Your $50 gift voucher was ... とあるので，正解は (C)。gift voucher = gift certificate を見抜こう。

---

187. Where do the proceeds of the event go?

(A) To the local community
(B) To a holiday event
(C) To three photographers
(D) To a charity organization

イベントの収益はどこへ行きますか。

(A) 地元のコミュニティー
(B) 祝日のイベント
(C) 3 人の写真家
(D) 慈善団体

正解：(D)

● 着眼点！　キーワードでサーチせよ！　レベル ★☆☆☆

解説　設問のキーワード proceeds をサーチしよう。手紙の第 4 段落に，The proceeds go to a different charity every year. とある。charity は「慈愛，慈善の心」を意味する名詞で，慈善に関する行為，事業，団体などに対しても使われる言葉。正解は (D)。

---

188. What is enclosed in the letter?

(A) A pamphlet of the charity organization
(B) A document explaining the plight of African refugees
(C) A leaflet and two invitation tickets to a display
(D) An accounting report of the bingo event

手紙に同封されているのは何ですか。

(A) 慈善団体のパンフレット
(B) アフリカ難民の窮状を説明する書類
(C) 展覧会のチラシと 2 枚の招待券
(D) ビンゴイベントの会計報告書

正解：(C)

● 着眼点！ 「同封」されていたものを見抜け！

[解説] キーワード enclosed をサーチしよう。手紙の第5段落に，We have enclosed a flyer ... and two invitations とあるので，これを言い換えた (C) が正解。We have enclosed「～を同封します」は手紙でよく使われる表現なので覚えよう。

[語句] □ plight 图 苦境，窮状

---

189. Who organized the exhibition? 展覧会を開催するのはだれですか。

(A) Three photographers
(B) The organizing committee of the bingo event
(C) The local community
(D) First Bank Center

(A) 3人の写真家
(B) ビンゴイベントの組織委員会
(C) 地元のコミュニティー
(D) First Bank Center

正解：(A)

● 着眼点！ チラシを見よう！

[解説] 礼状の差出人が Committee Chairman となっているからと，そこだけから判断すると不正解の (B) を選んでしまう。チラシの最終文を見よう。Three photographers have traveled ... と紹介してから，They have put together this exhibition とあるのが目に留まる。ここから正解は (A)。

[語句] □ put together ～をまとめ上げる，企画する

---

190. When will Mr. Taylor see the exhibition for free? Taylor さんはいつ展覧会を無料で見に行きますか。

(A) On November 24
(B) On November 25
(C) On December 2
(D) On December 3

(A) 11月24日
(B) 11月25日
(C) 12月2日
(D) 12月3日

正解：(A)

● 着眼点！ クロス問題に慣れよう！

[解説] 「日付」はクロスリファレンス問題の定番。Taylor さんが展覧会に行く日が問われているので，手紙を見よう。第5段落に two invitations for the previous day of the opening とある。チラシを見ると展覧会が開催されるのは November 25 to December 3 であるから，11月25日の前日の11月24日に見に行くと考えられるため，(A) が正解。

問題 191-195 は次のメモと手紙に関するものです。

メモ

担当者：支配人 Daisy Sparks
宛名：Buchow Hotel 全従業員
日付：6月5日（月）
件名：改修と点検の予定表

今週，下記の改修と点検がホテルの資産に対して行われます。改修または点検の当日には，該当施設が閉鎖されますので，ご注意ください。私たちのお客様が当ホテルでの安全で快適な宿泊を引き続きお楽しみいただけるように，今回の改修および点検は行われます。しかしながら，ご不便をおかけしてしまうこともありますので，お客様のご要望にはいつも以上に気を配ってください。

日付	詳細
6月6日	メインエレベーターの安全点検
6月7日	会議室のカーペットの張り替え
6月8日	ビジネスセンターに4台の新しいコンピューターを設置
6月9日	ホテルのフィットネスセンターの設備の点検

6月21日
Daisy Sparks 様
郵便番号 52873
ミネソタ州 Montrose 郡
Nelson 大通り 267 番
The Buchow Hotel

Sparks 様

私の名前は Ed Banks と申します。何度か Buchow Hotel に滞在したことがあります。従業員の方から心よりお助けいただいたことや，その豪華な雰囲気のおかげで貴ホテルをずっと気に入っていました。前者には変わりがなかったことは喜ばしいのですが，後者には顕著な凋落が見られました。

最後に宿泊した際，ロビーの家具を掃除する必要があるように思えました。客室はいつも通り快適でしたが，ブランド物のシャンプーとコンディショナーが安物のノーブランドのものに交換されていました。さらに，夜部屋にベーコンサンドイッチを注文したら，一時間後に冷たい状態で届きました。

ビジネス会議に出席したあと，貴ホテルに戻って運動するのを楽しみにしていましたが，フィットネス施設は何の事前通知もなしに閉鎖されていました。

心を寄せる顧客として，貴ホテルの今後の営業にここに記した私の意見がお役に立てるよう願っております。

敬具
Ed Banks （署名）
Ed Banks

> **語句**
> □ agenda 名 予定表, 議題　□ renovation 名 改修, 修繕, 修復
> □ perform 動 ~を実行する, 行う　□ asset 名 資産, 財産
> □ respective 形 それぞれの　□ check 名 点検, 検査, 健康診断
> □ ensure 動 ~を確実にする, ~を確かめる　□ attentive 形 注意深い, 気を使う
> □ set up ~　~を設置する　□ equipment 名 器具, 設備, 装置
> □ occasion 名 場合, 時　□ genuine 形 心からの, 本物の
> □ helpfulness 名 助けになること, 有用性　□ generic 形 一般的な, ノーブランドの

191. What is the purpose of the memo?　メモの目的は何ですか。

(A) To call an employee meeting　(A) 従業員会議を招集すること。
(B) To inform of a change in management　(B) 経営陣の変更を知らせること。
(C) To announce a maintenance schedule　(C) メンテナンスの日程を周知すること。
(D) To schedule a safety inspection　(D) 安全検査の日程を決めること。

正解：(C)

● 着眼点！ Subjectと冒頭をチェック！　レベル ★★☆☆

解説　冒頭に件名がある場合は，まずチェック。**Re: Renovations and Checks Agenda** とあり，改修と点検についてのメモであることがわかる。**agenda** は「協議事項，予定（表）」の意味。ここから，(C) か (D) に絞られる。さらに，2文目に **respective facilities will be closed on the day of renovations or checks** とあり，メンテナンスの日程はすでに決まっていることがわかる。よって，(C) が正解。

---

192. In the memo, the word "assets" in paragraph 1, line 1, is closest in meaning to　メモの第1段落・1行目の assets に最も近い意味の語は

(A) property　(A) 資産, 所有物
(B) rooms　(B) 部屋
(C) services　(C) サービス
(D) administration　(D) 管理

正解：(A)

● 着眼点！ フレーズ／コロケーションが出る！　レベル ★★★★

解説　セオリー通り，文脈を見よう。**assets** が，件名や第1段落・1文目にある **renovations**「（建物や家具，部屋などの）改修，修繕」の対象であることをヒントに，(A) か (B) に絞られる。またそのあとの内容を読むと，改修の範囲が (B)「部屋」に限らず，ホテルのさまざまな施設に及んでいることから，(A) が正解だとわかる。**hotel assets** というフレーズ／コロケーションは頻出。しっかり覚えよう！

193. Why was the letter written?

(A) To report a safety concern
(B) To complain about construction noise
(C) To offer a customer opinion
(D) To demand a refund

手紙はなぜ書かれたのですか。

(A) 安全性の問題を報告するため。
(B) 建築工事の騒音について苦情を言うため。
(C) 顧客の意見を述べるため。
(D) 返金を要求するため。

正解：(C)

● 着眼点！ 「手紙」の目的をつかめ！

レベル ★★★☆

解説　BanksさんがBuchow HotelのSparksさんに宛てた手紙。冒頭ではホテルをほめているが、主旨はそのあとのホテルに対する不満である。特に第4段落、As a concerned customer, I hope my opinions here will benefit the future operation of your hotel. と述べているので、顧客としてホテルのサービスに意見していることがわかる。よって（C）が正解。冒頭を読んでも目的や理由が明らかでないときは、結論部分を読んでみよう。

---

194. What was Mr. Banks satisfied with?

(A) Hotel personnel
(B) Conference room
(C) Bathroom amenities
(D) In-room dining

Banksさんが満足していたのは何ですか。

(A) ホテルの職員
(B) 会議室
(C) 浴室のアメニティ
(D) ルームサービス

正解：(A)

● 着眼点！ 「プラス」を見抜け！

レベル ★★☆☆

解説　手紙から、Banksさんがホテルをほめている箇所（プラスの箇所）を見抜こう。冒頭、I have always favored the hotel for the genuine helpfulness of its employees and its deluxe atmosphere. がポイント。従業員と雰囲気をほめている。ここから、（A）が正解。（B）は本文で触れられておらず、（C）と（D）は不満であった点として述べられているので誤り。

語句　□ amenity 图 アメニティ

---

195. On which day did Mr. Banks most likely stay at the hotel?

(A) June 6　　(B) June 7
(C) June 8　　(D) June 9

Banksさんは何日にホテルに宿泊したと思われますか。

(A) 6月6日
(B) 6月7日
(C) 6月8日
(D) 6月9日

正解：(D)

● 着眼点！ 「日付」はクロス問題の定番！

レベル ★★☆☆

解説　手紙には「日付」の情報がないので、まずメモを見よう。日付と詳細を確認。次に手紙を見ると、第3段落でフィットネス施設が利用できなかったとわかる。フィットネス施設の点検があったのは、6月9日。よって、正解は（D）。

問題 196-200 は次のお知らせと E メールに関するものです。

発行者：IIMG 社，シカゴ本社，人事部
発行日：6 月 1 日
社員各位

ロサンゼルスサプライチェーン部門における管理職の空位について

当社ロサンゼルス支店では現在，サービス地域拡大の計画に際し，サプライチェーン責任者を求めています。業務は 9 月 1 日より開始の予定です。
職務は西海岸地域における流通業務全般の監督となります。加えて，既存および見込み客対応，四半期の査定についても主たる責任者となります。適任者は次の要件を満たすこととします。

- 流通，物流管理，販売，他関連業務分野における最低 5 年の勤務経験
- 熟達した管理職としての経験，およびチームをまとめる手腕
- 家族と同居している応募者は，配偶者，子ども，ほかの同居家族のロサンゼルスへの転居の同意（最初の 1 か月間，宿泊場所は会社が用意します）
- 経営学修士取得者が望ましい

応募について：
興味のある社員は簡単な自己紹介を添えて，Rachel Harper 人事部長（rachharper@hr.iimg.com）宛てに 6 月 28 日までに E メールを送ること。Harper 人事部長と Chris McCartney ロサンゼルス支店長が，本社にて 7 月 3 日から 5 日の間に 1 回個人面接を行います。決定した面接日程は追って知らせることとします。

送信者：Ryu Xin Chu < xincryu@sp.iimg.com >
件名：ロサンゼルス SCM 職への応募
日付：6 月 24 日
宛先：Ms. Rachel Harper < rachharper@hr.iimg.com >

Harper 様

私は販売部副部長 Ryu Xin Chu と申します。6 月 1 日付で募集されているロサンゼルスのポジションに大変興味がありこのメールを送信しています。
私は McMillan School of Business を卒業後，経営学修士号を取得し，この 7 年間 IIMG 社で働いております。最初の 3 年はサプライチェーン部に配属され，中西部における当社サービスの競争力維持プロジェクトに携わりました。プロジェクトにおける交渉責任者としての私の役割は，当該期間中地域での販売において有効であったと証明されました。次の 4 年間は販売部で働き，より費用効率の高い宣伝計画の策定に向け，チームを指揮することに専念いたしました。私は新しい販売促進方法を導入することにより，この 4 年にわたり新規顧客数拡大に成功いたしました。
私の家族は新たな挑戦に臨む私の願いを支えてくれることをお約束いたします。私の夫と子どもたちはもともと南カリフォルニアの出身なので，ロサンゼルスへの引っ越しに前向きです。
お返事をお待ちしております。

敬具
Ryu Xin Chu

> 語句
> ☐ HR Department (Human Resources Department)　人事部
> ☐ be accountable for ～　～に責任がある (= be responsible for ～)
> ☐ requirement　名 要件
> ☐ accommodation　名 宿泊設備
> ☐ devote oneself to ～　～に専念する
> ☐ cost-effective　形 費用効率の高い

196. What is the main topic of the notice?

お知らせの主な話題は何ですか。

(A) Relocation of the headquarters
(B) Study abroad programs for employees
(C) Evaluation interviews
(D) In-house staff recruitment

(A) 本社の移転
(B) 職員の海外留学プログラム
(C) 査定の面接
(D) 社内公募

正解：(D)

● 着眼点！　見出しと冒頭を見よ！

レベル ★★☆☆

解説　まず，お知らせが To the staff「社員各位」とある点を見よう。さらに，お知らせの第1段落・1文目に，Our Los Angeles branch is currently seeking a supply chain director とあるので，社内公募だということがわかる。(D) が正解。

---

197. In the notice, the word "prospective" in paragraph 2, line 3, is closest in meaning to

お知らせの第2段落・3行目の prospective に最も近い意味の語は

(A) credentials
(B) potential
(C) confidential
(D) essential

(A) 資格，資質
(B) 可能性がある
(C) 秘密の
(D) 必須の

正解：(B)

● 着眼点！　基本ワードは即答！

レベル ★★★☆

解説　prospective = potential は TOEIC の基本ワード。即答して次へ行こう。prospective client「見込み客」と current client「既存客」の対比も大事。正解は (B)。

---

198. According to the notice, what is NOT suggested about the interview?

お知らせによると，面接に関してわからないことは何ですか。

(A) Questions to be asked
(B) Interviewers
(C) Number of times
(D) Location

(A) 質問事項
(B) 面接官
(C) 面接の回数
(D) 場所

正解：(A)

● **着眼点！** 事務連絡をチェック！

レベル ★★☆☆

解説　お知らせの最終段落は，面接についての事務連絡。本文と選択肢を比較しよう。(B), (C) と (D) は，2文目の Ms. Harper and Mr. Chris McCartney will do a one-time interview with each applicant at our headquarters を見れば OK。記述されていないのは「質問事項」で (A) が正解。

---

199. For which responsibility does Ms. Ryu Xin Chu most likely have the greatest confidence?　どの職責について Ryu Xin Chu さんは最も自信を持っていると思われますか。

(A) Information collection
(B) External affairs
(C) Producing electronic documents
(D) Organizing outgoing mail

(A) 情報収集
(B) 渉外
(C) 電子文書作成
(D) 送信メールの整理

正解：(B)

● **着眼点！** 職務内容をサーチ！

レベル ★★★☆

解説　Chu さんの職務内容は，E メールの第2段落を見よう。3文目の My role as chief negotiator in the project proved to be beneficial to regional sales over that period. から，正解は (B) と判断できる。negotiator は「交渉者」，つまり外部とのやり取り（＝ external affairs）を行っているので，これをアピールとすれば正解がわかる。

---

200. What is true about Ms. Ryu Xin Chu?　Ryu Xin Chu さんに当てはまることは何ですか。

(A) She used to work in the LA branch.
(B) She cannot live with her family in LA.
(C) She meets all the requirements.
(D) She comes recommended by her supervisor.

(A) 以前ロサンゼルス支店で働いていた。
(B) ロサンゼルスでは家族と一緒に生活することができない。
(C) すべての要件を満たしている。
(D) 上司から推薦されている。

正解：(C)

● **着眼点！** 採用の「要件」を見よ！

レベル ★★★☆

解説　お知らせの採用の要件をチェックしよう。Chu さんのメールとその要件を比較すると，Chu さんはすべてクリアーしているとわかる。ここから (C) を選ぶ。

READING TEST

模試 3
解答と解説

- 問題は，別冊の 66 〜 97 ページに掲載されています。

模試 3 解答と解説

PART 5

101. Christine has finished ------- paychecks for all employees.
(A) preparing (B) to prepare
(C) prepare (D) prepared

Christine は全従業員分の給与支払小切手を準備し終えたばかりです。

正解：(A)

● 着眼点！ 基本文法を確認せよ！

レベル ★☆☆☆

解説 空所直前の動詞 finish についての文法知識が問われる問題。動詞 finish が「〜し終える」という意味を表す場合，動名詞が続く。正解は (A)。(C) 動詞の原形，(B) to 不定詞や，(D) 過去形・過去分詞は動詞 finish のあとには続かない。

語句 □ paycheck 名 給与支払小切手

---

102. Technical support is available ------- a 24-hour basis for all registered users.
(A) from (B) for
(C) on (D) in

テクニカルサポートは，すべての登録ユーザーに 24 時間体制で提供されています。

正解：(C)

● 着眼点！ 前置詞とセットで語感を磨け！

レベル ★★☆☆

解説 文章は〈S (Technical support) + V (is) + C (available)〉と完成しているので，空所以下は修飾語句だと判断できる。空所の後ろに basis という語があることに注目。on a ~ basis で「原則〜で，〜方式で」という意味になる。よって，正解は (C)。on a 24-hour basis は「24 時間体制で」という意味。

語句 □ available 形 利用できる □ register 動 〜を登録する

---

103. The property ------- by the real estate agent is fairly close to what we had in mind.
(A) will show (B) shown
(C) shows (D) showing

不動産業者に見せてもらった物件は，私たちが思い描いていたものにかなり近いです。

正解：(B)

● 着眼点！ 空所に入る動詞の活用・変化を特定せよ！

レベル ★★☆☆

解説 動詞の形が問われている。空所前に名詞 property と空所後に by があるので，ここは形容詞の働きがあり，後ろから前を修飾できる過去分詞 (B) が最も適切。動詞 show の (A) 未来形，(B) 過去分詞，(C) 三人称・単数・現在形，(D) ing 形。

語句 □ property 名 物件，資産 □ real estate agent 不動産業者
□ fairly 副 かなり

104. Many ------- sales techniques, particularly Internet advertising, were introduced in the training session.
(A) usage (B) useful
(C) use (D) usefully

多くの役に立つ営業テクニック，特にインターネット広告が研修会で紹介されました。

正解：(B)

● 着眼点！ 品詞を見極めよ！

レベル ★☆☆☆

解説　次に続く語が sales techniques「営業テクニック」と名詞句であることから，空所は形容詞であるとわかる。形容詞は (B) の useful のみである。この問題は品詞を見極めれば，空所の前後を読んだだけで正解できる。解答時間短縮が高得点に結びつくので，わかるところは全部読まない思い切りも必要。(A) 名詞「言葉の使い方，(物の) 使い方」，(B) 形容詞「有用な，役に立つ」，(C) 名詞「使用，用途」，(D) 副詞「有効に」。

105. Joanne Stanley dedicated herself ------- helping the company launch a new business.
(A) for (B) on
(C) to (D) of

Joanne Stanley は，新しい事業を立ち上げるのを手伝うことに専心しました。

正解：(C)

● 着眼点！ 語彙力は高得点への近道！

レベル ★★☆☆

解説　この設問では，語彙力が問われている。よく出題される表現 dedicate oneself to ～ は，「～に専念する，打ち込む」という意味を表す語句。(C) to 以外の前置詞は，この表現では用いられない。動詞とともに用いられる前置詞の組み合わせに注意しよう。

106. Jack patiently explained to new employees how spyware -------, because he knew it would take time to understand.
(A) works (B) to work
(C) be worked (D) working

理解するのに時間がかかることを知っていたので，Jack はスパイウェアがどのように働くのかを粘り強く新入社員に説明しました。

正解：(A)

● 着眼点！ 全文を読むな！

レベル ★★★☆

解説　動詞 work の適切な形を選択する問題。how 以下は Jack が何を説明したかを述べている。explain の目的語となる〈疑問詞 how + S + V〉の名詞節であることがわかれば，S の spyware に対応した動詞の形 (A) works だと判断できる。spyware は software と同様，不可算名詞。(A) 三人称・単数・現在形，(B) to 不定詞，(C) 受け身形，(D) ing 形。

語句　□ patiently 副 粘り強く　□ explain 動 ～を説明する
□ spyware 名 スパイウェア

107. The protection of ------- heritage is regarded as one of the most important tasks of this community.
(A) historical　　(B) historically
(C) histories　　(D) history

歴史的遺産の保護は，このコミュニティの最も重要な課題の1つと見なされています。

正解：(A)

● 着眼点！ 品詞選択は前後を見る！

レベル ★☆☆☆

解説　空所には後ろの名詞 heritage「遺産」を修飾する形容詞が入る。選択肢の中で形容詞は (A) の historical のみ。historical heritage「歴史的遺産」でひとかたまりとして覚えよう。(A) 形容詞「歴史的な」，(B) 副詞「歴史的に，伝統的に」，(C) 名詞 history「歴史」の複数形，(D) 名詞 history「歴史」の単数形。

語句　□ protection 图 保護　□ be regarded as ~ ～と見なされる
□ task 图 職務，課題

---

108. The two parties have ------- reached an agreement on the diplomatic policy submitted to a committee a year ago.
(A) finalized　　(B) finally
(C) final　　(D) finality

2党は，1年前に委員会に提出されていた外交政策についての合意についに達しました。

正解：(B)

● 着眼点！ 空所の単語の役割を見極めよ！

レベル ★☆☆☆

解説　空所に何も入らなくても文が完結するため，空所には副詞が入るとわかる。正解は (B)。reach an agreement on/about ~「～に関しての合意に達する」という表現も重要なので覚えておこう。(A) 動詞「～を完結させる」の過去形・過去分詞，(B) 副詞「ついに」，(C) 形容詞「最後の」，(D) 名詞「最終的なこと」。

---

109. An R&D project of new product lineups is in ------- in order to expand to foreign markets.
(A) short　　(B) progress
(C) return　　(D) tune

外国の市場へ拡大するために，新しい商品ラインナップの研究開発プロジェクトが進行中です。

正解：(B)

● 着眼点！ イディオムに精通せよ！

レベル ★★★☆

解説　選択肢はいずれも in に続くことで特定の意味を表す。イディオムの意味を正しく理解していることが，正解へのカギとなる。適切なのは (B)。(A) は in short で「要するに」，(B) in progress で「進行中の」，(C) in return で「引き換えに」，(D) in tune で「調和している」。

語句　□ R&D 研究開発（research and development の省略形）

---

110. After interviewing all the applicants, we will determine ------- ones to hire.
(A) whose　　(B) when
(C) which　　(D) what

すべての志願者を面接したあと，私たちはどの人を採用するか決定します。

正解：(C)

● 着眼点！ 文意から判断せよ！

レベル ★☆☆☆

解説　空所直後の ones は，カンマの前の the applicants を表していることがわかる。ここから，ある特定のグループから選ぶときに用いる which「どの，どちらの」が適切。したがって，(C) が正解。

111. Jupiter Group has set a new target for ------- in energy use, including electricity.
(A) reduce
(B) reduced
(C) reduction
(D) reducing

Jupiter Group 社は、電力を含むエネルギー消費量の削減について新しい目標を設定しました。

正解：(C)

● 着眼点！ 品詞の選択は前後から判断せよ！

【解説】 品詞を問う問題。空所の前が前置詞 for なので、名詞がくると判断できる。また、空所のあとに in energy use が続くので、ここは直接目的語を取る動名詞は不可。したがって、(C) に絞られる。(A) 動詞 reduce「〜を減らす、減少させる」の原形、(B) 動詞の過去形・過去分詞、(C) 名詞「縮小、低下、削減」、(D) 動詞の ing 形。

【語句】 □ target 名 目標　□ electricity 名 電気、電力

112. This program was designed to help our athletes be better prepared both physically ------- mentally.
(A) so
(B) and
(C) or
(D) but

このプログラムは、選手が身体的にも精神的にもよりよい準備ができるよう、手助けをするために考案されたものです。

正解：(B)

● 着眼点！ 並列表現を整理して覚えよ！

【解説】 文中に both があるので、ここは (B) の and。both A and B で「AとBの両方」となる。either A or B「AかBかどちらか」、neither A nor B「AとBのどちらでもない」、not A but B「Aだけでなく Bも」という表現も TOEIC に頻出。help + A（人）+動詞の原形で「Aが〜するのを手伝う」という形にも注意。

【語句】 □ design 動 〜を設計する、デザインする、計画する　□ athlete 名 運動選手

113. An annual maximum of two months' sick leave is paid in ------- with current company rules and regulations.
(A) accordance
(B) accord
(C) accordingly
(D) accorded

年間最長の2か月間の病気休暇は、現在の社内規定に従って付与されます。

正解：(A)

● 着眼点！ 3語から成る群前置詞に精通せよ！

【解説】 選択肢には accord の派生語が並んでいる。空所の前後は in ------- with なので、この形になるイディオムを知らなければ正解するのが難しい問題。in accordance with 〜 で「〜に従って」という意味になる。(A) が正解。

【語句】 □ annual 形 年間の　□ sick leave 病気休暇
□ rules and regulations 規定、規則

114. ------- half of the employees at Murata Trading Co. can speak two different languages.
(A) Much
(B) Every
(C) Almost
(D) Most

Murata 貿易会社の従業員の半数近くが，2つの異なる言語を話します。

正解：(C)

●着眼点！ 文脈を捉えよ！

レベル ★★☆☆

解説　選択肢の中から文意が通るものを選ぼう。空所のあと，half of the employees 以降の意味と合わせて，文意が通るのは (C) のみ。

---

115. HQ Organic Corp. has ------- high standards in environmental sanitation in order to insure the safety of their food products.
(A) restricted
(B) abandoned
(C) remained
(D) maintained

HQ Organic 社は，食料品の安全性を保証するために，環境公衆衛生について高い基準を維持してきました。

正解：(D)

●着眼点！ 文意を捉えよ！

レベル ★★★☆

解説　適切な動詞を選ぶ問題。文意が通るのは，(D)。(A) restrict「～を制限する」，(B) abandon「～を捨てる」，(C) remain「～のままである」，(D) maintain「～を維持する」。(A) と (B) はそれぞれ形容詞としても用いられ，restricted は「制限された」，abandoned は「見捨てられた」という意味になることも覚えておこう。

語句　□ insure 動 ～を保証する

---

116. The author points out that ------- of the news articles distributed on websites are not based on fact.
(A) one
(B) each
(C) every
(D) some

その著者は，ウェブサイトで配信されるニュース記事の中には事実に基づいていないものがあると指摘しています。

正解：(D)

●着眼点！ 文章を整理せよ！

レベル ★★☆☆

解説　空所のある that 節を整理しよう。that 節の主語は ------- of the news articles で，動詞は are となる。これに対応した複数形の主語にできるのは (D) の some。point out「指摘する」，not based on fact は「事実に基づいていない，でたらめである」という意味。

語句　□ author 名 著者　□ article 名 記事　□ distribute 動 ～を配る，配信する

---

117. Please note that discount rates ------- in this pamphlet do not include tax and are subject to change.
(A) listed
(B) list
(C) listing
(D) to list

このパンフレットに記されている割引価格は税金を含まず，変更される場合があることにご注意ください。

正解：(A)

●着眼点！ 文意を把握して正解を導け！

レベル ★★★☆

解説　動詞 list「～を記載する，一覧表にする」の形が問われている。that 節内の主語は discount rates ------- in this pamphlet と長いので要注意。空所には名詞句 discount rates を修飾できる過去分詞 (A) が入る。

語句　□ be subject to ～　～することがある，～しやすい

118. Please keep in mind that parking violations in this particular area are ------- penalized.
  (A) cautiously
  (B) severely
  (C) necessarily
  (D) accurately

この特定のエリアでの駐車違反は、厳しく罰せられることをご留意ください。

正解：(B)

レベル ★★★★

● 着眼点！ 語彙力で即答せよ！

[解説] 副詞を選ぶ問題。be penalized で「罰せられる」という意味を表す。この文意を踏まえると，penalized を適切に修飾する副詞は (B) だとわかる。(A)「慎重に」，(B)「厳しく」，(C)「必然的に」，(D)「正確に」。

[語句] □ violation 图 違反（行為）

---

119. You must turn off any electronic devices and refrain ------- using mobile phones while you are in a hospital.
  (A) of
  (B) in
  (C) from
  (D) to

病院内ではすべての電子機器の電源を切り，携帯電話の使用をお控えください。

正解：(C)

レベル ★★★☆

● 着眼点！ 定型表現を素早く見つけよ！

[解説] 語法に関する問題。refrain from ~ で「~を控える，慎む」という意味なので，正解は (C)。この from のあとには，名詞・動名詞が続く。turn off ~ は「~を切る，止める」という意味。

---

120. The labor union ------- up against a new labor law that would make it harder to keep a job.
  (A) rising
  (B) were risen
  (C) raised
  (D) rose

労働組合は，職を維持することがより困難となる新労働法に対抗して立ち上がりました。

正解：(D)

レベル ★★★☆

● 着眼点！ 自動詞と他動詞を見極めよ！

[解説] 正しい動詞を選ぶ問題。空所の後ろに前置詞 up があるので自動詞がくる。rise up against ~ で「~に対抗して立ち上がる」という意味で，自動詞 rise の過去形 (D) rose が正解。rise の過去分詞形は risen。(C) raised は他動詞 raise「~を起こす，立てる，引き上げる」の過去形・過去分詞。rise と raise は類似の意味を持つが，前者は自動詞，後者は他動詞なので違いに注意しよう。

[語句] □ labor law 労働法

121. ------- who want to use the company car must make a reservation at least a week in advance.
(A) They
(B) Those
(C) These
(D) That

社用車を使用したい人は，少なくとも1週間前には予約をしなければなりません。

正解：(B)

● 着眼点！ 定型表現をマスターせよ！

解説　正しい定型表現を選ぶ問題。those who ～で「～する人（たち）」という意味を表す。正解は（B）。空所周辺と選択肢から，定型表現を素早く見つけよう。

語句　□ in advance　事前に，あらかじめ

---

122. The program offered at Bomona College teaches sales representatives various ways to streamline ------- marketing plans for maximum benefit.
(A) themselves
(B) they
(C) them
(D) their

Bomona大学で開講されているプログラムは，営業担当者に最大限の利益を出すための彼らのマーケティング計画を効率化するさまざまな方法を教えています。

正解：(D)

● 着眼点！ 空所周辺から考えよ！

解説　人称代名詞の問題。空所周辺から答えが導ける。空所後に名詞句 marketing plans があることから，所有の意味を表す（D）their が適切だとわかる。その他の選択肢は名詞を修飾できないので，即答しよう。

語句　□ streamline　動 ～を効率化する

---

123. The guest speaker for today's investment seminar is expected to arrive at the hall at ------- 9:00 A.M.
(A) recently
(B) newly
(C) approximately
(D) properly

本日の投資セミナーのゲストスピーカーは，午前9時ごろにホールに到着する見込みです。

正解：(C)

● 着眼点！ 空所直後の語に注目せよ！

解説　副詞の語彙問題。空所のあとに時刻が続いているので，空所に入る可能性があるのは「約，およそ」という意味の（C）。approximately（= about）はこのように時刻の前で使われる。

語句　□ investment　名 投資

---

124. The workshop includes a free, one-hour private consultation to answer any questions a ------- may have.
(A) participation
(B) participates
(C) participating
(D) participant

その研修会には，参加者が抱くであろうあらゆる疑問に答えるため，1時間の無料個人相談が含まれています。

正解：(D)

着眼点！ 対応する動詞と目的語から主語を選べ！

解説 空所の直前には冠詞 a, 後ろは動詞 may have のため，空所には主語となる名詞が入る。また，have の後ろには目的語がないので，any questions を目的語とする関係詞が省略されていることがわかる。名詞は (A) か (D) のどちらかだが，have any questions の主語として適切なのは人を表す (D)「参加者」。(A) 名詞「参加」，(B) 動詞 participate「参加する」の三人称・単数・現在形，(C) 動詞の ing 形，(D) 名詞「参加者」。

語句 □ consultation 名 相談

---

125. Our economist, Mike James, is going to summarize the expected ------- of devaluing the Chinese yuan.
(A) effective   (B) effectively
(C) effects   (D) to effect

中国元の切り下げに伴い，予想される効果について，当社のエコノミスト Mike James が手短にお話しします。

正解：(C)

着眼点！ まず品詞を決定せよ！

解説 空所には動詞 summarize「～を要約する，かいつまんで言う」の目的語となり，かつ形容詞 expected を受ける名詞が適切。名詞は (C) effects のみ。品詞がわかれば正解できる。(A) 形容詞「有効な，効率的な」，(B) 副詞「効果的に」，(C) 名詞「効果」，(D) 動詞「～を生じる」の to 不定詞。

語句 □ devalue 動 (通貨を) 切り下げる □ yuan 名 元 (中国の通貨単位)

---

126. If you need some technical assistance, you can contact us by phone or e-mail, ------- you prefer.
(A) however   (B) where
(C) whoever   (D) whichever

技術的なサポートが必要であれば，お電話またはメールのどちらでも構いませんので，当社までご連絡ください。

正解：(D)

着眼点！ 空所周辺のヒントを見逃すな！

解説 空所を含む節は，他動詞 prefer「～を好む，選ぶ」の後ろに目的語がないため，空所にはその前の phone or e-mail を目的語とする関係詞が入る。文意に沿っているのは，「どちらの～でも」という意味の (D)。

---

127. Signs have been ------- stating that the beaches are closed because of the strong winds.
(A) performed   (B) practiced
(C) proceeded   (D) posted

強風のために浜は閉鎖されたという看板が掲示されました。

正解：(D)

着眼点！ コロケーションで語感を磨け！

解説 主語の sign は「看板，表示」の意味なので，選択肢の中で組み合わせて使われ得る動詞を探す。空所には (D) posted を入れるのが最適。各選択肢の原形とその意味は，(A) perform「～を実行する」，(B) practice「～を練習する，実施する」，(C) proceed「進む，続けて行う」，(D) post「～を掲示する」。

128. ------- a clerical error, the ordered items were delivered to the wrong address.
(A) Since   (B) As
(C) Whereas   (D) Because of

事務の手違いのため，注文の品物は誤った住所に配達されました。

正解：(D)

● 着眼点！ 原因と結果を読み解け！
レベル ★★☆☆

解説　カンマより前の a clerical error「事務の手違い」は，それ以降の「注文の品が誤った住所に配達された」の原因を述べている。(C) を除く選択肢は原因を述べる時に使われるが，(A) と (B) は接続詞のため，後ろに主語と動詞が必要。名詞（句）に用いることが出来るのは (D) のみ。同じ使い方が出来る due to, owing to もあわせて覚えよう。(A) 接続詞「～なので」，(B) 接続詞「～なので」，(C) 接続詞「～だが一方」，(D) 群前置詞「～のために」。

---

129. Tucker & Benson is accused of breaching its ------- to protect shareholder rights.
(A) reputation   (B) ambition
(C) transition   (D) obligation

Tucker & Benson 社は，株主の権利を守る義務に違反したとして告発されています。

正解：(D)

● 着眼点！ 名詞選択は文意の理解から！
レベル ★★★★

解説　名詞を選ぶ問題。空所のあとの to protect shareholder rights「株主の権利を守る」に適切につながるのは (D)。be accused of ～ で「～（の罪）で訴えられる，告発される」の意味。(A)「名声，評判」，(B)「野心，野望」，(C)「移り変わり，移行」，(D)「義務」。

語句　□ breach 動（法律・契約などに）違反する

---

130. Ms. Atkinson is tied ------- preparing for the autumn exhibition, so Ms. Johnson will be in charge of the store for a while.
(A) in   (B) back
(C) up   (D) on

Atkinson さんは秋の展示会に向けた準備で忙しいため，Johnson さんがしばらくの間お店を取り仕切ります。

正解：(C)

● 着眼点！ 使えるイディオムを増やせ！
レベル ★★☆☆

解説　英語表現の知識が試されている問題。be tied up「忙しい，手が離せない」という表現がポイント。この表現を知ってさえいればすぐに解ける問題。解答時間の短縮は高得点につながるので，イディオムは確実に身につけよう。

---

131. Any employees who have worked at the company for more than three years are ------- to apply for the assistant manager position at the Newport Branch.
(A) eligible   (B) manageable
(C) affordable   (D) accessible

3 年以上勤続したすべての従業員は，Newport 支店の係長職に応募する資格があります。

正解：(A)

● 着眼点！ 頻出表現をマスターせよ！
レベル ★★★☆

解説　be eligible to do「～する資格のある」という語句を知っていれば簡単に解ける。正解は (A)。apply for ～ は「～を志願する，求める」の意味。(A)「資格のある」，(B)「扱いやすい」，(C)「購入しやすい」，(D)「接近できる」。

132. The board was not ------- the management team had the right plan to get the company out of financial trouble.
　(A) convincing　　　(B) conviction
　(C) convinced　　　(D) convincible

委員会には，経営陣が会社を財政困難から救い出すためのしかるべき計画があるという確信はありませんでした。

正解：(C)

●着眼点！　省略された that を見抜け！

レベル ★★★☆

[解説] 空所の後ろは文が完結している。よって，that が省略されているとわかる。計画があるのは経営陣なので，the board は convince される側だということになる。したがって was not convinced と受け身になる (C) が正解。convince は that 節をとることを覚えておこう。(A) 動詞 convince「〜を確信させる」の ing 形，(B) 名詞「確信」，(C) 動詞の過去形・過去分詞，(D) 形容詞「説得できる」。

[語句] □ management team　経営陣

---

133. The sales figures for the ------- computer from Oregon Computing are skyrocketing as a result of having more functions than previous models.
　(A) latest　　　　　(B) later
　(C) late　　　　　　(D) lately

以前のモデルより多くの機能があることを受けて，Oregon Computing 社の最新コンピューターの売上高は急激に上昇しています。

正解：(A)

●着眼点！　対になる表現を探せ！

レベル ★★☆☆

[解説] ヒントは文末の than previous models「以前のモデルよりも」という部分。以前のモデルと対比されるのは「最新の」という意味を表す (A) latest。(A) 形容詞「最新の」，(B) 形容詞「より遅い」，(C) 形容詞「遅れた」，(D) 副詞「最近」。

[語句] □ skyrocket　動 急増する

---

134. Nick Hilton got promoted for his ------- ideas for the company's new product which will be marketed in Singapore.
　(A) creativity　　　(B) creative
　(C) creatively　　　(D) create

Nick Hilton はシンガポールで販売される会社の新製品に関する創造力のあるアイディアにより昇進しました。

正解：(B)

●着眼点！　前後を確認して品詞を特定せよ！

レベル ★☆☆☆

[解説] 品詞を問う問題。空所の後ろには名詞 ideas が続いていることから，空所は形容詞であると判断する。選択肢の中で形容詞は (B) creative のみである。get promoted で「昇進する」の意味。(A) 名詞「創造力」，(B) 形容詞「創造力のある」，(C) 副詞「創造的に」，(D) 動詞「〜を創造する」。

135. EZ Net's main shopping menu is temporarily unavailable ------- system maintenance.
(A) as for   (B) in case
(C) as well   (D) due to

EZ Net 社の主要なショッピングメニューは，システムメンテナンスのため，一時的にご利用できません。

正解：(D)

● 着眼点！ 因果関係を読み取れ！
レベル ★★☆☆

解説　空所の前後の temporarily unavailable と system maintenance は，結果と原因を示してしていることに着目したい。この関係を適切につなぐことができるのは原因・理由を表す (D) のみ。(A)「〜に関しては」，(B)「〜に備えて」，(C)「〜もまた」，(D)「〜のため」。

語句　□ temporarily 副 一時的に　□ unavailable 形 利用できない
□ maintenance 名 保守，メンテナンス

---

136. At least 50 companies were affected to some ------- by the bankruptcy of TJ Electronics.
(A) presence   (B) extent
(C) aspect   (D) width

TJ Electronics 社の倒産により，少なくとも 50 社がある程度の影響を受けました。

正解：(B)

● 着眼点！ 定型表現を攻略せよ！
レベル ★★★☆

解説　空所の直前の to some に注目するとよい。to some extent で「ある程度」という定型表現となるので，正解は (B)。to some degree もほぼ同じ意味の表現なので，覚えておくとよい。選択肢はすべて名詞で，(A)「存在，出席」，(B)「程度，範囲」，(C)「見地，様相」，(D)「幅，広さ」の意味。

語句　□ affect 動 〜に影響をおよぼす　□ bankruptcy 名 倒産

---

137. The Lighton Hotel is famous for its courteous service and many critics say that it is ------- one of the greatest hotels in the region.
(A) define   (B) definition
(C) definitely (D) definite

Lighton ホテルは，丁寧なサービスで知られ，多くの批評家も間違いなくその地域で最高のホテルの 1 つだと述べています。

正解：(C)

● 着眼点！ 常用単語に強くなれ！
レベル ★☆☆☆

解説　適切な品詞を選ぶ問題。空所に何も入らなくても文が完結するため，副詞の (C) definitely が適切。この強調の副詞はよく使われるので覚えよう。courteous は「礼儀正しい，丁寧な」という意味の形容詞。(A) 動詞「〜を定義する」，(B) 名詞「定義」，(C) 副詞「確かに」，(D) 形容詞「間違いない，疑いない」。

138. Mr. Anderson was the head of his own small, yet successful Internet start-up company ------- he turned twenty-five years old.
(A) whether
(B) whereas
(C) by the time
(D) in the end

Anderson さんは，25 歳になるころには，自らの小さいながらもうまくいっているインターネット新興企業のトップでした。

正解：(C)

● 着眼点！ 接続詞の選択は結ぶ文節の読解がカギ！

レベル ★★★☆

解説　空所後の he turned twenty-five years old は，「時」を表す副詞節と考えられるので，「時」を導く接続詞（句）が必要。(C) が正解。(A) 接続詞「～かどうか」，(B) 接続詞「～であるのに対して」，(C)「～する時までに」，(D)「最後に」。

語句　□ successful 形 成功した

---

139. Details of the partnership agreement ------- need to be carefully reviewed, but both parties hope to sign a contract by the end of the month.
(A) once
(B) still
(C) ever
(D) even

提携協定の詳細はまだ慎重に検討を重ねる必要がありますが，双方とも月末までに契約を結ぶことを望んでいます。

正解：(B)

● 着眼点！ 文意を読み取れ！

レベル ★★★☆

解説　副詞を選ぶ問題。主語 Details of the partnership agreement に対し，現在形の動詞 need「～の必要がある」が続いている。また，月末までに契約したいと考えていることから，現在も進行中のことだとわかるので，意味が通るのは (B) のみ。(A)「いったん（～すれば）」，(B)「まだ」，(C)「かつて」，(D)「～さえ」。

語句　□ partnership 名 提携　□ agreement 名 協定

---

140. ------- the support of the Pinage Art Association and the local government, the exposition on 19th century paintings would not have succeeded.
(A) Without
(B) Despite
(C) Unless
(D) Otherwise

19 世紀の絵画展は Pinage 芸術協会と地方自治体の支援なしには成功していなかったでしょう。

正解：(A)

● 着眼点！ 仮定法の慣用表現に注意！

レベル ★★★★

解説　カンマのあとの文から仮定法過去完了だとわかる。空所からカンマまでの部分に注目。the support of the Pinage Art Association and the local government は「Pinage 芸術協会と地方自治体の支援」という名詞句で，この文が仮定法過去完了であることから空所には (A) が入る。この場合 without = but for で「もし（あの時）～がなかったら」の意。(A) 前置詞「もし～がなかったら」，(B) 前置詞「～にもかかわらず」，(C) 接続詞「～でない限り」，(D) 副詞「さもなければ」。

PART 6

Questions 141-143 refer to the following memo.
問題 **141-143** は次のメモに関するものです。

BUSHBY, GERARD & DWYER INTER-OFFICE MEMO
Date: August 11
Subject: Air Conditioning Repair
To: All Employees and Staff

As some of you may have noticed, the air conditioning has not been working properly in our main office [141] last weekend.
Temperatures in the office rose to a maximum of 39 degrees Celsius, which is not healthy or conducive to work. Due to the extreme heat, the main office of BUSHBY, GERARD & DWYER will close temporarily for repairs. The main office will re-open early next week.
[142] it re-opens, we would like all employees and staff to work in rotation at the branch office.
Shifts are divided into morning and afternoon, so that each person [143] half a day.

BUSHBY, GERARD & DWYER 社 社内メモ
日付：8月11日
件名：エアコン修理
宛先：全社員およびスタッフ

お気づきの方もいらっしゃると思いますが，先週末から，当社の本社ではエアコンが正しく作動していません。
社内の温度は最高で摂氏39度まで上がり，これは健康に悪く，働く上でも能率的ではありません。非常に高温のため，BUSHBY, GERARD & DWYER 社の本社は修理に向け，一時的に閉鎖いたします。来週早々には営業を再開します。
本社の営業が再開されるまで，全社員とスタッフは支店で，ローテーションを組んで仕事をしていただきたいと思います。
それぞれの人が半日働くことになるように，シフトは午前番と午後番とに分けられています。

語句
- □ Celsius　名 摂氏
- □ conducive　形 貢献する，助けになる
- □ shift　名 交替制の勤務時間

141.
(A) before
(B) since
(C) by
(D) after

正解：(B)

● 着眼点！ 時制に対応する前置詞を整理せよ！

解説 空所の直後にある last weekend とともに用いられ、文脈に合う前置詞を選ぶ。前置詞の前には the air conditioning has not been working properly とあり、〈has + been ＋現在分詞〉による三人称単数・現在完了進行形で、「動作の継続」を表す。よって、現在完了とともに用いられる前置詞 (B) since が適切。(A)「〜より前に」、(B)「〜から」、(C)「〜までには」、(D)「〜のあとに」。

142.
(A) Although
(B) Instead
(C) Until
(D) Since

正解：(C)

● 着眼点！ 期間を示す接続詞 until をマスターせよ！

解説 本社は来週営業を再開すると記されている。ローテーションを組んで支店で働くのは「再開するまで」だと考えられるので、「〜するまで」と期間を示す接続詞 (C) until が正解。「〜までには」と期限を示す前置詞 by と間違えやすいので、例文とあわせて覚えよう。(A) 接続詞「〜だけれども」、(B) 副詞「その代わりに」、(C) 接続詞「〜するまで」、(D) 接続詞「〜だから」。

143.
(A) works
(B) has worked
(C) was working
(D) will work

正解：(D)

● 着眼点！ 時制を読み取れ！

解説 so that 〜 で「〜するように」という意味を表す。「それぞれの人が半日働くことになるように」という意味になるので、未来形の (D) will work が適切。選択肢はそれぞれ動詞 work「働く」の (A) 三人称・単数・現在形、(B) 三人称・単数・現在完了形、(C) 三人称・単数・過去進行形、(D) 未来形。

Questions 144-146 refer to the following notice.
問題 144-146 は次のお知らせに関するものです。

Notice to All Employees

We will be offering a new health insurance policy beginning September 1. There are various options including vision and dental plans for you to consider. On July 12, Ms. Martha Akers will be here for the day to advise 144 seeking consultation about new plans.
To make an appointment with Ms. Akers, send an e-mail to MAkers@omnihealth.biz with 3 145 for appointment times.
Ms. Akers will see employees for 15 minutes from 8:30 A.M. to 4:30 P.M. (unavailable during lunch break 12:30 P.M.-1:30 P.M.). Please cc your supervisor in all correspondence and Ms. Akers will use the "reply all" function to make sure that you are 146 from work at that time.

全従業員へのお知らせ

9月1日より，新しい健康保険を提供します。眼科と歯科プランを含むさまざまなオプションが用意されています。7月12日，Martha Akers さんが新しいプランについて相談希望者にアドバイスをするため，終日ここにいらっしゃる予定です。
Akers さんとの面会の予約は，面会の希望時間を3つ記して MAkers@omnihealth.biz に E メールをお送りください。
午前8時30分から午後4時30分までの間（午前12時30分から午後1時30分のお昼休憩中は除く）Akers さんは従業員の皆さんと15分間ずつお会いします。すべてのやり取りにおいて，皆さんの上司にも CC でメールを送信してください。Akers さんは，皆さんがその時間仕事の退出を許されるように「全員に返信」機能を使用して連絡します。

144. (A) the one
(B) who
(C) anyone
(D) that

正解：(C)

● 着眼点！ 文構造から絞りこめ！

［解説］ 選択肢から空所には，（新しいプランについて相談を求めている）「人」を表す語が入ることがわかる。一見，(B) か (D) の関係代名詞が入りそうだが，空所の後ろには動詞がないので，関係詞節を作ることができない。つまり，(B) と (D) は適さない。また，特定の 1 人を指す (A) も不可。したがって，(C) が正解。

145. (A) prefers
(B) preferable
(C) preferences
(D) preferably

正解：(C)

● 着眼点！ 派生語の品詞選びは前後から判断せよ！

［解説］ prefer の派生語から適切な品詞を選ぶ問題。空所の直前の 3 は空所の単語を修飾している。名詞である (C) の **preferences** が正解。(A) 動詞「～を好む」の三人称・単数・現在形，(B) 形容詞「好ましい」，(C) 名詞「希望，好み」の複数形，(D) 副詞「できれば」。

146. (A) excuse
(B) to excuse
(C) excusing
(D) excused

正解：(D)

● 着眼点！ 動詞の意味から正しい形を選べ！

［解説］ ここの **excuse** は「（義務・出席などを）免ずる，退出を許す」の意味。空所の前は **you are -------** となっているので，ここは「あなたは退出を許される」という受け身形の (D) **excused** がふさわしい。動詞 excuse「～を免ずる」の (A) 原形，(B) to 不定詞，(C) ing 形，(D) 過去形・過去分詞。

Questions 147-149 refer to the following e-mail.
問題 147-149 は次の E メールに関するものです。

To: Mark Stuart
From: Jonathan Woods
Subject: Incorrect Numbers in Master Chemicals' Order

I have just received a call from Mr. Pitt regarding an inaccurate order quantity for plastic bottles. The correct amount is 100,000 pieces, not 10,000 and they are ⬚147 that the complete amount be delivered as originally scheduled.
Master Chemicals has been one of our most valued clients and we are entirely ⬚148 here. I urge you to talk with the production line manager immediately to fulfill this order on time. Please report to me on the changes in production schedule, so Mr. Pitt can be updated on the situation shortly.
⬚149, remember that such a fundamental error only lowers our corporate value. From now on, I hope you will take the necessary measures to ensure this kind of error never happens again.

宛先：Mark Stuart
送信者：Jonathan Woods
件名：Master Chemicals 社からの発注数誤りの件

先ほど Pitt さんから，ペットボトルの発注数に間違いがあった件で電話がありました。正しくは 1 万個ではなく 10 万個で，当初のスケジュールで一括納品してほしいとのことです。
Master Chemicals 社は当社の一番の得意先の 1 つであり，今回のことはすべてこちらに非があります。この注文品の納入を間に合わせるために，すぐに生産ラインの責任者と話をしてください。Pitt さんに最新の状況を説明できるよう，生産スケジュールの変更に関して直ちに私に報告してください。
同時に，このような根本的ミスは当社の企業価値を下げるものであることを覚えておいてください。今後は，こうしたことが二度と起こらないよう，必要な措置を取るよう望みます。

> 語句
> ☐ **plastic bottle**　ペットボトル
> ☐ **fulfill**　動 ～を果たす，かなえる
> ☐ **fundamental**　形 根本的な，基本的な
> ☐ **take the measures**　（何らかの）措置をとる，対処する

147. (A) demanding
(B) decreasing
(C) canceling
(D) increasing

正解：(A)

●着眼点！ 消去法を活用せよ！

[解説] 空所の直前に they are とあり，後ろに「当初のスケジュール通りに一括納品される」という意味の that 節が続く。文脈から「要求している」とわかるので，(C) canceling「取り消している」は不適切。また，(B) decreasing「減少している」，(D) increasing「増加している」も除外。(A)「求めている」が正解。

148. (A) at fault
(B) hopeful
(C) with success
(D) on schedule

正解：(A)

●着眼点！ 話題のニュアンスを即座に判断せよ！

[解説] (A) at fault は「間違って，誤って」という意味。話の内容から (B) hopeful「希望に満ちた」，(C) with success「成功して」というポジティブな語は当てはまらないとわかるはず。(D) on schedule「スケジュール通りに」も，前後の文章を読めば適していないと判断できる。よって，正解は (A)。

149. (A) Otherwise
(B) Therefore
(C) However
(D) Meanwhile

正解：(D)

●着眼点！ 文章の構成を読み解け！

[解説] 空所までの文章は現状の説明と指示をし，空所以降の文章は「このようなことは企業価値を下げる。二度と起こさないように」と注意を喚起する内容で，それまでの内容を受けたまとめの部分として独立している。よって，(D) の Meanwhile のみ文意が通る。選択肢はすべて副詞で，(A)「さもなければ」，(B)「したがって」，(C)「しかしながら」，(D)「同時に」。

Questions 150-152 refer to the following article.
問題 150-152 は次の記事に関するものです。

Gourmet Stores to Open in U.K.

Gourmet Stores announced plans to open its stores in the U.K. early next year. ⎿150⏌ its spokesperson, the company will start with 3 outlets in London and gradually increase the number to 50 within 3 years.
⎿151⏌ 15 years ago, Gourmet Stores has been successful for providing fresh and exotic produce from around the world. It currently has 100 stores in 20 major U.S. cities. This will be the first time for the company to expand its business abroad. While the franchise is well-known among the American upper class, it is relatively unknown elsewhere.
Through its first international operation the company aims to provide goods that are not easily ⎿152⏌ at local supermarkets.

Gourmet Stores 社が英国に出店

Gourmet Stores 社は来年初めに英国に出店する計画を発表した。同社広報によれば，London の3店舗からスタートして，今後3年間のうちに50店まで徐々に店舗数を増やしていく予定。
Gourmet Stores 社は15年前に設立され，世界中から集めた新鮮な外国産の食材を提供して成功を収めている。現在，アメリカ国内の主要20都市に100店舗を展開しているが，今回の計画は同社初の海外進出となる。
同社の店舗はアメリカの上流層にはおなじみだが，他ではあまり知られていない。
同社初の海外事業を通じて，地元のスーパーでは簡単に手に入らない食材を提供することを目指している。

語句
- relatively 副 比較的，割合に
- elsewhere 副 どこか他で

150.
(A) Accorded by
(B) Accorded to
(C) Accordingly
(D) According to

正解：(D)

● 着眼点！ 決まり文句は瞬時に正解を導け！

レベル ★☆☆☆

[解説] 空所を含む文を読んで，カンマの後ろの内容を **spokesperson** が言っているという文意を読み取ろう。according to ～ は，「～によれば」という意味の決まり文句。よって，正解は (D)。**TOEIC** 超頻出表現なので，確実に覚えておきたい。(C) **accordingly**「それに従い」という副詞もよく使われるので，あわせて確認しておこう。

151.
(A) Regulated
(B) Announced
(C) Enforced
(D) Founded

正解：(D)

● 着眼点！ 解答のアタリをつけながら問題文を読め！

レベル ★★☆☆

[解説] 選択肢はすべて動詞の過去形・過去分詞。空所からカンマまでは分詞構文であり，空所が受ける主語はカンマの後ろにある **Gourmet Stores** という名前の会社なので，found「～を設立する」の過去分詞 (D) が適切。その他は，(A) **regulate**「～を規定する」，(B) **announce**「～を公表する」，(C) **enforce**「～を施行する」。

152.
(A) charged
(B) applicable
(C) obtainable
(D) ready

正解：(C)

● 着眼点！ 空所の前後の意味から正解を導け！

レベル ★★★☆

[解説] 選択肢はすべて形容詞。関係代名詞の **that** 以下は **goods**「食材」を修飾しているので，空所には食材を説明する単語が入る。また，空所の直前は **not easily**，空所の後ろが **at local supermarkets** なので，「地元のスーパーで，簡単に～でない食材」という意味を表すことがわかる。文脈に合うのは (C) の **obtainable**「入手可能な」。(A)「請求された」，(B)「適用できる，適切な」，(D)「準備のできた，手早い」。

PART 7

問題 153-154 は次の広告に関するものです。

Fisher's Country Club
成人向けゴルフキャンプ！
ゴルフを習ってみたいですか？
もっと上手になりたいですか？
いいスイングになるように練習してみたいですか？
Fisher's のゴルフキャンプなら，これらすべてを体験することができます！

ゴルフについて知っておくべきことのすべてを，Fisher's のプロ・インストラクターたちが素晴らしい施設であなたに教えます。施設には，18ホールのチャンピオンシップコース，300ヤードのドライビングレンジ，練習用パッティンググリーン，広々としたショートゲーム練習場が，あります。

Fisher's のキャンプには，最低2日間のものから1週間のものまであります。それぞれのキャンプのまず最初に，皆さんのスイングをビデオに録画して弱点を特定，この弱点をキャンプ期間中に集中して練習していきます。また，毎日，ショートゲームの練習，そして午後には，Fisher's のチャンピオンシップコースでの練習ラウンドがあります。

そして私たちが提供するのはこれだけではありません。私たちの宿泊施設はこの地域でも最高級施設の一つです。惜しみなくぜいたくにしつらえた内装，豪華なスパ，フィットネスセンター，スイミングプール，そして3つのレストランが，ゴルファーの皆さんだけでなく，皆さんのパートナー，お友だち，そして奥様やご主人様など，ただリラックスしたいという方たちも魅了します。

詳しくは，いますぐ，キャンプ事務所にご連絡ください。

語句
- □ fabulous 形 とても素晴らしい
- □ facility 名 施設
- □ accommodation 名 宿泊施設
- □ lavishly 副 ぜいたくに
- □ appointed 形 設備のある
- □ luxurious 形 豪華で快適な
- □ spouse 名 配偶者

153. What is suggested about Golf Camp?

ゴルフキャンプについて何がわかりますか。

(A) It offers a one-day trial camp.
(B) It extends instruction from professional tennis players.
(C) It assists in correcting swings with audiovisuals.
(D) It provides rental gear for activities.

(A) お試し日帰りキャンプがある。
(B) プロのテニス選手からの指導を受けられる。
(C) 視聴覚機器を使ってフォームの矯正を手助けする。
(D) 用具レンタルのサービスがある。

正解：(C)

● 着眼点！ キャンプの「説明」をサーチ！

[解説] 定番の suggest 問題。本文と選択肢を対応させよう。Golf Camp をサーチして，キャンプの説明箇所を見抜く。第 2 段落の冒頭，Our camp を目印に読みすすめ，2 文目に your swing will be videotaped to identify the weak areas you will work on improving during your stay をチェック。ビデオ録画に言及しているので，正解は (C)。

[語句] □ extend 動 ～を施す，示す，供与する

---

154. What is NOT indicated about the accommodation offered?

提供されている宿泊施設について示されていないことは何ですか。

(A) Luxurious furnishings
(B) Several cafeterias
(C) Souvenir shops
(D) Gymnasium facilities

(A) ゴージャスな内装
(B) いくつかの食事処
(C) 土産物売り場
(D) トレーニングジム

正解：(C)

● 着眼点！ NOT 問題は効率を優先せよ！

[解説] NOT 問題は，本文と選択肢の比較検討が必要。わかる箇所から効率よく比較しよう。(A)，(B)，(D) は 第 3 段落・2 文目の Our lavishly appointed rooms, luxurious spa, fitness center, swimming pool, and three restaurants からわかる。(C) は記述がないため，これが正解。

[語句] □ furnishing 名 家具調度品 □ souvenir 名 土産物

問題 155-156 は次の E メールに関するものです。

差出人： Rosenberg Hotel
宛先： J. Simmons 様
件名： 宿泊ご予約の件
日付： 2月16日（木）

Simmons 様

下記の通り，お客様のご予約を確認させていただきます。
お名前：　　　John Simmons 様ご夫妻
部屋タイプ：　ガーデンビュー・ツイン1部屋
ご宿泊日数：　4泊
チェックイン：　11月18日
チェックアウト：　11月22日

この予約を確定するため，ご連絡いただいたお客様のクレジットカードに1泊分の予約金（税込み）をご請求させていただきます。私どものキャンセルポリシーについては，ホテルのウェブサイトをご参照ください。私どもでは，空港とホテルを結ぶ無料のシャトルサービスをご用意しております。このサービスをご利用になりたい場合には，飛行機の便名と到着時間をご連絡ください。係の者が到着エリアにお迎えに上がります。このほかに何か私どもがお役に立てることがございましたら，ご連絡ください。
Rosenberg Hotel へのご来館を，一同，心よりお待ち申し上げます。

敬具

John Patterson
予約担当マネージャー

[語句]
- □ reservation　名 予約
- □ confirm　動 〜を確認する
- □ guarantee　動 〜を確約する
- □ cancellation　名 取り消し
- □ complimentary　形 無料の
- □ pick 〜 up　〜を迎えに行く

155. Why was the e-mail sent to Mr. J. Simmons?

(A) To verify the booking request
(B) To inquire about an arrival time
(C) To notify him of the cancellation policy
(D) To publicize the hotel brand

このEメールはなぜJ. Simmonsさんに送られましたか。

(A) 予約の確認をするため。
(B) 到着予定時間を聞くため。
(C) キャンセルポリシーを伝えるため。
(D) ホテルの宣伝をするため。

正解：(A)

● 着眼点！ ビジネスメールの目的は冒頭を見よ！

[解説] メールの目的を問う問題。セオリー通り冒頭を見よう。We are happy to confirm your reservation as follows. とあるので（A）が正解。

[語句] □ publicize 動 〜を宣伝する

---

156. How will the Rosenberg Hotel secure the room?

(A) By asking for responses from guests with reservations
(B) By giving warnings about cancellations in advance
(C) By charging prepayment to credit accounts
(D) By requesting credit card numbers from guests

Rosenberg Hotelはどうやって部屋を確保しますか。

(A) 予約客に返信を求める。
(B) 事前にキャンセルについての警告をする。
(C) 前払金をクレジットカードにチャージする。
(D) 客のクレジット番号を求める。

正解：(C)

● 着眼点！ 設問の意味をつかもう！

[解説] 設問の secure the room「部屋を確保する」とは「予約する」と同義。その「方法」が問われているので、選択肢の By 〜ing だけを「タテ読み」しても正解の予想がつく。本文の冒頭、To guarantee this reservation, the hotel will charge a one-night deposit fee plus tax to the credit card number you have provided. がポイント。クレジットに請求があるとのことなので、正解は（C）。

問題 157-158 は次の招待状に関するものです。

Black & Crawford 法律事務所は，
謹んであなたを当事務所創立の父，
尊敬すべき Julius Black のサプライズ誕生パーティーに
ご招待いたします。

時：10 月 3 日 午後 6 時 30 分 − 10 時（7 時 30 分よりビュッフェディナー）

場所：Oxdale Country Club

服装：準正装

Black 氏は 1957 年，26 歳で当事務所を設立し，現役弁護士のメンバーとして，一流会社や「夢のある子どもたち」といった慈善団体にもアドバイスしてまいりました。当日，Black 氏は 6 時 45 分に到着予定です。Black 氏の息子（でありパートナーでもある）Howard の音頭で乾杯のあと，カクテルが午後 7 時から配られます。皆様の配偶者やお子様もディナーに歓迎いたしますのでご参加ください。Black 氏の家族は，誕生日プレゼントの代わりに，次の慈善団体に寄付をしてくださるよう望んでおります。「夢のある子どもたち」です。

語句
- ☐ counsel 名 法廷弁護士
- ☐ blue-chip 形 一流の
- ☐ philanthropic 形 慈善事業の

157. What is the main purpose of the party?

(A) To commemorate the 50th anniversary of the firm
(B) To honor Julius' retiring father
(C) To celebrate the firm founder's birthday
(D) To welcome Howard's entrance into the firm

パーティーの主な目的は何ですか。

(A) 事務所の創立50周年を記念すること。
(B) 退職するJuliusの父をたたえること。
(C) 事務所設立者の誕生日を祝うこと。
(D) Howardの事務所入所を歓迎すること。

正解：(C)

● 着眼点！ 招待状のタイトルを見よ！

解説　パーティーの招待状なので，タイトルを見ればOK。Surprise Birthday Party For the Firm's Founding Father The Honorable Julius Black とあるので，Founding Father「創立者」のパーティーとわかる。よって，(C) が正解。

語句　□ commemorate 動 ～を記念する，祝う

---

158. What is indicated about the party?

(A) Donating to a benevolent group is recommended.
(B) Dress code should be business casual.
(C) Guests are expected to bring gifts.
(D) Guests can bring friends.

パーティーについて示されていることは何ですか。

(A) ある慈善団体への寄付を勧められている。
(B) 服装はオフィスカジュアルがよい。
(C) 各自プレゼントを用意する必要がある。
(D) 友人を誘って参加してもよい。

正解：(A)

● 着眼点！ 選択肢を先にチェック！

解説　indicate 問題なので，本文と選択肢の比較が必要。まず，選択肢のキーワードをチェックしよう。(A) Donating や (B) Dress code を本文でサーチすればOK。最後の文に Mr. Black's family has asked that instead of gifts, donations be made to the following philanthropic organization: Children with Dreams. とあるので，寄付に言及している (A) が正解。

語句　□ benevolent 形 慈善のための

問題 **159-160** は次のクーポンに関するものです。

Guadix 空港駐車場
729番　Pine 通り

31 日間駐車して，たったの **99.99** ドル！*

無料の 24 時間シャトルバスサービスでターミナルまで
荷物運搬補助あり
敷地内には監視カメラを設置

*1 回限り有効。本クーポンをご利用の場合，優待駐車ポイントはございません。

[語句]
- ☐ complimentary　形 無料の
- ☐ shuttle bus service　シャトルバスサービス
- ☐ luggage assistance　荷物運搬補助
- ☐ surveillance　名 監視
- ☐ premises　名 敷地
- ☐ valid　形 有効な

159. For whom is the coupon intended?　　　このクーポンはだれに向けられたものですか。

　　(A) Frequent customers　　　　　　　　　(A) 常連客
　　(B) Long-term service users　　　　　　　(B) 長期サービス利用者
　　(C) Tourist groups　　　　　　　　　　　(C) 団体旅行者
　　(D) Airport workers　　　　　　　　　　　(D) 空港従業員

正解：(B)

● 着眼点！ クーポンの対象を見抜け！　　　　　　　　　　　レベル ★★☆☆

解説　クーポンの対象が問われている。このクーポンは，Guadix Airport Parking という見出しから，「駐車場」のクーポンだとわかる。見出しの下には，Park for up to 31 days for only $99.99! とある。31日間駐車でも 99.99 ドルなので，長期旅行者向けと推測できる。ここから (B) を選ぼう。

---

160. What does the parking lot NOT offer?　　　駐車場が提供していないものは何ですか。

　　(A) Free airport rides　　　　　　　　　　(A) 無料の空港への送迎
　　(B) Security cameras　　　　　　　　　　(B) 監視カメラ
　　(C) Porter services　　　　　　　　　　　(C) 荷物運搬サービス
　　(D) Security patrol　　　　　　　　　　　(D) 巡回警備

正解：(D)

● 着眼点！ 「並列」箇所をチェック！　　　　　　　　　　　レベル ★★☆☆

解説　NOT 問題なので，本文と選択肢を対応させよう。選択肢を先にチェックしてから，項目が「並んで」書かれている箇所を見る。本文中盤，Complimentary 24 hour shuttle bus service, Luggage assistance, Surveillance cameras がそれぞれ (A)，(C)，(B) に対応。消去法で，正解は (D)。

問題 161-163 は次のプレスリリースに関するものです。

Arlington Mall にまもなく 3 つの新規テナントが入ります。

Wildbane はカナダで 1 番のスポーツ用品店です。4 月に，アメリカ初の店舗が 2 階 North Hammer の隣にオープンします。

5 月には，2 階 Morgan Electronics 向かいの 2,600 平方フィートの敷地に，子供服の小売店の Littleton が出店します。

同月に，Giorgio's Trattoria にてイタリア料理もお楽しみいただけるようになります。このレストランは下の階の南の端になります。
新規テナントでは，開店から 1 週間，お手頃な特別価格でお品物やサービスをご提供いたしますので，どうぞこの機会をご利用くださいませ。

[語句]
- tenant 名 テナント，借用者，入居者
- retailer 名 小売業者，小売店
- occupy 動 〜を占有する

161. What is mentioned about the Arlington Mall?

Arlington Mall についてどんなことが述べられていますか。

(A) It will add a second floor.
(B) It will expand the food court.
(C) It will extend business hours.
(D) It will enhance the line-up of stores.

(A) 2 階を増設する。
(B) フードコートを拡張する。
(C) 営業時間を延長する。
(D) 店舗のラインナップを強化する。

正解：(D)

● 着眼点！ まずは見出しを見よ！

レベル ★★☆☆

[解説] 見出しから情報を取ろう。Arlington Mall will soon gain three new tenants. とあり，まもなく 3 つのテナントが新しく出店することがわかる。この内容を言い換え，テナント店舗について述べている (D) が正解。

[語句]
- enhance 動 〜を高める，強化する，増す

162. What is NOT indicated in the press release?

(A) Wildbane is a popular shop in Canada.
(B) Littleton sells garments for kids.
(C) Morgan Electronics is located on the lower floor.
(D) Giorgio's Trattoria offers Italian cuisine.

プレスリリースで示されていないことは何ですか。

(A) Wildbane がカナダで人気店であること。
(B) Littleton は子供向け衣服を販売していること。
(C) Morgan Electronics は下の階にあること。
(D) Giorgio's Trattoria がイタリア料理を提供すること。

正解：(C)

● 着眼点！ 選択肢のキーワードをサーチ！

レベル ★★☆☆

解説　定番の **NOT** 問題。選択肢が長いので，名詞キーワードをチェック＆サーチしよう。(A) Wildbane，(B) Littleton，(C) Morgan Electronics，(D) Giorgio's Trattoria。これらを本文でサーチすると，(C) の内容が一致しない。よって，(C) が正解。

語句　□ garment 名 衣服

---

163. According to the press release, when will the sale take place?

(A) In autumn
(B) In winter
(C) In spring
(D) In summer

プレスリリースによると，セールはいつ行われますか。

(A) 秋
(B) 冬
(C) 春
(D) 夏

正解：(C)

● 着眼点！ セール時期を見抜け！

レベル ★☆☆☆

解説　当然，季節や月がヒントになる。セール・割引の注意点は，最後の段落に **The new tenants will offer goods and services at special low prices for the first week after opening** と記されている。各店舗の開店時期は，それぞれ 4 月と 5 月であり，それから 1 週間の (C)「春」の間にセールが行われる。よって，(C) が正解。

問題 164-166 は次のお知らせに関するものです。

お知らせ

宛先：Brown 通り 54 番アパート住人の皆様
発信者：Jackson Waterworks 社
日付：4 月 12 日

以下の日時に予定されている必要な排水管修理のため，建物への給水を停止いたします。

　　　日付：5 月 15 日
　　　時間：午後 2 時からおよそ 3 時間

サービス復旧時に水が溢れ出るのを避けるために，この時間帯の間に，ご家庭の蛇口が閉まっていることをご確認ください。
お問い合わせは，555-7839 までお電話ください。

ご不便をおかけしまして申し訳ありません。

語句
- resident 名 住人
- water supply 給水，上水道
- plumbing 名 排管，下水
- repair 名 修理，修繕
- water tap 蛇口，栓
- reinstate 動 (制度を) 復活させる，(人を) 復位させる

164. What is the purpose of the notice?

(A) To report a water leakage
(B) To caution about a power outage
(C) To inform of a service disruption
(D) To announce a wall work

このお知らせの目的は何ですか。

(A) 水漏れを報告すること。
(B) 停電について注意をすること。
(C) サービス障害について知らせること。
(D) 壁の工事を周知すること。

正解：(C)

● 着眼点！ 最初の 1 文に集中！

レベル ★★★☆

解説　notice は事務的なお知らせが多いので, 最初の 1 文に集中しよう。The water supply to the building will be shut off とあるので, 水道の給水停止とわかる。これを service disruption「サービス障害」と言い換えた (C) が正解。

語句　□ power outage　停電, 電源異常

165. What is suggested about the repair work?

(A) It will be done along with road construction.
(B) It will be rescheduled in case of rain.
(C) It will be carried out by several contractors.
(D) It will be finished by the end of the day.

修繕工事についてどんなことがわかりますか。

(A) 道路工事と一緒に行われる。
(B) 雨天の場合, 予定が変更される。
(C) 複数の請負業者により行われる。
(D) 実施の当日中に完了する。

正解：(D)

● 着眼点！ 対応関係を見抜け！

レベル ★★☆☆

解説　セオリー通り, 本文と選択肢を比較しよう。(A)「道路工事」, (B)「天候」については触れられていないため×。(C)「請負業者」については, Jackson Waterworks 社以外の名は記載されておらず, 判断できない。工事が午後 2 時に始まり 3 時間余りで終わることを言い換えた (D) だけが本文と一致し, これが正解。

166. What are the residents asked to do?

(A) Turn off faucets
(B) Leave their residence
(C) Save sufficient water
(D) Switch off electricity

住人は何をするように求められていますか。

(A) 蛇口を閉める。
(B) 住居を離れる。
(C) 十分な水を貯める。
(D) 電気を切る。

正解：(A)

● 着眼点！ 「お願い」表現をサーチ！

レベル ★☆☆☆

解説　住人への「お願い」が問われているので, 「お願い」表現の Please 〜 をサーチしよう。最終段落に, Please make sure water taps in your home are turned off とあり, 蛇口が閉まっていることを確かめるように求められている。つまり, (A) が正解。

語句　□ faucet 名 蛇口　□ sufficient 形 十分な

問題 **167-170** は次の情報に関するものです。

週間ベストセラートップ3
当店の6月第1週における3冊のベストセラー

順位	題名	著者	価格	先週順位
1	『紅葉』	Stephan Brownstone	28 ドル	3
2	『名作おとぎ話 第1巻』		25 ドル	10
3	『イタリア料理のコツ』	Luciana Russo	35 ドル	2

『紅葉』
Stephan Brownstone 著
ハードカバー：389ページ
28 ドル

ある母親と音楽スターになることを夢見る娘の関係を描いた悲しい物語『紅葉』は，**Stephan Brownstone** の小説デビュー作です。家族問題に関するノンフィクション作品の著者として知られる **Brownstone** が，今度はフィクションの世界にもその活動の場を広げてきました。この小説は，かつて著者が行った，さまざまな経歴を持つ家族に関する精緻な調査が下地となっているのかと思わせるような作品です。

『名作おとぎ話 第1巻』
ハードカバー：70ページ
25 ドル

『名作おとぎ話 第1巻』には，世界中で最も親しまれている童話が10話入っています。声に出して読むように編集されており，読者を物語に夢中にさせるのは古風で風変わりなイラストです。第2巻は来春発売予定。

『イタリア料理のコツ』
Luciana Russo 著
ハードカバー：150ページ
35 ドル

本場のイタリア料理の作り方を覚えてみませんか。『イタリア料理のコツ』は，料理の経験を問わず，だれもが楽しめること必至です。お料理初心者の皆さんのために，基本のレシピは料理の手順に沿って順番に写真で紹介されています。料理が得意という皆さん向けには，皆さんがお試しできるように，**Russo** が基本のレシピを使った，オリジナルのおいしい応用レシピを用意しています。これは間違いなくキッチンに置いておきたくなるようなクッキングブックです。

語句
□ heartbreaking 形 胸の張り裂けるような　□ expand 動 広がる
□ meticulous 形 非常に綿密な　□ background 名 背景　□ foundation 名 基盤
□ quaint 形 一風変わった　□ entice 動 ～を誘う　□ authentic 形 本物の
□ regardless of ～ ～にかかわらず　□ first-time 形 初めての
□ step-by-step 形 一歩一歩の　□ definitely 副 間違いなく

167. Who most likely published this information?　　この情報はだれが公表したものだと思われますか。

(A) A publisher　　(A) 出版社
(B) A library　　(B) 図書館
(C) A bookstore　　(C) 書店
(D) A school teacher　　(D) 学校の教師

正解：(C)

● 着眼点！　情報の「発信者」を意識しよう！

解説　「だれ」が「だれ」に向けた情報かを意識しよう。ここでは表題 The three bestselling books in the first week of June at our store の at our store に注目。一般読者に向けて，書店が公表したものなので，(C) が正解。

---

168. What is Stephan Brownstone famous for?　　Stephan Brownstone は何で有名ですか。

(A) His interviews with famous families of the world　　(A) 世界中の名家との対談
(B) His TV documentaries on Family problems　　(B) 家族問題のテレビドキュメンタリー
(C) His research on social behavior　　(C) 社会行動に関する研究
(D) His non-fiction works on family matters　　(D) 家族問題についてのノンフィクション作品

正解：(D)

● 着眼点！　キーワードをサーチ＆ファインド！

解説　キーワード Stephan Brownstone をサーチしよう。すぐに The Autumn Leaves の著者とわかる。本の説明を読み進めると，Stephan Brownstone について Brownstone, known as the author of several non-fiction books on family issues とある。family issues を family matters に言い換えた (D) が正解。

---

169. What is true about *Classic Fairy Tales Volume 1*?　　『名作おとぎ話 第1巻』について当てはまることは何ですか。

(A) It raised its rank more than any other book.　　(A) 他の本よりランクを上げた。
(B) It is a work of renowned authors.　　(B) 著名な作家の作品である。
(C) It covers numerous eccentric photographs.　　(C) 風変わりな写真がたくさんある。
(D) It is the most expensive book on the list.　　(D) リストの中で本の価格が一番高い。

正解：(A)

● 着眼点！　表もチェックせよ！

解説　本文に集中していると「表」の情報を見落とすので注意しよう。表の Classic Fairy Tales Volume 1 のところを見ると，先週は 10 位であり，他の 2 冊と比べて一番順位を上げているこ

とがわかるので，(A) が正解。ここに気づかない場合，消去法でも解ける。

---

170. What did Luciana Russo prepare to satisfy experienced cooks?

(A) Numerous variations of food
(B) Recipes from famous Italian restaurants
(C) Advice on using new cooking gadgets
(D) Information on organic farms

Luciana Russo は料理の得意な人々を満足させるために何を用意しましたか。

(A) 多くのさまざまな料理
(B) 有名なイタリアンレストランからのレシピ
(C) 新しい調理器具の使用についてのアドバイス
(D) 有機栽培農家に関する情報

正解：(A)

● 着眼点！ 設問の「動詞」に注目！

レベル ★★☆☆

解説　キーワード・サーチは名詞が基本だが，「何を用意したか」というシンプルな設問では「動詞」も目印になる。Luciana Russo の本の説明で，For veteran cooks, Russo has prepared original and tasty variations of basic recipes とある。prepared をサーチすれば簡単。ここから (A) が選べる。

問題 171-175 は次のお知らせに関するものです。

9月20日

Maxi フードプロセッサの任意リコール
（製品番号 TSN 590 から TSN 650）

Maxi Kitchen Appliances 社は，社内検査を行った際，フードプロセッサの回転刃を支える結合部分が正常に機能しない可能性があると判断しました。この製品に関してけがや事故は未だ報告されておりませんが，Maxi Kitchen Appliances 本社は，お客様の安全を第一と考え，Maxi フードプロセッサ（製品番号 TSN 590 から TSN 650）1 万台のリコールを発表しました。リコールは政府の消費者安全委員会に報告され，現在無償での代替物の準備をしております。本件にかかわるご迷惑に対し心よりお詫び申し上げます。

危険：
内部電機部品の過熱，発火により火事を引き起こす可能性があります。
製品タイプ：Maxi フードプロセッサ（製品番号 TSN 590 から TSN 650）
Maxi フードプロセッサのリコール対象製品 1 万台はテレビ通販，および当社公式通販サイトで 1 月 15 日から 8 月 13 日にかけて販売，流通したものです。製造番号は TSN590 から TSN650 となっております。製造番号は製品の後部側面左側，電気コードの隣に記されています。

お手続き：
製造番号が TSN590 から TSN650 までの製品をお持ちのお客様は，すぐに使用を中止してください。お買い上げいただいた小売店に製品を返品し，返品証明書を受領してください。その証明書を送っていただきますと全額返金または同等代替製品との交換ができます。書類は以下の住所まで郵送ください。
宛先：リコール　製品番号 TSN590
Maxi Kitchen Appliances 社
1123 Baker 通り
Christchurch 2020
連絡先：
ご質問等ございましたら，ご遠慮なく品質管理部の担当者までお尋ねください。電話は 1-888-555-6255 です。または当社サイトの http://service.MaxiKitchen.co.nz. でも対応いたしております。リコールに関するお客様相談室は 9 月 20 日から 12 月 20 日までとなっておりますのでご了承ください。

Maxi Kitchen Appliances 社

語句
- voluntarily　副 自発的に
- consistently　副 一貫性のある，絶えず
- hazard　名 危険
- pose　動 ～を引き起こす，もたらす
- distribute　動 ～を流通させる

171. Who most likely issued the announcement?

このお知らせはだれが書いたものと思われますか。

(A) A consumer electronics retailer
(B) A newspaper publisher
(C) A manufacturer
(D) A trading company

(A) 家電量販店
(B) 新聞社
(C) メーカー
(D) 商事会社

正解：(C)

● 着眼点！ 見出しをチェック！

レベル ★★☆☆

解説 セオリー通り，「見出し」を見よう。**Voluntarily Recall of Maxi Food Processor** とあり，「リコール」がトピックとわかればOK。さらに文末が **Maxi Kitchen Appliances** と社名なので，メーカーからのお知らせとわかる。よって，（C）が正解。

---

172. Why are Maxi Food Processors being recalled?

Maxi Food Processors がリコールされる理由は何ですか。

(A) The safety lock can fail.
(B) The unit is a fire risk.
(C) The blades may come loose gradually.
(D) The switch can malfunction.

(A) 安全ロックが機能しない可能性があるから。
(B) 火災の危険があるから。
(C) 刃が徐々にゆるんでくる可能性があるから。
(D) スイッチが誤作動する可能性があるから。

正解：(B)

● 着眼点！ 「マイナス」をサーチ！

レベル ★★★☆

解説 「リコール」の理由が問われている。「何が問題か」（＝マイナス）をサーチしよう。冒頭，**the joint parts supporting the processor's rotating blades do not consistently work** とあるが，注目すべきは **Hazard** のパラグラフ。**The internal electrical component can overheat and ignite, posing a potential fire hazard.** を見れば，「部品の加熱，発火」が問題とわかる。よって，（B）が正解。

---

173. The word "representative" in paragraph 5, line 1, is closest in meaning to

第5段落・1行目の representative に最も近い意味の語は

(A) secretary
(B) executive
(C) clerk
(D) supervisor

(A) 秘書
(B) 役員
(C) 事務員，係
(D) 上司

正解：(C)

● 着眼点！ 定型文を覚えよう！

レベル ★★★★

解説 please do not hesitate to speak to representative「ご遠慮なく担当者にお問い合わせ

ください」は，文末の定型文。ここで **representative** は「担当者」の意味。一番近いのは（C）。

---

174. What is NOT indicated in the announcement?　　このお知らせに述べられていないことは何ですか。

(A) Production facilities　　　　　　　　　　(A) 製造工場
(B) Consumer support period　　　　　　　　(B) お客様サポートの期間
(C) Recalled product quantity　　　　　　　 (C) リコール対象商品の数量
(D) Causes of harm　　　　　　　　　　　　(D) 被害の原因

正解：(A)

● 着眼点！　選択肢の「名詞」をサーチ！　　　　　　　　　　　　レベル ★★★☆

[解説] 定番の **NOT** 問題。セオリー通り，選択肢の名詞をサーチしよう。（A）から順にサーチすると，意外と早く正解が選べる。（A）**Production facilities**「製造の施設」，つまり製造工場のこと。これについては何の記載もないので，（A）が正解。（B）**consumer support** は，**customer service** と同じ意味で，最後の文章で期間が述べられている。（C）は第1段落で，**a recall of 10,000 Maxi Food Processors** とある。（D）は第1段落・1文目に **detected that the joint parts supporting the processors' rotating blades do not consistently work** と原因が述べられている。

---

175. How can consumers receive compensation?　　顧客はどのようにして補償を受けることができますか。

(A) By mailing the verification of return to the company　　(A) 返品証明書を会社宛てに郵送する。
(B) By completing the online registration for reimbursement　(B) 費用返還をオンラインで登録する。
(C) By visiting stores and getting a refund there　　　　　　(C) 販売店に行き返金を受ける。
(D) By making a phone call to the public office　　　　　　(D) 役所に電話をかける。

正解：(A)

● 着眼点！　「補償」は後半を見よ！　　　　　　　　　　　　　レベル ★★★☆

[解説] リコールの「補償」については，**What to do** のパラグラフを見よう。返品の方法が詳しく書かれている。**a certificate of returned item**「返品証明書」をもらって，それを次の住所へ送るようにと指示がある。**customers may send ...** や **Please send the document ...** が見えれば簡単。正解は（A）。

問題 176-180 は次のメモに関するものです。

メモ

差出人：人事部 Valerie Sanchez
宛先：ICE Electronics 社全従業員
日付：10月20日
件名：10月30日をもって Act Green マラソン終了の件

10月30日付で，Act Green マラソンは半世紀の歴史に幕を閉じます。この期間に Act Green マラソンにご参加くださり，ICE 社の全社員にお礼申し上げます。
Act Green マラソンのアイディアは，地球を守るという社会意識を高めるために行ってきました。目標を達成するために，本会員制度では，すべての環境に優しい選択にはポイントを付与してきました。たとえば，車を運転する代わりに公共の交通機関を利用する，買い物の際は買い物バッグを利用する，などです。各会員様の参加累積ポイントが加算されるのに従い，当社は世界中の慈善団体に寄付をしてきました。会員様の総力の結果として，貧困層の子どもたちにワクチンを提供したり，絶滅危惧種を保護したり，熱帯雨林の保全に貢献することができました。今や，当初の目標は達成されました。
それでも，グローバル企業として，我々はエネルギー保全活動を推進する取り組みを近隣地区で継続していくつもりです。そこで，Eco チームプロジェクトを立ち上げます。新しいエコフレンドリーな週末活動に興味がある方は，ICE 社 Eco チームにご参加ください。ICE 社 Eco チームは毎週土曜日の朝に集まり，**Springton Park** を中心にビジネス街で，緑化運動や花壇の手入れを行っています。詳細は，内線番号 **7829** の **Andy** までお問い合わせください。

語句
- act green　環境に優しい行動を取る
- marathon　名 マラソン，長時間続く活動
- half century-long　半世紀に及ぶ
- period　名 期間
- raise awareness　意識（関心）を高める
- membership　名 会員
- green　形 環境にやさしい
- commitment　名 参加，献身，傾倒
- cumulative　形 累積の
- philanthropic　形 慈善の，博愛の
- collective　形 集合的な，集団の
- vaccination　名 ワクチン
- endangered　形 絶滅の危機に瀕した
- objective　名 目標
- primary　形 当初の，第1位の
- energy-conserving　形 エネルギー保全の
- eco-friendly　形 環境に優しい
- chiefly　副 主として

176. What is the purpose of the memo?　　このメモの目的は何ですか。

(A) To announce the date of the city marathon　　(A) シティマラソンの日程を周知すること。
(B) To notify of renewed company activity　　(B) 一新された企業活動について告知すること。
(C) To encourage workers to exercise daily　　(C) 従業員に日々運動することを推奨すること。
(D) To invite people to a charity event　　(D) チャリティーイベントに招待すること。

正解：(B)

● 着眼点！ 例外にも落ち着いて対応！

レベル ★★★★

[解説] メモの目的が問われているが，冒頭ではなく全体を読んで答える問題。これは「主題は冒頭チェック」というセオリーに当てはまらない例外ケース。ただし，件名と第 1 段落の冒頭部分から，Act Green マラソンの終了を伝えていることはわかる。続く第 3 段落では，別の形態での環境保護活動の継続が述べられている。これらを「企業活動の一新」と表した (B) が正解。(A) はスポーツ競技のマラソンを表し，本文の内容と合わない。(C) も本文で推奨されているのは「環境に優しい行動」であるので×。(D)「チャリティーイベント」については述べられていない。

---

177. How can ICE employees collect points?　　ICE 社の従業員はどうすればポイントを集めることができますか。

(A) By conserving energy　　(A) エネルギーを大切に使う。
(B) By selling ICE products　　(B) ICE 社製品を販売する。
(C) By working as a volunteer　　(C) ボランティアとして働く。
(D) By showing leadership　　(D) リーダーシップを見せる。

正解：(A)

● 着眼点！ 「ポイント」をサーチ！

レベル ★★★☆

[解説] points について述べられている箇所をサーチしよう。第 1 段落・2 文目 We'd like to thank all ICE employees for participating in the Act Green Marathon とあり，ICE 社全従業員が Act Green マラソンに参加していたことがわかる。次に第 2 段落・2 文目 membership has offered points to every green choice という表現から，会員は環境に優しい選択をするとポイントがもらえることがわかる。したがって，(A) が最も適切。

---

178. What is mentioned about the accomplishment of the Act Green Marathon?　　Act Green マラソンの成果についてどんなことが述べられていますか。

(A) It raised money for charity.　　(A) チャリティーへの資金を調達した。
(B) It made employees healthier.　　(B) 従業員を健康にした。
(C) It improved the company's image.　　(C) 企業イメージを向上させた。
(D) It resulted in worldwide races and events.　　(D) 世界規模でのレースとイベントになった。

正解：(A)

● 着眼点！ 「成果」を見抜け！ レベル ★★☆☆

[解説] キーワード Act Green Marathon をサーチ。その「成果」について，第 2 段落・3 文目に the company has donated to philanthropic organizations around the world と述べられており，会社は慈善団体に寄付をしたことがわかる。その直後の, As a result of … , we have contributed to … もヒント。よって，（A）が正解。

---

179. What is indicated about ICE? ICE 社についてどんなことが示されていますか。

(A) It is an organizer of sporting events. (A) スポーツイベントの主催者である。
(B) It was founded 50 years ago. (B) 50 年前に設立された。
(C) It is an international company. (C) 国際的な企業である。
(D) It is shutting down its business. (D) 事業を終わらせようとしている。

正解：（C）

● 着眼点！ 会社の「概要」を見抜け！ レベル ★☆☆☆

[解説] 選択肢の名詞をキーワードとして，ICE 社の概要をチェック！ 第 3 段落・1 文目の As a global company を言い換えた（C）が正解だとすぐに判断できる。スピーディに判断しよう。（A）は本文中の Act Green Marathon はスポーツイベントではないため誤り。（B）も環境保護活動が 50 年続いたのであり，会社自体の沿革については触れられていないので×。（D）は終わりを迎えるのは Act Green Marathon で，会社の事業ではないので，これも誤り。

---

180. What is true about the ICE Eco team? ICE 社 Eco チームについて当てはまることは何ですか。

(A) They meet biweekly. (A) 2 週間に 1 度会う。
(B) They grow vegetables. (B) 野菜を育てている。
(C) They operate locally. (C) 地域での活動をしている。
(D) They clean a park. (D) 公園の掃除をしている。

正解：（C）

● 着眼点！ キーワードをサーチ！ レベル ★★☆☆

[解説] Eco team をキーワードにサーチする。第 3 段落・1 文目の we will continue our efforts to promote energy-conserving actions in our neighborhoods with the launch of our Eco team project から，地域での活動をしていることがわかる。これを表した（C）が正解。同じく第 3 段落から，行っているのは（A）「隔週」でなく毎週で，（B）「野菜を育て」たり，（D）「掃除」をしているのではなく，植樹と造園をしているとわかるため，他の選択肢は誤り。

問題 181-185 は次の 2 つの E メールに関するものです。

宛先：Evan Garfield <egarfield@clarksville.ll.com>
差出人：カスタマーサービス担当　Drew <drew@speedycards.biz>
件名：Speedy Online Business Cards の確認　注文番号　22401
日付：10 月 22 日

Garfield 様

ご注文ありがとうございます。お客様の名刺は，これから 48 時間以内にお客様のもとに発送される予定です。

注文番号：22401
出荷状況：処理中，出荷待ち
サンプル：下記をご覧ください。

> 道化師 Evan「オリジナルの誕生日パーティーを！」
> 皆が童心に返る風船やお楽しみがあります。
> Evan Garfield
>
> 510-555-8354
> egarfield@clarksville.ll.com
> www.evandown.com

ご注意：
名刺の色があせないよう，直射日光を避けて保存されるようお勧めします。直射日光や日常の光が毎日当たる机に数か月置いておきますと，名刺の色はかなりあせてしまう場合があります。

ご注文いただき，誠にありがとうございます。

宛先：カスタマーサービス担当　Drew <drew@speedycards.biz>
差出人：Evan Garfield <egarfield@clarksville.ll.com>
件名：Speedy Online Business Card に関しての問題
日付：11 月 2 日

Drew 様

　注文番号 22401 に関していくつかの問題点を指摘したいと思います。
　まず第 1 に，だれかが私のウェブサイトアドレスを打ち直したとしか想像できません。というのは，名刺には www.evanclown.com ではなく，www.evandown.com とあるからです。"c" と "l" がすぐ隣同士にくると "d" に見えるのだと思いますが，私はあなたが文書を電子的にコピーするものと思っていました。私のホームページの URL が間違っていると，名刺は役目を果たしません。
　残念ながら，他にも 2 点問題があります。あなたは色が変化することがあると言っておられましたが，私の場合，最初の 50 枚については非常に鮮やかな色でしたが，残りの 450 枚は日光に当たったことがないにもかかわらず，配達された時点ですでに，かなり色あせていました。さらに，確認の E メールではまもなく発送する予定であるとありましたが，名刺は 11 月 1 日まで届きませんでした。
私は御社のサービスと製品の品質にひどくがっかりしています。正しい URL を記載し，色の安定している

ものと早急に取り替えてください。
よろしくお願いします。

Evan Garfield

> 語句
> □ confirmation 名 確認　□ ship 動 〜を出荷する　□ fade 動 (色が) あせる
> □ considerably 副 かなり，相当　□ variation 名 変化
> □ vibrant 形 (色が) 鮮明な，生き生きとした　□ prompt 形 即座の

181. Why was the first e-mail sent to Mr. Garfield?　1つ目のEメールはなぜGarfieldさんに送られましたか。

(A) To consult about the design of his card　(A) 名刺のデザインについて相談するため。
(B) To advertise entertainment at a party　(B) パーティーでの娯楽を宣伝するため。
(C) To deliver a message from children　(C) 子どもたちからのメッセージを伝えるため。
(D) To inform him that his order was being properly processed　(D) 彼の注文品がきちんと処理されていると知らせるため。

正解：(D)

● 着眼点！　まずsubjectをチェック！　レベル ★★☆☆

> 解説　ビジネスメールなので，まずsubjectを見よう。**Subject: Speedy Online Business Cards Confirmation Order 22401** とあり，オーダーの確認メールであることがわかる。確認メールには，オーダーのその後の予定も書かれる。**Thank you for your order. Your card will be shipped to you in the next 48 hours.** とあり，注文品 (名刺) が発送されますという内容だとわかる。それを「きちんと処理されている」と言い換えている (D) が正解。

182. According to the first e-mail, when are orders usually sent out?　1つ目のEメールによると，注文品は通常いつ発送されますか。

(A) On the day of purchase　(A) 購入したその日
(B) In a couple of hours　(B) 数時間のうちに
(C) Within two days　(C) 2日以内
(D) A week later　(D) 1週間後

正解：(C)

● 着眼点！　定番の「数字」の言い換え！　レベル ★☆☆☆

> 解説　TOEICでは「数字」は言い換えられる。1つ目のEメールには **Your card will be shipped to you in the next 48 hours.** とあるので，48時間＝2日以内ということになる。したがって，正解は (C)。**48 hours = two days** に反応しよう。

183. What does Mr. Garfield say about the color?　Garfieldさんは色について何と言っていますか。

(A) It didn't match what he had requested.　(A) 依頼したものと合っていない。
(B) It was faded from the beginning.　(B) 初めから色あせていた。
(C) It should be a lighter shade.　(C) もっと明るい色にしてほしい。
(D) It was vivid on every single item.　(D) どの1枚をとっても色が鮮やかだった。

正解：(B)

● 着眼点！　クレーム内容を把握せよ！

解説　Garfieldさんのメールはクレームを伝えている。その内容を把握することが肝心。色は3つのクレームのうちの1つ。第3段落で，the next 450 were already quite faded from the moment they were delivered と書かれているので，配達された時点でほとんどの名刺の色があせていたとわかる。したがって，(B) が正解。

---

184. When does Mr. Garfield say his cards were delivered?　Garfieldさんは，彼の名刺がいつ届いたと言っていますか。

(A) Within 48 hours of confirmation　(A) 確認から48時間以内
(B) Four days from confirmation　(B) 確認から4日後
(C) Within a week of confirmation　(C) 確認から1週間以内
(D) About ten days after confirmation　(D) 確認から約10日後

正解：(D)

● 着眼点！　クロス問題は「数字」が大事！

解説　クロスリファレンス問題では「数字」をヒントに答えを探るパターンが多い。確認のメールの日付は10月22日で，それから48時間以内に発送されると書かれているので，遅くとも10月24日までに届く（予定）。だが，Garfieldさんからのメールには11月1日に届いたとある。両方のメールから総合すると，約10日間かかっていることになる。よって，(D) が正解。

---

185. What is NOT mentioned in the second e-mail?　2つ目のEメールで述べられていないことは何ですか。

(A) Delay of delivery　(A) 配達の遅れ
(B) Additional 50 more cards ordered　(B) 名刺50枚の追加注文
(C) Descriptions of the correct web address　(C) 正しいURLの記載
(D) Request for replacement　(D) 交換の依頼

正解：(B)

● 着眼点！　選択肢のキーワードをサーチ！

解説　NOT問題なので，本文と選択肢の比較が必要。選択肢のキーワードをサーチしよう。(A) は2つ目のEメールの第3段落を見ると，the cards did not arrive until Nov. 1 とあり，内容と一致。(C) のURLに関しては，同じく2つ目のEメールの第2段落，(D) の交換についても，最後に述べられている。Additional 50 は消去法でも選べるが，サーチすれば即答できる。追加注文の事実はないので，(B) が正解。

問題 186-190 は次の 2 つの E メールに関するものです。

宛先：Scott Parsons, K&G Design Associates 社
送信者：Andy Itoh, Knight Owl Internet Cafe
件名：改装プラン
日付：12月9日

Parsons 様

先週は来ていただき本当にありがとうございました。仮の改修計画を送ります。あなたの専門知識を本当に頼りにしていますので, それについての助言をいただきたいと思います。どんな提案でも非常に助かります。

1 階の 1 人部屋個室については，もし 1 室あたり 800 ドル以下の費用であれば，堅木のフローリングにしようと考えています。もし他に安い材質の種類を見つけたら，教えてください。

もう 1 つの大きな改修は 2 階と 3 階の 2 人部屋個室です。私たちは数を 5 部屋から 10 部屋へ倍増させようと計画しています。すべての 2 人部屋の中に, 個室の洗面所を備え付けたいと思っています。2 人部屋を改装するための私たちの予算は 1 室あたり 3000 ドルです。

最後に，サービスの部分を新しくしたいと思っています。私たちの軽食サービスは上流顧客のために質を高めるべきだと思っています。あなたに，それぞれ 2000 ドル以内の予算で，ロビーにある軽食ラウンジを一新してもらい，2 階に新しいドリンクカウンターを取り付けてもらいたいんです。また，これらの部分の隣に同額で洗面所を備え付けることも重要です。

改めて，あなたの貴重な時間と援助を本当にありがとうございます。

Andy

宛先：Andy Itoh, Knight Owl Internet Cafe
送信者：Scott Parsons, K&G Design Associates 社
件名：Re：改装プラン
日付：12月14日

Itoh 様

あなたの改装プランを精査し，何ができるかを決めました。

改装について，次の点を考慮に入れることをお勧めします。
まず初めに, あなたの予算内で堅木のフローリングにすることはできないだろうと思います。その代わりに, 他の材料を提案します。表面が堅木のプラスチック素材です。1 室あたり 400 ドルで，簡単に手入れや掃除ができます。
2 つ目に, 2 人部屋の改装案については賛成です。しかし, 何部屋を追加したいかをもう一度検討してもよいと思います。
最後に, 私たちが提案するのはドリンクカウンターに関連したものです。軽食ラウンジの隣にそれを備え付けるならばより低い費用を提示できます。軽食ラウンジの費用に加えて 1800 ドルになります。しかしながら，つまりは 200 ドル節約できます。

私たちの提案にご興味があるかどうか聞けるのを楽しみにしています。

敬具

Scott

| 語句 | ☐ preliminary 形 予備の　☐ renovation 名 改修　☐ expertise 名 専門知識
☐ hardwood 名 堅木　☐ refurbish 動 ～を一新する
☐ fit out ～　～に必要な設備を取り付ける　☐ sort out ～　～を決める
☐ alternative 形 代替の　☐ maintain 動 ～を保守管理する |

186. Why did Mr. Itoh write the e-mail?　　Itoh さんはなぜ E メールを書きましたか。

(A) To consult on a remodeling
(B) To suggest an innovative room design
(C) To charge for extra services
(D) To offer Internet services

(A) 改装について相談するため。
(B) 革新的な部屋の設計を提案するため。
(C) 特別なサービスについて請求するため。
(D) インターネットサービスを提供するため。

正解：(A)

● 着眼点！　メールの目的は冒頭から！

解説　まず，メールの差出人と受取人を確認。個人からデザイン会社へのメールであるとわかる。第 1 段落・2 文目に Here is our preliminary renovation plan. とあり，続けて 3 文目に We really value your expertise, so could you give us some advice on it? とあるため (A) が正解。

187. In the first e-mail, the word "install" in paragraph 2, line 1, is closest in meaning to

1 つ目の E メールの第 2 段落・1 行目の install に最も近い意味の語は

(A) input
(B) convert
(C) place
(D) remove

(A) ～を提供する
(B) ～を変える
(C) ～を置く
(D) ～を取り除く

正解：(C)

● 着眼点！　頻出ワードは即答！

解説　文脈から解くのがセオリーだが，install「～を備え付ける」は頻出ワード。install hardwood floors のフレーズからも意味が推測できる。正解は (C)。

188. What most likely will be remodeled as it is planned?

何が計画通りに改装されると思われますか。

(A) Renewal of flooring material
(B) Private rooms with new flooring
(C) Drink counters on the second floor
(D) Lavatories for paired customers

(A) 床材の更新
(B) 新しいフローリングの個室
(C) 2 階のドリンクカウンター
(D) 2 人部屋の洗面所

正解：(D)

> 🔵 **着眼点！** 意見の一致を見抜け！
>
> レベル ★★★☆

解説 1つ目のメール（改修プラン）→2つ目のメール（プランへの応答）という流れを押さえる。2つ目のメールで、プランの不可についてコメントしているので、同意している箇所をサーチしよう。中盤、Secondly, I agree with the remodeling ideas for your couple's rooms. とあり、2人部屋には反対していない。ここから（D）を選ぼう。

語句 ☐ lavatory 　图 洗面所

---

189. What does Mr. Parsons say about hardwood flooring?　　Parsons さんは堅木のフローリングについて何と言っていますか。

(A) It is easy to clean.　　　　　　(A) 掃除がしやすい。
(B) It is too expensive.　　　　　　(B) 高価すぎる。
(C) It is made from plastic.　　　　(C) プラスチックで作られている。
(D) It is a substitution.　　　　　　(D) 代わりのものである。

正解：(B)

> 🔵 **着眼点！** メールを特定して、キーワード・サーチ！
>
> レベル ★★★☆

解説 まず、Parsons さんのメールを特定しよう。From: Scott Parsons とあるので、2つ目のメール。次に、hardwood flooring をサーチしよう。第3段落・1文目に I don't think we will be able to install hardwood flooring within your budget. とあるため、(B) が正解。

語句 ☐ substitution 　图 代用品

---

190. Where will the new drink counter most likely be installed?　　新しいドリンクカウンターはどこに備え付けられると思われますか。

(A) In the restaurant　　　　(A) レストランの中
(B) On the second floor　　　(B) 2階
(C) On the third floor　　　　(C) 3階
(D) In the lobby　　　　　　 (D) ロビーの中

正解：(D)

> 🔵 **着眼点！** キーワードをサーチ＆ファインド！
>
> レベル ★★★☆

解説 「依頼→返答」のメールの流れにおいて、今後の展開は「返答」を見る。2つ目のEメールの第5段落で、ドリンクカウンターについて、We can offer you a lower price if you choose to place it in the area next to the snack lounge. 「軽食ラウンジの隣に配置すれば低価格で提供できる」とあるが、軽食ラウンジがどこにあるかは述べられていない。1つ目のEメールを見ると、第4段落・3文目に our snack lounge in the lobby とあり、ロビーにあるとわかるので、(D) が正解。クロス問題の好例。ヒントをピンポイントでサーチしよう。

問題 191-195 は次のお知らせとリストに関するものです。

お知らせ

Arbor View マンションの住人の皆様へ

来月の第1週に，リサイクル可能なごみの収集に関する新しいルールがこのマンションで始まります。以下のガイドラインを参照してください。今週後半に建物の管理部が各マンションにボックスを設置していきます。回収日の午前6時までに，当マンションの裏路地にある大きな回収コンテナにボックスの中身を直接移さなくてはなりません。毎週月曜日は担当のリサイクル業者が来て行うため，細目まで仕分けをしなくても構いません。残念ながら，別の曜日にリサイクルを請け負う業者は分別をしないので，これらの曜日には適切なコンテナにリサイクル可能なものを分別してください。すべてのコンテナにはラベルが貼ってあります。同封のリストに従って，ごみを分別してください。

電気製品は毎月最終週に無料でリサイクルに出すことができます。しかし，裏路地が通行できなくなるのを防ぐため，回収日前日の夜まで電気製品を持ち出さないでください。詳細についてはリストをご覧ください。

ご質問は建物管理部（555-8688）にご連絡ください。

リサイクル

月曜日	プラスチック：ウォーターボトル，家庭用洗剤ボトル，ヨーグルトカップ，バター容器など。これらのボトルや容器のふたはしっかりと閉めてください。ラベルはついたままでも構いません。発泡スチロールはリサイクルできませんので，ご注意ください。
火曜日	ガラス：透明・色つきのガラスボトル，容器やビン。金属のふたやラベルはついたままで構いません。ただし，中身は空にしてください。電球や陶器や耐熱ガラスは回収しません。
水曜日	紙類：新聞，雑誌，包装紙，電話帳，シリアル用箱，段ボールなど。ホッチキス留めされていても回収いたします。ティッシュペーパーやお菓子の包装紙，ペーパーカップ，細断された紙や使用済みの紙皿は回収しません。
木曜日	電気製品：テレビ，冷蔵庫，**DVD** プレーヤーなど。
金曜日	カン：炭酸飲料，スープ，コーヒー，などのカン。すべてのカンは空にしてください。ラベルはそのままでも構いません。噴霧器用のカンやアルミニウムホイルは回収しません。

リサイクル業者電話番号
Plastics Redone 社：555-9063
Glass Works 社：555-0021
Recycled Paper 社：555-8214
Metal Disposal 社：555-3679
Electronic Recycling 社：555-1132

語句
- □ collection 名（ごみの）収集 □ recyclable 形 リサイクル可能な
- □ apartment complex マンション □ refer to ~ ~を参照する，問い合わせる
- □ empty 動 ~を移す，空にする □ alley 名 裏通り，路地
- □ pickup 名（ごみの）収集 □ handle 動 ~を担当する，取り扱う
- □ separate 動 ~を分類する，区別する □ enclosed 形 同封された
- □ at no cost 無料で □ secure 動 ~をしっかり閉める
- □ Styrofoam 名 発泡スチロール（商標） □ lid 名 ふた
- □ Pyrex 名 パイレックス（耐熱ガラス製品の商標） □ cardboard 名 段ボール，厚紙

191. What is the purpose of the notice?　このお知らせの目的は何ですか。

(A) To inform residents of a meeting　(A) 集会について住人に知らせること。
(B) To announce the launching of new rules　(B) 新しいルールの始まりを周知すること。
(C) To solicit volunteers among residents　(C) 住人の中からボランティアを勧誘すること。
(D) To promote a new garbage company　(D) 新しいごみ業者を宣伝すること。

正解：(B)

● 着眼点　文書の主旨は冒頭を見よ！

レベル ★☆☆☆

[解説] お知らせの第1段落・1文目 a new policy for the collection of recyclables will be started in this apartment complex から、リサイクル可能なゴミの収集についての新しいルールが始まることがわかる。これを言い換えた (B) が正解。その他の選択肢の内容については本文に記載されていないため誤り。

---

192. The word "keep" in the notice, paragraph 2, line 2, is closest in meaning to　お知らせの第2段落・2行目の keep に最も近い意味の語は

(A) oppose　(A) 〜に反対する、〜と競う
(B) prevent　(B) 〜を防ぐ、引き止める
(C) cancel　(C) 〜を取り消す、無効にする
(D) remove　(D) 〜を取り去る、取り除く

正解：(B)

● 着眼点　語彙は文脈から見る！

レベル ★★☆☆

[解説] keep という基本語が問われているので、文脈を見よう。in order to keep the alley from getting blocked から、keep ... from 〜「…に〜をさせない」という意味がわかれば OK。この意味に最も近いのは、(B) prevent「〜を防ぐ」で、これが正解。

---

193. When in the month will electronics be picked up free of charge?　電気製品が無料で回収されるのは、月のいつですか。

(A) The last Friday　(A) 最終金曜日
(B) The first Thursday　(B) 第1木曜日
(C) The last Thursday　(C) 最終木曜日
(D) The third Wednesday　(D) 第3水曜日

正解：(C)

● 着眼点　「曜日」はクロス問題で出る！

レベル ★☆☆☆

[解説] 設問キーワード electronics をサーチしよう。お知らせの第2段落・1文目に Electronics can be put out for recycling the last week of each month at no cost. とあり、毎月最終週は無料で回収されることがわかる。次に、リストを見ると電気製品の回収は木曜日であることから、(C) が正解。

194. According to the list, what are residents required to do?

(A) Shred their magazines
(B) Remove the labels from their cans
(C) Take the staples out of papers
(D) Put the lids on plastic bottles

リストによると，住人は何をするように要求されていますか。

(A) 雑誌を細断する。
(B) カンからラベルをはがす。
(C) 紙からホッチキスを外す。
(D) プラスチックボトルにふたをつける。

正解：(D)

● 着眼点！ 「指示」を読みとれ！

レベル ★★★☆

解説 リストと選択肢を比較して答えを見つけよう。リストは曜日ごとに，分類と品目名に注意事項が続く形式で書かれている。選択肢の品目と注意事項に焦点を当てて，正解を判断する。(A) と (C) は水曜日の紙類，(B) は金曜日のカン，(D) は月曜日のプラスチック製品についての記述とそれぞれ比較する。このうち (D) のみが 2 文目の **Please be sure to secure the lids tightly on these bottles and containers.** と一致し，正解だとわかる。「指示」が書かれている箇所にねらいをつけるとよい。

---

195. Which days can residents most likely recycle flyers?

(A) On Tuesdays
(B) On Wednesdays
(C) On Thursdays
(D) On Fridays

住人は毎週何曜日にチラシをリサイクルできると思われますか。

(A) 毎週火曜日
(B) 毎週水曜日
(C) 毎週木曜日
(D) 毎週金曜日

正解：(B)

● 着眼点！ ゴミの種類を見抜け！

レベル ★★☆☆

解説 リストを参考に，**flyers** がどのゴミに分類されるかをチェックしよう。**flyer** が「チラシ」だと知っていれば，**paper** 「紙類」であるので，(B)「毎週水曜日」が正解とわかる。しかし，**flyer** 「チラシ」を誤って **fryer** 「揚げ物用鍋」と勘違いしてしまうと，(C) や (D) を選んでしまう。**flyer** 「チラシ」はよく出る語句なので覚えておこう。

問題 196-200 は次のお知らせと E メールに関するものです。

20 周年記念セール

Tom & Tailor は来る水曜日に創立 20 周年を祝います。当店の洋服の型は有名会社の役員やまた一般の人々の間で大変幅広くご好評をいただいております。ここで，日頃のお客様方のご愛顧に対し深くお礼を申し上げたいと思います。ありがとうございます!!

感謝の印として，今月は値札より **10%** 引きのサービスをさせていただきます。また今週に限り，午後 **5** 時までのお客様には店舗内全商品につきましてさらに **10%** オフとさせていただきます。ぜひこの特別の機会をご利用いただきたく，ご来店をお待ちしております。

当店のポリシーはどんな体型，どんなサイズのお客様にも対応することであり，これからもそのことを続けていく所存でございます。当店の商売の大半はお客様との交流であり，それによりお客様方が何を求めているかを見つけ出すことができるのです。当店の熟練テーラーは喜んで皆様のお役に立ちたいと考えております。ご質問などありましたらご遠慮なく **tom@tailor.com** までご連絡ください。

当店の創立 20 周年を共に祝ってくださる古くからの，また新しいお客様方にも同様にお役に立てるのを楽しみにしております!!

宛先：Tom & Tailor service<ttservice@tailor.com>
送信者：James White<james@coolmail.com>
日付：9 月 21 日
件名：**10%** の割引

関係者各位

先週のことですが，とてもよくデザインされているビジネスシャツを **2** 枚購入しました。レシートを整理していたら，水曜日の午後 **4** 時頃に購入したシャツに対して十分な割引を受けていないことを発見しました。

今回の購入で，こうした間違いが起きたことに驚いております。明日，お店に伺いますので，速やかに対処していただきますようお願いいたします。

James White

語句	□ anniversary 名 記念日
	□ patronage 名 ご愛顧，引き立て
	□ as a token of 〜 〜の印として

196. What is the main purpose of this notice? / このお知らせの主な目的は何ですか。

(A) To let customers know the great deal is over
(B) To invite people to a special occasion
(C) To greet new customers
(D) To explain available sizes at a store

(A) 特別セールが終わったことを客に知らせること。
(B) 特別な行事に招待すること。
(C) 新規の客へ挨拶すること。
(D) 店舗に在庫のあるサイズの説明をすること。

正解：(B)

● 着眼点！　まずは見出しを見よ！

レベル ★★☆☆

[解説] The 20th Anniversary Sale「20周年記念セール」という見出しを見れば，ほぼ解ける。第2段落・最終文，Please come and take advantage of this special occasion. と第4段落，We are all looking forward to serving old and new customers alike to celebrate our 20th anniversary together という文から，客を招待しているということがわかる。正解は (B)。

---

197. According to the notice, which does the store value the most? / お知らせによると，店はどれを一番大切にしていますか。

(A) Carrying the latest fashion
(B) Interacting with customers
(C) Training professional tailors
(D) Serving more new clients

(A) 最新ファッションを取り扱うこと。
(B) 客と交流をすること。
(C) プロのテーラーを養成すること。
(D) より多くの新規の客に対応すること。

正解：(B)

● 着眼点！　重点ポイントをつかめ！

レベル ★★☆☆

[解説] the store value the most なので，店が重点を置いているポイントをつかもう。第3段落・2文目で，The best part of our business is interacting with you, と述べている。ここでの you は，customers を指している。したがって，(B) が正解。

---

198. Who is Mr. White? / White さんとはだれですか。

(A) A regular customer
(B) A well-experienced tailor
(C) A new neighbor
(D) An executive

(A) 常連客
(B) 経験豊富なテーラー
(C) 新しい隣人
(D) 会社の幹部

正解：(A)

● 着眼点！　クロスリファレンスを活用せよ！

レベル ★★☆☆

[解説] Who 設問なので，「職業」を見抜く。Mr. White は，メールの送信者。冒頭を読むと，割引を受けていないことに文句を言っている。notice に appreciate the patronage「日頃のご愛顧に感謝して」とあるので，何度か買い物をした客とわかる。クロスリファレンスを要する問題。正解は (A)。

199. Why is Mr. White visiting Tom & Tailor?

なぜ White さんは Tom & Tailor を訪問しようとしていますか。

(A) To respond to the advisement
(B) To clarify the opening hours of the store
(C) To order extra shirts
(D) To get a refund for the difference

(A) 助言に応えるため。
(B) 店の開店時間を明確にするため。
(C) 追加のシャツを注文するため。
(D) 差額を払い戻してもらうため。

正解：(D)

● 着眼点！ 次の展開を見抜け！

レベル ★★★☆

解説　メールの最後を見よう。White さんは，明日店を訪問すると書かれている。彼は割引を受けるために店に行くので，正解は（D）。次の展開をイメージすることが大事。

---

200. What is the discount rate Mr. White should have received?

White さんはどのくらいの割引を受けるべきだったのでしょうか。

(A) 20%
(B) 10%
(C) 30%
(D) 15%

(A) 20%
(B) 10%
(C) 30%
(D) 15%

正解：(A)

● 着眼点！ たし算を忘れるな！

レベル ★☆☆☆

解説　割引については，お知らせの第 2 段落を見よう。we would like to offer our customers 10% off our price tag, さらに Only this week, if you shop before 5 P.M., you can get an additional 10% discount on every item in our store. とある。つまり，今週に限り午後 5 時前に買い物をする客は 10+10 の 20％の割引になることになる。White さんが買い物をしたのは，purchased on Wednesday around 4 o'clock とあるので，20％の割引を受けられたはずである。正解は（A）。

READING TEST

模試 4
解答と解説

- 問題は，別冊の 98 ～ 129 ページに掲載されています。

模試 4 解答と解説

PART 5

101. Professor Fontaine of Tucker University ------- one of our external auditors since last February.
(A) was
(B) has been
(C) is
(D) will be

Tucker 大学の Fontaine 教授は，この前の 2 月以降，当社の社外監査役を務めています。

正解：(B)

●着眼点！ 時制のチェックはまず時間の表現から！
レベル ★☆☆☆

[解説] be 動詞の時制を問う問題。最後が since last February となっていることに着目。since「～以来」を含む文には完了形が使われるので，(B) が適切。

[語句] □ external auditor 社外監査役

---

102. The pictures must be chosen ------- tomorrow morning so that they can be included in our press release.
(A) until
(B) for
(C) in
(D) by

会社のプレスリリースに入れられるよう，明日の朝までに写真を選んでおかねばなりません。

正解：(D)

●着眼点！ 紛らわしい単語はセットで攻略せよ！
レベル ★★☆☆

[解説] 空所の後ろの tomorrow morning につながる前置詞を選ぶ。具体的な時を表して名詞を伴えるのは (A) の until と (D) の by。期限を示す by に対して，(A) の until は「～まで（の間，継続的に）」という意味なので，ここでは不適切。間違いやすいので，あわせて覚えよう。

[語句] □ press release プレスリリース

---

103. Anyone ------- in the position should contact Ms. Lee Monday through Friday between 10:00 A.M. and 4:00 P.M.
(A) interest
(B) interesting
(C) interested
(D) to interest

その役職に関心のある人は，月曜から金曜の午前 10 時から午後 4 時の間に Lee さんに連絡すること。

正解：(C)

●着眼点！ 文意から読み解く！
レベル ★★☆☆

[解説] 空所は人称代名詞 Anyone を修飾している。「関心のある人は応募すること」という文意をつかもう。選択肢の中で文意に適する表現は (C)。(A) 名詞「関心，興味」，(B) 形容詞「興味を引き起こす」，(C) 形容詞「興味を持っている」，(D) 動詞 interest「～に興味を持たせる」の to 不定詞。

[語句] □ position 名 役職，地位

104. Sales representatives are encouraged to ------- up with new ideas about advertising strategies.
(A) raise
(B) go
(C) come
(D) think

営業担当者は，広告戦略について新しいアイディアを提案することを奨励されています。

正解：**(C)**

● 着眼点！ **イディオムを見つけて正解せよ！** レベル ★★☆☆

解説　空所に当てはまる動詞を選ぶ問題。ここは come up with ～「～を発見する，提案する」という意味のイディオムを知っていることがポイントになる。正解は（C）。sales representative「営業担当者，外交員」という職種も頻出なので覚えておこう。

---

105. Ken Automotive Supplies has been a client of ------- for over 20 years in the South American region.
(A) we
(B) our
(C) ours
(D) us

Ken Automotive Supplies 社は，南米地域における当社の20年来の取引先です。

正解：**(C)**

● 着眼点！ **まず空所前後を確認せよ！** レベル ★☆☆☆

解説　まず，空所前後をチェックしてヒントを探そう。空所前の a client of のあとに所有代名詞を続けて「～の取引先」の意を表す（C）が正解。複数取引先がある中の1つを意味する表現となる。

---

106. A ten percent discount and free delivery service is offered ------- for customers with a membership card.
(A) exclude
(B) exclusion
(C) exclusive
(D) exclusively

10パーセントの割引と無料配送サービスは，メンバーシップカードをお持ちのお客様のみにご提供しております。

正解：**(D)**

● 着眼点！ **品詞の選択は前後から！** レベル ★★☆☆

解説　選択肢の中から適切な品詞を選ぶ問題。空所直前の述語動詞 is offered を修飾する副詞の（D）exclusively が適切。exclusively for ～という語句は「～専用，～だけ」という意味を表す。名詞 discount「割引」は，a XX% discount「XX% オフ」という形で用いられる。（A）動詞「～を除外する」，（B）名詞「除外」，（C）形容詞「排他的な」，（D）副詞「もっぱら，独占的に」。

---

107. Mr. Chen was extremely ------- to receive a job offer from a well-known beverage company in New York.
(A) happier
(B) happiest
(C) happily
(D) happy

Chen さんは，ニューヨークにあるよく知られた飲料会社からの仕事のオファーを非常に喜んで受けました。

正解：**(D)**

● 着眼点！ **常用単語に強くなれ！** レベル ★☆☆☆

解説　形容詞 happy に関連する選択肢が並んでいる。文全体から，空所は補語であり，形容詞が入ることがわかる。また，比較対象となる表現も含まれていないことから，（D）が適切。happy to do「喜んで～する」は覚えておこう。

108. Please be reminded that MSG Corporation ------- the contents of the service in the coming year.
(A) discontinue
(B) to discontinue
(C) have discontinued
(D) will discontinue

来年度 MSG 社は，サービスの内容を継続しないことにご注意ください。

正解：(D)

● 着眼点！ 全文を読んで時制を選べ！

レベル ★★★☆

解説　時制を選ぶ問題。文末 in the coming year から来年のことについて述べていることがわかる。よって，主節より未来のことを表す選択肢（D）が適切。文末まで目を通して，ヒントを見逃さないようにしよう。

---

109. The Korean restaurant is closed ------- further notice due to building repairs.
(A) by
(B) next
(C) until
(D) to

その韓国料理店は建物の修理のため，追って通知があるまで閉店しています。

正解：(C)

● 着眼点！ 全文を読んでイディオムを見つけよ！

レベル ★★★☆

解説　選択肢には，時に関わる語が並んでいる。建物の修理のためレストランが閉店しているという文意から，一時的な閉鎖だとわかる。空所後の further notice に関わるイディオム，until further notice は，「追って通知があるまで」という意味を表す。したがって，(C) が適切。

---

110. To show our appreciation to our ------- customers, we're offering free tickets to a popular comedy show held downtown.
(A) value
(B) valuate
(C) valuing
(D) valued

お得意様に私たちの感謝の気持ちを伝えるために，ダウンタウンで開かれる人気のコメディショーの無料券をお渡ししております。

正解：(D)

● 着眼点！ まず空所の前後をチェック！

レベル ★★★★

解説　空所前後をまず確認。our ------- customers と，空所には customers を修飾する形容詞が入ることがわかる。ここから，(D) を選ぼう。(A) 名詞「価値，値段」，(B) 動詞「〜を評価する」，(C) 動詞 value の ing 形，(D) 形容詞「貴重な」。

語句　☐ valued customer　得意先

---

111. One of the growing concerns for people who are worried about the earth is the ------- of our air and water.
(A) quality
(B) quantity
(C) quest
(D) questionnaire

地球のことを心配している人たちがますます懸念していることの1つは，空気と水の質です。

正解：(A)

● 着眼点！ 文脈から判断せよ！

レベル ★★★☆

解説　適切な名詞を選ぶ語彙問題。人々が空気と水の何について懸念しているかを判断して，正解を導く。選択肢はそれぞれ，(A)「質」，(B)「量」，(C)「探究」，(D)「アンケート」の意味。ここで文意が通るのは (A) のみで，これが正解。

語句　☐ concern　名 懸念

112. A group of consumers criticized the government for being indifferent ------- public opinion.
(A) to
(B) for
(C) from
(D) with

消費者グループは政府が世論に対して無関心であると非難しました。

正解：(A)

● 着眼点！ 形容詞と前置詞の相性に注意！

レベル ★★★☆

[解説] 空所の前の indifferent「無関心な，無頓着な」は後ろに，to/toward を伴う。ここでは (A) to が適切。前置詞とセットで覚えておこう。indifferent は different「異なった」の反意語ではないので，注意しよう。

[語句] □ consumer 名 消費者　□ criticize 動 〜を非難する　□ public opinion 世論

---

113. With the appearance of a competing company, it has become ------- important for BWU Corporation to expand its business to different fields.
(A) increase
(B) increasingly
(C) increasing
(D) increased

競合会社の出現により，BWU社にとって事業を他分野へ拡張することがますます重要になってきました。

正解：(B)

● 着眼点！ 品詞がわかれば即決できる！

レベル ★☆☆☆

[解説] 派生語問題はまず品詞を特定しよう。空所がなくても文意が完結するうえ，直後が形容詞 important であることから，空所には副詞が入るとわかる。(B) が正解。(A) 動詞「増す」，(B) 副詞「ますます」，(C) 形容詞「ますます増加する」，(D) 形容詞「増加した」。

---

114. Any person ------- income falls below the poverty line qualifies for this program.
(A) whom
(B) whose
(C) who
(D) whoever

その所得が法定貧困レベルを下回る人はだれでもこのプログラムの受給資格があります。

正解：(B)

● 着眼点！ 関係代名詞を攻略せよ！

レベル ★★☆☆

[解説] 主語 any person と述語動詞 qualifies の間の部分は，主語を修飾する語句を構成している。income falls below から，income は動詞ではなく名詞であることがわかる。したがって，これに先立つ空所には，関係代名詞の所有格である (B) whose が適切。

[語句] □ fall below 〜 〜を下回る　□ qualify 動 資格がある，適任である

115. This new technology enabled us to ------- an e-payment system which best fits your business needs.
　(A) be delivered　　　(B) delivered
　(C) delivering　　　　(D) deliver

この新しい技術により，皆様のビジネスニーズに最適な電子支払いシステムをお届けすることができました。

正解：(D)

着眼点！ 動詞の活用形はまず語の前後を見よ！

レベル ★★☆☆

解説 空所の前に to があり，後ろに目的語となる名詞句の an e-payment system があることから空所には動詞の原形が入り to 不定詞を構成することがわかる。よって (B)，(C) は不適切。空所の動詞 deliver の意味上の主語は us であることから受動態の (A) も×。正解は enable ＋人＋ to 不定詞で，「(人が) 〜するのを可能にする」という表現を作る動詞の原形 (D) deliver。

語句 ☐ e-payment 名 電子支払い

---

116. Please make sure the format of the new edition is ------- with the first edition.
　(A) consistently　　　(B) consistent
　(C) consistence　　　(D) consist

新版のフォーマットは初版と一致するようにしてください。

正解：(B)

着眼点！ 2 ステップで正解を導け！

レベル ★★☆☆

解説 正しい品詞を選択する問題。be 動詞の直後，かつ前置詞の前なので，空所に入るのは名詞か形容詞である。be consistent with 〜「〜と一貫した」となる (B) consistent が正解。(A) 副詞「一貫して」，(B) 形容詞「一貫した」，(C) 名詞「一貫性」，(D) 動詞「成る，成り立つ，一致する」。

語句 ☐ edition 名 (刊行物の) 版　☐ make sure 〜　〜を確かめる，確認する

---

117. The city council announced that the reform of its health services would take ------- the following fiscal year.
　(A) place　　　(B) occasion
　(C) hold　　　 (D) event

市議会は，公共医療サービスの改革が次の会計年度から行われることを発表しました。

正解：(A)

着眼点！ イディオムの知識がカギ！

レベル ★★☆☆

解説 空所に当てはまる名詞を選ぶ問題。take place で「行われる，起こる」という表現を知っているかどうかがポイントとなる。(A) が正解。(A)「場所」，(B)「時」，(C)「持つ所」，(D)「出来事」。

語句 ☐ fiscal year 会計年度，事業年度

---

118. The Siam Palace Resort & Club Pattaya is ------- for its excellent location combined with the tranquility of a private beach.
　(A) renown　　　(B) renewal
　(C) renowned　　(D) renovated

The Siam Palace Resort & Club Pattaya は，静かなプライベートビーチを含む優れた立地で有名です。

正解：(C)

178

● 着眼点！ 品詞と意味から正解を導け！

[解説] be 動詞の直後に来て，そのあとに for its … と続くので，空所に当てはまるのは形容詞。be renowned for ～ で「～で有名」という意味なので，正解は (C)。be famous for ～，be known for ～と同じく「～で有名である」という意味だが，どれも広告などでよく使われる表現なので押さえておこう。(A) の renown は名詞。形容詞や動詞と勘違いしないようにしよう。tranquility of ～ は「～の静けさ」という意味。(A) 名詞「有名，名声」，(B) 名詞「更新，再開」，(C) 形容詞「有名な」，(D) 動詞 renovate「～を修繕する，刷新する」の過去形・過去分詞。

[語句] □ excellent 形 優れた，素晴らしい　□ combine 動 ～を結合させる
□ tranquility 名 静けさ，平穏，安定

---

119. Financial projections show that if the market ------- to decline, the retail division will find itself with a negative cash flow.
(A) continued　　　(B) continuing
(C) continual　　　(D) continues

財務予測によると，もし市場が下落し続けたならば，小売り部門は負のキャッシュフローに至るでしょう。

正解：(D)

● 着眼点！ 消去法で選べ！

[解説] 空所は if 節の中にあり the market を主語とする動詞が入る。(C) の形容詞は不適切。直前に be 動詞がないので，(B) の ing 形も不可。主節の動詞は will fine と未来形になっているので，空所に入る動詞は過去形ではなく現在形でなければならない。よって (D) が正解。(A) 動詞 continue「～を続ける」の過去形，(B) 動詞の ing 形，(C) 形容詞「継続的な」，(D) 動詞の三人称・単数・現在形。

[語句] □ financial projection 財務予測　□ retail 名 小売り
□ negative cash flow 負のキャッシュフロー

---

120. ------- people would prefer to work in the communities where they live, but this is not always possible.
(A) Many of　　　(B) Much of
(C) Most　　　　(D) Almost

ほとんどの人は自分が住んでいる地域で働きたいと思っていますが，これは常に可能というわけではありません。

正解：(C)

● 着眼点！ 直後の語から正解を導け！

[解説] 直後に people があることに注目する。(A) は直後に the が必要であり，(B) のあとにくるのは不可算名詞でなければならないので，どちらも選択できない。(D) は副詞なので，名詞の people を修飾することはできない。(C) の Most はここでは形容詞でかつ many の最上級として用いられているので，名詞 people を修飾できるので (C) が正解。(A)「(可算名詞の) 多く」，(B)「(不可算名詞の) 多く」，(C) 形容詞「ほとんどの」，(D) 副詞「ほとんど」。

[語句] □ community 名 地域社会

121. Richmond Corporation's new warehouse is comparatively large among ------- of other companies nearby.

(A) those　　(B) what
(C) who　　(D) whom

Richmond 社の新倉庫は，近隣他社の<u>もの</u>の中では比較的大きいです。

正解：(A)

● 着眼点！　適切な代名詞を選べ！

レベル ★★★☆

[解説] 適切な代名詞を選択する問題。Richmond 社の新倉庫の大きさと近隣他社のものとが比較されていることがポイント。(A) those は前方にあるものを反復して表すときに用いられる。よって，正解は (A)。

---

122. The neighbors formed a community organization ------- protect their families from increasing incidents of crime.

(A) now　　(B) so that
(C) in order to　　(D) which

地域の人たちは最近多発してきている犯罪から家族を守る<u>ため</u>，地域市民組織を作りました。

正解：(C)

● 着眼点！　文の構造に注目して正解を勝ち取れ！

レベル ★★☆☆

[解説] 地域市民組織を作ったことと，家族を守る手段との関係を考える。家族を守ることは，組織を作ることの目的だと考えられるので，(C) が正解。(B) も目的を表すが，so that のあとには節（主語＋動詞）がくる。(D) も一見可能だが，続く動詞の活用が protect と原形であることから不適であることがわかる。(A)「今では」，(B)「～できるように」，(C)「～するために」，(D)「～するところの」。

[語句] □ incident 名 事件

---

123. ------- candidates are required to write a mandatory essay for the interview scheduled next Wednesday.

(A) Potential　　(B) Potentially
(C) Potentiality　　(D) Potentiate

応募<u>希望</u>者は，次の水曜日に予定されている面接に必須の小論文を書くよう求められています。

正解：(A)

● 着眼点！　品詞問題は前後を見よ！

レベル ★★☆☆

[解説] 適切な品詞の語を選ぶ問題。文頭であり，かつ空所直後に名詞 candidates「応募者，志願者」が続くので，(C) 名詞「可能性，潜在性」，(D) 動詞「～を可能にする」は不可。文意から (A) 形容詞「潜在的な，可能な」が正解。(B) 副詞「潜在的に」。

[語句] □ mandatory 形 必須の，義務的な

---

124. Because the massage services in the Sunshine Spa are very popular on weekends, you need to consider ------- a space in advance.

(A) reserved　　(B) reserves
(C) reserving　　(D) reserve

Sunshine Spa のマッサージサービスは週末にはとても人気があるので，事前にスペースを<u>予約すること</u>を検討する必要があります。

正解：(C)

180

- **着眼点！** consider の用法に注意！ ★★★☆
  - **解説** 品詞問題。consider という動詞は後ろに動名詞を目的語にとる。よって、ing 形である (C) が正解。consider +〜ing で「〜することを検討する」という意味。
  - **語句** □ consider 動 〜を検討する □ in advance 事前に □ reserve 動 〜を予約する

125. The chairperson of the board of directors declared she does not ------- to seek another term, though she will remain on the board.
(A) attend (B) intend
(C) predict (D) concur

取締役会の議長は、自分は取締役会には残るが、もう1期務めるつもりはないと発表しました。

正解：(B)

- **着眼点！** to 不定詞を目的語にとる動詞を攻略せよ！ ★★★☆
  - **解説** 適切な動詞を選ぶ問題。直後に to 不定詞があるので、to 不定詞を目的語にとる動詞を選ぶ。to 不定詞を目的語にとるのは (B) のみ。intend to 〜 で「〜するつもりである」という意味になる。(A)「〜に出席する」、(B)「〜を意図する、〜するつもりである」、(C)「〜を予言する」、(D)「賛同する」。
  - **語句** □ chairperson 名 代表者, 議長 □ board of directors 取締役会 □ term 名 期

126. By State Law, you need a ------- in order to purchase contact lenses.
(A) definition (B) prescription
(C) conception (D) motivation

州法の定めにより、コンタクトレンズを購入するには処方せんが必要です。

正解：(B)

- **着眼点！** 文意から導き出せ！ ★★★☆
  - **解説** 選択肢には名詞が並んでいるが、空所に入る名詞は、By State Law「州法により」、to purchase contact lenses「コンタクトレンズの購入」に you need「必要がある」ものでなければならない。この文意に合致するのは (B) のみ。(A)「定義」、(B)「処方せん」、(C)「概念、着想、妊娠」、(D)「動機づけ、やる気」。
  - **語句** □ purchase 動 〜を買う

127. ------- an effort as to overhaul vocational training programs does not seem to be sufficient.
(A) So (B) Much
(C) Same (D) Such

職業訓練プログラムを徹底的に見直すというような努力は十分ではないようです。

正解：(D)

- **着眼点！** イディオムで攻略せよ！ ★★★☆
  - **解説** ヒントは an effort のあとに続く as to の部分。Such + A（名詞）+ as to do で「〜するような A、〜するほどの A」という形でこの文はできているので、正解は (D)。(A) の so や (C) の same も as to と組み合わせて用いられることもあるが、ここでは文意に合わない。また、(B) much は数えられない名詞を修飾するので不可。
  - **語句** □ effort 名 努力 □ overhaul 動 〜を徹底的に見直す, 詳しく調べる, 追いつく □ vocational training 職業訓練 □ sufficient 形 十分な

128. The ------- price tag on the project is expected to range somewhere between 2.5 and 3 million dollars.
(A) estimating　　(B) estimate
(C) estimation　　(D) estimated

そのプロジェクトの見積り価格は 250 万から 300 万ドルの間と予想されます。

正解：(D)

レベル ★★★☆

● 着眼点！　形容詞的用法の分詞は意味で選べ！

解説　The と price tag の間に入る語なので，price tag を修飾する形容詞だとわかる。選択肢の中で形容詞の役割を果たせるのは (A) と (D)。estimate は「〜を見積もる」という意味なので，「価格」は「見積もられる」と「される側」なので過去分詞にする。(A) 動詞 estimate「〜を見積もる」の ing 形，(B) 動詞の原形，(C) 名詞「見積り」，(D) 動詞の過去形・過去分詞。

語句　□ price tag　価格，値札

---

129. The certification demonstrates that Gutierrez Dairy meets the highest social ------- environmental standards in the industry.
(A) but　　(B) toward
(C) and　　(D) such

証明書は，Gutierrez 乳業が業界で最も高い社会的かつ環境的基準を満たしていることを示しています。

正解：(C)

レベル ★★☆☆

● 着眼点！　品詞混合の選択ではまず品詞を確定して意味で選ぶ！

解説　空所をはさんで social と environmental という 2 つの形容詞が並んでいる。この 2 つの形容詞を結びつけるには接続詞が必要。内容的に反対の意味を表す (A) but が入るとは考えにくい。「社会的な，そして環境的な基準を満たす」とすると文意が通る。よって，(C) and が入る。(A) 接続詞「しかし」，(B) 前置詞「〜の方へ」，(C) 接続詞「そして」，(D) 形容詞「そのような」。

---

130. Mr. White was awarded the company's Best Salesperson of the Year for three ------- years.
(A) entire　　(B) precise
(C) consecutive　　(D) restless

White さんは 3 年連続で会社の年間最優秀販売員賞を授与されました。

正解：(C)

レベル ★★★☆

● 着眼点！　コロケーションで正解せよ！

解説　years を修飾する形容詞を選択する語彙問題。文意から空所に適切に当てはまるのは (C)。for three consecutive years は「3 年連続で」の意味。(A)「全体の，完全な」も紛らわしいが修飾する語をひとつのかたまりとして捉え，単数形の名詞が続く。ここでは，複数形 (years) となっているので不可。(B)「正確な」(C)「連続した」，(D)「落ち着かない，休むことのない」。

語句　□ award　動 〜を授与する　□ salesperson　名 販売員，店員

---

131. Jackie looked ------- when she finally realized that nobody was paying attention to her opinion.
(A) embarrass　　(B) embarrassing
(C) to be embarrassed　　(D) embarrassed

だれも自分の意見に注意を払っていないことにようやく気がついた時，Jackie は当惑しているように見えました。

正解：(D)

- **着眼点！** 形容詞的用法の分詞を見分けよ！ ★★☆☆

解説 動詞 embarrass「〜を当惑させる」の派生語の問題。look は後ろに補語（形容詞など）を取る。look embarrassed で「当惑しているように見える，気まずそうに見える」の意味。知覚動詞 look の後ろには現在分詞も補語として来ることがあるが，文意からここでは不適切。正解は (D)。

語句 □ pay attention to 〜　〜に注意を払う，注目する　□ opinion 名 意見

---

132. We believe that the new lineup of our AF digital camera series will ------- catch everyone's attention.

(A) patiently　　　(B) gratefully
(C) definitely　　　(D) deliberately

当社の AF デジタルカメラシリーズの新ラインナップは，間違いなく，皆さんの注目を集めると確信しています。

正解：(C)

- **着眼点！** 文意を把握せよ！ ★★★☆

解説 副詞の語彙問題。空所後の catch 以下と文意が合うのは (C)。(A)「しんぼう強く」，(B)「感謝して，喜んで，ありがたく」，(C)「間違いなく，確かに」，(D)「故意に，わざと」。

語句 □ lineup 名 ラインナップ，顔ぶれ，構成，人の列

---

133. Cape Clothing Store will have to undergo drastic downsizing due to a long-term economic -------.

(A) downturn　　　(B) growth
(C) market　　　(D) scale

Cape Clothing Store 社は，長期にわたる景気の停滞が理由で，思い切った人員削減を行わなければならなくなるでしょう。

正解：(A)

- **着眼点！** コロケーションを攻略せよ！ ★★☆☆

解説 語彙問題。due to 以下は，「長期間の経済的な〜が理由で」という意味。ここで economic という単語とのつながりから文意に合う (A) を選びたい。economic downturn で「経済の悪化，景気の停滞，不況」という意味の頻出表現。(B)「成長」，(C)「市場」，(D)「規模」。

語句 □ undergo 動 〜に耐える，〜を経験する　□ drastic 形 思い切った，極端な
□ downsizing 名 人員削減，経営合理化　□ long-term 形 長期間の

---

134. Known as a skilled technician, Mason Ford has no ------- of accounting.

(A) confidence　　　(B) knowledge
(C) expectation　　　(D) evidence

腕のよい技術者と知られている Mason Ford は会計の知識が全くありませんでした。

正解：(B)

- **着眼点！** 語彙力向上は得点力向上！ ★★★☆

解説 語彙力が問われている問題。文意に沿った意味を持つ選択肢を選ぼう。正解は (B)。has no knowledge of 〜 で「〜の知識を全く持たない」という意味になる。(A)「信頼，自信」，(C)「期待」，(D)「証拠」。

135. Jens Technology Group, Inc. announced today its ------- into Southeast Asian markets.
(A) expand (B) expandable
(C) expansively (D) expansion

Jens Technology Group 社は，本日，東南アジア市場への事業拡大を発表しました。

正解：(D)

● 着眼点！ 品詞がわかれば正解できる！

レベル ★☆☆☆

解説　空所は所有格 its のあとに続くので，名詞が適切である。よって (D) expansion が正解。(A) 動詞「～を拡大する，拡張する」，(B) 形容詞「拡張できる，発展性のある」，(C) 副詞「広大に，拡張的に，発展的に」，(D) 名詞「拡大，発展，伸張」。

語句　□ announce 動 ～を発表する

---

136. Workers need to comply ------- the safety regulations and report to the factory manager any defects they find in the machine.
(A) for (B) to
(C) along (D) with

従業員は安全規則にのっとって，機械に見つかったいかなる欠陥も工場長まで報告する必要があります。

正解：(D)

● 着眼点！ 自動詞は前置詞とペアで覚えよ！

レベル ★★★☆

解説　自動詞は，伴う前置詞によって意味が変わるが，comply は通例 with を伴う。イディオムとして覚えておくと comply を見ただけで正解の (D) with を導くことができる。comply with ～「～に従う，応じる」。近年，日本語でも使われるようになった compliance「コンプライアンス（法令遵守）」は comply の名詞形。report to ～「～に報告する」という語句もあわせて覚えよう。

---

137. Travelers can easily book ------- at the cheapest rate by using a rate comparison tool on Web sites.
(A) rewards (B) contents
(C) accommodations (D) destinations

旅行者は，ウェブサイトの料金比較ツールを利用することによって，簡単に最安値で宿泊の予約をすることができます。

正解：(C)

● 着眼点！ 仲間とペアで覚えよ！

レベル ★★☆☆

解説　語彙問題。空所の前の部分は「旅行者は簡単に予約できる」という意味なので，旅行者が予約するものを選択肢から選ぶ。「宿泊施設」という意味の (C) accommodations が最適。(A)「報酬」，(B)「内容」，(D)「目的地」。

語句　□ rate 名 料金，価格　□ comparison 名 比較

---

138. A typhoon ------- by strong winds is likely to arrive in Okinawa by tomorrow morning.
(A) accompanied (B) to accompany
(C) accompanying (D) will accompany

強風を伴った台風は，明朝までに沖縄に上陸する見込みです。

正解：(A)

● 着眼点！ 空所前後をまず確認！

レベル ★★☆☆

解説　空所前後にヒントがある。空所前 a typhoon と空所後 by strong winds を確認しよう。動詞 accompany は，(be) accompanied by ～という形で「～を伴う」という意味を表す。つまり，正解は (A)。

139. Always at the forefront of health-consciousness, California has become the first state to ------- ban trans fats in restaurants.
(A) complete
(B) completed
(C) completely
(D) be completed

常に健康志向の先端にいるカリフォルニア州は，レストランでトランス脂肪酸を完全に禁止する最初の州になりました。

正解：(C)

● 着眼点！ 空所の前後から品詞を確定せよ！

[解説] 空所の後ろの ban「～を禁止する」は動詞。to 不定詞の to と動詞の間に入る語なので，動詞を修飾する副詞（C）が正解。(A) 動詞 complete「～を完成させる」，(B) 動詞の過去形・過去分詞，(C) 副詞「完全に」，(D) 動詞の受動態。

[語句]
- forefront 图 先端，第一線
- health-consciousness 图 健康志向
- trans fat トランス脂肪酸

---

140. ------- being knowledgeable about the latest industry trends, it is important to treat our customers fairly and honestly.
(A) Otherwise
(B) Along with
(C) Wherever
(D) As a result

最新の業界トレンドに精通していることに加えて，当社のお客様に対して公正かつ誠実に接することが重要です。

正解：(B)

● 着眼点！ 文の構造に着目せよ！

[解説] 文頭からカンマまでは，文全体を修飾する副詞句を構成していることに着目。文意から空所の直後の being につながる適切な語句は (B) Along with「～に加えて，～と一緒に」。(A)「さもなければ，別の方法で」，(C)「どこへ～しようとも，～するところはどこでも」，(D)「結果として」。

[語句]
- knowledgeable 形 精通している，よく知っている
- treat 動 ～を扱う，待遇する，接する
- fairly 副 公平に，公正に
- honestly 副 正直に，誠実に

PART 6

Questions 141-143 refer to the following e-mail.
問題 141-143 は次の E メールに関するものです。

To: Zack Anderson
From: Karen Milestone
Subject: Our Apologies

Dear Mr. Anderson,

I am writing on behalf of Pro-Fast Delivery Systems, Inc., to apologize for the mix-up ⬚141 resulted in your packages being delivered late.
As a long-time valued customer, you probably know that we at Pro-Fast endeavor to deliver all packages on schedule, on or ⬚142 the estimated delivery date. Unfortunately, due to intense storms caused by the hurricane, there was a delay in delivering your packages. As a result, please accept this $30 printable voucher as a ⬚143 of our apology and goodwill.

宛先：Zack Anderson
差出人：Karen Milestone
件名：お詫び

Anderson 様

Pro-Fast Delivery Systems 社を代表して，混乱からお客様のお荷物の配達が遅れましたことをお詫びするためにメールをお送りしています。
長年ご利用をいただいている大切なお客様ですので，私ども Pro-Fast 社がすべての荷物をスケジュール通り，配達予定日またはそれ以前に配達する努力をしていることはおわかりいただいていることと存じます。
残念ながら，ハリケーンによる激しい嵐のため，お客様のお荷物の配達に遅れが生じました。つきましては，こちらのプリント可能な 30 ドルのクーポンを，私どものお詫びと誠意の印としてお受け取りください。

【語句】
- ☐ mix-up 名 混乱，取り違え
- ☐ endeavor 動 努力する
- ☐ intense 形 極めて強い
- ☐ voucher 名 クーポン券，割引券

141. (A) which
(B) so that
(C) being
(D) when

正解：(A)

● 着眼点！ 文の構造を把握せよ！ レベル ★★☆☆

[解説] 空所に入る語は，接続詞の役割と，resulted の主語の役割の両方を果たさなければならない。そのような働きをするのは，関係代名詞である。選択肢の中で resulted の主語になり得るのは (A) だけ。(A) 関係代名詞「～するところの」，(B)「～するように」，(C) be の ing 形，(D) 関係副詞「～する時」。

142. (A) during
(B) after
(C) before
(D) while

正解：(C)

● 着眼点！ 時を示す前置詞を区別せよ！ レベル ★★☆☆

[解説] 後ろが名詞句なので空所には前置詞が入る。ここは，「到着予定日時か，そうでなければそれよりも前に到着させる努力をしている」という文意だと推測できる。よって正解は (C)。(A) でも「その日のうち」という意味にとれるが，それは結果的に on と同じことになるので不可。(D) は前置詞ではなく接続詞なので，後ろに〈主語＋動詞〉が必要。(A) 前置詞「～の間」，(B) 前置詞「～のあと」，(C) 前置詞「～の前」，(D) 接続詞「～する間」。

143. (A) mark
(B) choice
(C) reason
(D) token

正解：(D)

● 着眼点！ コロケーションから解け！ レベル ★★★★

[解説] as a token of ～ で，「～の印に」という意味になる。ひとかたまりで覚えよう。正解は (D)。また as a token of appreciation で「感謝の印として」という意味になり，これもよく使われる。選択肢はすべて名詞で，それぞれ (A)「印」，(B)「選択」，(C)「理由」，(D)「印」の意味。

Questions 144-146 refer to the following notice.
問題 **144-146** は次のお知らせに関するものです。

Our New Hours and Dinner Menu.

Green Thumb Gourmet is proud to announce its new dinner menu. A ⎡ 144 ⎤ of cooked-from-scratch dishes are served from 5:00 P.M. to 8:00 P.M. To name a few from the menu, there is the Four Cheese Lasagna, the Sag Tofu Indian Curry and the Lebanese Stuffed Vegetables. ⎡ 145 ⎤, we will continue to serve our original organic salad and soup to everyone who orders their meal.
In addition, we will remain open during the late afternoon, so we can offer our hot takeouts to those ⎡ 146 ⎤ a late lunch or an early dinner. Our new hours are 10:30 A.M. to 8:00 P.M.

Green Thumb Gourmet
439 E. Moss St
555-9600

新しい営業時間とディナーメニュー

Green Thumb Gourmet は自信を持って新しいディナーメニューをお知らせします。午後5時から8時までは一から手作りしたさまざまな料理をお召し上がりいただけます。メニューをほんの2, 3例挙げると，4種類のチーズラザニア，サーグ・トーフ・インドカレー，レバノン風野菜の詰め物などがあります。さらに，料理を注文してくださったすべてのお客様に，当店オリジナルオーガニックサラダとスープを引き続きご提供いたします。
その上，午後は遅くまで営業し，遅い昼食や早い夕食をご希望の方々に当店の温かいテイクアウト料理をご提供いたします。新しい営業時間は午前10時半より午後8時までとなります。

Green Thumb Gourmet
439 E. Moss 通り
555-9600

語句
☐ from scratch　ゼロから，最初から
☐ takeout　名 テイクアウト料理

144. (A) various
(B) variety
(C) varied
(D) variable

正解：(B)

● 着眼点！ 品詞特定は正解への近道！

レベル ★★☆☆

解説　空所は a ------- of なので，名詞しか入らないとわかる。したがって，(B) variety が正解。a variety of ～ で「さまざまな～」の意味になる。(A) 形容詞「さまざまな」，(B) 名詞「多様さ」，(C) 形容詞「多様な」，(D) 名詞「変化するもの」または形容詞「変えられる」。

---

145. (A) However
(B) If
(C) Moreover
(D) While

正解：(C)

● 着眼点！ 文のつながりを見極めよ！

レベル ★★★☆

解説　空所の前では，料理のメニューをいくつか紹介しており，空所のあとでは，「サラダとスープを引き続き提供する」という内容を述べている。空所の前と後ろをつなぐのに適切なのは接続副詞である (C) Moreover。(A) 副詞「しかしながら」，(B) 接続詞「もし」，(C) 副詞「さらに」，(D) 接続詞「～だけれども」。

---

146. (A) desire
(B) to desire
(C) desiring
(D) desired

正解：(C)

● 着眼点！ 動詞の主体を見よ！

レベル ★★★☆

解説　空所部分を含む those ------- a late lunch or an early dinner は「遅い昼食や早い夕食をご希望の方々」の意味。those は「人々」の意味で「望んでいる人」とするには現在分詞の (C) desiring が適切。過去分詞の desired を使うと「望まれた」という受け身の意味になってしまうので，不適切。(A) 動詞 desire「～を切望する」の原形，(B) to 不定詞，(C) ing 形，(D) 過去形・過去分詞。

Questions 147-149 refer to the following letter.
問題 147-149 は次の手紙に関するものです。

To our customers,

Thank you for using Natural Equipment products.
This is to inform you there has been a change in our maintenance personnel. James Brandon, who has been servicing your units for the past five years, will be transferred to our Atlanta branch, ⬚ 147 ⬚ September 1.
Brad Wayne will be replacing him. Since the beginning of his service, Brad has been a dedicated ⬚ 148 ⬚ who makes sure your units continue to operate smoothly. Please be assured this change will not affect our services in any way.
If you have any further questions, please ⬚ 149 ⬚ to call our office at 555-5545. We hope to continue providing you with the quality service for which we are known.

Sincerely,

Adam Schultz
General Manager
Maintenance Division

お客様各位

Natural Equipment 社の製品をご利用いただき、ありがとうございます。
本日は、メンテナンス担当職員の変更についてお知らせします。この5年間お客様の設備を担当していた James Brandon が、9月1日付けで Atlanta 支店に転勤になります。
後任には Brad Wayne があたります。Brad は入社以来、仕事熱心な専門家であり、お客様が現在お使いの機器類を今後もスムーズに操作していただけるよう、万全を尽くします。今回の変更は弊社のサービスにいかなる影響も与えることはありませんので、どうぞご安心ください。
さらなるご質問がございましたら、お気軽に 555-5545 の弊社事業所までお電話ください。
今後も引き続きご好評いただいております当社の質の高いサービスを提供してまいりますので、どうぞよろしくお願いいたします。

敬具

Adam Schultz
メンテナンス事業部統括マネージャー

> 語句
> ☐ dedicated 形 献身的な
> ☐ affect 動 〜に影響を及ぼす、作用する

147. (A) ever since
(B) effective
(C) in
(D) always on

正解：(B)

● 着眼点！　日付を表す表現を覚えよ！　レベル ★★★☆

解説　ここでは，前任者の転勤がいつからかということを説明している。(A) ever since は「～以来ずっと」の意味。転勤は過去のことではなくこれからのことなので不適切。(C) 日付には in ではなく on を用いる。(D) は always が含まれているのが文意に合わず不適切。正解の (B) effective「～日付けで」はビジネスでの常用イディオムなので覚えよう。

---

148. (A) swimmer
(B) teacher
(C) professional
(D) driver

正解：(C)

● 着眼点！　単語の見た目に惑わされるな！　レベル ★★☆☆

解説　正解 (C) の professional は，「専門家，プロ選手」という意味の名詞。他の選択肢は，「お客様が現在お使いの機器類を今後もスムーズに操作していただけるよう努める」という，設備会社のメンテナンス担当者を言い表すにはいずれも不適切。

---

149. (A) hope
(B) do not
(C) expect
(D) feel free

正解：(D)

● 着眼点！　ビジネスの常用イディオムをマスターせよ！　レベル ★☆☆☆

解説　「さらにご質問のある方はお気軽に会社までお電話ください」という文章の一部となるので，ここは feel free to ～「気軽に～してください」が適切。よって，正解は (D)。ビジネスの常用イディオムである。(B) は文法上不可。(A)，(C) も文意に合わない。

Questions 150-152 refer to the following memo.
問題 150-152 は次のメモに関するものです。

Subject: Company Retreat

All staff

In our history, this year has been our best   150 . This is all thanks to your hard work.
I have always had   151   in our head chef Hiroaki Takagi, and I am proud of the service quality of our staff. I am also pleased that Natalie Borden has newly joined us as our Banquet Service manager.
Customers have been responding positively to our improved selection of food and beverages. I cannot think of any better way   152   your effort than a three-day vacation in Miami, Florida.
Needless to say, travel expenses and accommodation will be covered by the company. I hope all of you will participate and celebrate our success together.

With my appreciation,
Jean Bedeau, Owner Chef

件名：社員旅行

全スタッフの皆さんへ

お店の歴史上，この一年は これまでで 最もよい年となりました。これはすべて皆さんの熱心な仕事ぶりのおかげです。
私は常にヘッド・シェフである **Hiroaki Takagi** に 信頼 を置いていますし，スタッフのサービスの質にも誇りを持っています。また，今年 **Natalie Borden** が宴会サービスのマネージャーとして私たちのチームに加わってくれたことも嬉しく思っています。
お客様はより良くなった当店の料理と飲み物のセレクションに好意的な反応を示しています。私はフロリダ州マイアミへ3日間の休暇旅行にお連れするのが，皆さんの尽力に お礼をする 一番よい方法だと思います。
もちろん，旅費と宿泊費は会社負担です。皆さん全員が参加して，共に私たちの成功を祝ってくださるように願っています。

感謝を込めて
Jean Bedeau，オーナーシェフ

語句	□ company retreat　社員旅行
	□ banquet　名 宴会

150. (A) throughout
(B) else
(C) after
(D) yet

正解：(D)

● 着眼点！ 「過去最高」の表現を選べ！　レベル ★★★★

[解説] 空所に入る語として適切なものを選ぶ問題。(A) は「〜の間中」という意味の前置詞，(C) は「あとで」という意味の前置詞で，どちらも名詞を伴う必要があるので不適切。(B) は「他に」という意味の副詞だが，文脈に合わない。(D) は最上級の best の後ろについて「今までの中で」という意味になる。

---

151. (A) confidence
(B) confidential
(C) confident
(D) confided

正解：(A)

● 着眼点！ 空所の前から品詞を特定せよ！　レベル ★☆☆☆

[解説] 空所に入る語は動詞 had の目的語なので，名詞がくるとわかる。選択肢で名詞は (A) だけ。(A) 名詞「信頼」，(B) 形容詞「親展の」，(C) 形容詞「自信のある」，(D) 動詞 confide 「〜を信頼する」の過去形・過去分詞。have [put, place] confidence in 〜 で「〜を信頼する」という意味のイディオムを覚えておきたい。

---

152. (A) repaying
(B) repayment
(C) to repay
(D) repaid

正解：(C)

● 着眼点！ 修飾関係を捉えよ！　レベル ★★★☆

[解説] 空所を含む文の意味は，「フロリダ州マイアミへの 3 日間の休暇よりも皆さんの尽力に〜するよい方法を思いつかなかった」。ここから空所には better way を修飾する to 不定詞の形容詞的用法が適切で，「お礼をするための」方法になると判断しよう。したがって (C) が正解。(A) 動詞 repay「〜に報いる」の ing 形，(B) 名詞「返済」，(C) 動詞の to 不定詞，(D) 動詞の過去形・過去分詞。

PART 7

問題 153-154 は次の広告に関するものです。

Guinevere's の驚くべき食用菜園

自然食品を育てる家庭菜園に必要なものをお探しでしたら何でもそろう，Guinevere's にお越しください。私どもは，有機野菜が種から食卓に上るまで，あなたの庭を開発していくことを専門としています。フランスの集約的ガーデニング法をお教えします。これはそもそも，パリの都会の狭い地区で用いられた方法です。水を節約するために，作物を詰めて植えます。そうすることで，根が深く伸び，雑草を抑え収穫を上げます。お客様のニーズに合った最高の自然食用菜園の設計を行い，施工，維持，そして害虫を防ぎ，収穫するお手伝いをいたします。お客様の土壌を診断し，栽培する植物や有機肥料をお勧めすることができます。私どもは，料理人のための至福の菜園，子ども向けの菜園，スパイスを集めた菜園といった，あらゆるグループや趣味に合ったプランを用意しております。

語句
- □ edible 形 食用の
- □ organic food 自然食品，有機食品
- □ school 動 ～に教え込む
- □ deter 動 ～するのを思いとどまらせる，～を防げる
- □ pest 名 害虫
- □ zesty 形 ピリッとした風味の

153. What is being advertised?　　　　　何が広告されていますか。

　　(A) Organic catering　　　　　　　　(A) 自然食品の宅配
　　(B) French lessons　　　　　　　　　(B) フランス語のレッスン
　　(C) Garden tours　　　　　　　　　　(C) 庭園ツアー
　　(D) Gardening services　　　　　　　(D) ガーデニングのサービス

正解：(D)

● 着眼点！　広告のジャンルを見抜け！　　　　　　　　　　　　　　レベル ★☆☆☆

解説　何の広告かは，冒頭を見れば OK。タイトルと 1 文目から，オーガニックフードのガーデニングに関するビジネスだとわかる。2 文目の **developing your garden from seed to food for your table** でサービスを説明し，さらに後半で詳しく内容を述べている。客のニーズに合わせて，さまざまな庭を造る「庭造り」がサービスの根幹なので，(D) が正解。

---

154. Which is NOT a service mentioned in the　　広告の中に述べられていないサービスは
advertisement?　　　　　　　　　　　　　　　　どれですか。

　　(A) Waste removal　　　　　　　　　(A) 廃棄物の除去
　　(B) Pest control　　　　　　　　　　　(B) 害虫駆除
　　(C) Construction　　　　　　　　　　(C) 建造
　　(D) Soil diagnostics　　　　　　　　　(D) 土壌診断

正解：(A)

● 着眼点！　サービスを順にサーチしよう！　　　　　　　　　　　レベル ★★☆☆

解説　選択肢のサービス項目を順にサーチしよう。ガーデニング法については，本文中盤で菜園の設計，施工，害虫駆除，土壌診断が順に述べられている。選択肢と比較すれば OK。(A) だけが書かれておらず，これが正解。

問題 155-156 は次の E メールに関するものです。

宛先：rcrawford@pr.nextcellular.com
差出人：catehodgeson@tech.nextcellular.com
件名：製品リコール
日付：5月7日

Ron さん

技術部の Cate です。すでにご存じとは思いますが，バッテリー過熱の問題があり，携帯電話 NT Quasar 10 万台を回収しなければなりません。これは当社にとって経済的および技術的な痛手であるだけでなく，広報の問題でもあります。このリコールには，全国の何千という携帯電話店および電子機器店に影響を与えます。小売店とお客様に，当社の一番の関心事は安全だということと，欠陥バッテリーを回収して新しいものと交換するきちんとした計画があるということを確信してもらう必要があります。このリコールに関して技術面での解決が見えたら，直接連絡します。

Cate Hodgeson
技術部長

語句
- setback 名 痛手
- public relations 広報活動，渉外事務
- retailer 名 小売業者
- concern 名 関心事
- faulty 形 欠陥のある

155. What is the e-mail about?

(A) Planning a new cell phone launch
(B) Planning to ask for the return of products
(C) Asking a retailer to carry a product
(D) Apologizing to customers

このEメールは何に関するものですか。

(A) 新しい携帯電話の発売計画
(B) 製品の回収計画
(C) 小売業者に製品を扱ってもらうための依頼
(D) 顧客への謝罪

正解：(B)

● 着眼点！ subject（件名）を見よう！

レベル ★★★☆

[解説] Eメールの主題はsubjectに集約されている。Recall of productとあるので，製品の回収に関するメールだとわかる。さらに，本文冒頭でも，As you know by now we have to recall over 100,000 NT Quasar cellular phonesからも確認できる。よって，正解は(B)。recall productsがask for the return of productsと言い換えられている。recallという語の知識がカギ。

---

156. What is wrong with the product?

(A) It is not being marketed properly.
(B) Its screen is faulty.
(C) It is too expensive.
(D) Its battery is not safe to use.

製品はどこが悪いのですか。

(A) 販売の仕方が適切でない。
(B) スクリーンに欠陥がある。
(C) 値段が高すぎる。
(D) バッテリーが使用に際し危険である。

正解：(D)

● 着眼点！ トラブルの原因を読み取ろう！

レベル ★☆☆☆

[解説] トラブルの原因／理由をサーチしよう。2文目，because of a problem with overheating batteriesをチェックすればOK。これをnot safeと言い換えた（D）が正解。

問題 157-158 は次のメモに関するものです。

メモ

差出人：**Linda Perry**，人事部長
宛先：全スタッフ
日付：**8 月 25 日（月）**
件名：月例スタッフミーティング

来月の第 1 月曜日は労働者の日のため，9 月の月例会議は，第 2 月曜日の 9 時に延期いたします。

議題は，いつもとは異なります。ご存じの通り，今回は最も利益をもたらした部門に賞を贈ります。昨年は，営業チームが 5 つ星ホテルでの夕食招待券を獲得しました。

CEO が現在のビジネスの状況とそれが当社に与える影響について，プレゼンテーションを行います。

この半年間ご尽力くださり，ありがとうございます。

語句
- **Labor Day** （アメリカ・カナダにおける）労働者の日
- **agenda** 名 議題，予定，協議事項
- **present ... with ~** …に~を贈呈する
- **productive** 形 利益をもたらす，生産的な
- **obtain** 動 ~を得る，手に入れる

157. What is the main purpose of the memo?　このメモの主な目的は何ですか。

(A) To announce a change in schedule　(A) 予定の変更を知らせること。
(B) To recognize an employee　(B) 従業員を表彰すること。
(C) To hold an emergent meeting　(C) 緊急会議を開くこと。
(D) To invite a company excursion　(D) 会社の小旅行に招待すること。

正解：(A)

● 着眼点！　メモの目的は冒頭！

レベル ★★☆☆

[解説] 冒頭部分をチェックしてメモの目的をつかもう。第 1 段落，our usual monthly meeting in September will be postponed とあり，9 月の月例会議が延期になったことがわかる。この内容に最も適しているのは，(A)。(B) は紛らわしいが，9 月の月例会議のテーマの一つであって，このメモはあくまでも日程変更を中心に伝えているので×。

[語句]
□ recognize　動 ～を表彰する，評価する
□ excursion　名 (団体の) 小旅行，観光旅行

---

158. What information is NOT included in the memo?　メモに含まれていないのは何の情報ですか。

(A) The day of the next staff meeting　(A) 次回の職員会議の日程
(B) The topic of the CEO's presentation　(B) CEO のプレゼンテーションのトピック
(C) The department to be commended　(C) 称賛される部門
(D) The expression of gratitude to the staff　(D) 職員に対する謝意の表現

正解：(C)

● 着眼点！　NOT 問題は本文に当てはまるものから除外せよ！

レベル ★★★☆

[解説] 選択肢の名詞を本文中でサーチしよう。(A) staff meeting は第 1 段落，(B) presentation は第 3 段落，(D) gratitude は言い換えられて最終文に対応する。消去法で，正解は (C)。

[語句]
□ commend　動 ～を称賛する，～を推薦する
□ gratitude　名 感謝の気持ち，謝意

問題 **159-160** は次の手紙に関するものです。

Westfield Housing Loans 社
88 Jasper Ave.
Bluebell, Ohio
213-555-7623

6月30日

North 様

Westfield Housing Loans 社のローンにお申し込みいただき，ありがとうございます。私どもはあなた様のお取り引きに感謝し，お手伝いしたいと思います。しかし，お送りいただきましたローン関係書類が数ページ抜けていることがわかりました。私どもがこれまでに受け取りました情報は，申込書と職歴のみです。これまでの住所リストと，クレジット記録を調査するためのご本人の署名入りの宣誓書が必要です。これらの用紙を手紙に同封いたしました。必要な情報がすべて整いましてから，ローン認可までの過程は，約2，3週間となります。その後に，あなた様に認可される借入金額を郵便にてお知らせいたします。

書類や認可の過程について何かご質問がございましたら，**800-555-0902** のカスタマーサービスまでご連絡くださるか，私どものウェブサイト **www.westfieldhousing.org** をご覧ください。

敬具
Jody Brown 融資担当者

[語句]
- ☐ **apply for** ～　～に申し込む，～を申請する
- ☐ **notify**　動 ～に知らせる
- ☐ **approval**　名 承認，認定

159. What is the purpose of this letter?

(A) To advertise a loan
(B) To request some more documents
(C) To send more information to Mr. North
(D) To explain how long a process takes

この手紙の目的は何ですか。

(A) ローンの広告をすること。
(B) 追加の書類を要求すること。
(C) North さんにもっと情報を送ること。
(D) 処理過程に何日かかるかを説明すること。

正解：(B)

●着眼点！ 手紙の目的は冒頭を見よ！

レベル ★☆☆☆

解説　ビジネスレターの目的は，冒頭で述べられる。挨拶のあと，**However** 以下に注目しよう。it has come to our attention that the loan documentation you sent in is missing a few pages とあり，そのあとに何が足りないかについての説明があるので，(B) が正解。(A) はこの手紙は申込者宛てなので誤り。(C) は情報を送らなければならないのは **North** さんの方。処理日数についても述べられてはいるが，この日数を伝えることが目的ではない。よって，(D) も不正解。

---

160. Why is a signature needed?

(A) To record previous addresses
(B) To pay off a loan
(C) To view a job record
(D) To inquire about credit history

署名はなぜ必要ですか。

(A) 以前の住所を記録するため。
(B) ローンを完済するため。
(C) 職歴を閲覧するため。
(D) クレジット記録を照会するため。

正解：(D)

●着眼点！ signature がわかれば解ける！

レベル ★★☆☆

解説　設問の表現は，本文で言い換えられていることを意識しよう。**signature** が本文では **a signed statement** と言い換えられている。これがわかれば正解を見抜くのは簡単。本文中盤に，We need a list of your previous addresses and a signed statement personally allowing us to look at your credit records とある。(D) credit history は「クレジット記録」という意味で，これが正解。(B) pay off a loan 「ローンを完済する」。

問題 161-163 は次の広告に関するものです。

House Repair 社 住まいの修繕サービス
どんな小さな仕事も私たちにお任せください！

換気扇のお掃除から棚の据え付けまで，お住まいのことで何かお困りでしたら，今すぐ House Repair 社にお電話ください。

修理，据え付け，お掃除，リフォームなど，自分でもできるけれど，暇がなくてなかなか手が回らない，そんなお仕事をお引き受けします。当社の専門サービス担当者は，お住まいのあらゆる問題に対処できるよう訓練を受けており，必要な道具も装備しております。

お申し込みはお電話で。当社は 24 時間営業，年中無休です。お住まいでお困りのことをお話しいただければ，電話ですぐに簡単なお見積もりをいたします。たいていの場合は，1 回のご訪問で解決します！

語句
- home repair　家の修繕
- exhaust fan　換気扇
- require　動 ～を必要とする，要求する
- tackle　動 ～に取り組む

161. Who will most likely be calling House Repair?　House Repair 社に電話をする可能性が高いのはどんな人ですか。

(A) Building janitors
(B) Home owners
(C) Architectural design offices
(D) Cleaning companies

(A) ビルの管理人
(B) 住宅所有者
(C) 建築設計事務所
(D) 清掃会社

正解：(B)

● 着眼点！　広告の「対象」を予測せよ！

解説　広告の「対象」が問われている。セオリー通り，見出しに注目。House Repair, The Home Repair Service とあるので，住まいの修繕サービスの広告とわかる。本文冒頭でも，一般向けのサービスと判断できるので，正解は (B)。

162. What is true about House Repair?

(A) They will accept all trivial requests.
(B) They provide cheap and quick repairs.
(C) They will send courteous staff.
(D) They will charge extra for estimates.

House Repair 社についてどんなことが当てはまりますか。

(A) どんな小さな要望も引き受ける。
(B) 安価で迅速な修理サービスを提供する。
(C) 礼儀正しいスタッフを派遣する。
(D) 見積料金を取る。

正解：(A)

● 着眼点！　サービスをサーチ！

レベル ★★★☆

[解説] House Repair 社のサービスをサーチしよう。(B) cheap and quick repairs ではない。(C) courteous staff とは言っていない。(D) については，見積もりは取るが，見積料金を取るとは書かれていない。よって，正解は (A)。見出しからでも (A) を選べるが，キーワード・サーチで比較する方がよい。

---

163. What is indicated about the service for regular home problems?

(A) Repairs will end in one hour.
(B) Problems will be repaired in one visit.
(C) It will take two days to diagnose.
(D) Reservation should be made a week before.

通常の住まいの問題に対するサービスについて述べられていることは何ですか。

(A) 修理は 1 時間で終了する。
(B) 問題は 1 回の訪問で解決する。
(C) 診断に 2 日を要する。
(D) 1 週間前に予約が必要である。

正解：(B)

● 着眼点！　最後の文を見逃すな！

レベル ★★☆☆

[解説] 選択肢の「数」をサーチしよう。(A) one hour，(B) one visit，(C) two days，(D) a week。この中で，本文中で言及されているのは (B) のみ，最終文に書かれている。よって，正解は (B)。

問題 164-166 は次の情報に関するものです。

**Lakeland Shore チャリティーアートオークションは
Clive Tavares さんをお迎えします**

第 13 回，年次 Lakeland Shore チャリティーアートオークションは，2 月 11 日午後 6 時に開催されます。

場所：East Torrance 通りに面した LS アートギャラリー，Pine 通りと 21 番通りの間

特別ゲスト：彫刻家 Clive Tavares さん

午後 6 時：開会式
午後 6 時 30 分：Clive Tavares さんによる挨拶
午後 7 時：オークション開始
午後 10 時：閉会式

Tavares さんはご親切にも最近のブロンズ作品：『手』，『母子』，『バラ』，そして最新作『朝食』の 4 点をオークションに寄付してくださいました。これらの作品の入札は，7,000 ドルからの開始となります。他にも，Salle，Roth，Freilicher の絵画を含む 500 点以上の美術作品がオークションに登場します。Lakeland Shore 美術館会員の入場は無料（非会員は 10 ドル）です。オークションに出品される全作品は，国際地震救済資金の協力のもと，Lakeland Shore 美術館により提供されます。

[語句]
- sculptor 名 彫刻家
- admission 名 入場料

---

164. How often is the Lakeland Shore Charity Art Auction held?

Lakeland Shore チャリティーアートオークションはどのくらいの頻度で開催されますか。

(A) Once a year
(B) Twice a year
(C) Every other year
(D) Every four years

(A) 年 1 回
(B) 年 2 回
(C) 隔年
(D) 4 年に 1 度

正解：(A)

●着眼点！ annual を見落とすな！

[解説] How often の頻出問題。タイトルの下，The 13th annual Lakeland Shore Charity Art Auction を見れば OK。annual とは，「年 1 回の」という意味。したがって (A) が正解となる。annual と once a year の言い換えに注意！

165. Which is the most recent work of Mr. Tavares?

(A) *The Hand*
(B) *Roses*
(C) *Breakfast*
(D) *Mother & Child*

Tavares さんの最も新しい作品はどれですか。

(A) 手
(B) バラ
(C) 朝食
(D) 母子

正解：(C)

● 着眼点！ 「作品」をサーチ！

解説　Mr. Tavares の作品について書かれているところを素早く探そう。本文中では，*The Hand*，*Mother & Child*，*Roses*，and his latest art piece，*Breakfast* となっている。カンマの前の his latest art piece は「最新作」の意味。よって，(C) が正解。

---

166. What is mentioned about the auction?

(A) The collection adds up to 7,000.
(B) Entrance fees are equally charged.
(C) An artist makes a speech.
(D) One institution provides all the items.

オークションについて述べられていることは何ですか。

(A) 売却される所蔵品は 7,000 に上る。
(B) 入場料はすべて一律である。
(C) ある芸術家がスピーチを行う。
(D) 1 つの団体がすべての作品を用意する。

正解：(C)

● 着眼点！ 選択肢の名詞をサーチ！

解説　定番の mention 問題。選択肢と本文を一致させよう。選択肢の名詞キーワード，(A) 7,000，(B) equally charged，(C) speech，(D) One institution を中心にサーチ。(A) は $7,000 のひっかけ。(B) は会員は Admission is free で非会員は 10 ドルなので×。(D) は最終文と異なる。よって，正解は (C)。タイムスケジュールにある Remarks は，make a speech の言い換え。

問題 167-170 は次の手紙に関するものです。

Pacific Airlines 社
空の旅をお選びください

5月9日

Sarah Watson 様
53 Oak Street,
Pittsburgh, PA

Watson 様

ようこそ Pacific Airlines 社の Frequent Flyer プログラムへ！

弊社のプログラムは，ご搭乗されてから 10 日以内に再びご利用いただいた場合，ボーナスマイルが獲得できる唯一のプログラムです（制限あり）。さらに，ご家族を登録していただくと，獲得したマイルを皆さん共同でお使いになれます。また地上で Pacific Airlines 社のクレジットカードを利用することでもマイルを獲得することができます。

その上，長い距離を飛べば飛ぶほど，より多くの無料サービスを受けることができます。初めはブロンズレベルからスタートしていただき，シルバー，ゴールドと続いていきます。ゴールドレベル（1 年間で 10 万マイル以上のフライトをご利用になった場合）になると，空港のラウンジを無料でお使いいただけるほか，アップグレード券 2 枚と指定のホテルでの 2 名様 1 泊分のご宿泊が無料となります。

弊社の Frequent Flyer プログラムでは，たまったマイルと特典との交換もより簡単な手続きでできるようになりました。弊社ウェブサイトにログオンして予約を入れるだけです。ご旅行の予定はありませんか？それならば，たまったマイルを全国の小売店でご利用できる商品券と交換するという選択もできます。

弊社の Frequent Flyer プログラム についての小冊子を同封します。お知りになりたいような情報はこの冊子にすべて載っています。

Pacific 航空のクレジットカードは 2 週間以内に書留郵便でお手元に届きます。
Pacific 航空のフライトで近々お目にかかれることを楽しみにしております！

敬具
Edward Paine
社長兼最高経営責任者

語句
- award 動 (賞などを) 与える，名 賞
- restriction 名 制限，制約
- be entitled to ～　～する権利がある
- designated 形 指定の
- redeem 動 ～を商品に換える，払い戻す，回復する
- gift certificate 商品券

167.

What is the main purpose of this letter?

(A) To thank Ms. Watson for joining the Frequent Flyer Program
(B) To respond to Ms. Watson's inquiry
(C) To explain how to redeem awards
(D) To explain their program's benefits compared to competitors

この手紙の主な目的は何ですか。

(A) Watson さんに Frequent Flyer プログラムへの参加を感謝すること。
(B) Watson さんの問い合わせに答えること。
(C) 特典との交換方法を説明すること。
(D) プログラムの競合他社と比べての優位性を説明すること。

正解：(A)

● 着眼点！ 手紙の主旨は冒頭！

レベル ★★☆☆

[解説] Pacific Airlines 社が Watson さんに送った手紙であることを確認しよう。主旨は冒頭なので，Welcome to Pacific Airlines' Frequent Flyer Program! をチェック。Watson さんがプログラムに最近参加して，そのことに感謝していることがわかる。正解は（A）。

168.

How can miles add up without flying?

(A) By registering family members
(B) By using the Pacific Airlines' credit card
(C) By using gift certificates
(D) By shopping at certain retail outlets

どうすれば飛行機に搭乗しないでマイルがたまりますか。

(A) 家族メンバーを登録する。
(B) Pacific Airlines のクレジットカードを使う。
(C) 商品券を使う。
(D) 特定の小売店で買い物をする。

正解：(B)

● 着眼点！ without flying に注目！

レベル ★★★☆

[解説] マイルの獲得方法が問われている。ポイントは without flying。例外的な事柄である点を意識しよう。手紙の第 1 段落はマイルの獲得方法を説明している。最後の文で，You can also earn miles on the ground every time you use the Pacific Airlines' credit card. と述べられており，(B) が正解とわかる。(A)，(C)，(D) も文中に登場した話題ばかりなので紛らわしいが，マイルを獲得する方法ではない。

169.

What are customers advised to do in order to use miles accumulated?

(A) Mail an application form
(B) Visit the airline office
(C) Call the Awards Desk
(D) Go to the Web site

たまったマイルを交換するために顧客は何をするよう勧められていますか。

(A) 手紙で申込用紙を送る。
(B) 航空会社の事務所を訪ねる。
(C) マイル交換担当部署に電話する。
(D) ウェブサイトに行く。

正解：(D)

● 着眼点！ マイルの変換方法をサーチ！

レベル ★★☆☆

[解説] マイルの変換方法が問われている。use miles → redeem awards「商品と引き換える」がわ

かるかどうかがポイント。第3段落, Just log on to our Web site とあるので, (D) が正解。

170. What is most likely written in the enclosed booklet?

同封の小冊子には何が書かれていると考えられますか。

(A) Corporate profile and financial information
(B) Credit card details
(C) How to apply for the program
(D) Details of the program

(A) 会社の概要と財務情報
(B) クレジットカードの詳細
(C) このプログラムへの申し込み方法
(D) プログラムの詳細

正解：(D)

● 着眼点！ キーワードをサーチせよ！

レベル ★★★★

[解説] 設問のキーワード enclosed booklet をサーチしよう。第4段落に We have enclosed a booklet on our Frequent Flyer Program とある。その直後で, you will find everything you need to know about it と述べているように, それはプログラムの詳細について説明しているものと推測できる。よって, (D) が正解。(A) と (B) は除外。(C) もありそうだが, すでにプログラムに参加している客への手紙なので,「参加申し込み方法」が載っているというのは不適切である。

問題 171-175 は次のパンフレットに関するものです。

石油科学技術における化学工学の学士／修士

ここ **Dinmore** 大学でのユニークな5年間の学位プログラムは，化学工学の学士と修士を組み合わせたものです。世界のエネルギー市場において石油とガスが果たしている重要な役割のため，この分野での熟練者への需要は増してきました。これらの貴重な資源を利用し保存するには，技術の進歩と多くの異なった科学の分野の参加が不可欠です。化学工学専攻の卒業生は，さまざまな燃料・エネルギー会社で職を探せます。

最初の3年間は，他の化学工学プログラムとあまり変わりませんが，特別コースやセミナーを選択することができます。4年目に始まる専門分野では，貯蔵槽からの石油やガスの生産といった高度なテーマを扱います。このとき学生たちは高度な化学工学も勉強し続けます。さらに，化石燃料エネルギー分野における新製品の開発から生まれた問題を扱う実用的事柄に関するコースもあります。学生たちは5年目に終える個人の研究プロジェクトを始めます。

最終学年を通じて，学生たちは研究プロジェクトを完成させ，専門のエネルギーのテーマに取り組みます。このときに，プログラムに参加している全員が『石油産業における技術』と呼ばれるコースを取ります。卒業時には，**Dinmore** の学生たちは高い確率で，石油やガス生産産業の会社の重要なポストを見つけることができます。

オンラインでの申し込みは www.Petrotech.Dinmore.edu へ。

語句
- ☐ B.S. (= Bachelor of Science) 名 科学学士
- ☐ M.S. (= Master of Science) 名 科学修士
- ☐ petroleum 名 石油
- ☐ preserve 動 〜を保存する
- ☐ valuable 形 貴重な
- ☐ reservoir 名 貯蔵槽
- ☐ conclude 動 〜を終える
- ☐ specialized 形 専門的な

171. What is the main topic of this brochure?

(A) Methods of procuring oil and gas from reservoirs
(B) Ways of using new fossil fuel products
(C) Features of a chemical engineering program
(D) All scientific fields that support the oil industry

このパンフレットの主な話題は何ですか。

(A) 貯蔵槽から石油とガスを調達する方法。
(B) 新しい化石燃料製品の使い道。
(C) 化学工学プログラムの特徴。
(D) 石油産業を支えるすべての科学分野。

正解：(C)

● 着眼点！ 見出しと冒頭を見よ！

レベル ★★★☆

> **解説** パンフレットの表題 Chemical Engineering B.S./M.S. in Petroleum Technology と冒頭の The unique five-year degree program here at Dinmore University から，新しい化学工学プログラムの内容について説明していることがわかる。正解は（C）。（A）についても触れているが，4年目から始まる専門分野のテーマだと言っているだけで，パンフレットの中心のテーマではない。

> **語句** □ procure 動 〜を手に入れる

---

172. What does the brochure say about the initial three years of the program?

プログラムの最初の3年間についてパンフレットには何とありますか。

(A) They are very specialized in petroleum technology.
(B) They are similar to other chemical engineering programs.
(C) They offer students job-seeking opportunities.
(D) They change depending upon what is happening in the oil industry.

(A) 石油技術に非常に特化している。
(B) 他の化学工学プログラムと似ている。
(C) 学生に求職の機会を与える。
(D) 石油産業で何が起こっているかによって変わる。

正解：(B)

> **着眼点！** 迷わず three years をサーチ！

> **解説** 設問キーワード three years をサーチしよう。第2段落の冒頭 The first three years are much the same as other chemical engineering programs から始まる文に注目。最初の3年間は他の化学工学プログラムとほぼ同じだと述べている。この内容に合致するのは（B）。

---

173. What is indicated about students working on their research?

研究に取り組んでいる学生について何が示されていますか。

(A) Their areas of study are limited to practical matters.
(B) They finish their projects in two years.
(C) Their funding is provided from affiliated corporations.
(D) They conduct experiments in a small group.

(A) 専門分野が実用的事柄に限られている。
(B) 2年でプロジェクトを終える。
(C) 関連企業から資金を援助してもらえる。
(D) 少人数でグループワークを行う。

正解：(B)

> **着眼点！** まず research をチェックして！

> **解説** 学生について問われているので，第2段落以降を意識して，キーワード research をサーチ。第2段落の最終文に，Students start their individual research projects which are concluded in the fifth year. とある。学生たちは4年生の時に始めたプロジェクトを5年生の時に終えるとわかるので（B）が正解。

174. The word "positions" in paragraph 3, line 4, is closest in meaning to

(A) poses
(B) points
(C) locations
(D) jobs

第3段落・4行目の positions に最も近い意味の語は

(A) 姿勢
(B) 点
(C) 場所
(D) 仕事

正解：(D)

● 着眼点！ 文脈にも注意しよう！

レベル ★☆☆☆

[解説] 瞬時に解ける時はスピード優先。それ以外では，前後を意識して，文脈から判断しよう。key positions in companies の部分に注目。会社の中で見つける position とは「職, 勤め口」のこと。正解は (D)。

---

175. What is suggested about Dinmore graduates?

(A) They start up industry-university collaboration projects.
(B) They succeed in finding good positions in some industries.
(C) They are in need of support from career counselors.
(D) They are hired by the university as faculty.

Dinmore の卒業生についてどんなことがわかりますか。

(A) 産学協同プロジェクトを開始する。
(B) いくつかの業界でよい仕事を見つけられる。
(C) 職業カウンセラーによる支援が必要である。
(D) 大学に教授として雇われる。

正解：(B)

● 着眼点！ 今後の展望については最後を見よ！

レベル ★★☆☆

[解説] 勧誘のパンフレット，広告では，末尾に効能，効果が書かれるのがパターン。最後の部分を見ると，Upon graduation, Dinmore students have a high success rate in finding key positions in companies in the oil and gas production industry. と述べている。就職しやすいことを強調しているので，正解は (B)。(A), (C), (D) については述べられていない。

問題 176-180 は次の記事に関するものです。

地元の技術革新者がコミュニティーでの偉業で表彰

地元の人たちにとって，Ernie Samson は今もずっと Gregston の労働者階級地区で育った情熱的な少年だ。ただ，市内の他の人たちにとっては，彼は，市内で最も貧しいいくつかの学校でコンピューターサイエンスプログラムを始め，今年 E. Lawrence Community Service を受賞した人だ。メキシコ出身の母親を持つ Ernie は，ラテン系出身者初の受賞者である。

大学卒業以来，Ernie と彼の技術会社は，恵まれない状況にある高校の生徒たちにプログラミング，ウェブサイトデザイン，それにグラフィックデザインを教えるコースの設備を整え，指導者を配置するのを促すために，100 万ドル以上の資金を寄付してきた。Ernie は単にお金を寄付するだけで他の人に仕事をさせるのではなく，実際に週 1 回，テクノロジービジネスを開始・運営する方法について授業を行うボランティアをしている。彼の会社はまた，最も優秀な生徒たちを選んで，彼の会社で放課後や休暇中にアルバイトをさせている。来年から，Ernie の会社はコンピューター科学の最も優秀な生徒たちに大学の奨学金を与える。

Ernie は，子供たちに小さいうちにテクノロジーに興味を持たせることが大切だと信じている。彼は，自分がテクノロジービジネスで成功したのは，9 年生のときにコンピューターサイエンスを教えていた Dan Paulson 先生のおかげだと言う。Paulson 先生は Ernie にコンピューターについて学ぶことを勧めただけではなく，彼が放課後に家でコンピュータープログラムを作れるように，中古のコンピューターを与えたのである。

語句
- local 名 土地の人，地元の人
- descendant 名 子孫
- contribute 動 〜を寄付する
- disadvantaged 形 恵まれない，貧しい，不利な
- part-time 形 アルバイトの
- scholarship 名 奨学金
- attribute 〜 to ... 〜を…のおかげだと考える

176. Where did Mr. Samson grow up?

(A) In the inner city
(B) In a working class area
(C) In an affluent suburb
(D) In a foreign country

Samson さんはどこで育ちましたか。

(A) 都心に近いスラム街
(B) 労働者の居住地区
(C) 裕福な郊外
(D) 外国

正解：(B)

● 着眼点！ 「生い立ち」をサーチ！

レベル ★☆☆☆

[解説] キーワード Mr. Samson をサーチすると，第 1 段落・1 文目に，Ernie Samson will always be the passionate kid who grew up in a working class neighborhood of Gregston とある。労働階級地区とあるので，(B) が正解。

---

177. Why has Mr. Samson and his company contributed a large sum of money?

(A) To recruit the top-ranked students at schools
(B) To offer internship programs to young adults
(C) To improve the learning conditions in the city
(D) To advertise their new programs

なぜ Samson さんと彼の会社は多額のお金を寄付してきたのですか。

(A) 学校で最も優秀な生徒を採用するため。
(B) 青少年にインターンシッププログラムを提供するため。
(C) 市の学習環境を改善するため。
(D) 彼らの新しいプログラムを宣伝するため。

正解：(C)

● 着眼点！ 寄付の理由は何？

レベル ★★★☆

[解説] 寄付の理由が問われている。第 2 段落冒頭でいきなり contributed が見つかる。Since graduating from college, Ernie and his tech company have contributed over a million dollars to help provide equipment and instructors to disadvantaged high schools … とあるので，貧しく，恵まれない環境にある学校を改善するために寄付してきたのだとわかる。したがって，正解は (C)。

---

178. What did Mr. Samson receive?

(A) A scholarship to college
(B) A job promotion
(C) A computer science degree
(D) Recognition for service

Samson さんは何を受けましたか。

(A) 大学への奨学金
(B) 仕事での昇進
(C) コンピューターサイエンスの学位
(D) 貢献に対する表彰

正解：(D)

● 着眼点！ 受賞のジャンルは出る！

レベル ★★★☆

[解説] 表題から，受賞者の紹介だということがわかる。また，第 1 段落・2 文目に he is best known as this year's winner of the E. Lawrence Community Service award とあり，賞を

受けたとわかる。ここから（D）を選ぶ。recognition「表彰」や service = contribution「貢献」がわからないとダメ。

---

179. What does Mr. Samson do once a week?

(A) Attends computer science classes
(B) Teaches a business class
(C) Prepares to start a new program
(D) Chooses a new intern

Samson さんは週1回何をしていますか。

(A) コンピューターサイエンスのクラスに出席している。
(B) ビジネスクラスを教えている。
(C) 新しいプログラムを始める準備をしている。
(D) 新しいインターンを選んでいる。

正解：(B)

●着眼点！ once a week を目印に！

レベル ★★☆☆

[解説] 設問キーワード once a week をサーチ。第2段落中盤，but actually volunteers once a week to teach a course とあるので，授業ボランティアをしているとわかる。ここから（B）が正解。

---

180. The word, "attributes" in paragraph 3, line 3, is closest in meaning to

(A) credits
(B) measures
(C) achieves
(D) celebrates

第3段落・3行目の attributes に最も近い意味の語は

(A) 〜に帰する
(B) 〜を測る，見当をつける
(C) 〜を達成する
(D) 〜を祝う，ほめたたえる

正解：(A)

●着眼点！ 文脈から意味を取ろう！

レベル ★★★★

[解説] attributes のある文章を見よう。He attributes his success in the tech business to his ninth grade computer science teacher, Mr. Dan Paulson. とあり，attribute A to B「A は B のおかげである」のフレーズが見える。この attribute と同じ意味を持つのは（A）だけ。

問題 181-185 は次のお知らせと記事に関するものです。

エントリー募集
第 4 回 Hopton 映画祭
新たな才能を探しています！

Hopton 映画祭は現在，オリジナルの映像作品を受け付けています。各カテゴリーの入賞者には **1,000** ドルと銀の表彰トロフィーが授与されます。受賞作品は，3 月の Hopton 映画祭で上映されます。この映画祭では，参加者は一流の監督やシナリオライターと会う機会を得るでしょう。

以下のカテゴリーへのエントリーを募集しています。

カテゴリー	説明
メイン・カテゴリー	他のカテゴリーに指定されていないすべての映画
アニメーション・カテゴリー	アニメ映画
短編映画・カテゴリー	7 分未満の映画
ユース・カテゴリー	18 歳未満の方が制作した映画

<u>料金と締切り</u>
エントリー料：55 ドル
締切り：9 月 18 日（すべての資料は締切り当日の消印まで有効）

印刷用申込フォームや第 4 回 Hopton 映画祭に関するその他の詳細については，www.hoptonfestival.com をご覧ください。

映画祭受賞作 Flying Wings
Tobias Payne 記

今年の Hopton 映画祭の受賞作品の中で，注目は Danny Evans の *Flying Wings* です。他のほとんどの出場者と違い，Evans はこれまで映画製作の経験がありませんでした。
「受賞すると思いませんでしたので，すごく驚きました。今，両親の励ましの言葉に感謝しています。」と，Evans はコメントしました。
Flying Wings は世界を旅するために，高給の金融アナリストとしての仕事を辞めた Mauli Jones という架空の人物についての話です。Mauli はエキゾチックな国々を訪れ，そこで地元の珍味を試し，素晴らしい新たな友人を作ります。
たった 6 分の長さにもかかわらず，*Flying Wings* はユーモアを交えてよく構成された映画です。Evans の今後の作品を見ずにはいられません。

語句
- recognition 名 表彰，承認
- director 名 （映画などの）監督，（組織の）責任者
- screenwriter 名 シナリオライター，脚本作家
- postmark 動 〜に消印を押す
- printable 形 印刷可能な
- prior 形 前の，先の
- grateful to ... for 〜 …に〜のことで感謝する
- delicacy 名 珍味，気配り

181. What is indicated in the notice?

(A) The applicants will fill in the online entry forms.
(B) The judges will be people from the entertainment sector.
(C) The winners will receive prize money and an award.
(D) The organizers are hoping to discover talented actors.

お知らせには何が示されていますか。

(A) 申込者は，オンラインの申込フォームに記入する。
(B) 審査員はエンターテイメント部門の人である。
(C) 入賞者は賞金と表彰トロフィーを授与される。
(D) 主催者は才能ある役者を発掘しようと思っている。

正解：(C)

● 着眼点！ サッと全体を見る意識が大事！　レベル ★★★☆

[解説] indicate 問題は，文書全体に目を通そう。お知らせの第1段落・2文目に The winners from each category will be awarded 1,000 dollars and a silver trophy of recognition. とあるので，これを言い換えた (C) が正解。(A)「申込」は，最終段落に「オンライン申込」ではなく印刷用申込フォームで行うとあるので×。(B) は記載がなく，またこの映画祭は，(D)「役者」ではなく映画作品制作者のコンクールなので，ともに誤り。

[語句] □ sector 名 部門，活動分野　□ organizer 名 主催者

---

182. In the notice, the word "presented" in paragraph 1, line 3, is closest in meaning to

(A) endorsed
(B) shown
(C) rolled
(D) produced

お知らせの第1段落・3行目の presented に最も近い意味の語は

(A) 是認される
(B) 上映される
(C) 丸められる
(D) 制作される

正解：(B)

● 着眼点！ 文脈からスパッと解こう！　レベル ★★☆☆

[解説] films will be presented at ... とあるので，文脈を取るのは簡単。ここでは「フィルムが上映される」と考えれば OK。よって，(B) が正解。

---

183. According to the article, what is unique about Mr. Evans?

(A) He experienced studying abroad.
(B) He quit his job to shoot a film.
(C) He borrowed money from his parents.
(D) He had never made a film before.

記事によると，Evans さんについて特徴的なことは何ですか。

(A) 留学を経験した。
(B) 映画を撮るために仕事を辞めた。
(C) 両親からお金を借りた。
(D) 映画を作ったことが一度もない。

正解：(D)

> **着眼点！** ユニークな点を見抜け！

解説 「記事」は Danny Evance の作品評なので，「ユニーク」な点を見抜けば OK。第 1 段落・2 文目の Unlike most other contestants, Evans had no prior experience in creating films until now. とあり，ここから (D) が正解だとわかる。(A)「留学」と (C)「両親からの借り入れ」は記載がなく，(B)「仕事を辞めた」のは映画の登場人物のことなので誤り。

---

184. What most likely is the topic of *Flying Wings*?

Flying Wings のトピックは何だと考えられますか。

(A) Traveling on a budget
(B) Getting a pilot's license
(C) Discovering new cultures
(D) Working overseas

(A) 予算内での旅行
(B) パイロットの資格取得
(C) 新しい文化の発見
(D) 海外での就労

正解：(C)

> **着眼点！** トピックを読み解け！

解説 *Flying Wings* のトピックが問われている。作品の内容については，「記事」の第 3 段落に目を向けよう。ここでは，物語の主人公は世界を旅するために仕事を辞め，エキゾチックな国々で珍味を食べ，友人作りをするという内容が書かれている。これを言い換えた (C) が正解。(B)「資格取得」は全く関係ないので×。(A) と (D) についても，「予算内」や「就労」が不適切。

---

185. Which category did Mr. Evans enter?

Evans さんはどのカテゴリーに応募しましたか。

(A) Main
(B) Animation
(C) Short-film
(D) Youth

(A) メイン
(B) アニメーション
(C) 短編映画
(D) ユース

正解：(C)

> **着眼点！** クロス問題を意識して！

解説 クロスリファレンス問題。2 つの文章から必要な情報を，素早く見つけることが解答する上で欠かせない。まず，「記事」の第 4 段落から Evans さんの作品が 6 分間であることがわかる。次に，「お知らせ」の表を見てみると，7 分未満の映画は **Short-film Category** に区分されることがわかる。したがって，(C) が正解。要点を押さえて，スパッと解こう。

問題 186-190 は次の旅程表と E メールに関するものです。

Keith 様
こちらが旅程表です。
質問や変更があれば，いつでもご連絡ください。
よろしくお願いします。
Bob Cassidy

J.D. WATKINS 証券会社 東アジア公式訪問

日程
9月3日 – 6日（2泊4日）

1日目：9月3日
　午前11時15分　　サンフランシスコ発
（9月4日）
　午後3時15分　　東京着
　午後6時　　　　New Tokyo Oriental ホテルチェックイン
　　　　　　　　　夕食

2日目：9月5日
　　　　　　　　　Terrace レストランでの朝食
プレゼンテーション
　午前9時 – 午前10時30分
　　　　　　　　　• Allen Keefer Associates 社：「裁定取引の現状」
　　　　　　　　　• Vanderburg Consulting 社：「日本の不動産への投資」
　午前10時40分 – 正午
　　　　　　　　　• Honda Securities 社：「原油の輸入が日本市場に与える影響」
　　　　　　　　　• Takizawa & Murphy 法律事務所：「バイリンガル弁護士の雇用」
　午後1時　　　　チェックアウト
　　　　　　　　　昼食
　午後1時30分 – 午後5時30分
　　　　　　　　　Honda Securities 社の方々との株式市場見学
　午後7時　　　　東京発
　　　　　　　　　機内での夕食
　午後10時15分　香港着
　午後11時　　　Hong Kong Grand Dragon ホテルチェックイン

3日目：9月6日
　　　　　　　　　Aqua Azure での朝食
プレゼンテーション：
　午前9時 – 午前10時30分
　　　　　　　　　• South China Securities 社：「海外市場への中国の投資」
　午前10時40分 – 正午
　　　　　　　　　• Grover Wu Consulting 社：「中国の最新株式情報」
　　　　　　　　　• Jackson Cole 投資銀行：「東アジアにおける英国銀行業」
　午後1時　　　　チェックアウト
　　　　　　　　　昼食

午後 2 時 50 分　　香港発

午前 11 時 50 分　　サンフランシスコ着

宛先：Bob Cassidy
送信者：Keith Woodridge
件名：旅程表についてのいくつかの修正
日付：8 月 26 日

Bob 様

旅程表についていくつか変更点をこの E メールでお知らせします。
Tyrone Taylor から電話でよい知らせと悪い知らせがありました。

まず悪い知らせから。**South China Securities** 社と **Grover Wu Consulting** 社の両社が最近の金融危機を受けて会合から手を引きました。これによって香港での会合は 1 つのみとなります。

次によい知らせです。お得意様である **Mansfield & Lo** 社の **Billy Lo** さんが 9 月 7 日に香港証券取引所を案内してくださいます。素晴らしい機会ですよね。私はその件に関して彼に応えるべきだと思います。あなたのスケジュールとバッティングするかどうかについては，今月末までに折り返しお返事をください。もししなければ，彼の申し出を受けるために帰国日を再調整します。

変更はともかく，私たちはこれまでの仕事で最もわくわくする出張を手配いたしました。

よろしくお願いします。

Keith

語句
- arbitrage　名 裁定取引
- attorney　名 弁護士
- pull out of ～　～から撤退する
- take ～ up　～に応じる
- as to ～　～について，～に関して

186. What is the main topic of the itinerary?

(A) A private tour to East Asia
(B) A conference schedule
(C) A business trip plan
(D) An international trade negotiation

旅程表の主なトピックは何ですか。

(A) 東アジアへの個人的な旅行
(B) 会合の日程
(C) 出張計画
(D) 国際取り引きの交渉

正解：(C)

● 着眼点！ 旅程表の表題を見落とすな！

レベル ★★☆☆

解説　旅程表の表題に J.D. WATKINS SECURITIES CORP.（社名）の OFFICIAL VISIT TO EAST ASIA とあり，プレゼンテーションのスケジュールを中心に書かれていることがわかる。また E メールの第 4 段落にも business trip とあることから，出張の旅程表だとわかる。(A) は個人的な旅行ではないため誤り。(B) 会合の日程はプレゼンテーションの時間が書かれているが，旅程表の一部についてのみ述べたものである。(D) も海外への旅程表であるが，取り引きの交渉という内容は含まれていない。上述の内容を端的に表現した (C) が正解。

---

187. In the itinerary, the word "SECURITIES" in line 6, is closest in meaning to

(A) savings
(B) safety
(C) stocks
(D) defense

旅程表の 6 行目の SECURITIES に最も近い意味の語は

(A) 節約
(B) 安全
(C) 株式
(D) 防衛

正解：(C)

● 着眼点！ 誤答を誘う選択肢に注意！

レベル ★★☆☆

解説　「安全」，「守る」の意味に関連する選択肢が並ぶが，問題文の securities を「安全」と読み間違えた場合のひっかけ。ここでの securities は「安全」ではなく「有価証券」の意味。よって (C) が正解。

---

188. In the e-mail, what is implied about the itinerary?

(A) Some parties' withdrawal from the schedule
(B) Closing a mutual contract by the end of month
(C) Changes in the careers fair venue
(D) A one-day tour to Asian street markets

E メールで，旅程表について何がわかりますか。

(A) 何人かの当事者が計画から撤退すること
(B) 月末までの相互契約のクロージング
(C) キャリアフェアの会場の変更
(D) アジアのストリートマーケットの 1 日見学

正解：(A)

● 着眼点！ E メールの伝達事項を読み取れ！

レベル ★★★☆

解説　E メールでは，旅程に関して，悪い知らせとして 2 社の不参加，よい知らせとして得意先からの

オファーが記されている。この区分に従って，選択肢と比較検討する。悪い知らせの内容と一致する (**A**) が正解。(**B**) は月末までにするのはこのメールに対する返信であって，相互契約のクロージングではない。(**C**) はキャリアフェアについても会場についても何も書かれていないため全くの誤り。(**D**) は見学するのはストリートマーケットではなく証券取引市場であるため誤り。

---

189. Why does Mr. Woodridge ask for a reply?　Woodridge さんはなぜ返事を求めていますか。

(A) He wants to decide the arrival date in San Francisco.
(B) He needs to introduce a new client in Hong Kong.
(C) He ought to contact the presenters in China.
(D) He has to arrange another business trip to Tokyo.

(A) サンフランシスコへの到着日程を確定したいため。
(B) 香港で新規の顧客を紹介する必要があるため。
(C) 中国でプレゼンターに連絡するべきであるため。
(D) 東京への別の出張を手配しなければならないため。

正解：(A)

● 着眼点！　「お願い」を探せ！

レベル ★★★☆

解説　「お願い」が求められているので，本文に please を探そう。E メールの第 3 段落に，Please write back as to whether it will conflict with your schedule by the end of this month. If not, I will reschedule the return date to accept his offer. とあり日程の決定のために返信を求めているのがわかる。よって (**A**) が正解。(**B**) は Billy Lo は新規顧客でなく得意先であるし，(**C**) と (**D**) については本文に書かれていない。

---

190. Which presentation in Hong Kong is held as scheduled?　香港でどのプレゼンテーションが予定通り行われますか。

(A) The Current State of Arbitrage
(B) Chinese Hot Stock Tips
(C) Recruiting Bi-Lingual Attorneys
(D) British Banking in East Asia

(A) 「裁定取引の現状」
(B) 「中国の最新株式情報」
(C) 「バイリンガル弁護士の雇用」
(D) 「東アジアにおける英国銀行業」

正解：(D)

● 着眼点！　Hong Kong をクロスせよ！

レベル ★☆☆☆

解説　まず，Hong Kong をサーチ。旅程表を見ると，9 月 6 日に 3 つのプレゼンがあるとわかる。選択肢の (**A**) と (**C**) は，香港ではなく東京で行われるものであるため誤り。次に E メールを見よう。(**B**) はプレゼンターが参加を取りやめたため中止となることがわかる。正解は (**D**)。

問題 191-195 は次のメモとスケジュールに関するものです。

メモ

差出人：Bob Tyler ＜総務部＞
受取人：Steve Briggs ＜法務部＞
件名：「Company Employee Handbook」の改訂
日付：2月6日

Steve へ

今週成立したプライバシー法の修正にしたがって，「Company Employee Handbook」の内容を見直し，必要な修正を加える必要があります。

当社の企業弁護士より，新たな法律が民間の有限責任会社に一体何を求めているのかについて，簡略化した分析資料がまもなく送られてきます。手短に言いますと，修正には IT，経理，管理部門および顧客データを取り扱う可能性のあるその他の従業員を対象とする，従業員研修プログラムが含まれることが必至です。こうした現状において，まず新しくリスクマネジメント研修を実行しなければなりません。

スケジュールの初稿を添付しました。お目通しをいただき，何か問題があれば私までご連絡ください。すべて問題が無ければ，お教えください。あなたが研修を続け，新しいコンプライアンス・プログラムを実行している間に，私の方で経営陣が集まるよう手配をし，会場を予約します。スケジュールには，いくつかまだ決まっていない予定がありますが，それらの対処はお任せします。

スケジュール（2月6日稿）

日付	詳細
6月2日	将来予測と研修プログラム開始の理由について，全部門，全社員を対象とする会議
6月3日	**IT 部門**（全日）：未決定
6月4日	**経理部門**（午前）：a) ファイル保管庫について，b) 文書廃棄手順について **受付**（午後）：a) 来訪者の確認について，b) 適切な登録について
6月5日	**管理部門**（午前）：未決定 **営業部門**（午後）：a) 携帯端末の使用にあたってのヒントについて，b) 職場からデータを持ち出す際の適切な手続きについて
6月6日	**カスタマーサービス部門**（午前）：未決定
6月9日	各部門からレポートの回収
6月12日	結果の概要と提案書を提出

語句
- □ **compliance** 名 法令順守，コンプライアンス
- □ **amendment** 名 修正，改正
- □ **pass** 動（議会を）通過する
- □ **review** 動 ～を見直す，再検討する
- □ **corporate lawyer** 企業弁護士
- □ **simplified** 形 簡略化された
- □ **breakdown** 名 分析，内訳，故障，消耗
- □ **expect ... from ～** …に～を期待する
- □ **briefly** 副 手短に言えば，簡潔に

- □ handle 動 ～を取り扱う，対処する
- □ circumstance 名 状況
- □ carry out ～ ～を実行する
- □ look ～ over ～を調べる，ざっと目を通す
- □ arrange for ... to ～ …が～するように手配する
- □ venue 名 開催場所，現場
- □ count on ～ ～を頼りにする
- □ disposal 名 処分，処理
- □ proposal 名 提案，計画

191. What is the main purpose of the memo?　メモの主な目的は何ですか。

(A) To inform the deadline　(A) 締切り日を通知すること。
(B) To request Mr. Briggs to work　(B) Briggs さんに仕事を依頼すること。
(C) To call an urgent meeting　(C) 緊急会議を招集すること。
(D) To introduce an article　(D) 記事を紹介すること。

正解：(B)

●着眼点！ セオリーの例外！

[解説] 主旨が冒頭にはっきりと書かれていない例外ケース。件名と第1段落から，Company Employee Handbook に修正を加える件で連絡していることがわかる。案件の概要が説明されたあと，具体的な要件に入るのは第3段落以降。I have attached my first draft of the schedule. Please look it over and get back to me if there is a problem. から，(B) 「Briggs さんに仕事を依頼している」ことがわかり，これが正解。(C) 「緊急会議の招集」も紛らわしいが，予定の確定後に経営陣を招集するという流れなので，(B) の方がより適切。

192. Why will the Company Employee Handbook be changed?　Company Employee Handbook はなぜ変更されるのですか。

(A) To incorporate the incoming legal changes　(A) これから始まる法律の変更を取り入れるため。
(B) To reflect new management policies　(B) 新しい管理方針を反映させるため。
(C) To make the modifications in design and format　(C) デザインと形式の変更を加えるため。
(D) To raise the employees' motivation　(D) 従業員のモチベーションを高めるため。

正解：(A)

●着眼点！ 変更の「理由」をつかめ！

[解説] キーワード Company Employee Handbook をサーチ。メモの第1段落・1文目の Following the amendments to the privacy law passed this week から，成立した法律の修正にしたがって変更が行われることがわかる。選択肢が紛らわしいので，ひっかからないように。(A) が正解。

223

193. In the memo, the word "implement" in paragraph 3, line 3, is closest in meaning to

(A) announce
(B) execute
(C) choose
(D) explain

メモの第3段落・3行目の implement に最も近い意味の語は

(A) 〜を公表する，周知する
(B) 〜を実施する，行う
(C) 〜を選ぶ，選挙する
(D) 〜を説明する，明らかにする

正解：(B)

● 着眼点！ 基本ワードは即答せよ！

解説　TOEIC 頻出の implement。carry out「実行する」とイコールなので，最も近いのは (B)。また，implement the new compliance program というフレーズから文脈をたどっても，見当がつくはず。

---

194. What is NOT indicated on the schedule?

(A) Attendees are required to file a report.
(B) The situation will be explained on the first day.
(C) Each department has its own subjects.
(D) An achievement test will be conducted.

スケジュールに示されていないことはどんなことですか。

(A) 参加者はレポートを提出するよう求められている。
(B) 初日に状況の説明がある。
(C) 各部門は独自の学習テーマがある。
(D) 確認テストが行われる。

正解：(D)

● 着眼点！ 選択肢の「タテ読み」を活用せよ！

解説　NOT 問題は，先に選択肢を読んで内容を把握してから本文を読もう。スケジュールをざっと見ながら，選択肢と対応させよう。(A)「レポートの提出」は June 9 の詳細欄に示されている。(B)「状況の説明」は，初日 June 2 の詳細欄に書かれている。部門ごとで研修テーマがわかれているため，(C) も本文と一致する。(D)「確認テスト」は本文に記載がなく，これが正解。

195. What will Mr. Briggs probably do?

(A) Search for a convention center
(B) Issue revised company guidelines
(C) Select topics for some sessions
(D) Rearrange the schedule for lecturers

Briggs さんはおそらく何をすると考えられますか。

(A) 会場を探す。
(B) 修正した社則を発行する。
(C) いくつかの研修内容を決める。
(D) 講師のために予定を変更する。

正解：(C)

● 着眼点！　次の展開を見抜け！

レベル ★★☆☆

[解説] probably do とあるので，次の展開をイメージしよう。「メモ」は Tyler さんから Briggs さんに宛てたもので，仕事を依頼しているのは明白。その詳細は，第 3 段落の As there remain undecided agendas on the schedule, I'm counting on you to handle these. から，未決定事項を決めるようにとのこと。次に，スケジュールを見ると，IT，管理，カスタマーサービスの各部門のテーマがまだ決まっていない (not yet fixed)。したがって，(C) が正解。

問題 196-200 は次の 2 つの E メールに関するものです。

宛先：Amanda Cole
送信者：Johnathan Parks
件名：当社新製品の報道発表
日付：4 月 14 日

こんばんは，Amanda。

6 月 1 日に当社はエアコンの新商品，UX200 を発売します。それに先立ち，新製品を一般に紹介し，宣伝する報道発表を行うことを計画中です。ついては，その手配をお手伝い願えないでしょうか。

報道発表は 5 月 16 日の月曜日から 5 月 20 日の金曜日の間のどこか 1 日に行う予定です。FN 家電本社近辺で行いたいと思っています。場所は約 90 名の記者と 30 名から 40 名のカメラマンを収容できる十分な広さが必要です。もし私たちの要望に合う場所が見つからないようであれば，部長と代替案を検討しますので，知らせてください。

詳細情報が必要，あるいは何か質問があるようでしたらメールをください。よろしくお願いします。

Johnathan Parks
副部長
業務管理部

宛先：Johnathan Parks
送信者：Amanda Cole
件名：Re: 当社新製品の報道発表
日付：4 月 15 日

こんにちは，John。

新製品の報道発表準備に関する昨日のメールを受け取りました。場所と日時の確認，またこの件に関して現時点でいくつかの質問をさせていただきたく，メールを書いています。

条件に見合う数か所に問い合わせたところ，5 月 18 日水曜日に Edmond Hill ビルのイベントホール A に空きがあることがわかりました。そのホールは 150 席収容できますので十分な広さだと思います。すでに午前 10 時から予約を入れましたので，もし他の時間を希望でしたらできるだけ早くメールをいただきたいと思います。

またビデオプロジェクターを使用する予定はありますか。もし使用するのであれば，私が手配いたしましょうか。他に必要な機器に関しては，必要数をおっしゃっていただければこちらで手配をすることが可能です。お返事は 4 月 25 日月曜日までにいただけると大変助かります。

再度，ご協力を感謝いたします。

Amanda Cole
宣伝部

> **語句**
> □ prior to ～　～に先立ち
> □ vicinity　名 周辺，近辺
> □ approximately　副 およそ
> □ comply with ～　～に適合する
> □ alternative　形 代替の
> □ Thank you in advance.　よろしくお願いします。
> □ requirement　名 要件
> □ prefer　動 むしろ～の方を好む

196. Why did Mr. Parks send an e-mail to Ms. Cole?

(A) To give details of a new product release
(B) To announce the press release schedule
(C) To request arrangements for an upcoming event
(D) To discuss an advertising plan

Parks さんは，なぜ Cole さんにメールを送ったのですか。

(A) 新製品発売の詳細を伝えるため。
(B) 報道発表スケジュールについて知らせるため。
(C) 来るイベントの手配を依頼するため。
(D) 宣伝計画を話し合うため。

正解：(C)

● 着眼点！　E メールの目的は冒頭！

レベル ★★★★

解説　1 つ目の E メール，第 1 段落最後の文で，I was wondering if you could help us set it up と手配を依頼している。この it は前文の a press release「報道発表」を指している。これを言い換えたのが (C) の an upcoming event である。したがって，正解は (C)。

---

197. What is NOT suggested about the press release?

(A) A new household appliance will be presented.
(B) The hall has already been booked.
(C) The starting time can be rearranged.
(D) Investors are the main audience.

報道発表に関して示されていないことは何ですか。

(A) 新しい家庭用機器がプレゼンされる。
(B) ホールはすでに予約されている。
(C) 開始時間は調整可能である。
(D) 投資家が主な聴衆である。

正解：(D)

● 着眼点！　選択肢のキーワードをサーチ！

レベル ★★★☆

解説　press release について問われているので，2 つの E メールを見なければならない。選択肢の名詞キーワードを軸に素早くサーチしよう。エアコンの新商品を発表するので，(A) は OK。2 つ目の E メール，第 2 段落・3 文目で述べられているように会場ホールは予約されているので，(B) も当てはまる。また，同じ文の後半に，if you prefer a different time, please e-mail me とあり，調整可能であると推測できる。よって (C) も OK。(D) の investors は登場しないので，これが当てはまらず，正解となる。

227

198. What new information is indicated in the second e-mail?

(A) The preferable dates
(B) The rental fee amount
(C) The number of attendants
(D) The hours to hold the event

2つ目のEメールで新たに述べられているのは何ですか。

(A) 望ましい日程
(B) レンタル料金
(C) 出席者の人数
(D) イベント開催の時刻

正解：(D)

● 着眼点！ クロスリファレンスを活用せよ！　レベル ★★★★

[解説] 選択肢のキーワード，(A) dates，(B) fee，(C) number，(D) hours をサーチ。(A)，(C) は1つ目のメールに情報があるので×。(B) は2つ目のEメールでビデオプロジェクターの使用有無を聞いているが，レンタル料金については何も言っていない。2つ目のEメールの第2段落・3文目に **I have already reserved it from 10 A.M.** とあり，1つ目のメールでは時間については何も触れていないので，これが新しい情報。したがって，正解は (D)。

---

199. In the second e-mail, the word "meet" in paragraph 2, line 1, is closest in meaning to

(A) answer   (B) satisfy
(C) gather   (D) see

2つ目のEメールの第2段落・1行目の meet に最も近い意味の語は

(A) 答える   (B) 満たす
(C) 集まる   (D) 会う, 見る

正解：(B)

● 着眼点！ コロケーションに慣れよう！　レベル ★★☆☆

[解説] TOEICのリーディングでは，フレーズ／コロケーション力が重要。ここでは，**meet your requirements** で，「要件を満たす」という意味になる。**satisfy requirements** も同じ意味。よく使われるフレーズなので覚えておきたい。正解は (B)。

---

200. What is indicated about the Edmond Hill Building?

(A) It only holds 100 people.
(B) It opens after 11 A.M.
(C) It is close to the headquarters.
(D) It is a historical building.

Edmond Hill ビルについて何が述べられていますか。

(A) 100人しか収容できない。
(B) 午前11時以降にオープンする。
(C) 本社に近い。
(D) 歴史的建造物である。

正解：(C)

● 着眼点！ 無理せず，消去法を使おう！　レベル ★★★☆

[解説] Edmond Hill をサーチ。2つ目のEメールの第2段落だけでは，正解が選べない。だが，1つ目のEメールの第2段落で，**We would like to hold it in the vicinity of FN Consumer Electronics headquarters** とある。**vicinity** は「周辺，近辺」の意味。よって，正解は (C)。消去法でも解くことができる。

READING TEST
模試 5
解答と解説

- 問題は，別冊の 130 〜 161 ページに掲載されています。

模試 5 解答と解説

PART 5

101. If you are eligible ------- Medicare, please fill in this form.
(A) to
(B) for
(C) of
(D) about

Medicareの受給資格がおありでしたら，この用紙に記入してください。

正解：(B)

● 着眼点！ イディオム be eligible for
レベル ★★☆☆

解説 前置詞選択問題。eligible は「資格のある，適格な」という意味の形容詞。be eligible for ~ で「~の資格がある」，be eligible to do で「~する資格がある」の意味となる。ここでは直後に Medicare という名詞が来るので，(B) for が適切。前置詞とあわせてイディオムとして覚えよう。Medicare「メディケア」は，米国政府が提供する高齢者向け医療保険制度のこと。

語句 □ fill in ~ ~に記入する

102. The island of Sun ------- for its beautiful scenery, historical heritage, and natural hot springs.
(A) has known
(B) will know
(C) is known
(D) knowing

太陽の島は，美しい景観，歴史的遺産，そして天然温泉で知られています。

正解：(C)

● 着眼点！ 語感を鍛えて即答せよ！
レベル ★☆☆☆

解説 動詞 know の正しい形を選ぶ問題。空所後の for がポイント。be known for ~ で「~で知られている」という意味を表す。よって，正解は (C)。(A) は現在完了形，(B) 未来形，(C) 現在形の受動態，(D) ing 形。

103. Beverage industry giant Gordon Sax ------- a pilot shop of its coffee chain in downtown Bangkok next week.
(A) opened
(B) to open
(C) is going to open
(D) to be opening

飲料業界大手の Gordon Sax 社は来週，バンコクの繁華街で同社のコーヒーチェーンのパイロット店を開く予定です。

正解：(C)

● 着眼点！ 文中のヒントを見逃すな！
レベル ★☆☆☆

解説 動詞の適切な形を選ぶ問題。next week と未来を表す語句があるので，動詞も未来形でなければならない。選択肢の中でこれに当てはまるのは (C) のみ。pilot shop は顧客の反応を見るための実験的店舗のこと。

104. The Music Scholarship Competition is held every year for all high school seniors ------- are going to college.
(A) which
(B) whose
(C) who
(D) they

音楽奨学金コンペは毎年，大学に進学する予定の高校 3 年生全員を対象に開催されています。

正解：(C)

> **着眼点** 先行詞から関係代名詞を選べ！

解説 空所に入るのは are going to college に対して主語の役割をする関係代名詞。先行詞は seniors「3年生の生徒」なので, 関係代名詞は主格で人を先行詞にとる（C）who が適切。

語句 □ competition 名 コンペ, 競技会　□ senior 名 最上級生

---

105. Mr. Brook has suggested ------- help from the consultants to put together a revolutionary marketing plan.
(A) getting　　　(B) gotten
(C) to get　　　(D) get

Brook さんは, 革新的なマーケティング計画をまとめるために, コンサルタントの援助を得ようと提案しました。

正解：(A)

> **着眼点** suggest の用法をチェックせよ！

解説 suggest のあとに続く get の正しい形を選ぶ問題。suggest は後ろに動名詞または名詞を取る他動詞なので,（A）の動名詞 getting が適切。類例に avoid「〜を避ける」, consider「〜を考える」, postpone「〜を延期する」などがある。覚えておこう。

語句 □ consultant 名 コンサルタント　□ revolutionary 形 革新的な, 画期的な

---

106. All employees are expected to make a ------- to superior customer service.
(A) commitment　　　(B) commit
(C) committing　　　(D) committed

全従業員は, よりよい顧客サービスに本気で取り組むことを期待されています。

正解：(A)

> **着眼点** 品詞選択は空所前後にヒント！

解説 品詞を選ぶ問題では, 空所の前後の語が大きな手がかりとなる。この文では直前に冠詞 a があるので, 空所には名詞が入ることがわかる。make a commitment to 〜 で「〜に本気で取り組む, 深く関与する」という意味を知っていれば, すぐに解答できる。（A）が正解。（A）名詞「献身」,（B）動詞「〜に献身する」,（C）動詞の ing 形,（D）形容詞「献身した」。

語句 □ superior 形（より）優れた

---

107. Due to ------- maintenance of the air conditioning, smoking in this building will be temporarily prohibited.
(A) regular　　　(B) regularize
(C) regularly　　　(D) regularity

エアコンの定期点検により, この建物内での喫煙は一時的に禁止されています。

正解：(A)

> **着眼点** 派生語問題は空所前後から品詞選択が決め手！

解説 適切な品詞を選ぶ問題。空所のあとには名詞 maintenance「点検」が続いている。選択肢のうち名詞を修飾できるのは形容詞。よって（A）が正解。（A）形容詞「定期的な」,（B）動詞「〜を規則正しくする, 合法化する」,（C）副詞「定期的に」,（D）名詞「規則正しさ」。

108. Unfortunately, the product ------- did not meet our standards of quality.
(A) itself
(B) yourself
(C) themselves
(D) himself

残念ながら，その製品そのものが私たちの品質基準を満たしていませんでした。

正解：(A)

● 着眼点！ 代名詞が指すものを見抜け！

レベル ★☆☆☆

[解説] 選択肢はすべて再帰代名詞。再帰代名詞は名詞の直後で用いると，強調の意味を表す。ここでは，空所前の the product を強調しているので，(A) itself が正解となる。

109. Initially, MG Electronics was planning to sell its new product only during the summer, but increased production ------- it sold well.
(A) regarding
(B) before
(C) despite
(D) when

当初，MG Electronics 社は新製品を夏の間だけ販売する計画でしたが，売れ行きが好調だったため増産しました。

正解：(D)

● 着眼点！ 節をつなぐのは，接続詞！

レベル ★★☆☆

[解説] 空所のあとは節のため，接続詞が入る。接続詞である (B) と (D) のうち，文意から (D) がより適切。選択肢はそれぞれ，(A) 前置詞「〜に関しては」，(B) 接続詞「〜よりも前に」，(C) 前置詞「〜にもかかわらず」，(D) 接続詞「〜するとき，〜なので」。

110. A timetable released by the construction company shows even more ------- in a project that started years ago.
(A) to delay
(B) delaying
(C) delays
(D) delayed

建設会社が発表した予定表は，数年前に始まったプロジェクトのよりいっそうの遅れを示しています。

正解：(C)

● 着眼点！ 複数の要素がある場合はまず品詞を特定せよ！

レベル ★★☆☆

[解説] 空所に入るのは show の目的語となり形容詞 more および形容詞句 in a project に修飾される品詞であることから名詞とわかる。選択肢の中で名詞は (C) のみ。動詞 delay「〜を遅らせる」の (A) to 不定詞，(B) ing 形，(C) 名詞「遅れ」の複数形，(D) 過去形・過去分詞。

[語句] □ timetable 名 時間割，予定表

111. Purchased items can be returned to FS Interiors free of ------- if it is within two weeks of purchase.
(A) payment
(B) fee
(C) fair
(D) charge

ご購入された商品は，ご購入から2週間以内であれば，FS Interiors 社へ無料でご返品いただけます。

正解：(D)

● 着眼点！ イディオム free of charge をすばやく解答せよ！

レベル ★★☆☆

[解説] 似たような意味の語から，適切なものを選ぶ問題。正解は (D)。charge という単語はいろいろな意味で用いられるので，注意したい。名詞として用いられると，「経費，料金」や「責任，管理」などの意味を表し，動詞の場合「〜を請求する」という意味で用いられることがある。free of charge で「無料で」の意。選択肢はすべて名詞で，(A)「支払い」，(B)「手数料」，(C)「品評会」，(D)「料金」の意味。

112. Professor Wilson of Carlton University was awarded $100,000 for ------- contributions to the study of the human genome.
(A) legitimate　　　(B) actual
(C) extraordinary　(D) tentative

Carlton 大学の Wilson 教授は、ヒトゲノム研究に対するたぐいまれな貢献により 10 万ドルを授与されました。

正解：(C)

●着眼点！　形容詞選択問題は文の理解がカギ！

解説　適切な形容詞を選択する問題。どのような形容詞が入るかは、文の理解がカギ。ヒントを文中の他の部分で探そう。前半の was awarded $100,000「10 万ドルを授与された」がポイント。文意に合うのは、(C) の extraordinary。(A)「合法的な、正当な」、(B)「実際の」、(C)「たぐいまれな、非凡な」、(D)「試験的な」。ちなみに、award は名詞なら「賞、賞金」の意味。

語句　□ award 動 ～を授与する　□ contribution 名 貢献　□ genome 名 ゲノム

---

113. Mr. Kean, the president of Dubmen Company, was introduced to the audience ------- after the screening of the corporate promotion movie.
(A) shorter　　　(B) shortened
(C) shortly　　　(D) shortness

Dubmen 社の Kean 社長が、企業広告映像の上映後まもなく観衆に紹介されました。

正解：(C)

●着眼点！　空所の直後の after に注目せよ！

解説　空所直後の after the screening of the corporate promotion movie に注目。(C) shortly は after ～ や before ～ などの前にある時、「～の少しあと／前」を表す。正解は (C)。(A) 形容詞 short の比較級、(B) 動詞 shorten「～を短縮する」の過去形・過去分詞、(C) 副詞「まもなく」、(D) 名詞「短いこと」。

---

114. The new cellular phone is designed to meet the most ------- requirements of our clients.
(A) independent　(B) extinct
(C) demanding　　(D) intensive

その新しい携帯電話は、私たちの顧客の最も厳しい要求を満たすように設計されています。

正解：(C)

●着眼点！　コロケーションで考えよ！

解説　選択肢はすべて形容詞。文意から、requirements を修飾するのに適切な形容詞は (C) demanding である。(A)「独立した」、(B)「絶滅した」、(C)「要求の厳しい、きつい」、(D)「集中的な」。

語句　□ meet 動 ～を満足させる、(要求を) 満たす　□ requirement 名 要求、条件

115. The football game was delayed 4 hours ------- account of heavy snow.
(A) for　　　　　(B) in
(C) on　　　　　(D) by

フットボールの試合は，大雪のため4時間遅れました。
正解：(C)

● 着眼点！　イディオム　on account of
レベル ★★☆☆

解説　適切な前置詞を選ぶ問題。正解は (C)。on account of ～ は「～の理由で，～のために」という意味の定型表現で，because of と同じ意味。

---

116. Of the ------- candidates who had applied for the position, only three were left for the final interview.
(A) much　　　　(B) most
(C) more　　　　(D) many

このポストに応募してきた多数の候補者の中で，3人だけが最終面接に残りました。
正解：(D)

● 着眼点！　形容詞は修飾する名詞がカギ！
レベル ★★☆☆

解説　空所が修飾する candidates が解答のカギである。candidate は可算名詞なので，不可算名詞にのみ用いられる (A) の much は不可。(B) most「ほとんど，最も」は文意に合わないし，(C) の more は比較する対象がないので不可。これを正しく修飾する数量形容詞は可算名詞の複数形のみに使う (D) の many。position は，ここではある「職種」や「ポスト」のこと。文頭の of は「～の中で」の意。

語句　□ candidate 图 候補者　□ final interview 最終面接

---

117. A social-media venture eventually recorded its greatest profits for the last quarter and ------- its competitors.
(A) to surpass　　　(B) surpassing
(C) was surpassed　(D) surpassed

あるソーシャルメディアのベンチャー企業は前四半期に最高益を記録し，ライバル会社を追い抜きました。
正解：(D)

● 着眼点！　動詞の形を選ぶときは時制と態をチェックせよ！
レベル ★★☆☆

解説　動詞の適切な形を選ぶ問題。この文は A social-media venture を主語として，動詞 recorded と空所の語が and で並列に結ばれている。recorded が過去形なので，空所に入る動詞も過去形であることがわかる。よって，(C)，(D) のどちらか。次に，空所の直後にある its competitors「その競争相手」を目的語にとれるのは能動態の (D) surpassed。動詞 surpass「～を追い抜く」の (A) to 不定詞，(B) ing 形，(C) 過去形の受動態，(D) 過去形・過去分詞。

---

118. It took ------- amount of effort on my part before Mr. Taylor finally agreed to let the project continue.
(A) an enormous　　(B) a conservative
(C) a heavy　　　　(D) a stable

Taylor さんがプロジェクトの続行に最終的に同意するまで，私は大変な努力を要しました。
正解：(A)

> **着眼点** 形容詞と名詞のコロケーションで答えよ！

解説 適切な意味を持つ形容詞を選ぶ問題。空所直後の amount of effort との組み合わせを考える。amount は量を表しているので，(B)，(D) は不可。effort の意味を考えて適切なものは (A) のみである。take effort で「努力を要する」，on my part で「私の方では」の意味。(A)「莫大な」，(B)「保守的な」，(C)「重い」，(D)「安定した」。

119. Mr. Bennet got promoted to vice president not because of his age ------- because of his outstanding achievements.
  (A) so   (B) or
  (C) and   (D) but

Bennet さんは年齢ではなく，飛び抜けた業績が理由で副社長に昇進しました。

正解：(D)

> **着眼点** 文の構造をまず把握せよ！

解説 つなぎ語を選ぶ問題なので，文全体の構造に目を向けよう。空所の前にもあとにも because of があることに注目したい。1つ目の because of の前には not があるので，これに対応した語が空所に入ると考えられる。not A but B で「A ではなく B」という意味になる (D) が正解。相方探しの問題とも言える。

語句
□ get promoted to ~ ~に昇進する
□ outstanding 形 飛び抜けた，極めて優れた   □ achievement 名 業績

120. The Andersons tried to ------- eating fast food, so they always brought healthy snacks with them when they traveled.
  (A) avoid   (B) actualize
  (C) attract   (D) accept

Anderson 家の人々はファストフードを食べないようにしていたので，旅行をする時にはいつも健康的なおやつを持参していました。

正解：(A)

> **着眼点** avoid + ing をチェックせよ！

解説 so 以下の文から，ファストフードは食べないということが推測できる。したがって，選択肢の中では (A) avoid が適切。105. でも説明したように avoid は動名詞を目的語にするので，そのことがわかればすばやく解答できる。(A)「~を避ける」，(B)「~を実現する」，(C)「~を引きつける」，(D)「~を受け入れる」。

121. Please allow one week from the time of submission of your application for -------.
  (A) approve   (B) approval
  (C) approved   (D) approver

申込書の提出時から承認まで1週間かかります。

正解：(B)

> **着眼点** 品詞選択はまず空所周辺から！

解説 品詞問題。空所には前置詞 for の目的語が入るので，名詞または名詞に相当するものを選ぶ。選択肢のうち，申込書提出時から1週間かかるという文意に適しているのは (B)。(A) 動詞「~を承認する」，(B) 名詞「承認」，(C) 形容詞「承認された」，(D) 名詞「承認者」。

122. Thunderstorms are ------- likely to occur in the Midwestern states today as a cold front blows through the entire region.
(A) most
(B) few
(C) many
(D) some

寒冷前線が地域全体にかかっているため、本日、中西部の州に雷雨が発生する恐れがあります。

正解：(A)

●着眼点！ 定型表現 be most likely to ～

[解説] be most likely to ～「～しそうである」は、設問文にも用いられる頻出表現。ほかに likely を修飾する語句として、very や more も覚えておきたい。イディオムに関する知識を養おう。

[語句] □ thunderstorm 名 雷雨　□ cold front 寒冷前線

---

123. Ms. Clooney updated the company's Web site by ------- because the person in charge was out of town on vacation.
(A) themselves
(B) himself
(C) itself
(D) herself

担当者が休暇中で町にいなかったため、Clooney さんは会社のウェブサイトを彼女自身で更新しました。

正解：(D)

●着眼点！ 全文を読んで特定せよ！

[解説] 全文を読んで、by oneself「～自身で」の主語を見つけよう。不在の担当者ではなく、Ms. Clooney がウェブサイトを更新したことがわかる。つまり、彼女自身を表す (D) herself が適切。

---

124. Ndjamena Coffee Trade Inc. has specialized ------- Ethiopian beans for decades and successfully led the market with its refined products.
(A) in
(B) at
(C) upon
(D) on

Ndjamena コーヒー商社は、数十年にわたりエチオピア産の豆を専門に扱い、洗練された商品で市場をうまくけん引してきました。

正解：(A)

●着眼点！ 語彙力で即答せよ！

[解説] この問題では、動詞 specialize の語法が問われている。適切なのは (A)。空所前の specialize は自動詞。specialize in ～「～を専門にする、専門に扱う」という表現で用いられる。

---

125. In order to ------- a group study room in the library, you need to follow the instructions in the student's guidebook.
(A) appoint
(B) contact
(C) reserve
(D) reply

図書館のグループ学習室を予約するためには、学生ガイドブックの説明書に従ってください。

正解：(C)

●着眼点！ 語彙問題は文意から！

[解説] 空所に入る動詞を選ぶ語彙問題。文意に沿った意味を持つ動詞を見つけよう。ガイドブックの説明に従うという内容から、学習室の利用に関わることだとわかるので (C) が正解。(A)「～を指定する」、(B)「～に連絡する」、(C)「～を予約する」、(D)「～に返答する」。

126. Divlin Museum takes pride in its position as the most popular museum for three ------- years.
(A) success
(B) successful
(C) successive
(D) succeeding

Divlin 博は、3年連続で最も人気のある博物館としての地位に誇りを持っています。

正解：(C)

● 着眼点！ 形容詞は名詞との相性で選べ！

レベル ★★★☆

解説　空所の前後に注目すると形容詞であると判断できるため、(A) は不可。(B) と (D) は紛らわしいが、ここでは文意から、for ~ successive days/years で「~日／~年連続で」という意味を表す (C) が適切。consecutive も同意。(A) 名詞「成功」、(B) 形容詞「成功した」、(C) 形容詞「連続する」、(D) 形容詞「次の、あとに続く」。

語句　□ take pride in ~　~を誇りとする

---

127. BPI Group recently went ------- a massive reorganization after billions of dollars were wasted.
(A) through
(B) over
(C) around
(D) behind

数十億ドルが浪費されたのち、BPI Group 社は最近、大規模な組織再編成を行いました。

正解：(A)

● 着眼点！ イディオム go through で即答せよ！

レベル ★★☆☆

解説　go through は「(苦しみ、試練などを) 経験する、体験する」という意味の定型表現なので、(A) が適切。(B) は go over で「~を調査する」、(C) は go around で「~を周回する」、(D) は「~の裏を探る」となり、他の選択肢ではいずれも意味が通らない。

語句　□ massive 形 大規模な　□ reorganization 名 組織再編成
□ waste 動 ~を浪費する

---

128. We would like to remind you that this year's career fair will be ------- at The Mount Royal Hotel instead of The King Edward Hotel.
(A) holding
(B) holds
(C) held
(D) hold

今年のキャリアフェアは King Edward ホテルに代わって Mount Royal ホテルで開催されることをお知らせいたします。

正解：(C)

● 着眼点！ 多義語に注意！

レベル ★☆☆☆

解説　動詞 hold には「~を持つ」という意味だけでなく、多様な意味があるので要注意。「(イベントなどを) 開催する」という意味で頻出する。空所の前に動詞 be があることから、(B) と (D) は不適。また、主語 career fair は「開催される」という文意が正しいので、(C) が正解だとわかる。

129. ------- we get booked up quickly during the summer holiday season, we strongly recommend you make a reservation early.
(A) If　　　　　　　(B) After
(C) When　　　　　(D) As

夏の休暇シーズンはすぐに予約でいっぱいになりますので，お早めにご予約されるように強くお勧めします。

正解：(D)

● 着眼点！　接続詞を選ぶ前に全文を読め！

レベル ★★☆☆

解説　2つの文をつなぐ接続詞が問われている。空所以外の文意は，カンマの前が「夏の休暇シーズンの間はすぐに予約でいっぱいになる」で，後ろが「早く予約するように勧める」となる。これをつなぐのに最もふさわしいのは，原因・理由を表す (D)「〜なので」。

語句　□ get booked up　予約でいっぱいになる　□ recommend　動 〜を勧める
　　　□ make a reservation　予約をする

---

130. J&K Inc. and SGM Group plan to hold ------- negotiations on all the outstanding issues.
(A) intensive　　　(B) impressive
(C) instructive　　(D) expensive

J&K 社と SGM Group 社は，すべての未解決の問題に関して集中的な交渉を行う予定です。

正解：(A)

● 着眼点！　コロケーションから解け！

レベル ★★★☆

解説　形容詞を選択する問題。直後の negotiation「交渉」を修飾する形容詞として適切なのは，(A) のみである。(A)「集中的な，徹底的な」，(B)「印象的な」，(C)「教育的な，ためになる」，(D)「高価な，費用のかかる」。

語句　□ negotiation　名 交渉，折衝　□ outstanding　形 未解決の，傑出した

---

131. After having intervened in the FX market, the authorities are now considering ------- options to deal with the current account deficit.
(A) either　　　　(B) another
(C) every　　　　(D) other

外国為替市場に介入したのち，当局は現在，経常収支赤字に対処するための別の選択肢を検討しています。

正解：(D)

● 着眼点！　名詞と形容詞の相性を調べよ！

レベル ★★☆☆

解説　名詞 options「選択肢」を修飾する形容詞を選択する。(A) either は2つのもののうち「どちらか一方の」という意味なので，複数形に合わない。(B) another と (C) every も可算名詞の単数形しか修飾しないので不可。ここは後ろに複数形がとれる (D) other が正解。

語句　□ intervene　動 〜に介入する　□ authorities　名 当局
　　　□ consider　動 〜を熟考する，検討する　□ deficit　名 赤字，不足額

---

132. The Faculty of Medicine in Duxton University got a ------- to the Dental Journal.
(A) description　　(B) subscription
(C) legislation　　 (D) comprehension

Duxton 大学医学部は，Dental Journal 誌の定期購読を申し込みました。

正解：(B)

● **着眼点！** コロケーションで選べ！ ★★★☆

解説 動詞 got と空所のあとに続く to the Dental Journal がヒント。Dental Journal は雑誌名と推測されるので、(B) subscription が適切。get a subscription で「定期購読権を取得する」という意味。(A)「記述，描写」，(B)「定期購読，購読料，購読申し込み」，(C)「立法」，(D)「理解」。

語句 □ faculty 名 (大学の) 学部，職員，教授会　□ medicine 名 医学，薬

---

133. YN Textile Company was established ------- recently and has been developing very fast in the last few years.
(A) relatively　　(B) relative
(C) related　　　(D) relation

YN Textile 社は比較的最近設立され，ここ数年急激なスピードで成長し続けています。

正解：(A)

● **着眼点！** 副詞を修飾するのは副詞！ ★★★☆

解説 空所に当てはまる適切な品詞を選ぶ問題。空所直後の副詞 recently を修飾できるのは，同じ副詞。よって (A) relatively が正解。こういう形があることも覚えておこう。(A) 副詞「比較的」，(B) 形容詞「比較上の」，(C) 形容詞「関連した」，(D) 名詞「関係」。

---

134. I'd appreciate it if you checked the content of the ------- document files I forwarded to you this morning.
(A) attached　　(B) attach
(C) attaching　　(D) to attach

今朝転送した添付文書ファイルの中身をチェックしてくれると，ありがたいのですが。

正解：(A)

● **着眼点！** 空所前後だけで解け！ ★★☆☆

解説 品詞を答える問題。空所周辺の the ------- document files から，答えを導こう。空所には，名詞句 document files を修飾する語が入る。文意に適しているのは「添付の，付属の」を表す (A)。動詞 attach の (B) 原形，(C) ing 形，(D) to 不定詞。

語句 □ forward 動 〜を転送する

---

135. The Consumer Confidence Index is still well below the historical average ------- income and job security have significantly improved.
(A) even though　　(B) as a result of
(C) because of　　 (D) according to

所得と雇用保障が著しく改善したにもかかわらず，消費者信頼感指数は依然として過去の平均を大幅に下回っています。

正解：(A)

● **着眼点！** 空所の前後の順接／逆接を見抜け！ ★★☆☆

解説 空所の前後は，「消費者信頼感指数が低レベルにある」と「所得と雇用が改善した」という 2 つの逆接的な意味合いの節で構成されている。これらをつなぐのは接続詞。よって必然的に (B)，(C)，(D) は除外できる。接続詞と前置詞の区別を瞬時にできるようになろう。(A)「〜にもかかわらず」，(B)「〜の結果として」，(C)「〜のために」，(D)「〜によると」。

語句 □ job security 雇用保障　□ significantly 副 著しく
□ improve 動 改善する

136. We must ensure we meet the ------- by sharing workloads, or we will lose our credibility since competition is becoming fierce.
(A) deadline   (B) distribution
(C) proposal   (D) cancellation

仕事量を分担して，納期に間に合わせることを確実にしなければなりません。さもないと，競争が激化しているので信用を失うでしょう。

正解：(A)

● 着眼点！ 文意から読み取れ！

解説　語彙問題。選択詞に並んでいる語句はそれぞれ，(A)「締め切り」，(B)「配分」，(C)「提案」，(D)「取り消し」。文意に適しているのは，(A) deadline。イディオム meet a deadline で「締め切りに間に合う」という意味になる。

語句　□ workload 名 仕事量　□ credibility 名 信頼性
　　　□ fierce 形 激しい，し烈な

137. -------, Michael has been recognized for his high skills and has become a section chief in just a year of service in the company.
(A) Amazed   (B) Amazing
(C) Amazingly   (D) Amazement

驚いたことに，Michael は彼の高度な技量が認められ，わずか1年余りの勤務でセクションチーフになりました。

正解：(C)

● 着眼点！ 文全体を修飾する副詞は文頭に来ることが多い！

解説　空所には文全体を修飾する語が入る。それができるのは副詞。よって，(C) が適切。recognize は「〜を認める，評価する」という意味。(A) 動詞「〜を驚嘆させる」の過去形・過去分詞，(B) 形容詞「驚嘆すべき」，(C) 副詞「驚くほどに」，(D) 名詞「驚愕，仰天」。

138. A new taxation law that passed Congress this spring will come into ------- next September.
(A) influence   (B) effect
(C) outcome   (D) result

アメリカ議会を今春通過した新税法は，来年9月に施行されます。

正解：(B)

● 着眼点！ 似た意味を持つ単語からの選択はイディオムを探せ！

解説　英語表現についての問題。選択肢はすべて似たような意味を持つ語である。その中で，come into effect「（法律などが）効力を発する」というイディオムに気づくことがポイント。正解は (B)。選択肢はすべて名詞で，(A)「影響」，(B)「結果，影響」，(C)「結果」，(D)「結果」。

139. Alamo Footwear offers the ------- selection of brand name shoes, boots and sandals in the U.K.
(A) widely
(B) widest
(C) wider
(D) more widely

Alamo 靴店は，ブランドシューズ，ブーツとサンダルの英国における最も広範囲に及ぶ品揃えを提供しています。

正解：(B)

● 着眼点！ 文中のヒントを見逃すな！

レベル ★★☆☆

[解説] 文中に散りばめられたヒントを見つけよう。空所前 the と文末 in the U.K. から，「英国で最も～な」という意味を表す最上級の表現が入ることがわかる。形容詞 wide は wider, widest と活用するので，(B) が正解。

---

140. In most instances, ------- a country begins to open its market to free trade, social and political freedoms soon follow.
(A) only
(B) once
(C) first
(D) soon

ほとんどの場合，国が一度自由貿易に市場を開放し始めると，社会的，政治的自由もすぐあとに続きます。

正解：(B)

● 着眼点！ 条件を表す接続詞としての once

レベル ★★☆☆

[解説] a country begins to ... と social and political freedoms ... の2つの文をつなぐ語が欠けている。よって空所に必要な品詞は接続詞である。ここは「いったん～すると」と条件を表す接続詞の (B) once がふさわしい。(A) 副詞「ただ～だけ」，(B) 接続詞「いったん～すると」，(C) 副詞「最初に」，(D) 副詞「すぐに」。

[語句] □ instance 名 場合

PART 6

Questions 141-143 refer to the following e-mail.
問題 141-143 は次の E メールに関するものです。

To: david@freshcakedesign.org
From: hallenguyen@cybertree.net
Subject: Modeling for your brand

Dear David,
I'm Halle Nguyen, a freelance model. I saw an article about your brand in the online design and fashion magazine *Up & Up* and am interested in modeling for you. Your clothes, ⬚141⬚ the T-shirts, are creative and cute and I think my look would ⬚142⬚ well with your designs.
I have five years of experience and ⬚143⬚ last November was a regular model for the lifestyle magazine *Color/Life*. Attached are several photos of me, including pictures of a photo spread I did for July cover of *Color/Life*. I look forward to hearing from you.

Sincerely,
Halle

宛先：david@freshcakedesign.org
差出人：hallenguyen@cybertree.net
件名：貴社ブランド用モデル

David 様
私はフリーランスモデルの Halle Nguyen と申します。デザインとファッションのオンライン雑誌 *Up & Up* で貴社ブランドの記事を読み，貴社のモデルをしたいと思っています。貴社の洋服，特にTシャツは創造的でかわいらしく，私のルックスは貴社のデザインによく合うと思います。
モデルの経験は 5 年あり，去年の 11 月まではライフスタイル雑誌 *Color/Life* でレギュラーのモデルをしていました。*Color/Life* 7 月号の表紙のために撮ったグラビア写真を含めて，私の写真を数枚添付します。お返事をお待ちしています。

敬具
Halle

> 語句
> ☐ **freelance** 形 フリーランスの，自由契約の
> ☐ **photo spread** グラビア

141. (A) especially
(B) naturally
(C) relatively
(D) regularly

正解：(A)

●着眼点！ 前後の名詞の関係をつかめ！

レベル ★☆☆☆

解説　clothes と T-shirts との関係を考えると、T-shirts は clothes の一部。選択肢は (A)「特に」、(B)「自然に、当然」、(C)「比較的」、(D)「定期的に」なので、「衣類、特に T シャツ」とするのが自然。(A) が正解。

---

142. (A) stop
(B) get
(C) go
(D) run

正解：(C)

●着眼点！ イディオム　go well with で即答せよ！

レベル ★★☆☆

解説　自分を推薦するメールで、自分の外見が相手のデザインに「合う」と言っている。後ろに well with があるので、go well with ～「～と似合う」だと判断する。正解は (C)。

---

143. (A) by
(B) until
(C) for
(D) in

正解：(B)

●着眼点！ 文中に時を示す表現を探せ！

レベル ★★★☆

解説　時を示す前置詞の選択問題。文の構造を把握して、正解を導こう。空所を含む文の and 以下に注目すると、空所と last November が regular model であった時期を表していると考えられる。ここで主語の I は省略されている。現在は freelance model だと言っているので、「去年の 11 月まで専属モデルだった」と考えるのが自然。したがって、(B)「～まで」が最も適切。(A)「～までには」、(C)「～のために」、(D)「～の中に」。

Questions 144-146 refer to the following notice.
問題 144-146 は次のお知らせに関するものです。

Come Join Us at Our Annual Company Picnic

The season for the Annual Company Picnic is here!
     When: Sept. 30（Sat.）11:00 A.M.-3:00 P.M.
     Where: Ridgestone Park
This year, the Picnic Organizing Committee (that's us!) has specially invited Misty, the Magician to join us. She [144] a performance as well as making animal balloons for the kids. We also have a variety of fun games and sports [145]: face painting, tag football, mini-soccer, raffles and more!
For gourmet food lovers, Sawyer's is catering this year and the menu will include their famous Mexican tacos.
So [146] your family and friends for a day of fun! Reservations are necessary. Sign up with Kathy at the Administrative Division by Sept. 5.

毎年恒例の会社ピクニックへどうぞご参加ください

毎年恒例の会社ピクニックの季節になりました！
     日時：9月30日（土曜日）午前11時～午後3時
     場所：Ridgestone Park
今年，ピクニック実行委員会（私たちです！）は，特別ゲストに手品師の **Misty** さんをお招きしています。手品を披露してくれるほか，子供たちに動物の形の風船を作ってくれます。楽しいゲームやスポーツもいろいろそろえました。フェイスペインティング，タグフットボール，ミニサッカー，くじ引き，そのほか盛りだくさんです！
美食家の皆さんには，今年は **Sawyer's** がケータリングしてくれます。評判のメキシカンタコスもあります。
ご家族やお友だちを誘って，ぜひ楽しい1日をお過ごしください！ 参加には予約が必要です。
管理部の **Kathy** に，9月5日までにお申し込みください。

語句　□ raffle　名 くじ引き

144. (A) had given
(B) will be giving
(C) has been given
(D) was giving

正解：(B)

● 着眼点！ 基本文法をマスターせよ！

レベル ★★☆☆

[解説] 前後の文脈から正しい時制を選択する問題。まず，本文にはこれから開催されるイベントについての情報が記載されていることがポイント。選択肢の中で，これから起こること（＝未来）について表すことができるのは，(B) のみ。時制問題は頻出なので，間違えないようにしよう。

145. (A) right up
(B) lined up
(C) brought up
(D) heads up

正解：(B)

● 着眼点！ 日本語に定着している英語から類推せよ！

レベル ★★★☆

[解説] 選択肢の意味はそれぞれ，(A)「すぐに」，(B)「並んだ，用意された」，(C)「育てられた，持ち出された」，(D)「頭上注意」。文意から (B) とわかる。日本語でも「ラインナップ」という言葉が使われるので，ニュアンスはわかりやすい。商品説明や種類を表す時によく用いられる。

146. (A) carry out
(B) pick up
(C) bring along
(D) depend on

正解：(C)

● 着眼点！ 招待状の定型表現をマスターせよ！

レベル ★★☆☆

[解説] bring along your family and friends「ご家族，お友だちをご一緒にお連れください」は招待状によく使われる表現。(A) carry out ～「～を成し遂げる」，(B) pick up ～「～を拾い上げる」，(D) depend on ～「～を当てにする」は文の内容に合わない。

Questions 147-149 refer to the following e-mail.
問題 147-149 は次の E メールに関するものです。

To: Brian Fuller
From: John Monroe
Date: June 30
Subject: Property in Buena Park

Dear Brian,

I am interested in the property at 5 Oak Avenue in Buena Park, advertised on renthow.org. According to the website, it will be available 147 August 31 and I am hoping to move in September 14.
I'd be happy to see the property 148 my business trip to Buena Park shortly in July.
I will be there from July 1 to July 5. Please let me know your schedule for showing the house during my stay.
Also, please 149 me a rental application as well, so I will have everything ready if I do decide to rent.

Sincerely,
John Monroe

宛先：Brian Fuller
送信者：John Monroe
日付：6 月 30 日
件名：Buena Park の物件

Brian 様

renthow.org に載っていた Buena Park の Oak Avenue 5 番地の物件に興味があります。ウェブサイトによれば，8 月 31 日から利用できるとありました。私は 9 月 14 日に入居したいと思っています。
7 月に入ってまもなく出張で Buena Park に行く予定があるので，その折にぜひ，物件を見たいと思います。
7 月 1 日から 5 日までそちらの街に滞在しますので，その間に家を案内していただける日をお知らせください。
また，賃貸申込書もお送りください。そうすれば，その物件を借りると決めたときにすべて書類をそろえておけると思います。

敬具
John Monroe

語句
□ property 名 不動産物件
□ application 名 申込書，申請書

147.
(A) starting
(B) start
(C) to start
(D) started

正解：(A)

● 着眼点！ 前置詞的な starting に注目せよ！

レベル ★★☆☆

解説 日付の前なので，ここは前置詞の役割に相当する単語が入ると予想できる。(A) starting は「〜から」の意味で日付の前に置いて前置詞のように使う用法もあるので (A) が正解。(B) 動詞 start「〜を始める」の原形，(C) to 不定詞，(D) 過去形・過去分詞。

148.
(A) during
(B) along
(C) within
(D) while

正解：(A)

● 着眼点！ 前置詞を攻略せよ！

レベル ★★☆☆

解説 空所前後の関係がポイント。空所の後ろを見ると，my business trip ... in July と7月の出張という「時期」が記されている。日程などの期間の前には，「〜の間に」という意味を表す (A) during が入る。(D) の接続詞 while「〜している間に」は紛らわしいが，後ろに節が続いていないので誤り。

149.
(A) have
(B) get
(C) take
(D) send

正解：(D)

● 着眼点！ 動詞の選択は文意を読み取れ！

レベル ★☆☆☆

解説 空所の後ろに「物件を借りると決めたときに書類をそろえておける」とある。そのためには，rental application を先にもらいたいという意味だと推察できる。よってここは (D)「〜を送る」が適切。(A)「〜を持つ」，(B)「〜を得る」，(C)「〜を連れていく」は文意に合わない。

Questions 150-152 refer to the following article.
問題 150-152 は次の記事に関するものです。

Original Wear to Develop New Women's Brand

Original Wear has just announced its plans ⬚150 a new brand for women. The brand will target the low-end market and will be sold exclusively at Drayton retail outlets next spring.
Items include apparel, footwear and bags. The company will unveil the ⬚151 of its plans to work closely with Drayton before the details are disclosed next month.
Sales of this brand ⬚152 to grow continuously. Original Wear will take advantage of the marketing potential of Drayton, especially anticipating a chance to tap into a part of the market others haven't.

Original Wear 社，新しい婦人服ブランドを展開

Original Wear 社は婦人服の新ブランドを展開する計画を発表した。このブランドは低価格帯市場をターゲットとし，来春から Drayton 社の小売り店でのみ販売される。
対象商品は，衣類，靴とバッグとなる。同社は来月詳細が明らかにされる前に，Drayton 社との緊密な協力計画の概要を公表する。
このブランドの売り上げは伸び続けると予想されている。Original Wear 社は，Drayton 社の市場可能性をうまく活用していく意向で，これにより特に他社が手をつけていない市場に食い込む足がかりを得ることを見込んでいる。

[語句]
- □ low-end market 低価格帯市場
- □ exclusively 副 もっぱら～，～のみで
- □ outlet 名 直販店
- □ unveil 動 ～を公表する
- □ disclose 動 ～を明らかにする
- □ take advantage of ～ ～を利用する，活用する
- □ anticipate 動 ～を見込む
- □ tap into ～ ～に進出する

150.
(A) develop
(B) developed
(C) will develop
(D) to develop

正解：(D)

● 着眼点！ 正しい動詞の形を選べ！

レベル ★☆☆☆

[解説] 動詞 develop「〜を開発する」の形が問われている。空所の後ろは its plans を修飾しているということに気付くのがポイント。修飾できるのは過去分詞形の (B) と to 不定詞の (D) だが、文意に合う (D) が正解。この不定詞は、直前の名詞句 its plans がどのような計画なのか、具体的な内容を説明する「同格」を表す不定詞。

151.
(A) requirement
(B) summary
(C) celebration
(D) productivity

正解：(B)

● 着眼点！ 空所の前後の意味から正解を導け！

レベル ★★★☆

[解説] 語彙力が問われている。空所を含む文に注目して、文意を正しくつかもう。「詳細が来月公表される前に、会社が明らかにする」ものとしては、(B)「概要」が適切である。(A)「要件、要求」、(C)「お祝い、賞賛」、(D)「生産性」は、文意に適さない。

152.
(A) are expected
(B) expect
(C) expected
(D) have expected

正解：(A)

● 着眼点！ ふさわしい動詞の態と時制はどれかがポイント！

レベル ★★☆☆

[解説] 動詞の時制と態がポイントの問題。この文の主語は Sales of this brand であるので、文脈から、動詞 expect「〜を予想する」は受動態となるとわかる。受動態は選択肢の中で (A) 1つだけである。be expected to 〜 で「〜すると予想される」となり、(A) が正解。(B) 原形、(C) 過去形・過去分詞、(D) 現在完了形。

PART 7

問題 153-154 は次のウェブページに関するものです。

BAY 誌を定期購読しよう!
博物館の展示から映画館で上映中の作品まで,
一流レストランから **TV** の番組表まで,
BAY 誌はすべてのエンターテイメント情報をお届けします!

私たちについて	☒ はい, **BAY** 誌の無料お試し号を送ってください。
購読者限定	
購読	名前
お試し号	Milo Sanders
ブログ	住所
	278 November 通り, Toronto, ON M6Y7H5
	電話番号
	212-555-7829
	*ご記入いただいた情報は,上記の目的のためにのみ使用されます。
	送信

語句
- □ subscribe to 〜 〜を定期購読する, 予約する
- □ museum exhibition 博物館や美術館の展示
- □ listing 名 予定(番組)表, 一覧表
- □ subscriber 名 購読者, 予約者
- □ issue 名 発行物, 〜号, 〜刷

153. What kind of topic does *BAY* magazine most likely cover?

(A) Business
(B) Technology
(C) Entertainment
(D) Fashion

BAY 誌はどんな話題を扱っていると考えられますか。

(A) ビジネス
(B) テクノロジー
(C) エンターテインメント
(D) ファッション

正解：(C)

● 着眼点！ 選択肢をタテ読み！

[解説] *BAY* 誌のジャンルが問われている。まず，選択肢をタテ読みして，ジャンルをチェックしよう。ウェブページの見出しの下に *BAY* brings you all entertainment information! とある。したがって，(C) が正解。

[語句] □ cover 動 (問題などを) 扱う，取り上げる

---

154. What is implied about Mr. Sanders?

(A) He has started a subscription to *BAY*.
(B) He will get a free copy by mail.
(C) He will send an e-mail to the publisher.
(D) He has agreed to receive advertisements.

Sanders さんについてどんなことがわかりますか。

(A) *BAY* 誌の定期購読を始めた。
(B) 郵送で無料版を受け取る。
(C) メールを出版社に送る。
(D) 広告を受け取ることに同意した。

正解：(B)

● 着眼点！ キーワードをサーチ！

[解説] 設問キーワード Mr. Sanders という人物名をサーチする。中盤に，Yes, please send me a free trial issue of *BAY*. の箇所から，この人物がお試し号を申し込もうとしていることがわかる。このフォームには氏名に加えて，住所と電話番号が記入されているため，郵送で無料版が送られるだろうと推測できる。したがって，(B) が正解。

問題 155-156 は次の E メールに関するものです。

宛先：全新入社員
差出人：研修部
件名：営業研修
日付：9月4日

新入営業社員は次の金曜日，終日，営業研修に参加しなければなりません。研修の目的は，顧客の注意を引き，メッセージを伝え，契約を結ぶチャンスを増やすための実用的なテクニックを皆さんに示すことです。

研修は 2 部構成となっています。午前中の講義では話す技術についてご紹介します。午後は，15 年間戸別訪問セールスに従事した Patty Clark 営業副部長が中心となる実践型のセールスワークショップがあります。彼女は新しい仲間と自分の経験や知識を共有してくれるでしょう。次の金曜日，午前 9 時 30 分に 2 階の大会議室で会いましょう。

敬具

Rachel Sanchez
研修部部長

語句　□ get ~ across　（意味・考えなどを）わからせる，通じさせる
　　　□ close deal　契約をまとめる
　　　□ door-to-door　形 戸別の

155. What is the main purpose of the event?

イベントの主な目的は何ですか。

(A) To introduce new technologies
(B) To instruct newcomers in sales methods
(C) To spread business strategies
(D) To renew contracts with customers

(A) 新しい技術を紹介すること。
(B) 新人に販売方法を指導すること。
(C) ビジネス戦略を広めること。
(D) 顧客との契約を更新すること。

正解：(B)

● 着眼点！　メールの「宛先」と「件名」を見よう！

レベル ★★☆☆

[解説] メールを見ると，「全新入社員」に向けて，「営業研修」の案内とある。いわゆる新人研修の案内メールで本文の1行目を見ても，それが確認できる。ここから (B) を選ぶ。

---

156. What is mentioned about Ms. Clark?

Clark さんについて何が述べられていますか。

(A) She previously worked for another company.
(B) She has been training sales people for fifteen years.
(C) She had been selling product for a long time.
(D) She developed the company's sales methods.

(A) 以前は他の会社で働いていた。
(B) 15年間営業担当者を育ててきた。
(C) 長い間製品の販売をしてきた。
(D) 会社の販売方法を開発した。

正解：(C)

● 着眼点！　キーワードをサーチ！

レベル ★★★☆

[解説] 設問の人名キーワードをサーチしよう。第2段落に Patty Clark, our vice president of Sales, who had engaged in door-to-door sales for fifteen years. とある。Clark さんはベテランの営業担当者とわかる。for fifteen years を for a long time と言い換えている (C) が正解。

問題 **157-158** は次の手紙に関するものです。

Fairbanks デパート
609　Stratton 通り
Baltimore, MD 24242
8月30日

大切なお客様各位

Fairbanks デパートをご利用いただき，ありがとうございます。

長期にわたる改装のあとで，私どもの本店は，来る 10 月 1 日に営業再開いたしますことをお知らせ申し上げます。

Stratton 通りにございます私どもの店舗は，販売面積を 50 万平方フィートに拡大し，当デパート最大の店舗となります。各フロアとも広い通路と快適な試着室を備え，お買い物がしやすいように再設計されました。私どもの本店の目玉は，家族でお買い物を楽しむ自由な時間をご支援するためのプロの保育士がいる託児所で，子供用品売り場に開設されます。

5 つの国際的なブランドにともに開店を祝ってもらうべく，世界のファッションの中心であるロンドン，パリ，ミラノそして東京から衣料品を店舗に仕入れます。

開店の週には様々な特別イベントを準備しております。後日，招待状をお送りいたします。

新しい本店が，想像以上のお買い物の楽しみを皆様にお届けできるよう，心より願っております。

敬具

Robert Trent
Fairbanks デパート **CEO**

語句
- flagship　名 中心店舗，最も重要なもの
- comfortable　形 快適な
- centerpiece　名 最も重要なもの，目玉
- nursery　名 託児所
- childcare　名 保育，育児
- forthcoming　形 来るべき

157. What is the main purpose of this letter?　　手紙の主な目的は何ですか。

(A) To invite guests to an opening ceremony　　(A) 顧客を開店の式に招待すること。
(B) To announce a temporal move to a different address　　(B) 異なる住所への一時的な移動を発表すること。
(C) To advertise worldwide clothing brands　　(C) 世界の洋服ブランドを宣伝すること。
(D) To attract customers to a reopened store　　(D) 再開した店舗へ顧客を引き込むこと。

正解：(D)

●着眼点！　手紙の形の「広告」！

[解説] To all our valued customers「大切なお客様各位」とあるように, 本文は手紙の形をした「広告」。迷わず冒頭から主題を見抜こう。This is to inform you that our flagship store will be reopening on October 1 after a lengthy refurbishment. とあり, 本店の営業再開を知らせる手紙であるとわかるので, (D) が正解。

---

158. How can Fairbanks Department Store support family customers shopping?　　Fairbanks デパートはどのようにして家族で来る顧客の買い物を支援できますか。

(A) By providing sizeable and comfortable fitting rooms　　(A) 広くて快適な試着室を提供する。
(B) By providing childcare workers for babysitting services　　(B) 託児サービスのために保育士を供給する。
(C) By resizing shopping space for more goods　　(C) より多くの商品のために売り場の大きさを変える。
(D) By contracting to produce clothes for different generations　　(D) 様々な世代のための服を提供する契約を結ぶ。

正解：(B)

●着眼点！　設問文のキーワードでサーチ！

[解説] 設問キーワード support family customers shopping で本文をサーチしよう。手紙の中盤に, The centerpiece of our flagship is a nursery with childcare professionals. This facility aims to support family-shopping leisure and will open on the children's floor. とあり, これを言い換えた (B) が正解。

問題 159-160 は次の情報に関するものです。

世界的に有名なシェフが料理クラスを指導
Kulawy が North Dallas にスパイスを一振りします

Taj Mahal, Madras East, Curry Palace などの有名レストランの 72 歳のオーナー, Ranjit Kulawy さんが, 2 月 19 日に North Dallas コミュニティーセンターで料理クラスを開きます。クラスは一般公開されます。このクラスでは, インド料理, 特にカレー, ナン, タンドリーチキンに焦点を当てます。Kulawy さんは参加者に, ほうれん草, 豆（ダール）, そして野菜（トマトベース）の 3 種類の異なるカレーの作り方の基本を教える予定です。サンアントニオの住人で徹底したベジタリアンである Kulawy さんは, 9 歳のときに, 自分が生まれたムンバイで料理を始めました。彼は世界中のレストランで働き, パリ, ロンドン, ベルリン, モスクワ, カイロ, 東京, 北京, ロサンゼルス, ヒューストン, メキシコシティー, そしてリオデジャネイロなどの都市にある 100 以上の店のオーナーとなりました。

語句
- □ focus on ~　~に焦点を当てる
- □ cuisine　名 料理
- □ spinach　名 ほうれん草
- □ dal　名 ダール豆

159. According to the information, what kind of event takes place on February 19?

情報によると，どんなイベントが 2 月 19 日にありますか。

(A) A table manners course
(B) A travel orientation
(C) A spice trade fair
(D) A culinary lesson

(A) テーブルマナーの講座
(B) 旅行のオリエンテーション
(C) 香辛料の見本市
(D) 料理のレッスン

正解：(D)

● 着眼点！ 見出しからジャンルを見抜け！

レベル ★★★☆

解説　イベントのジャンルは，見出しを見れば OK。WORLD-RENOWNED CHEF TO LEAD COOKING CLASS とあるので，世界的に有名なシェフの料理教室だとわかる。さらに本文冒頭で，Mr. Ranjit Kulawy, ... will be holding a cooking class on February 19 と書かれている。ここから（D）を選ぼう。難しいのは正解の選択肢中の語 culinary「料理の」だが，上記から主題がわかっていれば，消去法でも容易に解答できる。

語句　□ culinary　形 料理の

---

160. Where does Mr. Kulawy live?

Kulawy さんはどこに住んでいますか。

(A) San Antonio
(B) Houston
(C) Dallas
(D) Mumbai

(A) サンアントニオ
(B) ヒューストン
(C) ダラス
(D) ムンバイ

正解：(A)

● 着眼点！ 地名は曲者！　あせってはダメ！

レベル ★☆☆☆

解説　地名問題はひっかけが多い。ここでは Kulawy さんが「どこに住んでいるか」が問われているので，「住む」に関連するワードに注意してリーディングしよう。本文中盤，(Being) A resident of San Antonio and a strict vegetarian, Mr. Kulawy began cooking ... とある。Kulawy さんは San Antonio の住人なので，正解は（A）。

問題 161-163 は次のメモに関するものです。

メモ

発信者：人事部 Rickey Sanchez
宛先：Ostox 社全従業員
日付：10月12日
件名：フードドライブ

来週フードドライブを行います！ 今回のテーマは，「Fall Bounty」です。集められた食料や品物は，地元のフードバンク World Without Hunger（WWH）に寄付されます。WWH の代表 John Wiley 氏は，野菜やスープの缶詰，プリンター用紙と食器用洗剤が特に必要だと告げました。
来週の月曜日までに，横断幕と寄贈品のための回収ボックスを各部に設置する人手が数名必要です。イベントの準備のお手伝いをしてくださる方は給与課の Melanie までお申し出ください。

[語句]
☐ food drive　フードドライブ（食料を提供する慈善活動）
☐ bounty　[名] 気前のよさ，恵み深さ，賞金
☐ food bank　フードバンク（困窮者に食料を提供する施設）
☐ banner　[名] 横断幕，垂れ幕

161. What is the main topic of the memo?　メモの主な内容は何ですか。

(A) An all-staff meeting
(B) A welfare activity
(C) A cooking event
(D) A new company rule

(A) 全従業員会議
(B) 慈善活動
(C) 料理イベント
(D) 新しい会社規則

正解：(B)

●着眼点！　冒頭をしっかり読もう！

レベル ★★☆

[解説]「件名」に Food Drive とあるが，慌ててはダメ。本文の冒頭を読めば，これがチャリティー・イベントだとわかる。第1段落・2文目 the collected foods and goods will be donated「食料品や品物を集めて寄付する」がポイント。これを言い換えた，(B) が正解。

[語句]　☐ welfare　[名] 福利，福祉

258

162. Who is John Wiley? John Wiley とはだれですか。

(A) A manager of a HR department
(B) A head of an organization
(C) A clerk at a local bank
(D) An owner of a grocery store

(A) 人事部長
(B) 組織の長
(C) 地元の銀行員
(D) 食料雑貨店主

正解：(B)

● 着眼点！ カンマの後ろを見よ！

レベル ★☆☆☆

解説　設問キーワード John Wiley をサーチしよう。本文中盤で，John Wiley, the head of WWH とある。「人名，役職名」の並びがポイント。カンマの後ろにヒントがある。ここから（B）を選ぼう。

語句　□ clerk 名 フロント係，店員　□ grocery 名 食料雑貨店，（複数形で）食料雑貨類

---

163. What is NOT requested by World Without Hunger? World Without Hunger が要望していないものは何ですか。

(A) Housekeeping items
(B) Stationery
(C) Used clothing
(D) Preserved foods

(A) 家事用品
(B) 文房具
(C) 古着
(D) 保存食

正解：(C)

● 着眼点！ 「並列」箇所を見抜け！

レベル ★★☆☆

解説　選択肢の 4 つの項目をサーチする際，「A, B, and C」のような「並列」箇所を探そう。第 1 段落・3 文目，especially in need of canned vegetables and soup, printer paper, and dish soap から，順に（D）「保存食」である野菜・スープの缶詰，（B）「文房具」であるプリンター用紙，（A）「家事用品」である食器用洗剤をチェック。（C）「古着」のみ記されておらず，これが正解。

問題 164-166 は次のお知らせに関するものです。

Prima Trading 社
Prima タワー
520 番地　10 番街
New York 市
New York 州　10018

Prima スーパーマーケットご利用のお客様へ！

弊社全 310 店舗でご利用いただけるポイントカードを導入いたします。現在ご加入いただきますと，商品ご購入時に期間限定のダブルポイントが貯まります。

期間限定の特別サービスにつき，6 週間後に終了いたします。同封のリーフレットに詳細がございます個人情報取り扱い方針に同意いただけるようでしたら，用紙へのご記入をお願いします。「取引条件について」も同封されております。ご署名の上，プレミアム会員様用の付属の封筒にてご返送ください

☑　Prima ポイントカードの送付を希望します。
☑　個人情報取り扱い方針および取引条件についてを読み，同意します。

名前：　　Jenny Miller
住所：　　1355 Oak Tree 通り，Washington, 98109
電話番号：555-3111

署名：Jenny Miller

語句
- loyalty card　ポイントカード
- privacy statement　個人情報取り扱い方針
- leaflet　名 リーフレット，小冊子
- terms and conditions　取引条件

164. What is NOT mentioned in the notice?

(A) Number of stores accepting the card
(B) Design of the loyalty card
(C) Promotion period
(D) Extra points per purchase

お知らせに記されていないことは何ですか。

(A) ポイントカードが使用できる店舗数
(B) ポイントカードのデザイン
(C) 販売促進期間
(D) 購入品あたりの追加ポイント

正解：(B)

● **着眼点！** NOT 問題に慣れよう！　レベル ★★☆☆

解説　NOT 問題は，(A) から順にサーチして解こう。キーワード・サーチは慣れれば簡単。(A)「店舗数」は第 1 段落・1 文目にある。(D)「追加ポイント」は，同じく 2 文目に DOUBLE POINTS と大文字で強調されている。(C)「販売促進期間」も，第 2 段落・1 文目に This is a limited offer and will end in 6 weeks.「6 週間後に終了」とあるので除外できる。よって，消去法で正解は (B)。

語句
- per 〜　前 〜につき，〜あたり

165. What does Prima Trading Co. ask customers to do?

(A) Send back a signed form
(B) Check its website for promotional codes
(C) Renew membership
(D) Write down current points

Prima Trading 社は顧客に何をするようお願いしていますか。

(A) 署名した書類を送り返す。
(B) ウェブサイトでキャンペーンコードを調べる。
(C) メンバーシップを更新する。
(D) 現在のポイント数を記入する。

正解：(A)

● 着眼点！ 「お願い」 → Please をサーチ！

レベル ★☆☆☆

〔解説〕 会社の「お願い（要望）」が問われている。Please 〜や Would you 〜をサーチしよう。第2段落・4文目に Please sign and mail it back to us in the attached envelope とあるので、この内容を言い換えた（A）が正解。（C）「更新」については紛らわしいが、第1段落・1文目に We are introducing our Loyalty Card 「ポイントカードを導入します」とあるため、本文の内容と一致しない。

---

166. What is implied about Jenny Miller?

(A) She is sending a complaint.
(B) She is signing up for the program.
(C) She is redeeming bonus points.
(D) She is getting novelties.

Jenny Miller についてどんなことがわかりますか。

(A) 苦情を送ろうとしている。
(B) プログラムに申し込もうとしている。
(C) ボーナスポイントを換金しようとしている。
(D) 販促商品を手に入れようとしている。

正解：(B)

● 着眼点！ 「人物」をサーチせよ！

レベル ★★★★

〔解説〕 設問キーワード Jenny Miller をサーチすると、お知らせの最後の部分に見つかる。名前の上にある2つのチェック欄にチェックをしていることから、ポイントカードへの申込希望者だとわかる。ここから、(B) が正解。

〔語句〕 □ novelty 名 (安価で、小さくて、珍しい) 商品、ギフト

問題 167-170 は次の E メールに関するものです。

送信者：Taisia Kaminski [Kaminski@archives-mg.com]
受信者：Louie Bombarger [Director@mg.com]
件名：企業アーカイブ
日付：1月31日

Louie へ

ここ数週間，アーカイブ部門が普通では考えられない大量の依頼を受領しています。添付のデータシートにありますように，一日あたり 70 件もの依頼を受ける日もあります。当部門ではこれらを処理するのに十分な人手がありません。

IT 部門の Jiro Zhao と話をしているのですが，彼はインターネット経由でだれもがアーカイブファイルにアクセスできるプログラムを考案できると思うとのことです。現状，情報資料が電子的にではなく物理的に送られていますので，この種のプログラムは，時間的にも労力的にも，利用者とスタッフの双方にとても役立つでしょう。さらに，資料を送付するための郵送料も大幅に削減できるでしょう。

他に緊急の懸案事項がなければ，木曜日の会議でこの件の詳細について話し合いたいと思っております。

よろしくお願いします。

Taisia Kaminski
アーカイブ部門
副部長

語句
- archive 名 アーカイブ，公文書，記録保存館
- personnel 名 人員，全職員
- come up with ~ （アイディアなどを）考え出す
- in terms of ~ ~の点について，~の立場から
- postage 名 郵便代，切手代，郵送
- pressing 形 差し迫った，しつこい

167. Why did Ms. Kaminski send the e-mail to Mr. Bombarger?

(A) To report a recent problem
(B) To describe an equipment malfunction
(C) To address an issue of the IT Department
(D) To complain about employee behavior

Kaminski さんはなぜ Bombarger さんにメールを送ったのですか。

(A) 最近の問題を報告するため。
(B) 装置の欠陥を述べるため。
(C) IT 部門の問題に取り組むため。
(D) 従業員の行動について苦情を言うため。

正解：(A)

着眼点！ メールの概要をつかめ！

レベル ★★☆☆

解説 メールの冒頭部分には必ず目を通そう。第 1 段落では，アーカイブ部門が大量の依頼を最近受けているが，人手が間に合っていないことが書かれている。つまり，部署の近況報告である。これを要約した（A）が正解。（C）は紛らわしいが，IT 部門の問題ではないため誤り。

168. What is mentioned about the Archives Department?

(A) It lacks funding.　(B) It is understaffed.
(C) It has safety concerns.　(D) It is overcrowded.

アーカイブ部門についてどんなことがわかりますか。
(A) 資金が不足している。
(B) 人員が不足している
(C) 安全性が懸念されている。
(D) とても混雑している。

正解：(B)

●着眼点！ 「言い換え」を見抜け！　レベル ★★☆☆

[解説] アーカイブ部門の近況は第1段落。3文目，Our department simply does not have enough personnel to handle these. から，人手が足りていないことがわかる。これを言い換えた (B) が正解。形容詞 understaffed の意味を知らなくても，under（未満で）＋ staff（人を配置する）から連想しよう。

[語句] □ understaffed 形 人員不足の，人手不足の

---

169. Who most likely is Jiro Zhao?

(A) A public servant　(B) A computer programmer
(C) A delivery person　(D) An administrative assistant

Jiro Zhao はだれだと考えられますか。
(A) 公務員
(B) コンピュータープログラマー
(C) 配達員
(D) 管理部スタッフ

正解：(B)

●着眼点！ 「職種」をイメージせよ！　レベル ★☆☆☆

[解説] 設問キーワードの Jiro Zhao をサーチしよう。第2段落・1文目に Jiro Zhao in the IT Department, and he thinks he can come up with a program とある。IT 部門で働いており，プログラムも考案できる人の職業としてふさわしい (B) が正解。

---

170. What will be the main advantage of the suggested solution?

(A) The public won't have to send requests for archive material by mail.
(B) The company will make money by charging the public.
(C) The Archives Department will have doubled staff.
(D) It will take only one day to physically send requested materials.

示された解決策の主な利点はどんなことですか。
(A) 利用者がアーカイブ資料について依頼を郵送する必要がなくなる。
(B) 利用者に利用料を課すことで会社が利益を上げる。
(C) アーカイブ部門の人員が2倍になる。
(D) 依頼された資料を物理的に送るのに1日しかかからなくなる。

正解：(A)

●着眼点！ 解決策を把握しよう！　レベル ★★★☆

[解説] 第1段落がアーカイブ部門の問題報告。第2段落がその解決策の報告である。1文目の a program which lets the public access the archive files through the Internet から，インターネット経由でアーカイブにアクセスできるプログラムの話が持ち上がったことがわかる。この利点については同じく2・3文目に，時間・労力・郵送料の削減が挙がっている。正解は (A)。(D) は紛らわしいが，インターネットの利用により郵送自体を止めるため×。

[語句] □ double 動 〜を2倍にする

問題 171-175 は次のメモに関するものです。

連絡メモ ― STEVENS & DOUGLASS 法律事務所
経営幹部より
全弁護士および職員へ

今年度の健康保険の補償範囲の変更に伴う従業員の新しいフィットネス奨励制度をお知らせします。

ご存じの通り，昨年，保険料見直しの結果，当事務所は健康保険会社を Ball State 社（20 年以上にわたって当事務所に保険を提供してきました）から Gotham Life & Equity 社に切り換えました。

Gotham Life & Equity 社は，従業員の 75％ 以上がスポーツクラブに参加し，週 3 日，1 日最低 30 分規則正しい運動を行っている会社には料金を 25％ 値引きすると発表しました。当事務所の最大のライバルである，Steele & Wiggins 事務所もすでに従業員の 80％ がこのプランに登録しています。

これを念頭に置き，私たちも事務所の全員と職員に Silver's Gym の会員権を半額で提供します。Silver's Gym は好都合なことに当事務所と同じビルの 15 階にあります。さらに営業時間も都合がよく，定休日なしで午前 5 時 30 分から午後 11 時 30 分まで営業しています。サウナと 25 メートルの室内プールに加え，Silver's Gym には個人トレーナーが居て，プロ用のウェイトリフティングやエアロビクス施設があります。

語句	
☐ insurance	名 保険
☐ coverage	名 補償範囲
☐ incentive	名 励み
☐ premium	名 保険料

171. What is the purpose of the memorandum?

(A) To encourage employees to exercise more
(B) To publicize an effective working policy
(C) To announce the merger with Steele & Wiggins
(D) To introduce the firm's newest client

連絡メモの目的は何ですか。

(A) 従業員がもっと運動するよう奨励すること。
(B) 効果的な労働方針を公表すること。
(C) Steele & Wiggins 事務所との合併を知らせること。
(D) 事務所の一番新しい顧客を紹介すること。

正解：(A)

● 着眼点！ メモの目的は冒頭！

レベル ★★☆☆

解説 連絡メモの目的は冒頭をチェックしよう。ここでもまず第1段落・1文目で the firm would like to announce a new employee fitness incentive と概要を伝えている。フィットネスを奨励しているので、正解は （A）。

語句 □ merger 名 合併

---

172. Why did the firm switch health insurance providers?

(A) It introduced a new system.
(B) It failed to reach a long-term agreement.
(C) It merged with a conflicting insurance company.
(D) It reconsidered payment for insurance.

なぜ事務所は健康保険会社を切り換えたのですか。

(A) 新しいシステムを導入したから。
(B) 長期契約の合意に至ることができなかったから。
(C) 競争相手の保険会社と合併したから。
(D) 保険料の支払いを再考したから。

正解：(D)

● 着眼点！ 「理由」をつかめ！

レベル ★★★☆

解説 保険会社を切り替えた「理由」が問われている。この件は、第2段落を見れば OK。as a result of reviewing the premium とあるので、「見直し」を言い換えた （D）が正解。

---

173. What is mentioned as an added benefit of the employee fitness program?

(A) Reduction in yearly electric bills
(B) Deducted premiums for implementation
(C) Lowered rates for regular health checkups
(D) Continuous increases in work-efficiency

従業員のフィットネスプログラムの付加利益として何が述べられていますか。

(A) 年間の電気代の削減
(B) 実行による保険料の控除
(C) 定期健康診断料金の減額
(D) 業務における効率性の継続的な向上

正解：(B)

● 着眼点！ 「利点」をサーチせよ！

レベル ★★★★

解説 フィットネスプログラムによる利点をつかもう。第3段落で、Gotham Life & Equity has

announced a 25% rate cut for companies ... がポイント。従業員が運動している会社の保険料は割り引くとあるので，正解は（B）。

[語句] □ deducted 形 控除された □ implementation 名 実行

---

174. In the memorandum, the word "competitor" in paragraph 3, line 4, is closest in meaning to

(A) entrepreneur
(B) interest
(C) rival
(D) administrator

連絡メモの第3段落・4行目にある competitor に最も近い意味の語は

(A) 起業家
(B) 同業者
(C) 競争相手
(D) 管理者

正解：(C)

● 着眼点！ 文脈から推測せよ！

レベル ★☆☆

[解説] 語彙問題は，文脈から解くのが基本。だが，即答できる時はためらわずにすぐ答えて，次へ行こう。**Our biggest competitor, Steele & Wiggins** とあるので，competitor と S&W 事務所は同格。よって，competitor「競争相手」に最も近い意味の語は，(C) rival。

---

175. What is NOT mentioned as a feature of Silver's Gym?

(A) Favorable opening hours
(B) Various course activities
(C) Accessible location
(D) Fully equipped facilities

Silver's Gym の特長として述べられていないことは何ですか。

(A) 都合のよい営業時間
(B) 様々なコース活動
(C) 行きやすい立地
(D) 豊富な設備のある施設

正解：(B)

● 着眼点！ 選択肢をサーチしよう！

レベル ★★☆

[解説] **Silver's Gym** については最終段落に紹介されているので，その部分と選択肢をそれぞれ比較検討しよう。(A) は **It operates in convenient hours as well**，(C) は **Silver's Gym is conveniently located**，(D) は **Silver's Gym has ... a sauna and a 25 meter indoor swimming pool** からわかるが，(B) については記述がない。よって，正解は (B)。

問題 176-180 は次の広告に関するものです。

Harrison's Vacation Ownership プログラム

Harrison's timeshare ownership システムで，毎年，一流の宿泊施設でのぜいたくな休暇を過ごしてみませんか。Harrison's 社は世界中に 30 余りの 5 つ星リゾートを所有し，それが今，あなたのものとしてお楽しみいただけます。バハマの清純なビーチからアジアのエキゾチックな目的地にいたるまで，「あなた自身の」家へと世界中を旅することができます。

Harrison's Vacation Ownership をご利用になれば，2 部屋または 3 部屋の寝室，美しいリビングダイニングルーム，完全装備のキッチン，大型のバスタブ／シャワーブース付きの 2〜3 のバスルーム完備のゴージャスなヴィラに滞在する権利を入手できます。ほとんどのヴィラには，眺めがよく，家族でバーベキューをするのにも十分な広さのバルコニーが付いています。寝室 2 つのヴィラで，6〜8 人の方が快適にお泊まりいただけます。狭苦しいホテルの部屋のことは忘れてください。あなたとご家族の皆さんは，ゆったりとしたスペースの中で，私どもの質の高いサービスを受けながら，夢のような休暇をお楽しみいただけるのです。もちろん，リゾート内にあるホテルの施設とサービスはすべてご利用いただけます。

タイムシェアでは，将来の休暇費用を前払いすることになります。ですから，将来，ホテルの料金の変動に関係なく，一定額を提示されます。タイムシェアでは，お好きな目的地 2 カ所に最低でも 1 週間ずつ滞在するプランからご用意しております。

詳しくは，弊社のウェブサイトをご覧いただくか，**1-800-555-8888** までお電話ください。

語句
- □ destination 名 目的地
- □ oversize 形 特大の
- □ house 動 〜を泊める
- □ cramped 形 狭苦しい，窮屈な
- □ pamper 動 〜を甘やかす，満足させる
- □ constant 形 一定の
- □ irrespective of 〜 〜に関係なく

176. What is the main purpose of this advertisement?

広告の主な目的は何ですか。

- (A) To draw readers to relaxing spas
- (B) To propose a long stay vacation to readers
- (C) To promote outdoor lodges on the beach
- (D) To guide readers in housing renovation

- (A) 快適なスパに読者をひきつけること。
- (B) 読者に長期休暇を提案すること。
- (C) ビーチにある戸外の宿について宣伝すること。
- (D) 読者に家の改装について案内すること。

正解：(B)

●着眼点！ 何の広告かをつかめ！

レベル ★★★☆

[解説] 広告は，見出しと冒頭チェックが基本。ここでは冒頭，Experience a luxurious vacation … with Harrison's timeshare ownership system. に注目しよう。timeshare ownership の広告であることがわかる。この部分が押さえられていれば，(A)，(C)，(D) をすべて除外できる。また Harrison's timeshare ownership system については第3段落・最終文に Timeshares start at a minimum of one week each at two exciting destinations of your choice. とあり，2 カ所のリゾートを最低でも一週間以上利用できることがわかる。(B) が正解。

---

177. According to the advertisement, what is Harrison's?

広告によると，Harrison's 社とは何ですか。

- (A) A hospitality enterprise
- (B) A charter flight service
- (C) A real estate agent
- (D) A film production company

- (A) サービス業の企業
- (B) チャーター機サービス
- (C) 不動産業者
- (D) 映画制作会社

正解：(A)

●着眼点！ 会社の「業種」をチェック！

レベル ★★★☆

[解説] どんな会社かが問われているので，「業種」を示すキーワードを探そう。第1段落・2文目に Harrison's has over 30 five-star resorts around the world, and now, they are yours to enjoy. とあることから，リゾート会社とわかる。これを言い換えた (A) が正解。

---

178. What is indicated about the accommodation?

宿泊施設について何が示されていますか。

- (A) A luxurious twin room at a hotel resort
- (B) A comfortable apartment near the city center
- (C) A first-class condominium
- (D) A multiple-room villa

- (A) リゾートホテルのぜいたくなツインルーム
- (B) 都市の中心部に近い快適なアパート
- (C) 高級コンドミニアム
- (D) 部屋数の多いヴィラ

正解：(D)

●着眼点！ ホテル情報は出る！

レベル ★★☆☆

| 解説 | ホテルの部屋についての詳細は定番の設問。選択肢を「タテ読み」して，広告をしっかり読もう。すると，(A) hotel，(B) apartment，(C) condominium については述べていないことがわかる。文中で説明があるのは gorgeous 2- or 3-bedroom villas のことのみなので，正解は (D) となる。

---

179. What is NOT true about Harrison's Vacation Ownership Program?

Harrison's Vacation Ownership プログラムについて正しくないものは何ですか。

(A) It targets families and large groups.
(B) It is a package deal of hotels and meals.
(C) It requires payment in advance.
(D) It offers rooms in many destinations.

(A) 家族や大きい団体を対象にしている。
(B) ホテルと食事がセットの一括商品である。
(C) 前払いが必要である。
(D) 多くの目的地で部屋を提供している。

正解：(B)

● 着眼点！ 関連ワードを素早くサーチ！

レベル ★★★☆

| 解説 | NOT 問題は選択肢と本文の比較検討が必要。選択肢のキーワードを素早くサーチして，正解を探そう。(A) は第2段落・5文目の You and your family can now enjoy a dream vacation, (C)は第3段落・1文目の you will be prepaying for your future vacations, (D)は第1段落・2文目の Harrison's has over 30 five-star resorts around the world, and now, they are yours to enjoy. がヒント。(B) については記載がないので，これが正解。

---

180. What does the advertisement say about the advantages of timeshare?

この広告ではタイムシェアの長所は何だと言っていますか。

(A) Flexible check-out times
(B) Flat room rates any time
(C) Extra bonus points every stay
(D) No cancellation fees

(A) 融通の利くチェックアウトの時間
(B) 一定額の部屋料金
(C) 滞在ごとのボーナスポイント
(D) キャンセル料の免除

正解：(B)

● 着眼点！ 「プラス」の情報を探せ！

レベル ★★★★

| 解説 | タイムシェアにはどんな利点があるのかをサーチしよう。「プラス」の情報を探すと，第3段落・2文目に you will receive constant rates, irrespective of any changes in room rates in the future とあることから (B) が正解。「商品の説明」→「商品の利点」という文章の流れをつかもう。

問題 181-185 は次の旅程表とEメールに関するものです。

I-Electronics 社
副社長 Michael Corwin 様 旅程表

Mike，香港へようこそ！　私たちの最新の工場に出張でいらっしゃるのを一同お待ちしています。以下の旅程表をご覧ください。東京での夕食も含めて，スケジュールはすべて手はずを整えています。日本の取引先についてのさらなる詳細については，**I-Electronics Tokyo** 社の **Nami Uchida** 人事部長にお問い合わせください。
何か変更を加えたい場合は，私までお気軽にご連絡ください。
(t_huang@iehongkong.com)

月曜日：
午後7時　香港国際空港に到着
　　　　　　シャトルバスで **New Pearl** ホテルへ
火曜日：
午前9時15分　**Kwun Tong** 工業センターに工場訪問
　　　　　　工場長の **Fang** さんが施設をご案内します。
午後4時　I-Electronics Hong Kong 社の副社長 **Liu** さんがラウンジまでお迎えいたします。
　　　　　　夕方の晩餐会（場所未定）まで，私ども一同と **Kowloon** オフィスで簡単な打ち合わせを行います。
水曜日：
午前7時15分　シャトルバスで，香港国際空港へ
　　　　　　東京へ向けて発
午前11時20分　新東京国際空港（成田）に到着
　　　　　　シャトルバスで，**Shinjuku Central** ホテルへ
午後3時　**I-Electronics Tokyo** 社を訪問
　　　　　　Nami Uchida 人事部長がロビーでお出迎えをし，いらっしゃる予定のお客様について簡単にご説明いたします。
午後6時　**Shabu Matsumoto** で **Horikoshi Metals** 社の方々と夕食

木曜日：
　　　　　　プライベートな時間
金曜日：
午後4時　シャトルバスで成田空港へ
　　　　　　L.A. に向けて発

Thomas Huang 作成
I-Electronics Hong Kong 社 秘書

宛先：Thomas Huang <t_huang@iehongkong.com>
送信者：Michael Corwin <m_corwin@ieamerica.com>
件名：旅程表
日付：6月8日

Thomas さんへ

スケジュールをお送りいただきありがとうございます。いくつかお願いしたい修正を除いて，完璧だと思います。ところで，あなたにご紹介いただいたおかげで，**Uchida** さんとお話しすることができました。もう

東京での私の方での手配もすべて整っています。

日曜の夕方に香港に到着し，月曜に観光の時間を取りたいと思います。妻の **Karen** が同伴しておりますことを覚えておいてください。**Karen** は商用で来るのではありませんが，**I-Electronics** 社の職員でもあります。彼女も晩餐会に参加でき，お近づきになっていただければ，とてもありがたく思います。

話は変わりますが，私の携帯電話は国際間でつながるはずなので，**+1-310-555-0987** でご連絡いただけます。

会合でお会いできるのを楽しみにしています。

敬具

Michael

語句
- connection 名 取引先
- banquet 名 晩餐会
- brief 動 ～に要点を話す，事前に必要な指示を与える
- prospective 形 見込みの

---

181. Why will Mr. Corwin visit Hong Kong?

Corwin さんはなぜ香港を訪れるのですか。

(A) To perform a yearly audit
(B) To negotiate a project launching
(C) To look around the latest plant
(D) To discuss restructuring worldwide operations

(A) 年次の監査を実施するため。
(B) プロジェクトの立ち上げについて交渉するため。
(C) 最新の工場を見て回るため。
(D) 世界規模の事業の再構築を議論するため。

正解：(C)

● **着眼点！** 旅程表のリードに注目せよ！

レベル ★★☆☆

解説 旅程表のリード部分に注目。冒頭に **Welcome back to Hong Kong, Mike! We all are waiting for your official visit to our newest factory.** とあることから，Corwin さんは最新の工場の視察が目的で香港を訪れるのだとわかる。これに一致する内容の選択肢は (C)。

---

182. Where will the banquet take place?

晩餐会はどこで開かれますか。

(A) At New Pearl Hotel
(B) At Mr. Liu's home
(C) At Shabu Matsumoto
(D) Undecided

(A) New Pearl ホテル
(B) Liu さんの家
(C) Shabu Matsumoto
(D) まだ決まっていない。

正解：(D)

● **着眼点！** キーワードを素早くサーチ！

レベル ★★☆☆

解説 設問キーワード **banquet** をサーチしよう。旅程表の火曜日に **an evening banquet (location to be determined)** と記載されている。つまり，会場はこれから決める＝まだ決まっていない，ということなので (D) が当てはまる。

183. According to the e-mail, what will change in the itinerary?

E メールによると，旅程表の何が変わりますか。

(A) The attendee　(B) The arrival date
(C) Contact information　(D) The return date

(A) 参加者　(B) 到着日
(C) 連絡先　(D) 帰国日

正解：(B)

● 着眼点！　変更点は出る！

レベル ★★★★

解説　クロスリファレンス問題。まず，E メールを見て変更点を探そう。第 2 段落・1 文目で We would like to be in Hong Kong Sunday evening and take time for sightseeing Monday. とあり，日曜日の到着後，月曜に観光がしたいと書かれている。旅程表には，月曜に香港到着とあるので，スケジュールの変更を希望しているとわかる。よって，正解は (B)。妻の同伴は旅程表に記載の行事には影響しないので，(A) は×。

---

184. What is suggested about Mr. and Mrs. Corwin?

Corwin さん夫妻についてどんなことがわかりますか。

(A) They want to participate in the factory tour.
(B) They would like to attend the company meeting.
(C) They want to socialize at the dinner party.
(D) They need guides in Hong Kong.

(A) 工場見学に参加したい。
(B) 株主総会に出席したい。
(C) 晩餐会で交流したい。
(D) 香港でのガイドを必要としている。

正解：(C)

● 着眼点！　「夫妻」がポイント！

レベル ★★☆☆

解説　設問で Mr. and Mrs. Corwin「Corwin 夫妻」とある点が重要。メールで Mr. Corwin の妻が言及されているのは，第 2 段落なので，そこを集中的に見れば OK。すると最後の文に I would greatly appreciate it if Karen could also join in the banquet so you can get to know each other. とあり，夫婦そろって晩餐会に参加し，交流を深めたいと希望していることがわかる。正解は，これを言い換えた (C)。

---

185. On what day does Mr. Corwin say he will see Mr. Huang?

Corwin さんは何曜日に Huang さんに会うと言っていますか。

(A) Sunday　(B) Monday
(C) Tuesday　(D) Wednesday

(A) 日曜日　(B) 月曜日
(C) 火曜日　(D) 水曜日

正解：(C)

● 着眼点！　クロスリファレンスを活用せよ！

レベル ★★★☆

解説　まず，Corwin さんのメールを見よう。E メールの最後に，I look forward to seeing you at the meeting. とある。meeting を頼りに旅程表をサーチ。すると，旅程表の火曜日に A briefing with us at our Kowloon office とあるので，この時に会うことがわかる。したがって，(C) が正解。クロスリファレンス問題は，「曜日」に関するものが多い。

問題 186-190 は次の 2 通の手紙に関するものです。

6月25日
Frank Richardson 博士
眼科医
Florentine 総合病院

Richardson 博士

9月に行う健康セミナーのゲストスピーカーとして，先生をお招きしたく思います。こちらは 9月15日 (金) 午後 1 時から午後 3 時まで Merlton ホテルの Rose Ballroom で開催されます。このイベントには 100 人以上の大勢の人が集まると思われます。

First Sports 社はミネソタ州で最も大きなフィットネスセンターの一つで，理学療法とリハビリテーションの施術をする認可を受けております。登録会員数は 500 名を超えています。健康的なライフスタイルを促進するという使命の一環として，当社では月に 1 度，健康セミナーを開催しています。

次回セミナーは「レーザー眼科手術」に焦点を当てており，David Hudson 博士より，先生にご連絡をするよう勧められました。Hudson 博士からは，先生がレーザー眼科手術に豊富な経験を持つ方であるということも教えていただきました。この話題について，1 時間ほどお話しいただき，会を締めくくりたいと思います。

通常，セミナーのテーマは私どもが事前に選んでおりますが，今回のこのテーマは私どものお客様にとって目下の関心事となっています。多くの方たちが，この処置について関心を示されていました。何人かの著名な運動選手がこの処置を受けているという最近の報道も，おそらく皆さんの関心を集めたものと思います。

最後に，9月のイベントにおける講演者になることをご承諾いただけましたら，大変光栄に存じます。スケジュールの都合がよろしくないようでしたら，お知らせください。前述の時間の範囲内で調整するよう誠心誠意対応いたします。

ご連絡，お待ちしております。

敬具

Stuart Harris
イベント・コーディネーター
First Sports 社

7月2日
Stuart Harris 様
イベント・コーディネーター
First Sports 社

Harris 様

6月25日付のお手紙をどうもありがとうございました。
そちらの健康セミナーについては Hudson 博士より伺っており，レーザー眼科手術についてお話しさせていただければ光栄に存じます。
しかしながら，9月15日は午後遅い時間のニューヨーク行きの飛行機に乗らなければいけないため，遅くとも午後 2 時 30 分にはホテルを出なければなりません。なんとかスケジュールを調整していただけますでしょうか。詳しい打ち合わせをするために，下記の番号まで私の携帯電話にお電話ください。
(054-555-2999)

敬具

Frank Richardson, 医学博士
眼科医

語句
- □ ophthalmologist 名 眼科医
- □ turnout 名（集会などの）参加者（数），出席者（数），動員
- □ certify 動 ～に資格を与える　□ physical therapy 物理療法，理学療法

---

186. How often does First Sports organize health seminars?

(A) Weekly　　　　(B) Monthly
(C) Annually　　　(D) Quarterly

正解：(B)

First Sports 社はどのくらいの頻度で健康セミナーを開催していますか。

(A) 1 週間に 1 度
(B) 1 カ月に 1 度
(C) 1 年に 1 度
(D) 3 カ月に 1 度

● 着眼点！「頻度」は頻出！

[解説] How often なので「頻度」問題。数字は基本的に言い換えを意識しよう。ここではセミナーに関する箇所をサーチ。最初の手紙の第 2 段落最後の文，As part of our mission to promote a healthy life-style, we host a health seminar once a month. を見れば OK。正解は (B)。monthly は，once a month の言い換え。

---

187. Who usually chooses the subjects for the health seminars?

(A) Customers　　　　(B) Event Organizers
(C) The general public　(D) Doctors

正解：(B)

いつもはだれが健康セミナーのテーマを選びますか。

(A) 顧客
(B) イベントの主催者
(C) 一般大衆
(D) 医師

● 着眼点！言い換えに反応せよ！

[解説] セミナーのテーマについて，該当箇所をサーチしよう。最初の手紙の第 4 段落に，While we usually select themes in advance とあり，この we は最初の手紙を書いている Stuart Harris が所属する First Sports だとわかる。正解は (B)。テーマをサーチする際，subjects = themes の言い換えを見抜こう。

---

188. What does Mr. Harris think caused the increased interest in laser eye surgery?

(A) Broad insurance coverage, including the surgery
(B) Recent approval by a government body
(C) Increases in the number of qualified ophthalmologists
(D) Reports on famous sports players having the operation

Harris さんはどんなことがレーザー眼科手術への関心を増大させたと思っていますか。

(A) 手術を含む手厚い保険補償
(B) 最近の政府機関の認可
(C) 手術を行う資格のある眼科医数の増大
(D) 多くの著名な運動選手たちがこの処置を受けたという報道

正解：(D)

● 着眼点！　レーザー手術への「関心」をサーチせよ！

解説　laser eye surgery というトピックを選んだ動機が述べられている，最初の手紙の第4段落に注目。2文目に Recent reports on some well-known athletes who have undergone this procedure may perhaps draw everyone's attention to it. とある。ここから，多くのアスリートが手術を受けたことがわかる。draw everyone's attention → cause the increased interest の言い換えに反応しよう。正解は (D)。

---

189. Why does Dr. Richardson write to Mr. Harris? / Richardson 博士はなぜ Harris さんに手紙を書いているのですか。

(A) To arrange the schedule
(B) To change the topic of the seminar
(C) To negotiate the fee
(D) To recommend another expert in the field

(A) スケジュールを調整するため。
(B) セミナーのトピックを変更するため。
(C) 講演料について交渉するため。
(D) その分野の別の専門家を推薦するため。

正解：(A)

● 着眼点！　博士の「要望」を見抜け！

解説　Richardson 博士の手紙を読むと，第2段落で would be honored to talk about laser eye surgery とあり講演のオファーを受諾している。しかし，第3段落・1文目で，however を伴って，提示された条件通りでは受けられない事情を説明している。その事情を読み取れば OK。遅くとも2時半までには会場を退出しなければならない旨が述べられている。(D) は本人が受諾しているので誤り。(B) と (C) については博士から特に何も述べていない。時間に関係する (A) の内容だけが手紙の趣旨と一致する。

---

190. What is suggested about Dr. Richardson's speech? / Richardson 博士の講演について考えられることは何ですか。

(A) It will be rescheduled to the morning.
(B) It will be held in a different location.
(C) It will be rearranged for a different day.
(D) It will be brought forward to the first half.

(A) 午前中に時間変更される。
(B) 別の場所で行われる。
(C) 別の日に再設定される。
(D) 前半に前倒しにされる。

正解：(D)

● 着眼点！　意外なヒントを見逃すな！

解説　Richardson 博士の都合を受けての相談は今後のことであるが，予測のヒントとなる文が最初の手紙の第5段落に見つかる。If there is a conflict with your schedule, please let us know. We will make every effort to rearrange things within the stated time period. とあり，Harris さんはおそらく時間内で博士の講演の時間を前倒しにすると考えられる。正解は (D)。(B) と (C) について，場所や日付の変更は申し出ていないため誤り。また (A) が紛らわしいが，あくまで午後1時から午後3時までの時間枠内での変更であるため不適切。

問題 191-195 は次の E メールと広告に関するものです。

受信者：habrams@lotmail.com
送信者：jgoldberg@tornioTA.com
日付：10月12日
件名：Re: 求職申し込み

Hafiza Abrams 様

契約社員の件で E メールにてお問い合わせをいただきましたので，ご回答いたします。**Ontario Daily** 紙に今朝掲載されていた求人広告を添付いたします。フレックスタイム制の職をお探しとのことですので，今回のいくつかの仕事にご関心を寄せていただけるものと思いました。

あなたの履歴書によりますと，以前 **Max Café** の接客係として勤務されていたのですね。カバーレターにこの職務経験について詳しくお書きになるとよいと思います。応募書類を書くにあたって支援が必要であれば，555-8966 番まで私宛にお電話ください。面談のお時間を決めましょう。

敬具
Joanna Goldberg
Tornio 人材派遣会社

El Vita ガラス美術館

El Vita ガラス美術館では現在，次の仕事で求人しています：
＜美術館＞
ツアーガイド
・お客様を館内全域にご案内します。現場研修があります。英語とスペイン語に堪能でなければなりません。他の外国語スキルはプラスになります。

＜美術館レストラン＆カフェテリア＞
宴会サービス係
・テーブル掃除やお客様に食事を提供します。さまざまなスケジュールが選べますが，週末や祝日の勤務があります。

厨房助手
・決められたレシピにしたがって，質の高い冷菜と温菜の調理ができなければなりません。3 年以上の職務経験が必要です。勤務時間は平日午前 11 時から午後 9 時までです。

＜美術館ギフトショップ＞
販売員
・現金での取引を取り扱い，お客様に製品の情報をお伝えします。優れたコミュニケーションスキルが必要です。ガラス製品に関する知識はプラスとなります。さまざまな勤務時間が選べます。

全従業員は開館時間中，美術館を無料で利用でき，美術館ギフトショップで割引が受けられます。

応募にあたっては，履歴書と給与要件をこちらまでお送りください。
郵便番号 **K7T 5A6**
オンタリオ州オタワ市 **Triton Square 243** 番
El Vita 美術館人事部　宛
または，**hr@elvita.org** までメールしてください。

語句
☐ flexible　形 融通の利く　☐ résumé　名 履歴書，要約
☐ elaborate　動 詳細に述べる　☐ cover letter　カバーレター，同封された説明の手紙
☐ duty　名 職務　☐ extensive　形 広範囲にわたる，大量の
☐ banquet　名 宴会，ごちそう　☐ prep cook　料理人見習い，厨房助手

191. Why did Ms. Goldberg send the e-mail?

(A) To respond to an application
(B) To apply for a part-time job
(C) To advertise an open position
(D) To help Ms. Abrams find employment

Goldberg さんはなぜEメールを出したのですか。

(A) 応募書類に返事をするため。
(B) アルバイトに応募するため。
(C) 欠員の職を公募するため。
(D) Abrams さんが仕事を探すのを手伝うため。

正解：(D)

● 着眼点！ Eメールの目的は冒頭をチェック！

レベル ★★★★

解説　冒頭からEメールの目的を読み取ろう。Eメールの第1段落・1文目 I'm responding to your e-mail inquiring about a contract worker. から，仕事探しに関する依頼に対する返信であることがわかる。よって，(D) が正解。(A) は紛らわしいが，Goldberg さんは「応募書類」を受理したのではないため×。

---

192. What does Ms. Abrams put stress on in her job search?

(A) Location
(B) Salary
(C) Job contents
(D) Hours on duty

Abrams さんが仕事探しで強調しているのは何ですか。

(A) 場所
(B) 給与
(C) 職務内容
(D) 勤務時間

正解：(D)

● 着眼点！ 仕事の「条件」を押さえて！

レベル ★★★☆

解説　Abrams さんの仕事の「条件」をサーチ。Eメールの第1段落・3文目 Since you are looking for a position that provides flexible working hours から，融通の利く勤務時間で仕事探しをしていることがわかる。つまり，(D) が正解。本文と選択肢で異なる言い回しや表現が使われていても，慌てずに正解の根拠を探そう。

語句　□ put stress on ~　~を強調する　□ on duty　勤務中の

---

193. What is mentioned in the advertisement?

(A) Applicants should call the Museum directly.
(B) All employees can receive complimentary food.
(C) Some staff may need to work on weekends.
(D) The institution provides external training programs.

広告ではどんなことが示されていますか。

(A) 応募者は美術館に直接電話をしなければならない。
(B) 全従業員には無料で食事が提供される。
(C) 週末に働く必要があるスタッフもいる。
(D) 施設は外部のトレーニングプログラムを提供する。

正解：(C)

> **着眼点！** 選択肢のキーワードをサーチ！　　レベル ★★★☆

解説 定番の mention 問題。慌てず，選択肢のキーワードをサーチしよう。(A) applicants，(B) complimentary food，(C) weekends，(D) training とそれぞれサーチすると，(A) は，広告文最後に，郵送または E メールで応募するようにあるので×。(B) は，従業員の「食事」ではないので×。(D)「トレーニング」については，Tour Guide の箇所に書かれているが on-site「現場」でのトレーニングなので×。(C) は Banquet Server の箇所で言及されているので正解。

語句 □ institution 图 施設，組織　□ external 形 外部の

---

194. According to the advertisement, what is required for the Tour Guide position?

広告によると，ツアーガイドの職には何が必要ですか。

(A) Linguistic proficiency
(B) Academic degrees
(C) Work experience
(D) Culinary skills

(A) 言語の習熟
(B) 学位
(C) 職務経験
(D) 料理の腕前

正解：(A)

> **着眼点！** 該当箇所に集中しよう！　　レベル ★★☆☆

解説 Tour Guide について述べた箇所をサーチし，選択肢を比較検討しよう。3 文目に Must be fluent in English and Spanish. とあり，英語とスペイン語に堪能であることが求められている。それを言い換えた表現の (A) が正解。

語句 □ linguistic 形 言語の　□ proficiency 图 技量，熟達　□ culinary 形 料理の

---

195. Which job will probably best suit Ms. Abrams?

Abrams さんにはどの職が最も適していると考えられますか。

(A) Tour Guide
(B) Banquet Server
(C) Prep Cook
(D) Sales Representative

(A) ツアーガイド
(B) 宴会サービス係
(C) 厨房助手
(D) 販売員

正解：(B)

> **着眼点！** クロスリファレンスを活用せよ！　　レベル ★☆☆☆

解説 クロスリファレンス問題。まず，Abrams さんの前職を確認しよう。E メールに waitress at Max Café とあるので，それに近いジャンルの仕事を「広告」でサーチ。週末・祝日勤務があるが，Banquet Server が彼女の希望に近いとわかる。よって，正解は (B)。

問題 196-200 は次の記事と E メールに関するものです。

市庁舎　風化損傷による存亡の危機

Costa Rosa, VI 発（6 月 15 日）　5 月 25 日, 市議会は保存計画を議論するため, 予備会合を開いた。経理担当者はその費用を 250 万ドルと試算したが, それは市の年次予算の 4 分の 1 を超すものである。議会メンバーたちはその費用を市が単独で負担するのは非現実的であるとした。

地元の学者たちは建物の文化的, 歴史的価値についての一連の会議を開催した。公文書保管人である Phillip Warhol は, Clairville 市庁舎の歴史的重要性を力説した。彼の表明した意見は学者間の議論の論調を代表しており, 象徴としての文化的記念建造物に焦点を当てている。

一方, その建造物とその近隣地域の再開発に対しての注目は少ない。街を行く歩行者の Rachel Gordon は再開発案を支持しているが次のように語った。「国内の他のたくさんの市がスポーツチームや娯楽ビジネス, そしてもちろんファッションブティックなどの誘致に成功しているわ。」

6 月 14 日, 市長は 6 月 26 日から市庁舎存廃に関する一連の会議に住民を招集することとした。地域住民は全員集会に自由に出席する資格があり, 意見を述べるよう促されている。議題や質問に関しては mayor_30@costarosa.vi までメールを送付すれば, Heath 市長が返信をする。

送信者：Robert Kendrick
宛先：Elizabeth Heath
件名：タウンミーティングへの専門家の参加
日付：6 月 18 日

Heath 様

私は Robert Kendrick と申します。Costa Rosa 美術館で絵画の専門家として働いています。ご参考までにお伝えしますが, この数日間, 当美術館で史跡保存のためのワークショップを開催いたしました。その成果として, 現在の Clairville 市庁舎の一件について一条の光を投じられることを願い, 保存に対しコスト効率の高い方法を研究しているプロの方を紹介させていただこうと思います。

Ming Wei Wang さんは, 今回のワークショップに参加したのですが, 彼女の西洋, 東洋両方の歴史的遺産に採用された保存技術においての経験は有名です。彼女は市庁舎保存計画について議論することに意欲を持っています。ベトナムでの彼女の携わったプロジェクトに Hang Seng の保存がありますが, 限られた予算内での質の高い仕事が評価されています。しかしながら, 彼女は新聞に記されていた要件を満たしていません。

そこで, 彼女が集会に出席して彼女の専門知識を我々と共有できるかどうかここにお尋ねしたく存じます。もし必要であれば, 彼女についての資料をお送りいたします。いずれにせよ, 時間が迫っていますので, できるだけ早いお返事を頂けると幸いです。

敬具
Robert Kendrick

語句
- city council　市議会
- preservation　名 保存
- preliminary　形 予備の
- budget　名 予算
- pedestrian　名 歩行者
- advocate　動 〜を支持する
- summon　動 〜を招集する
- eligible　形 資格がある
- heritage　名 文化・歴史的遺産
- expertise　名 専門知識

196. According to the article, what is the city's problem with its city hall?

記事によると，市が抱える市庁舎に関する問題は何ですか。

(A) Strong protests against preservation
(B) Remodeling city's monuments
(C) Financial limitations to its budget
(D) Delays in construction

(A) 保存に対する強い反対
(B) 市の記念建造物の改築
(C) 予算内での財政的限界
(D) 建設の遅延

正解：(C)

● 着眼点！ 「問題点」を見抜け！

レベル ★★★☆

[解説] 記事の見出しにある **City Hall** について，冒頭から，その **preservation plan** の議論だとわかる。問題点は第 1 段落に書かれている通り，250 万ドルとコストがかかること。2 文目以降に **more than a quarter of the yearly budget. Council members found it unrealistic for the city to cover the costs itself.** とあり，「コストが高く，予算内ではとても収まらず非現実的」とある。ここから正解は (**C**)。最初の段落だけで，スパッと決めよう。

---

197. Who most likely is Phillip Warhol?

Phillip Warhol はだれだと考えられますか。

(A) A council member
(B) An architect
(C) A representative of Costa Rosa
(D) A historian

(A) 市議会メンバー
(B) 建築家
(C) Costa Rosa 選出の国会議員
(D) 歴史家

正解：(D)

● 着眼点！ 名前の直後を見よ！

レベル ★★★☆

[解説] キーワード **Phillip Warhol** をサーチ。記事の第 2 段落で，**Phillip Warhol, an archivist, emphasized the history of Clairville City hall.** とある。**archivist** は「公文書保管人」。つまり，アーカイブの管理人である。歴史を扱うので，(**D**) を選ぼう。

---

198. In the article, the word "neighboring" in paragraph 3, line 3, is closest in meaning to

記事の第 3 段落・3 行目の neighboring に最も近い意味の語は

(A) traditional
(B) expansive
(C) adjacent
(D) subordinate

(A) 伝統的な
(B) 広範囲の
(C) 隣接した
(D) 下位の

正解：(C)

● 着眼点！ 単語はシンプルに考えよ！

レベル ★★★★

[解説] 語彙問題は文脈から解くのが基本。だが，それでも選べない場合は，単語をシンプルに考えよう。neighboring → neighbor「隣人，近所の人」から，「近い」イメージをつかもう。これに当て

はまるのは（C）。消去法でも選べる。

---

199. What is the purpose of the e-mail?

(A) To solicit support for the museum workshop
(B) To undertake construction work
(C) To promote new books written by experts
(D) To introduce an excellent authority in the field

E メールの目的は何ですか。

(A) 美術館のワークショップへのサポートをお願いすること。
(B) 建築工事を請け負うこと。
(C) 専門家によって書かれた新しい本を宣伝すること。
(D) その分野での優秀なエキスパートを紹介すること。

正解：(D)

● 着眼点！ E メールの目的は冒頭を読め！

レベル ★★★☆

解説　E メールの「目的」は，セオリー通り冒頭を中心に見よう。第1段落・3文目の I'd like to ～「〜したい」に目が留まれば正解を選択できる。I'd like to introduce you to a professional who has examined cost-efficient approaches in conservation, in the hope this will shed a light on the current Clairville City Hall issues. がポイント。「専門家を紹介する」とあるので，正解は（D）。

---

200. What is indicated about Ms. Ming Wei Wang?

(A) She does not reside in Costa Rosa.
(B) Her projects are highly regarded by Mayor Heath.
(C) She needs to work on the site in Vietnam.
(D) Her conservation plan was voted down by the council.

Ming Wei Wang さんについてどんなことが示されていますか。

(A) Costa Rosa の住民ではない。
(B) Heath 市長にプロジェクトが高く評価されている。
(C) ベトナムの現場で作業をする必要がある。
(D) 市議会により保全計画が却下された。

正解：(A)

● 着眼点！ 「人物」はクロス問題の定番！

レベル ★★★★

解説　「人物」と「曜日」は，クロスリファレンス問題の定番。ここでは，「E メール」の第2段落で，Ming Wei Wang が見つかる。その段落では，最後の文の However, she does not meet the needs reported in the paper. に注目。「彼女は新聞に記載の要件を満たしていない」とあるが，この要件とは何なのか「記事」に戻って見てみよう。「記事」の第4段落・2文目の All locals are welcome and eligible to attend the gatherings の箇所がその要件。よって，正解はこれを要約した（A）。他の選択肢について，（B）「プロジェクトの評価」は，Heath 市長が高く評価しているとは書かれていない。（C）「ベトナムでの業務」は過去の実績の一つ。（D）は，まだ保全計画について議論していないので誤り。

解答一覧

模試 1

Part5
- 101　B
- 102　B
- 103　C
- 104　D
- 105　B
- 106　D
- 107　B
- 108　C
- 109　C
- 110　A
- 111　A
- 112　C
- 113　C
- 114　B
- 115　D
- 116　D
- 117　A
- 118　B
- 119　D
- 120　B
- 121　D
- 122　C
- 123　B
- 124　B
- 125　B
- 126　A
- 127　D
- 128　B
- 129　B
- 130　C
- 131　B
- 132　C
- 133　C
- 134　C
- 135　D
- 136　D
- 137　B
- 138　B
- 139　D
- 140　C

Part6
- 141　B
- 142　D
- 143　C
- 144　A
- 145　B
- 146　B
- 147　B
- 148　A
- 149　B
- 150　B

Part7
- 151　A
- 152　D
- 153　C
- 154　B
- 155　C
- 156　A
- 157　C
- 158　D
- 159　D
- 160　B
- 161　C
- 162　C
- 163　D
- 164　D
- 165　C
- 166　D
- 167　A
- 168　B
- 169　A
- 170　B
- 171　C
- 172　B
- 173　B
- 174　C
- 175　D
- 176　C
- 177　C
- 178　B
- 179　D
- 180　A
- 181　D
- 182　A
- 183　C
- 184　D
- 185　A
- 186　A
- 187　C
- 188　B
- 189　C
- 190　B
- 191　C
- 192　A
- 193　C
- 194　D
- 195　C
- 196　B
- 197　B
- 198　A
- 199　C
- 200　B

模試 2

Part5
- 101　C
- 102　B
- 103　C
- 104　C
- 105　A
- 106　B
- 107　C
- 108　B
- 109　A
- 110　C
- 111　B
- 112　B
- 113　B
- 114　C
- 115　B
- 116　D
- 117　D
- 118　D
- 119　A
- 120　D
- 121　B
- 122　D
- 123　B
- 124　A
- 125　A
- 126　A
- 127　B
- 128　D
- 129　C
- 130　C
- 131　A
- 132　D
- 133　A
- 134　B
- 135　D
- 136　B
- 137　B
- 138　B
- 139　A
- 140　B

Part6
- 141　B
- 142　C
- 143　B
- 144　C
- 145　D
- 146　C
- 147　D
- 148　C
- 149　C
- 150　B

Part7
- 151　C
- 152　A
- 153　C
- 154　D
- 155　A
- 156　C
- 157　A
- 158　C
- 159　B
- 160　C
- 161　C
- 162　B
- 163　B
- 164　D
- 165　A
- 166　C
- 167　C
- 168　B
- 169　C
- 170　A
- 171　C
- 172　C
- 173　C
- 174　B
- 175　D
- 176　C
- 177　C
- 178　D
- 179　A
- 180　A
- 181　B
- 182　B
- 183　B
- 184　D
- 185　B
- 186　C
- 187　D
- 188　C
- 189　A
- 190　A
- 191　C
- 192　A
- 193　C
- 194　A
- 195　D
- 196　D
- 197　B
- 198　A
- 199　B
- 200　C

模試 3

Part5

#	Ans
101	A
102	C
103	B
104	B
105	C
106	A
107	A
108	B
109	B
110	C
111	C
112	B
113	A
114	C
115	D
116	D
117	A
118	B
119	C
120	D
121	B
122	D
123	C
124	D
125	C
126	D
127	D
128	B
129	D
130	C

Part6

#	Ans
131	A
132	C
133	A
134	B
135	D
136	B
137	C
138	C
139	B
140	A
141	B
142	C
143	D
144	C
145	C
146	D
147	A
148	A
149	D
150	D

Part7

#	Ans
151	D
152	C
153	C
154	C
155	A
156	C
157	C
158	A
159	B
160	D
161	D
162	C
163	C
164	C
165	D
166	A
167	C
168	D
169	A
170	A
171	C
172	B
173	C
174	A
175	A
176	B
177	A
178	A
179	C
180	C
181	D
182	C
183	B
184	D
185	B
186	A
187	C
188	D
189	B
190	D
191	B
192	B
193	C
194	D
195	B
196	B
197	B
198	A
199	D
200	A

模試 4

Part5

#	Ans
101	B
102	D
103	C
104	C
105	C
106	D
107	D
108	D
109	D
110	D
111	A
112	A
113	B
114	B
115	D
116	B
117	A
118	C
119	D
120	C
121	A
122	C
123	A
124	C
125	B
126	B
127	D
128	D
129	C
130	C

Part6

#	Ans
131	D
132	C
133	A
134	B
135	D
136	D
137	C
138	A
139	C
140	B
141	A
142	C
143	D
144	B
145	C
146	C
147	B
148	C
149	B
150	D

Part7

#	Ans
151	A
152	C
153	D
154	A
155	B
156	D
157	A
158	C
159	B
160	D
161	B
162	A
163	B
164	A
165	C
166	C
167	A
168	B
169	D
170	D
171	B
172	B
173	B
174	D
175	B
176	B
177	C
178	D
179	B
180	A
181	C
182	B
183	D
184	C
185	C
186	C
187	C
188	A
189	A
190	D
191	B
192	A
193	B
194	D
195	C
196	C
197	D
198	D
199	B
200	C

模試 5

Part 5
#	Ans
101	B
102	C
103	C
104	C
105	A
106	A
107	A
108	A
109	D
110	C
111	D
112	C
113	C
114	C
115	C
116	D
117	D
118	A
119	D
120	A
121	B
122	A
123	D
124	A
125	C
126	C
127	A
128	C
129	D
130	A
131	D
132	B
133	A
134	A
135	A
136	A
137	C
138	B
139	B
140	B

Part 6
#	Ans
141	A
142	C
143	B
144	B
145	B
146	C
147	A
148	A
149	D
150	D

Part 7
#	Ans
151	B
152	A
153	C
154	B
155	B
156	C
157	D
158	B
159	D
160	A
161	B
162	B
163	C
164	B
165	A
166	B
167	A
168	B
169	B
170	A
171	A
172	D
173	B
174	C
175	B
176	B
177	A
178	D
179	B
180	B
181	C
182	D
183	B
184	C
185	C
186	B
187	B
188	D
189	A
190	D
191	D
192	D
193	C
194	A
195	B
196	C
197	D
198	C
199	D
200	A

巻末ふろく

押さえておきたい！
TOEIC 頻出
単語 & フレーズ

　TOEICテストに頻出の単語・フレーズばかりを厳選しました。テスト本番までに，英語を見てパッと意味が言えるようになるまで繰り返し練習しましょう。

問題

次の単語・フレーズの意味を言ってみましょう。答えは右ページに！⇒

- [ ] 1 sign 動
- [ ] 2 candidate 名
- [ ] 3 independent 形
- [ ] 4 agent 名
- [ ] 5 evacuate 動
- [ ] 6 association 名
- [ ] 7 deal with ~
- [ ] 8 office supply
- [ ] 9 shareholder 名
- [ ] 10 update 動
- [ ] 11 competition 名
- [ ] 12 accountant 名
- [ ] 13 supervisor 名
- [ ] 14 immediately 副
- [ ] 15 benefit 名
- [ ] 16 offer 動
- [ ] 17 fuel 名
- [ ] 18 arrange for ~
- [ ] 19 personnel 名
- [ ] 20 designate 動
- [ ] 21 figure out ~
- [ ] 22 prize 名
- [ ] 23 transfer 動
- [ ] 24 merger 名
- [ ] 25 consultation 名
- [ ] 26 issue 動
- [ ] 27 submission 名
- [ ] 28 found 動
- [ ] 29 approximately 副
- [ ] 30 faculty 名
- [ ] 31 reconstruction 名
- [ ] 32 overview 名
- [ ] 33 sustainable 形
- [ ] 34 provide 動
- [ ] 35 facility 名
- [ ] 36 ongoing 形
- [ ] 37 entitle ~ to ...
- [ ] 38 preliminary 形
- [ ] 39 approval 名
- [ ] 40 conduct 動

答え

- [ ] 1 〜に署名する
- [ ] 2 志願者，候補者
- [ ] 3 独立した
- [ ] 4 代理人
- [ ] 5 避難する
- [ ] 6 つながり，関連性
- [ ] 7 〜を処理する，〜に対応する
- [ ] 8 事務用品
- [ ] 9 株主
- [ ] 10 〜を更新する
- [ ] 11 コンペティション，競技会
- [ ] 12 会計士
- [ ] 13 管理者，監督者，上司
- [ ] 14 ただちに
- [ ] 15 利益，福利厚生
- [ ] 16 〜を提供する
- [ ] 17 燃料
- [ ] 18 〜の準備をする
- [ ] 19 人事課
- [ ] 20 〜を指名する
- [ ] 21 〜を理解する，〜がわかる
- [ ] 22 賞品，景品
- [ ] 23 転勤する
- [ ] 24 合併
- [ ] 25 相談
- [ ] 26 〜を発行する
- [ ] 27 投稿，提出
- [ ] 28 〜を創設する
- [ ] 29 約，およそ
- [ ] 30 教授陣
- [ ] 31 再生，改造
- [ ] 32 概要
- [ ] 33 持続可能な
- [ ] 34 〜を提供する
- [ ] 35 施設
- [ ] 36 現在行われている，進行中の
- [ ] 37 〜に…する資格を与える
- [ ] 38 準備の，予備的な
- [ ] 39 承認
- [ ] 40 〜を行う，導く

次の単語・フレーズの意味を言ってみましょう。答えは右ページに！⇒

問題

- [ ] 41　potential　名
- [ ] 42　anticipation　名
- [ ] 43　state-of-the-art　形
- [ ] 44　thorough　形
- [ ] 45　decade　名
- [ ] 46　introduce　動
- [ ] 47　venue　名
- [ ] 48　sales figures
- [ ] 49　protection　名
- [ ] 50　reception　名
- [ ] 51　domestic　形
- [ ] 52　destination　名
- [ ] 53　recent　形
- [ ] 54　survey　名
- [ ] 55　extensive　形
- [ ] 56　expansion　名
- [ ] 57　advantage　名
- [ ] 58　establish　動
- [ ] 59　employ　動
- [ ] 60　encourage　動
- [ ] 61　device　名
- [ ] 62　extreme　形
- [ ] 63　circumstance　名
- [ ] 64　adjust　動
- [ ] 65　estimate　名
- [ ] 66　registration　名
- [ ] 67　procedure　名
- [ ] 68　manufacturer　名
- [ ] 69　merchandise　名
- [ ] 70　primary　形
- [ ] 71　handling　名
- [ ] 72　store　動
- [ ] 73　quote　名
- [ ] 74　contact method
- [ ] 75　overlook　動
- [ ] 76　cuisine　名
- [ ] 77　modestly　副
- [ ] 78　proceeds　名
- [ ] 79　enclose　動
- [ ] 80　renovation　名

答え

- [ ] 41　潜在能力，将来性
- [ ] 42　期待
- [ ] 43　最新技術の
- [ ] 44　丁寧な，完璧な
- [ ] 45　10年
- [ ] 46　〜を導入する
- [ ] 47　会場
- [ ] 48　売上高
- [ ] 49　保護
- [ ] 50　歓迎会，披露宴
- [ ] 51　国内の
- [ ] 52　目的地
- [ ] 53　最近の
- [ ] 54　調査
- [ ] 55　広範囲の
- [ ] 56　拡大，拡張
- [ ] 57　利点，強み
- [ ] 58　〜を設立する，確立する
- [ ] 59　〜を雇う
- [ ] 60　〜を促す
- [ ] 61　道具
- [ ] 62　極端な，極限的な
- [ ] 63　状況
- [ ] 64　〜を調整する
- [ ] 65　見積もり
- [ ] 66　登録
- [ ] 67　手続き，手順
- [ ] 68　製造業者，メーカー
- [ ] 69　商品
- [ ] 70　当初の，第1位の
- [ ] 71　手数料
- [ ] 72　〜を保管する，蓄える
- [ ] 73　見積額，引用文
- [ ] 74　連絡方法
- [ ] 75　〜を見おろす
- [ ] 76　料理
- [ ] 77　控えめに
- [ ] 78　収益
- [ ] 79　〜を同封する
- [ ] 80　改修，修繕，修復

問題

次の単語・フレーズの意味を言ってみましょう。答えは右ページに！⇒

- [ ] 81 check-up 名
- [ ] 82 agenda 名
- [ ] 83 perform 動
- [ ] 84 set up ～
- [ ] 85 accommodation 名
- [ ] 86 paycheck 名
- [ ] 87 register 動
- [ ] 88 property 名
- [ ] 89 annual 形
- [ ] 90 rules and regulations
- [ ] 91 distribute 動
- [ ] 92 in advance
- [ ] 93 investment 名
- [ ] 94 management 名
- [ ] 95 temporarily 副
- [ ] 96 unavailable 形
- [ ] 97 affect 動
- [ ] 98 agreement 名
- [ ] 99 preference 名
- [ ] 100 fulfill 動
- [ ] 101 souvenir 名
- [ ] 102 reservation 名
- [ ] 103 confirm 動
- [ ] 104 complimentary 形
- [ ] 105 pick ～ up
- [ ] 106 premises 名
- [ ] 107 valid 形
- [ ] 108 definitely 副
- [ ] 109 occupy 動
- [ ] 110 enhance 動
- [ ] 111 garment 名
- [ ] 112 repair 名
- [ ] 113 sufficient 形
- [ ] 114 expand 動
- [ ] 115 foundation 名
- [ ] 116 regardless of ～
- [ ] 117 period 名
- [ ] 118 confirmation 名
- [ ] 119 ship 動
- [ ] 120 considerably 副

答え

- [ ] 81 点検，検査，健康診断
- [ ] 82 予定，議題
- [ ] 83 ～を実行する，行う
- [ ] 84 ～を設置する
- [ ] 85 宿泊設備
- [ ] 86 給与支払小切手
- [ ] 87 ～を登録する
- [ ] 88 物件，資産
- [ ] 89 年間の
- [ ] 90 規定，規則
- [ ] 91 ～を配る，配信する
- [ ] 92 事前に，あらかじめ
- [ ] 93 投資
- [ ] 94 経営
- [ ] 95 一時的に
- [ ] 96 利用できない
- [ ] 97 ～に影響をおよぼす
- [ ] 98 協定
- [ ] 99 希望，優先事項
- [ ] 100 ～を果たす，かなえる
- [ ] 101 土産物
- [ ] 102 予約
- [ ] 103 ～を確認する
- [ ] 104 無料の
- [ ] 105 ～を迎えに行く
- [ ] 106 敷地
- [ ] 107 有効な
- [ ] 108 間違いなく
- [ ] 109 ～を占有する
- [ ] 110 ～を高める，強化する，増す
- [ ] 111 衣服
- [ ] 112 修理，修繕
- [ ] 113 十分な
- [ ] 114 広がる
- [ ] 115 基盤
- [ ] 116 ～にかかわらず
- [ ] 117 期間
- [ ] 118 確認
- [ ] 119 ～を出荷する
- [ ] 120 かなり，相当

問題

次の単語・フレーズの意味を言ってみましょう。答えは右ページに！⇒

- [ ] 121　prompt　形
- [ ] 122　alternative　形
- [ ] 123　refer to ～
- [ ] 124　secure　動
- [ ] 125　position　名
- [ ] 126　consumer　名
- [ ] 127　qualify　動
- [ ] 128　retail　名
- [ ] 129　reserve　動
- [ ] 130　salesperson　名
- [ ] 131　pay attention to ～
- [ ] 132　undergo　動
- [ ] 133　downsizing　名
- [ ] 134　rate　名
- [ ] 135　comparison　名
- [ ] 136　intense　形
- [ ] 137　voucher　名
- [ ] 138　dedicated　形
- [ ] 139　banquet　名
- [ ] 140　obtain　動
- [ ] 141　recognize　動
- [ ] 142　gratitude　名
- [ ] 143　apply for ～
- [ ] 144　notify　動
- [ ] 145　require　動
- [ ] 146　admission　名
- [ ] 147　award　動
- [ ] 148　designated　形
- [ ] 149　preserve　動
- [ ] 150　valuable　形
- [ ] 151　contribute　動
- [ ] 152　recognition　名
- [ ] 153　prior　形
- [ ] 154　grateful to ... for ～
- [ ] 155　organizer　名
- [ ] 156　compliance　名
- [ ] 157　review　動
- [ ] 158　expect ... from ～
- [ ] 159　handle　動
- [ ] 160　look over ～

答え

- [ ] 121 即座の
- [ ] 122 代替の
- [ ] 123 ～を参照する，問い合わせる
- [ ] 124 ～をしっかり閉める
- [ ] 125 役職，地位
- [ ] 126 消費者
- [ ] 127 資格を得る，適任である
- [ ] 128 小売り
- [ ] 129 ～を予約する
- [ ] 130 販売員，店員
- [ ] 131 ～に注意を払う，注目する
- [ ] 132 ～に耐える，～を経験する
- [ ] 133 人員削減，経営合理化
- [ ] 134 料金，価格
- [ ] 135 比較
- [ ] 136 極めて強い
- [ ] 137 クーポン券，割引券
- [ ] 138 献身的な
- [ ] 139 宴会
- [ ] 140 ～を得る，手に入れる
- [ ] 141 ～を表彰する，評価する
- [ ] 142 感謝の気持ち，謝意
- [ ] 143 ～に申し込む，～を申請する
- [ ] 144 ～に知らせる
- [ ] 145 ～を必要とする，要求する
- [ ] 146 入場料
- [ ] 147 （賞などを）与える
- [ ] 148 指定の
- [ ] 149 ～を保存する
- [ ] 150 貴重な
- [ ] 151 ～を寄付する
- [ ] 152 表彰，承認
- [ ] 153 前の，先の
- [ ] 154 …に～のことで感謝する
- [ ] 155 主催者
- [ ] 156 法令順守，コンプライアンス
- [ ] 157 ～を見直す，再検討する
- [ ] 158 …に～を期待する
- [ ] 159 ～を取り扱う，対処する
- [ ] 160 ～を調べる，ざっと目を通す

問題

次の単語・フレーズの意味を言ってみましょう。答えは右ページに！⇒

- [ ] 161 disposal 名
- [ ] 162 proposal 名
- [ ] 163 comply with ～
- [ ] 164 prefer 動
- [ ] 165 fill in ～
- [ ] 166 consultant 名
- [ ] 167 contribution 名
- [ ] 168 requirement 名
- [ ] 169 outstanding 形
- [ ] 170 achievement 名
- [ ] 171 reorganization 名
- [ ] 172 recommend 動
- [ ] 173 negotiation 名
- [ ] 174 consider 動
- [ ] 175 application 名
- [ ] 176 outlet 名
- [ ] 177 unveil 動
- [ ] 178 anticipate 動
- [ ] 179 subscribe to ～
- [ ] 180 forthcoming 形
- [ ] 181 donation 名
- [ ] 182 welfare 名
- [ ] 183 clerk 名
- [ ] 184 grocery 名
- [ ] 185 loyalty card
- [ ] 186 postage 名
- [ ] 187 understaffed 形
- [ ] 188 dispatch 動
- [ ] 189 insurance
- [ ] 190 connection 名
- [ ] 191 prospective 形
- [ ] 192 résumé 名
- [ ] 193 transaction 名
- [ ] 194 on duty
- [ ] 195 institution 名
- [ ] 196 proficiency 名
- [ ] 197 budget 名
- [ ] 198 pedestrian 名
- [ ] 199 advocate 動
- [ ] 200 preservation 名

答え

- [ ] 161　処分, 処理
- [ ] 162　提案, 計画
- [ ] 163　〜に適合する
- [ ] 164　むしろ〜の方を好む
- [ ] 165　〜に記入する
- [ ] 166　コンサルタント
- [ ] 167　貢献
- [ ] 168　要求, 条件
- [ ] 169　飛び抜けた, 極めて優れた
- [ ] 170　業績
- [ ] 171　組織再編
- [ ] 172　〜を勧める
- [ ] 173　交渉, 折衝
- [ ] 174　〜を熟考する, 検討する
- [ ] 175　申込書, 申請書
- [ ] 176　直販店
- [ ] 177　〜を公表する
- [ ] 178　〜を狙う, 〜を予測する
- [ ] 179　〜を定期購読する, 予約する
- [ ] 180　来るべき
- [ ] 181　寄付, 寄贈
- [ ] 182　福利, 福祉
- [ ] 183　フロント係, 店員
- [ ] 184　食料雑貨店, (複数形で) 食料雑貨類
- [ ] 185　ポイントカード
- [ ] 186　郵便代, 切手代
- [ ] 187　人員不足の, 人手不足の
- [ ] 188　〜を発送する
- [ ] 189　保険
- [ ] 190　取引先
- [ ] 191　見込みの
- [ ] 192　履歴書, 要約
- [ ] 193　処理, 取引
- [ ] 194　勤務中の
- [ ] 195　施設, 組織
- [ ] 196　技量, 熟達
- [ ] 197　予算
- [ ] 198　歩行者
- [ ] 199　〜を支持する, 提唱する
- [ ] 200　保存

監修者紹介

塚田 幸光（つかだ　ゆきひろ）

関西学院大学教授。立教大学大学院博士課程満期退学。
京都大学，神戸大学などでもTOEICテスト対策の集中講座を担当し，学生からの支持も絶大。
著書は，『TOEICテストPart7を1問1分で解けるようになる本』（小学館・共書），『TOEICテスト本番攻略 模試』（学研・共書），さらに大ヒットした『はじめての新TOEICテスト全パート総合対策』（アスク出版）など，多数。

高橋 基治（たかはし　もとはる）

東洋英和女学院大学教授。サンフランシスコ大学大学院修士課程修了。
専門は英語教育と第二言語習得。TOEICも含め英語関連の著書は30冊以上にのぼる。主な著書に『TOEICテスト「正解」のたねあかし』（小学館），『栄光の単語 TOEIC TEST リスニング編』（スリーエーネットワーク），『TOEICテストリスニング正解がわかるキーワード』（共著，コスモピア）など他多数。

編集協力	株式会社メディアビーコン
カバーデザイン	武藤一将デザイン室
本文デザイン	小林峰子
録音・編集	一般財団法人　英語教育協議会（ELEC）
ナレーター	Howard Colefield
DTP	株式会社四国写研
印刷所	株式会社　リーブルテック

落丁・乱丁本はお取りかえいたします。
© Gakken Education Publishing 2014, Printed in Japan
本書の無断転載，複製・複写（コピー），翻訳を禁じます。

TOEIC®テスト 600点攻略
リーディング 5回模試

模試1 …………………… 2
模試2 …………………… 34
模試3 …………………… 66
模試4 …………………… 98
模試5 …………………… 130

アンサーシート …………… 163

READING TEST

In the Reading test, you will be asked to demonstrate how well you comprehend written English. The Reading test is comprised of three parts and directions are given for each part. The entire test will last 75 minutes. Within the time allowed, you should answer as many questions as you can. You must mark your answers on the separate answer sheet provided. Do not write your answers in the test book.

PART 5

Directions: A word or phrase is missing in the following sentences. For each sentence, four answer choices are given below. Select the best answer to fill in the blank. You must mark your answer on the answer sheet.

101. If you cancel your order before installation, you ------- be charged.

(A) will
(B) will not
(C) would
(D) would not

102. The largest ------- in the area recently cut the jobs of 500 factory workers.

(A) employee
(B) employer
(C) employs
(D) employing

103. The company website will be unavailable to users on Friday, June 11th, between 11:00 P.M. ------- 2:00 A.M.

(A) or
(B) through
(C) and
(D) to

104. In the ------- of an accident, you must get a signed police report.

(A) course
(B) absence
(C) middle
(D) event

105. Any employees who have signed up can ------- in the dinner party next Friday.

(A) enter
(B) participate
(C) enjoy
(D) hold

106. DSA Pharmaceutical and Frontec Medical Corporation announced that they would ------- develop their new medicine.

(A) collaborate
(B) collaboration
(C) collaborative
(D) collaboratively

107. The presentation given by Joanne Keason, the sales manager, was very ------- for her subordinates.

(A) inform
(B) informative
(C) information
(D) informed

108. Candidates for teaching positions at AIS are expected to have at least a Bachelor's -------.

(A) certificate
(B) document
(C) degree
(D) grade

109. Tomorrow's weather will remain cloudy with a chance of rain ------- the day.

(A) across
(B) beside
(C) throughout
(D) into

110. If you want to ------- an independent agent nearest you, just click "Find My Agent" on the menu bar.

(A) locate
(B) decide
(C) talk to
(D) order

111. As a result of careful investigation, Ms. Wonder is ------- granted a license to operate a business in the neighborhood.

(A) officially
(B) official
(C) officer
(D) officiate

112. All recommendation letters should ------- separately in a sealed envelope.

(A) be placing
(B) place
(C) be placed
(D) placing

GO ON TO THE NEXT PAGE

113. The typhoon affected ------- 2 million people in China, with about 900,000 of them evacuated from their homes.

(A) as much
(B) mostly
(C) more than
(D) better than

114. ------- Ms. Chen's performance was indisputably excellent, she didn't get promoted.

(A) However
(B) Although
(C) With
(D) Nonetheless

115. Because of ------- association with an international banking scandal, Senator Bruno was questioned by concerned authorities.

(A) he
(B) him
(C) he's
(D) his

116. This new personnel evaluation method may help you assess ------- aspects of your employees' abilities.

(A) divert
(B) diversion
(C) diversity
(D) diverse

117. ------- you have any questions or comments about our products, please feel free to contact us anytime.

(A) Should
(B) Will
(C) May
(D) Must

118. A group of volunteers founded an NPO to support the unemployed and provide them with the ------- to live.

(A) income
(B) means
(C) wage
(D) talent

119. The Service Center is ------- for dealing with all inquiries and complaints from our customers.

(A) responsive
(B) responsibility
(C) response
(D) responsible

120. Because of an accident in the factory, TM Imports will not ------- new orders until further notice.

(A) processed
(B) be processing
(C) be processed
(D) processing

121. ------- to the success of their new line of office supplies, Abelco & Cain, Inc. shareholders enjoyed increased third-quarter profits.

(A) In addition
(B) Such
(C) According
(D) Due

122. Mr. Raymond P. Barlow is best known for his financial ------- to geophysical society.

(A) contribute
(B) contributed
(C) contribution
(D) contributing

123. I would appreciate your ------- me an updated copy of my account statement.

(A) send
(B) sending
(C) sold
(D) being sold

124. The chairman repeatedly emphasized the ------- of market trends in his speech.

(A) signify
(B) significance
(C) significantly
(D) significant

125. A world financial leader, Japan relies on oil-rich nations ------- Qatar for petroleum.

(A) even though
(B) such as
(C) already
(D) still

126. The president's speech focused on the fragile state of the economy, and he urged everyone to be ------- to make some sacrifices.

(A) prepared
(B) prepare
(C) preparation
(D) prepares

127. All members should actively take part in the discussion ------- we can improve our proposal before we take it to the competition.

(A) as if
(B) even so
(C) through
(D) so that

128. Tony Eagleton and Juan Dormirado, both high school students in Denmark, were honored last night for their volunteer work ------- behalf of the homeless.

(A) in
(B) on
(C) to
(D) for

GO ON TO THE NEXT PAGE

129. In an effort to reduce expenses, Whitman Film Co. has decided to halve its production ------- for the upcoming year.

(A) refunds
(B) costs
(C) rewards
(D) values

130. Instead of hiring an accountant, Ms. Iwata did her company's bookkeeping all by -------.

(A) her own
(B) her
(C) herself
(D) hers

131. Any expenditure ------- budget allotment should be reported to your supervisor immediately.

(A) toward
(B) beyond
(C) against
(D) within

132. The new air conditioner released last month has a special sensor that adjusts the room temperature and air volume -------.

(A) automatic
(B) automatically
(C) automate
(D) automation

133. Both the costs and the benefits should be considered ------- assess the effectiveness of the new inventory control system.

(A) as well as
(B) because of
(C) in order to
(D) as for

134. Environmentally friendly products are on the increase in many markets around the world, most -------, the U.S. and Japan.

(A) casually
(B) affordably
(C) notably
(D) worthy

135. The glasswork I received from Simon Jewellers Inc. was damaged, so I asked them to send me -------.

(A) the other
(B) one
(C) each other
(D) another

136. James Consulting Services Inc. offers ------- benefits programs to full-time workers, including dental coverage.

(A) attraction
(B) attract
(C) attracted
(D) attractive

137. These days, Magno Electronics has taken the ------ in dealing with the issue of a downturn in domestic demand.

(A) effective
(B) initiative
(C) incentive
(D) objective

138. The conference room ------- the panel discussion will be held is equipped with the latest computer technology.

(A) which
(B) where
(C) how
(D) when

139. Four earthquakes were ------- in the Greater Los Angeles Area last week and all occurred on Tuesday.

(A) happened
(B) given
(C) shaken
(D) felt

140. Catering to the rich, ------- of luxury resort hotels in Europe and the Caribbean has been on the rise.

(A) construct
(B) constructive
(C) construction
(D) constructor

GO ON TO THE NEXT PAGE

PART 6

Directions: A word or phrase is missing in sentences in the texts. For each sentence, four answer choices are given below. Select the best answer to fill in the blank. You must mark your answer on the answer sheet.

Questions 141-143 refer to the following memo.

To: All Branch Employees
Re: Annual Training Seminar

Due to the rising costs of fuel, we are arranging for branch staff transportation to the Annual Training Seminar several months ------- than usual. Someone in

141. (A) early
(B) earlier
(C) earliest
(D) earliness

personnel at each branch has been designated as the contact person. If you don't know who it is, contact the ------- of personnel at your branch to find out.

142. (A) lead
(B) charge
(C) front
(D) head

Training is required for all management level staff and ------- for other full time

143. (A) rational
(B) reasonable
(C) optional
(D) opposite

employees. Part time employees may only participate with special written permission from their supervisor. If there are any questions about eligibility, please speak with your immediate supervisor before contacting headquarters.

Questions 144-146 refer to the following article.

Do you ------- your lack of accomplishment on your habit of procrastinating? Do

144. (A) blame
(B) abuse
(C) praise
(D) attain

not feel bad, says an article by popular blogger Marvin Mansfield. In his latest entry, Mr. Mansfield writes that many of the most successful and productive people deal with the urge to whine about and avoid work projects every day. The difference between the chronic procrastinator and ------- who get to work is that

145. (A) them
(B) those
(C) one
(D) ones

the latter have figured out concrete tricks to get past TV watching, unneeded web surfing and daydreaming. One recommended method is to work on a task for ten minutes uninterrupted and take a two minute break (don't skip the break even if you feel like continuing). Do this five times and you'll ------- close to an hour of

146. (A) be
(B) have done
(C) have been doing
(D) have been done

productive work.

GO ON TO THE NEXT PAGE

Questions 147-149 refer to the following advertisement.

GRAND OPENING - NEIL'S BEACHFRONT NAIL SALON
4225 Ocean Avenue
Suite #12
Laguna Beach, California

Welcome to the Grand Opening of Neil's Beachfront Nail Salon! This week only, we offer you ------- on all nail art designs, as well as several prizes.
    147. (A) discount
        (B) discounts
        (C) to discount
        (D) discounted

For those of you who like Bubble Bunny, Captain Cod, and Ratman, we think you will be especially happy to hear our news. Believe it or not, all cartoon character nails will be at half price, ------- for finger and toe nails.
        148. (A) both
             (B) none
             (C) which
             (D) either

Also, the first one hundred men to come to the salon ------- a free nail art design of
                          149. (A) received
                                (B) will receive
                                (C) receive
                                (D) were received

their choice. We offer a variety of colors and sparkling rhinestones for men.

Questions 150-152 refer to the following letter.

Hummer Flax Inc.
18 Maple Ave.
Georgetown, VA

January 12

Dear Ms. Lund,

I received your request to transfer to our marketing division in Arizona. We are grateful for your ambition and enthusiasm to take on a challenge in a new environment.
Unfortunately, however, we have put a temporary freeze on hiring at the division, ------- our marketing department in Arizona is large in size and we usually recruit

150. (A) if
     (B) although
     (C) in spite of
     (D) since

most staff there. Our company is going ------- restructuring and consolidation of

                             151. (A) through
                                  (B) under
                                  (C) with
                                  (D) over

its organization due to a recent merger, and it hasn't been decided which position will be available yet. The availability of all positions will be ------- within 3

                                   152. (A) fixing
                                      (B) fix
                                      (C) to fix
                                      (D) fixed

months, so I would appreciate it if you could wait until then.
Thank you for your patience and interest in staying with the company.

Sincerely,

Bill Framer, Human Resources Manager

GO ON TO THE NEXT PAGE

PART 7

Directions: In this part, you are asked to answer questions based on a variety of texts, such as notices, e-mails, memos, and articles. Select the best answer for each question and mark your answer on the answer sheet.

Questions 153-154 refer to the following announcement.

BIAD
Consultation Seminar

Date: Monday, February 2
Place: Main Auditorium, Midway Art Center

The Boston Institute of Art and Design (BIAD) will host a consultation seminar for those who are interested in a career as a web designer.

On the day, the following questions will be answered:
- Where can I train to become a designer?
- What kind of financial support is available from the government?
- How do I advance my career once I complete my training?

Short individual counseling will also be available after the workshop.

153. What is being announced?

(A) A training opportunity for school consultants
(B) A workshop for experienced physicians
(C) An advice session for prospective designers
(D) A mandatory seminar for sports instructors

154. What information is NOT available at the event?

(A) Government support
(B) Job vacancies
(C) Training providers
(D) Career development

Questions 155-156 refer to the following article.

Reader's Review: Fox Mountain

The Fox Mountain Trail is good for both novice and experienced hikers. An overnight hike is possible with a permit. Rich in wild flower meadows and moss-ridden forests as well as beautiful foliage in Autumn, the area experiences heavy snowfall during the winter. Whitehill Lake is usually covered with snow and ice by November, presenting hikers with the danger of being on the lake without realizing it. Winter hikers should also be warned that the path descending from North Peak to West ridge is steep, and under heavy snow coverage, an ice axe is a must.

155. Where does the article most likely appear?

(A) In a road map
(B) In a company newsletter
(C) In an outdoor magazine
(D) In a scientific journal

156. What is NOT mentioned in the article?

(A) Overnight facilities
(B) Trail scenery
(C) Snow coverage
(D) Necessary equipment

Questions 157-159 refer to the following memo.

Dream Build

OFFICE MEMORANDUM

To: All Dream Build Staff
From: Peter Channing COO
Subject: Company Newsletter
Date: January 21

We have had many requests from staff for a company newsletter. We are pleased to announce that we will begin to issue a newsletter every other month. The following is a list of regular contents.

Top Stories: business news, company info, press releases
Employee News: promotions, new staff, job openings
New Products: innovations, staff ideas on products
Classifieds: anything to sell, items wanted
Spotlight: staff news and stories
Notice, Health & Safety: policy changes, health & safety tips

We urge all employees to contribute, so colleagues may well find your information valuable. According to a study, publishing a company magazine improves staff morale overall and arouses their interest in the workplace. We will hold a competition every 6 months for the best submission. The winner will get an invitation coupon from the Turin restaurant in town.

On a final note, we are also going to appoint a part-time editor. Consequently, we would really appreciate it if you could introduce a person interested in this position. If you know someone for the job, then contact Pamela Smith in the HR department by e-mail (smith-P@dream-build.com) or by internal phone at 175.

157. How often will the company newsletter be published?

(A) Every January
(B) Every month
(C) Every 2 months
(D) Every 6 months

158. Where will personnel transfers most likely appear?

(A) Top Stories
(B) New Products
(C) Classifieds
(D) Employee News

159. What does the company encourage employees to do?

(A) E-mail Pamela Smith
(B) Develop editing expertise
(C) Get coupons from a restaurant
(D) Write an article for a newsletter

Questions 160-162 refer to the following press release.

Major Chip Manufacturer Announces New High Speed Processor

By Harry Jonson
August 10

Portland, OR – Intelligent Chip has just announced the release of its latest high speed processor, using a completely new technology. Distribution of this cutting-edge processor will begin this week to all the major notebook manufacturers. Intelligent Chip company spokesperson, Iain Foster, reported that this brand new technology has taken several years to develop and that the benchmark test has proven it performs at up to 100 times faster than the current processors.

About Intelligent Chip Ltd. Intelligent Chip Ltd. has been in business for 29 years and was founded by the current CEO, Dave Stern, providing the computer industry with approximately 20% of all processors used in the world. The company expects that with the release of their new super-fast chip they will gain a larger share of the market. A miniature version of the same chip will follow next year. It has been developed specially for the rapidly changing mobile device market.

To learn more about this innovation, please contact:
Bill Murphy, Media Relations
1568 NW, Sandy Blvd. Ste. 300A
Office: (503) 555-5309
Fax: (503) 555-5609
murphyb@intelligentchip.com

160. What is NOT mentioned about the new product?

(A) Release time
(B) Sales price
(C) Development period
(D) Performance

161. What is true about Intelligent Chip Ltd.?

(A) Its founder has already retired.
(B) It makes a secret of its future plans.
(C) It anticipates an increase in the market share.
(D) It has recently entered the IT industry.

162. Who can provide more information about the new processor?

(A) Iain Foster
(B) Dave Stern
(C) Bill Murphy
(D) Harry Jonson

Questions 163-165 refer to the following schedule.

Schedule for Dr. Shreya Sen from Morgana University
August 1-4

Sunday, August 1	• 17:30 - Arrival at Denver International Airport and transportation to the St. Paul Hotel.
Monday, August 2	• 11:00 - Meeting with the faculty of Griffin University • 14:00 - Presentation of reforestation proposals by graduate students
Tuesday, August 3	• 9:00 - Transportation to Sanders • 11:30 - Lunch meeting with Sanders Forestry Association Director, Robert Kwon • 13:30 - Field trip to Redham forest where soil reconstruction activities are underway.
Wednesday, August 4	• 9:30 - 14:00 Visit to Blueridge paper mill. Manager Juan José will give a tour of the mill as well as provide an overview of Blueridge Co.'s sustainable forestry management schemes. • 15:30 - Transportation to Denver International Airport

163. Who most likely is Dr. Sen?

(A) A grounds keeper
(B) A factory manager
(C) A marine biologist
(D) A scientist

164. On which day will Dr. Sen take a factory tour?

(A) August 1
(B) August 2
(C) August 3
(D) August 4

165. What is suggested in the schedule?

(A) Juan José will pick Dr. Sen up at the St. Paul Hotel.
(B) Robert Kwon will visit Blueridge paper mill.
(C) Dr. Sen will meet other university professors.
(D) Graduate students will hear Dr. Sen's special lecture.

GO ON TO THE NEXT PAGE

Questions 166-168 refer to the following advertisement.

Wimhaven Tennis Club
Celebrating 100 Years

Have you ever dreamed of becoming a UK national tennis star?

The Wimhaven tennis club has been in business for 100 years, providing facilities to the international tournament circuit.

We are celebrating this year with a national tournament for tennis players of all ages from clubs in the British Isles. Some of our top seeded players and their coaches will be on hand to offer guidance and training during the tournament.

In addition, the National Tennis Association will offer the top 4 players a one-year schooling program with ongoing training from our professional coaches using our top quality facilities here in London.

Here at Wimhaven, we boast renowned grass courts for tournaments and practice.

To participate in the tournament, contact us through your own local tennis club.

Alexander Jones
Wimhaven Tennis Club
Wimhaven Avenue
London W15
020 555 4647

166. For whom is the advertisement intended?

(A) Young students wanting to be athletes
(B) Current Wimhaven Tennis Club Members
(C) Tournament officials
(D) Ordinary tennis club players

167. Who will offer tennis instructions during the competition?

(A) First-class professionals
(B) Retired star players
(C) Tournament winners
(D) Olympic medalists

168. How can people apply for the tournament?

(A) By sending an enrollment fee by post
(B) By asking their own club
(C) By becoming a Wimhaven club member
(D) By making a phone call to Mr. Jones

GO ON TO THE NEXT PAGE

Questions 169-171 refer to the following e-mail.

From:	customerservice@ortmart.com
To:	Jennifer Lowe<jlowe@yus.com>
Subject:	Silver Status Gift
Date:	June 24

Dear Member,

We thought you might like to know that we have begun shipping the Silver Status Gifts! We have hundreds of members who have reached the Silver Status this counting period, so it might take a little time -- if you don't get your order at the same time as your neighbors or friends, please be patient! We will send you another e-mail when your reward ships. All gifts will be shipped by July 10.

For those of you who did not reach the Silver Status during this counting period, please remember that the new counting period starts July 1! By earning over 10,000 points through shopping at our store between July 1 and November 31, you can earn Silver Status which will entitle you to the next Silver Status Gift!

We look forward to seeing you soon !

Vijay Khan
Manager
ORT Mart

169. What is the purpose of this e-mail?

(A) To inform that an item has been shipped
(B) To notify that a campaign term has changed
(C) To apologize for a change in the delivery date
(D) To congratulate a winner of a competition

170. What caused the shipment delays?

(A) Company holidays
(B) Many simultaneous deliveries
(C) Changes in the promotion goods
(D) Mistyped personal information

171. How can members reach Silver Status?

(A) By recruiting new members
(B) By contributing to the Web site
(C) By making large purchases
(D) By collecting stamps

GO ON TO THE NEXT PAGE

Questions 172-175 refer to the following memorandum.

November 30
To: Mr. J. Wyatt
General Manager, Human Resources Division
Power Net Co.
From: Paul Green
Peters & Lloyd

Dear Mr. Wyatt,

This is to update you on our ongoing search for someone to fill the position of director of your e-commerce department.
Currently, we have two candidates we feel meet your requirements. The following is a brief rundown of each.

1. Mr. Brian French, age 42
  - currently head of marketing division for a mail order company
  - residing in Orange County
  - MBA from Stapleton College of Commerce
  - was instrumental in expanding business to become the No. 1 mail order company
  - seems to be well liked among colleagues

2. Mr. Peter Matthews, age 36
  - currently vice president of an online store
  - residing in State County
  - MBA from Metropolitan University
  - created and developed the Bright brand which became one of the most popular among teenagers
  - known as a hard worker; worked his way up to his current position

This is only preliminary information. If you are interested in either of these candidates, we will directly approach them for more information with your approval. We have some inside information that Peter Matthews is currently looking for a new job. We know that he is a highly valued executive at the online store, but perhaps he is ready for a new challenge since he has been with this company for almost ten years.

We will continue to look for other suitable candidates but there are not that many executives living in this local area that meet your criteria. Both French and Matthews are professionals with excellent backgrounds and business experience.

Please let me know your thoughts on these candidates and how you want to proceed with this matter.

172. What kind of firm is Peters & Lloyd?

(A) Accounting house
(B) A head hunter
(C) A consulting firm
(D) An Internet service provider

173. What is NOT true about Mr. French?

(A) He earned a graduate degree in management.
(B) He is running a shop-by-mail service company.
(C) He lives in Orange County.
(D) He has a likable personality.

174. What is suggested about Mr. Green?

(A) He has worked with Peters & Lloyd over ten years.
(B) He has already contacted some other candidates.
(C) He highly values the two candidates.
(D) He is thoroughly acquainted with Mr. Matthews.

175. What will Mr. Wyatt most probably do next?

(A) He will lower the minimum hiring standards.
(B) He will raise the incentive for the position.
(C) He will interview the candidates.
(D) He will write Mr. Green back.

GO ON TO THE NEXT PAGE

Questions 176-180 refer to the following letter.

Copy and Print, Inc.

May 10
James Bryant
Flower Design Co.
515 Crest St.

Dear Mr. Bryant,

This is to inform you that the maintenance contract for your high-speed color copier (ID: CPS2000-5I4D) will expire on June 30. We would like to suggest that you renew the contract to keep your copier running smoothly. Please send us the attached document, Renewal Form of Maintenance Contract (RFMC), via post, facsimile, or e-mail.

Documentation:
1. The contractor information on the form is filled out based on the profile that is currently in our records: company name, address, and the information on contact personnel. If there is any change in what is written, please update the details.
2. Our maintenance service is mainly provided on a yearly basis. Only if you prefer a multi-year contract, you will be encouraged to check the box and complete the number of years.
3. Your current plan is listed in the section, Service Details. When you would like to upgrade the services, check off the boxes on what is to be added to your current plan.

Methods of Payment:
Starting this year, you can choose to pay by installment or by the single payment plan as before. Please note, however, that you will save money 10% when you make the full payment in advance. Once your RFMC is received, you will be sent the bill and asked to make payment at your bank accordingly.

Attention:
You can extend the contract years after your current one has expired. In that event, you are encouraged to sign the Form of Maintenance Contract.

Sincerely,

Heather Thomas

Maintenance Dept.
Copy & Print, Inc.

176. What is indicated about the maintenance contract?

(A) It is automatically extended.
(B) It allows for applications by phone.
(C) It is annually renewed in most cases.
(D) It provides customer support 7 days a week.

177. The word "expire" in paragraph 1, line 2, is closest in meaning to

(A) conclude
(B) fulfill
(C) end
(D) term

178. Which detail is mentioned as contractor information?

(A) The name of the sales representative
(B) The contact details of the person in charge
(C) The product ID under coverage
(D) The duration of the maintenance contract

179. What is true about the methods of payment?

(A) The outsourcing of collecting payment begins.
(B) The installment is deducted from one's bank account.
(C) The yearly sum is charged on one's bill.
(D) Documents will be sent before payment.

180. What will Copy & Print, Inc. do with late applications?

(A) Ask the customer to fill out another form
(B) Charge handling fees for late applications
(C) Send a bill stating additional rates
(D) Confirm it with a person in charge

GO ON TO THE NEXT PAGE

Questions 181-185 refer to the following e-mails.

From:	ratner@worldcheese.co.jp
To:	j.vandermeer@vonkagkaas.nl
Subject:	Visit request
Date:	Friday, October 31st

Dear Sir or Madam,

We are a Japanese cheese wholesaler, selling mainly to restaurants in the Tokyo area, and are interested in extending our range of European products. We are currently inviting several Dutch dairy farmers, hoping to add their products to our already extensive list of French and Italian kinds. We are interested only in exclusive deals.

I attended a food fair in Tokyo today, and had a brief talk with your people about my idea of adding your cheeses to our inventory. Could you please call to arrange a meeting before the end of next month? It would be more interesting if our marketing representative, Andrew Nonaka, and Louis Gasset, sales manager, could attend the initial meetings and presentations.

I'm looking forward to your response.

Kind regards,

J Ratner
World Cheese CEO
Tel: 030 5555 8787   Mob: 080 5555 4008
Mail: ratner@worldcheese.co.jp

From:	j.vandermeer@vonkagkaas.nl
To:	ratner@worldcheese.co.jp
Subject:	Re: Visit request
Date:	Monday, November 3rd

Dear Mr. Ratner,

Thank you for your interest in our homemade dairy products.

We would be delighted to visit you. To discuss things with you in more detail, we are happy to give you a presentation on our production units and excellent products. In fact, we would like to invite you to taste a range of our cheeses when we meet.

We will leave Japan at the end of this week, so I suggest a meeting this Thursday or Friday morning at the latest when your team will be available. Otherwise, I would like to invite you to Amsterdam.

I will of course follow up on your mail with a telephone call to you to confirm a suitable time. If you would like to ask immediate questions, please call my cell at 070 5555 4221.

Sincerely,

Johan Van der Meer
Sales Director
Department of International Trade, Vonk AG Kaas
030 5555 2411

---

181. What does Mr. Ratner indicate about World Cheese?

(A) It aims to diversify sales regions in Japan.
(B) It does not have an extensive list of French cheeses.
(C) It has participated in a trade show in Italy.
(D) It plans to trade Dutch foods.

182. Why did Mr. Ratner send an e-mail to Mr. Van der Meer?

(A) To set up negotiations
(B) To offer promotion goods
(C) To increase market shares
(D) To head-hunt personnel

183. What does Mr. Van der Meer propose to show at the meeting?

(A) A guided tour to the company's farmstead
(B) A release of the company's quality control process
(C) A variety of sample merchandise
(D) An official dinner at a restaurant

184. What is suggested about Vonk AG Kaas?

(A) They mass-produce several products.
(B) They conducted a marketing survey.
(C) They work with local restaurants.
(D) They made a short visit to an event.

185. Why will Mr. Van der Meer make a phone call to Mr. Ratner?

(A) To fix the time of an appointment
(B) To explain about the production lines
(C) To ask questions about the Japanese market
(D) To catch up on a trading event

GO ON TO THE NEXT PAGE

Questions 186-190 refer to the following e-mail and document.

To:	Ms. Sheila Barnett, General Manager, Human Resources
From:	William Brown, Division Manager, Asian Sales Division, Seoul
Date:	Monday, March 11
Subject:	Re: Recommendation for Personnel in Shanghai Office

Dear Ms. Barnett,

This is a response to your request to introduce a motivated junior employee to work in Human Resources at our Shanghai office. With careful consideration, I would like to recommend Ms. Dorothy Scott for the position. Attached to this e-mail is her performance evaluation record.

Ms. Scott joined our firm 3 years ago and has worked for me in the Asian Sales Division. She is a competent worker and has proven herself to be a team player. While her job experience is limited to sales, she has the capability to adjust to a new environment. I guarantee she will be fully committed to her new role without any problems.

Her excellence in Chinese further fulfills the requirement. Having studied for two years at Shanghai College of Commerce, she has a great command of Mandarin. She has been passionate about mastering the local dialect spoken in Shanghai and now understands basic business conversation and writing.

Needless to say, Ms. Scott is a valuable member of my team. Giving adequate thought to this transfer, I believe that it will not only be beneficial for her career, but certainly contribute to our business in Shanghai.

Your kind consideration is greatly appreciated.

Respectfully,

William Brown

Evaluation Record of Work Performance

NAME: Ms. Scott, Dorothy   ID No.: F8000987
Position: Sales Representative
Evaluation Date: March 9   (Place check where appropriate)

Performance	Evaluation				Score
	A	B	C	D	
Completes work/assignment accurately	✓				10
Completes work/assignment on time	✓				10
Work on projects on one's initiative		✓			8
Overall evaluation	✓				10

Evaluation (Scores 1-10)
  A=Excellent (9-10)   B=Very Good (7-8)   C=Satisfactory (4-6)   D=Poor (1-3)

Comments:
Ms. Scott completes her assignments accurately and on time. She is also qualified to handle problems with clients. At the same time, she has built good relationships with her clientele and on the whole, has potential. However, she needs to gain more leadership skills and through further training and experience. She can readily improve in this area if she asserts herself with more confidence.

Evaluated by: William R. Brown
Position: Division Manager, Asian Sales Div., Int'l Sales Dept.

186. What is the purpose of this e-mail?

(A) To recommend an employee for a position
(B) To request feedback on sales figures
(C) To evaluate a new worker from Shanghai
(D) To inquire about an evaluation record

187. Where does Mr. Brown work?

(A) Human Resources
(B) Corporate Planning
(C) Asian Sales
(D) General Affairs

188. In the evaluation form, the word "initiative" in line 7, is closest in meaning to

(A) collaborative
(B) readiness
(C) administrative
(D) politeness

189. What is implied about the evaluation record?

(A) It showed the best marks on all the performance criteria.
(B) It referred to Ms. Scott's recent promotion.
(C) It was submitted shortly before the e-mail was sent.
(D) It suggested conducting an interview to set a higher goal.

190. What is NOT suggested about Ms. Scott?

(A) She has cooperated with coworkers.
(B) She has gone through leadership training.
(C) She has worked in Asian Sales.
(D) She has studied abroad for years.

GO ON TO THE NEXT PAGE

Questions 191-195 refer to the following article and letter.

Town Weekly Column
Movie Going Magic at the New Cinestar by Brendan Hawk

The Cinestar Movie Complex opened last week to great anticipation and excitement. Cinestar does not disappoint as it has the second most theaters in the city, following Wonder Movies with nine screens. Besides this, all eight screens are equipped with a state-of-the-art surround sound system.

After the closing last spring of the venerable Plaza Theater, locals have been waiting for a worthy replacement. Then, Walter Investment, LLC. decided to bail out the theater. The company appointed Tracy Hepburn, then-chief producer of Walker Brothers, as the director of the new complex.

What Tracy Hepburn is most proud of is Cinestar's beautifully designed lobby. She points out that everything –including the sofas and the counters– has a retro look to it. For example, the walls are covered with posters of Hollywood classics from the 50s.

Both the ticket counter and the concessions corner have five stations so you will never have to wait long for your tickets or refreshments. There are video game machines and movie preview screens scattered about and plenty of those retro sofas for everyone to relax on while they're waiting for their show to start. Inside each theater, the seats are roomy, plush and angled just right for comfort, but not enough to put you to sleep right away.

Dear Mr. Brendan Hawk,

Thank you for your positive review of Cinestar. It's our goal to provide the best movie going experience there is and we're happy to see we're on our way to meeting that goal. Although your review was accurate and thorough, there are a few things we'd like to point out.

The correct number of screens is ten. The original plan for eight was expanded to ten and perhaps that caused some confusion. Two of our screens are oversized and those have four sofas each for couples and families. All of our screens have rows of seats accessible by wheelchair.

I also would like to let you know that every first Sunday of the month is half off the ticket price for viewers under eighteen. Children ages four and under and senior citizens always receive discounted admissions.

Again, thank you for your kind article and please come visit us anytime.

Sincerely,

Tracy Hepburn
Cinestar Movie Complex

191. What is the purpose of the article?

(A) To introduce a movie star
(B) To publicize a magic show
(C) To review a new cultural institution
(D) To announce a construction plan

192. In the article, the word "state-of-the-art" in paragraph 1, line 6, is closest in meaning to

(A) newest
(B) vintage
(C) expensive
(D) imported

193. Who is Ms. Hepburn?

(A) An architect
(B) An investor
(C) A facility director
(D) An interior designer

194. What is the main purpose of the e-mail?

(A) To sell a brand-new event plan
(B) To order the refurbishment of theatrical facilities
(C) To announce a thank-you party
(D) To highlight the inaccurate points in the article

195. What is true about Cinestar Movie Complex?

(A) It prohibits bringing in any food and drink.
(B) It offers discounts on Tuesdays.
(C) It has the most screens in the municipality.
(D) It screens the latest Hollywood movies.

GO ON TO THE NEXT PAGE

Questions 196-200 refer to the following flyer and review.

Bottles on the Shore
On the 1st floor of The Caesar Palace Hotel
On June 1st, REOPENS after a month-long renovation!!

Bottles on the Shore is an oceanfront seafood restaurant for which Nichola Fàbregas, a world famous chef, has worked as head cook. Our restaurant has been revitalized after refurbishment over the last month, and is now ready to re-open. Everyone is more than welcome to dine with us!

The grand-opening commemorates our 30th anniversary as a premier dining establishment. We have been in the same location for the past three decades and will continue to be. We still offer your favorite seasonal menus. The renovation, however, made a great change to our place; the patio seats boast the best ocean views in the summertime. Nevertheless, due to limited availability, we would like you to make a reservation for these seats in advance.

For the first two weeks after reopening, we would like to offer the following special deals:

➢ $70 - The full course dinner, following the original thirty year old recipe
➢ A special gift for the first 50 guests sitting in our patio seats every day
➢ 10% off your bill if you pay with cash (no discounts on bills paid with credit)

Thank you very much for having dinner with us! We would like you to tell us more about your dining experience at Bottles on the Shore. Please rate us below and provide your comments at the bottom of this sheet. We value all remarks with the greatest sincerity.

Scores (5=great, 1=bad)

VIEW	5	4̷	3	2	1
PRICE	5	4	3̷	2	1
FOOD	5̷	4	3	2	1
SERVICES	5	4̷	3	2	1

Comments

My friend and her husband had recommended seafood here, so my colleagues and I decided to have dinner at Bottles on the Shore for the first time. The view from the oceanfront patio was better than expected. My friends enjoyed the remarkable full course dinner, and so did we. It was quite unfortunate that we missed the gifts though, and to be honest, I was not quite sure of the taste when I only knew the price. A mere 10 % discount was not quite helpful, yet our food was exceptional! We were also satisfied with the gentle service. We won't miss the wonderful dinner experience at this restaurant in other seasons to come.

Again, a thousand thanks !!

196. What does the flyer indicate about the restaurant?

(A) It has welcomed a new head chef.
(B) It has been in the same place.
(C) It never accepts credit cards.
(D) It will reopen in two weeks time.

197. In the flyer, the word "revitalized" in paragraph 1, line 2, is closest in meaning to

(A) refreshment
(B) regenerated
(C) renown
(D) replicated

198. What is being suggested about the $70 full course?

(A) It is available only in June.
(B) It is served to those who bring the flyer.
(C) It is limited to the first 50 groups.
(D) It is for only three people or more.

199. According to the review, which of the following is the guest satisfied the most with?

(A) Sight from the seats
(B) Range in price
(C) Quality of dishes served
(D) Quality of services

200. According to the review, what is true about the guest?

(A) She dined with her husband.
(B) She made a reservation in advance.
(C) She wanted to come back alone.
(D) She paid with a credit card.

Stop! This is the end of the test. If you finish before time is called, you may go back to Parts 5, 6, and 7 check your work.

READING TEST

In the Reading test, you will be asked to demonstrate how well you comprehend written English. The Reading test is comprised of three parts and directions are given for each part. The entire test will last 75 minutes. Within the time allowed, you should answer as many questions as you can. You must mark your answers on the separate answer sheet provided. Do not write your answers in the test book.

PART 5

Directions: A word or phrase is missing in the following sentences. For each sentence, four answer choices are given below. Select the best answer to fill in the blank. You must mark your answer on the answer sheet.

101. Much of Jane's free time has been devoted to ------- care of her sick father.

(A) take
(B) took
(C) taking
(D) taken

102. Our new computer system, installed this morning, allows ------- to keep track of all orders.

(A) our
(B) us
(C) we
(D) ours

103. We would like to inform you that new voting laws have ------- since the last election.

(A) to introduce
(B) introduced
(C) been introduced
(D) introduce

104. Please present your invitation card to the receptionist as ------- as you reach the venue.

(A) long
(B) far
(C) soon
(D) much

105. MOSCOW PETROL decided to lower its ------- quota from 25 million to 24.5 million barrels per day.

(A) production
(B) produce
(C) producing
(D) produced

106. If the project -------, Mr. Jenkins would have informed us immediately.

(A) is going to be cancelled
(B) had been cancelled
(C) has cancelled
(D) was cancelled

107. I ------- passed the employment examination and was hired as a secretary at the Raywood Next Corporation.

(A) success
(B) successful
(C) successfully
(D) succeed

108. At yesterday's meeting, the sales team of APS Holdings ------- surprised to find that the sales figures were far better than expected.

(A) were
(B) was
(C) have been
(D) will be

109. All of the new workers are requested to take a medical checkup ------- to their first day at work.

(A) prior
(B) preceding
(C) advance
(D) before

110. The new vice president for advertising wants to put the focus on ------- a younger set of customers.

(A) attract
(B) attracts
(C) attracting
(D) attraction

111. Opening hours at the Brokfeld Museum will be extended ------- the holiday season.

(A) while
(B) during
(C) because
(D) yet

112. The application form should be filled out with the ------- information and turned in to the human resources department.

(A) necessity
(B) necessary
(C) necessitate
(D) necessarily

GO ON TO THE NEXT PAGE

113. Please be aware that ------- handling fees may be required for international mail orders.

    (A) legal
    (B) additional
    (C) original
    (D) current

114. Traveling slowly by boat, the visitors are given a lesson on identifying the wildlife that resides ------- the river.

    (A) among
    (B) about
    (C) along
    (D) with

115. National leaders are asking local governments to take the lead in developing and implementing ------- protection initiatives.

    (A) environment
    (B) environmental
    (C) environmentally
    (D) environmentalism

116. We regret to inform you that the tickets for the reception party have been -------.

    (A) up to par
    (B) laid off
    (C) out of stock
    (D) sold out

117. Please note that our production line in Myanmar will be ------- shut down this summer for repairs.

    (A) rarely
    (B) frequently
    (C) simply
    (D) temporarily

118. ------- the exception of the Sapporo branch, we had trouble getting in touch with our domestic offices by phone.

    (A) As
    (B) For
    (C) In
    (D) With

119. Better public speaking skills help you convey messages on any occasion, at formal gatherings in -------.

    (A) particular
    (B) specific
    (C) example
    (D) emphasis

120. In order to keep your application up-to-date, we recommend checking and installing the latest version -------.

    (A) allegedly
    (B) equally
    (C) occasionally
    (D) periodically

121. The new computer model produced by the Electro Best Company marked the best sales this season, ------- the active sales promotion of its competitors.

(A) although
(B) despite
(C) but
(D) because of

122. Now, we would like to proudly introduce this new model which is far superior ------- any other competing product.

(A) with
(B) than
(C) above
(D) to

123. Through its globally linked network, the Hutchison Group ------- a comprehensive range of financial services.

(A) receives
(B) provides
(C) explains
(D) includes

124. Due to the inclement weather, we had to take an ------- route to the destination.

(A) alternative
(B) alternation
(C) alternating
(D) alternately

125. The recent ------- of digital broadcast systems and networks has been explosive.

(A) evolution
(B) impression
(C) foundation
(D) pollution

126. The survey shows that 45 percent of adults disapprove of President Wilson's ------- on making tax cuts permanent.

(A) position
(B) positioning
(C) positioned
(D) positional

127. It has been ------- announced that PAS Bank and Pacific ML Bank will merge into a new bank, which will be the largest in the country.

(A) formalize
(B) formality
(C) formal
(D) formally

128. The nutritionist told me that the higher the temperature that food is cooked at, ------- it stays in the gut.

(A) much longer
(B) the longest
(C) as long as
(D) the longer

129. The project team will have to ------- extensive research before settling on a final plan.

(A) address
(B) accept
(C) conduct
(D) improve

130. The company's expansion includes creating a 10,000-square-foot production facility, ------- will create close to a hundred new jobs.

(A) that
(B) almost
(C) which
(D) so

131. With their growing production, gas and oil industries ------- the city's expansion and economic prosperity over many decades.

(A) have accelerated
(B) accelerating
(C) have been accelerated
(D) accelerate

132. Keeping up with the latest information technology will provide a ------- advantage for future employment.

(A) substance
(B) substantiate
(C) substantially
(D) substantial

133. In preparation for the banquet, Mr. Lopez visited some supermarkets that have ------- preferred beverage in stock.

(A) his
(B) them
(C) him
(D) their

134. A ------- approach to reducing CO_2 emissions was presented by the environmental agency.

(A) chronic
(B) rational
(C) intimate
(D) mental

135. ------- in the late 80s, Mikee Dragon Co. currently has more than 200 stores in the States.

(A) Been established
(B) Establishing
(C) Having established
(D) Established

136. The new residential development will adjoin our existing ones, ------- the plan is approved.

(A) although
(B) provided
(C) unless
(D) because of

137. Even though the project was ------- but easy to achieve, the enthusiasm of the whole planning department led it to great success.

(A) something
(B) nothing
(C) everything
(D) anything

138. While most candidates ------- opportunities to meet voters, they rarely venture beyond the safety of their own communities.

(A) trust
(B) seek
(C) submit
(D) comply

139. CyNet Inc. plans to open a new plant in Oregon that will employ 500 people ------- five years to handle their advertising business.

(A) within
(B) about
(C) at
(D) during

140. Mr. Berkley has the ------- to decide what is classified and what is not, so please get approval from him.

(A) assignment
(B) aspect
(C) audience
(D) authority

GO ON TO THE NEXT PAGE

PART 6

Directions: A word or phrase is missing in sentences in the texts. For each sentence, four answer choices are given below. Select the best answer to fill in the blank. You must mark your answer on the answer sheet.

Questions 141-143 refer to the following notice.

Park Notices and Park Activities

In recent weeks, there has been an issue with pet waste being found on lawns through the park. It is possible that stray dogs are coming into the park. In order to keep Trudeau Park dog friendly, the lawns need ------- clean. We encourage

    141. (A) remain
        (B) to remain
        (C) remaining
        (D) will remain

dog owners to clean up their dog's waste and to be sure to dispose of ------- else

    142. (A) anything
        (B) anymore
        (C) something
        (D) some more

they happen to see on the grass.
April 24 - there will be field trials conducted by the Kennel Club of Vancouver. Only registered dogs can participate, but spectators are ------- welcome.

    143. (A) then
        (B) also
       (C) for
       (D) along

May 10 - the Evening in the Park concert and performance series begins its season. All events are free. For further information, call us at 604-555-1347.

Questions 144-146 refer to the following letter.

KIRK PATRICK & LAING, ARCHITECTS
2001 Brownley Circle
Suite 903
Toronto, Ontario

Dear Sir or Madam,

I am writing to apply for a position at your firm. I am ------- a graduate student in
                        144. (A) eagerly
                             (B) actively
                             (C) currently
                             (D) correctly

architecture at Western Ontario University, and plan to graduate next month.
My primary ------- is in design. My master's project involves designing a
    145. (A) interesting
           (B) interested
           (C) to interest
           (D) interest

residential block of single-family homes.
I have two years of part-time experience at the architecture offices of Parker &
Soto, and am ------- in a number of design programs including Vectorworks.
        146. (A) proud
               (B) significant
               (C) proficient
               (D) outstanding

I would greatly appreciate it if you could kindly send me an application form for a position at your firm.

Sincerely,

Stephanie Sjobowicz

GO ON TO THE NEXT PAGE

Questions 147-149 refer to the following advertisement.

We believe in the saying, "The pen really is mightier than the sword." The Mighty Pen by the Write Company proves it. This revolutionary writing device has a titanium body that is literally strong enough to resist a strike by a sword. Yet, that's not all that makes it mighty.
The Mighty Pen writes well even ------- extreme conditions such as 50 degrees

    147. (A) over
        (B) on
        (C) with
        (D) under

Celsius. Moreover, the pen is not only extremely strong, ------- also extremely kind

    148. (A) although
        (B) so
        (C) but
        (D) for

to the writer. The contoured shape ------- to fit naturally in your hand and reduce

    149. (A) designs
        (B) is designing
        (C) is designed
        (D) will design

strain.
The Mighty Pen is $99.99 with free shipping. There is no doubt that the Mighty Pen is worth every penny as it is the best to write down your thoughts with.

Questions 150-152 refer to the following letter.

Dear Calvin,

I hope you are well. Thank you for the invitation to Nathan's graduation party. I am ------- to hear that Nathan is going to be a doctor soon!

150. (A) cooperative
 (B) delighted
 (C) positive
 (D) graceful

At first, I thought Grace and I would be able to make it to Los Angeles that weekend. Checking my schedule, however, I found out that it ------- with a

151. (A) conflict
 (B) conflicting
 (C) conflicted
 (D) was conflicted

conference in Seattle.
In ordinary circumstances, I would have just canceled my plans, as I've known Nathan since the days we all used to call him "Little Nate." However, as I am appointed as the featured speaker at this conference, I am unable to cancel this time.
Grace and I are so disappointed to find the party and my conference scheduled ------- the same time.

152. (A) at
 (B) on
 (C) in
 (D) of

Thank you anyway and hope we can get together sometime soon.

Best,
Mike

GO ON TO THE NEXT PAGE

PART 7

Directions: In this part, you are asked to answer questions based on a variety of texts, such as notices, e-mails, memos, and articles. Select the best answer for each question and mark your answer on the answer sheet.

Questions 153-154 refer to the following advertisement.

John's Professional Gardening
Originally founded in Termer, California
All work guaranteed!

Now servicing all of Claremont County and Northern Bucks County, Nevada

Garden and Lawn Maintenance
Average size lawn (20' x 10'): Weekly $20.00
Smaller and larger lawn costs are adjusted accordingly.
Monthly or semi-monthly services are also offered.

If you are a first-time user, call 878-555-4592. We will give you a free estimate on your plan.
Please do not forget to refer to the following code, 245542, for a 10 % discount.
The special rate is for anyone who mentions it regardless of user status.

- Landscaping
  Planting grass, flowers, ground cover, and trees
  Sprinkler repair
  Designing landscape plans
- Fertilizing plants and grass
- Tree Service
  Pruning
  Trimming
  Removing

153. What is the purpose of the advertisement?

(A) To explain a tree service
(B) To show an estimate
(C) To attract new customers
(D) To give prices

154. Who is eligible for discounts?

(A) Newly signed up clients
(B) Residents in California and Nevada
(C) Initial 10 people making a call
(D) Whoever mentions the promotional numbers

Questions 155-157 refer to the following Web site.

www.web_books.com/news

Web Books
The Specialist for Self Study Books

Web Books
Specialist Study Books
Call us on (250)-555-9812

| **Home** | Products | Services | Shop | Membership | About us |

You have found the premier web site for all fields of study books. You can search for all subjects and we have prices to suit everyone's pocket. We deal with new & used books.

Known as the largest web-book seller, we have now become the important place for not only students but also the general public.

We also offer our site members the opportunity to resell the books they have previously used. We have developed a simple system to enter the ISBN number of the book you wish to sell. This is then automatically matched to our database of books. Once you have completed the necessary fields, you will have the opportunity to sell your books to thousands of online buyers.

It's a simple system and very ECO friendly. Try it today.

You can also CLICK HERE to see our second hand software site.

155. For whom is the web site intended?

(A) Customers buying books
(B) Workers advertising a book fair
(C) Sales staff selling books
(D) Engineers providing software

156. What is suggested about Web Books?

(A) It specializes in environment related books.
(B) It has many branch shops around the country.
(C) It has created a system to trade used books.
(D) It is the second-biggest shop of web-books.

157. What is NOT mentioned on the web site?

(A) Web Books has established maximum prices.
(B) Registration is required to sell books.
(C) The procedure for selling books is easy.
(D) The books might be sold to many buyers.

GO ON TO THE NEXT PAGE

Questions 158-159 refer to the following article.

Citing increasing oil prices and the floundering economy, Advantage Airlines (AAL) recently announced that it will be adding fuel charges to its ticket prices. AAL is the last of the five major carriers to institute such charges. Unlike some of the other major carriers such as Delphi and Oracle Air, AAL will charge only for flights over 500 miles.* For flights under 500 miles, there will be no surcharge. Advantage CEO Donald Lee stated that the change was necessary to remain competitive in a tough market. Fuel charges of $200 for domestic flights ($300 for international) will come into effect September 15th. Advantage also announced in a press release that beginning September 1st, they will charge $100 for all luggage above the 20 kg limit (40 kg for international flights). In a publicity move designed to counter the negative effects of the fuel charges, AAL also announced complimentary snack services on all flights. Thanks to its partnership with Gremlin Food Corporation, all AAL passengers will enjoy unlimited soft drinks, as well as pretzels and candy bars.

*Skyclub Platinum Members are exempt.

158. What is stated about Advantage Airlines?

(A) It plans to merge with a food company.
(B) It owns and runs a hotel chain.
(C) It is a leading airline company.
(D) It started new domestic and international routes.

159. According to the article, what type of advantage will Skyclub Platinum members receive?

(A) Bonus points
(B) Fuel charge exemption
(C) Extra pieces of baggage
(D) Free light meals

Questions 160-162 refer to the following letter.

September 10

Mr. Zak Rojas
TTY Corporation
18 Rich Street, New Haven
Victoria 3665

Dear Mr. Rojas,

We are delighted to invite you to the Autumn Toy Fair, which will be held from October 8 to 12 at Backwater Plaza. Over 300 top manufacturers from the toy industry will display their quality products, ranging from classic toys to interactive entertainment.

Registration can be done online or at the door. Please note that the fair is for traders only and is not open to the public. No one under the age of 18 will be admitted.

The Autumn Toy Fair is expected to repeat its previous success and bring invaluable business opportunities to buyers from around the country. We hope to provide a most satisfactory sourcing trip!

Leonie Yung

Leonie Yung

National Toy Foundation

160. Why was the letter sent?

(A) To get some researchers together
(B) To inform buyers of toy festival
(C) To raise money for charity
(D) To develop a new product

161. What is true about registration?

(A) It is exclusively for business people.
(B) It cannot be done over the Internet.
(C) It must be completed in September.
(D) It will be open to small children.

162. What is indicated about the Autumn Toy Fair?

(A) It will last over a week.
(B) It has been held before.
(C) It is the largest in the country.
(D) It is an exhibition of vintage toys.

GO ON TO THE NEXT PAGE

Questions 163-165 refer to the following e-mail.

To: Customer Service, Light Fixtures Inc.
From: May Preston
Subject: Minimum order for light bulbs
Date: December 5

To whom it may concern,

I had been looking for a 34-watt linear fluorescent light bulb in daylight white color and fortunately, I was able to find this product through your online shopping site: Product No. L-5442-GE5. I am quite fond of this and its natural lighting which matches perfectly with the atmosphere in my room. Since an electronic shop in my town stopped selling it the other day and I couldn't find it at any other place, I was happy to see it available on your website. However, before I ordered, I noticed this particular product can only be purchased by the case (30 pcs.).
The light bulb is for my home and there are only so many that I need. I noticed there are some types of light bulbs that are sold by the piece. Would it be possible to do the same for the above product as well? I need 3 pieces and am willing to pay any extra handling costs for these.

Awaiting your soonest reply,

May Preston
123 Washington Blvd.
Jacksonville, CT 55555
Phone 123-555-4567

163. What is the main purpose of this e-mail?

(A) To request international shipping
(B) To order a fewer number of items
(C) To change the color of products
(D) To ask for storing items

164. What is indicated about L-5442-GE5?

(A) It is no longer available.
(B) It is durable.
(C) It is for business use.
(D) It is not widely available.

165. What is written in the e-mail?

(A) Contact information
(B) Payment methods
(C) Delivery period
(D) Order numbers

Questions 166-168 refer to the following form.

MarketPlace2020
5009 Peachtree Avenue, Atlanta,
GA 55903
Phone 1-800-555-3230
Fax 1-800-555-3240

ORDER INVOICE & BILL

Thank you for your purchase at MarketPlace2020. This is the invoice of your order.

DATE OF ORDER: January 20
SHIPPING DATE: January 21
PAYMENT DUE: February 17

ORDER NUMBER: 17-F9NC-540
ORDERED BY:
- Name: Ellen Dumont
- Address: 1973 Rosewood Drive
- City/State/Zip: Frankfort, IN 47948
- Phone/ Fax: 765-555-2975

Catalog Page	Item Number	Color	Quantity	Description	Price	Total
46	24920	NA	2	Popover Pan	14.99	29.98
25	24020	blue	1	Pie Plate	19.99	19.99

Merchandise total	$49.97
Shipping & Handling	$4.50
Sales Tax	$2.08
Total	$56.55

PAYMENT
Once you have made sure your order had been properly delivered, please make payment via bank transfer by February 17. Our account information is written on the catalog, where you can find the name of financial institution, account number, etc. Payment in cash is NOT accepted.

If you have any trouble with the ordered items, please do not hesitate to call us.

Thank you for your catalog order.
You can also order online at MarketPlace2020.com.

166. What is NOT mentioned in the form?

(A) Names of ordered products
(B) Customer's personal information
(C) Store e-mail address
(D) Detailed statement

167. What is suggested about the order?

(A) No commodity tax is charged.
(B) Discounts have been applied.
(C) Payment is made after delivery.
(D) The order was placed online.

168. What is true about the MarketPlace2020's payment?

(A) They return the service charges.
(B) They accept payment within one month.
(C) They take only cash payment.
(D) They hold a number of bank accounts.

GO ON TO THE NEXT PAGE

Questions 169-171 refer to the following review.

Jack Parker's
The Damaged River
By Erin Marks

I have not read a book this intriguing in years. This will be hard for anyone to match. The mystery is deep in this story and makes it hard to put down. It is a riveting book about love and betrayal. The theme itself would have sounded rather mediocre and commonplace if it were not written by the author. Yet, Jack Parker's sensational debut with *Behind the Door* is vividly remembered through this book even though it was a decade ago. He, once more, illustrates how love plays a key role in his new story, *The Damaged River*. Every line gives a rather picturesque account of an affair as it is told in his fashion. The contrast between scenery and characters deliberately weaves into a puzzle.

If you like a story derived from his previous work, you'll enjoy this book more. This time, he attempts to carry on the stories of the characters in previous works. For example, Ann Roberts who finally finds true love after many failed relationships.

It is from here on you cannot stop turning pages as the story gets more and more thrilling. Undoubtedly, I highly recommend it.

169. What is implied about *The Damaged River*?

(A) It is the first romance from the author.
(B) It is filled with many illustrations.
(C) It is an exciting mystery.
(D) It is unique to this genre.

170. Who is Ann Roberts?

(A) A character in the book
(B) An author
(C) A book reviewer
(D) An actress

171. What is suggested about Jack Parker?

(A) His writing style is plain.
(B) He is a professional painter.
(C) He has been in the field for ten years.
(D) He directs films based on his novels.

GO ON TO THE NEXT PAGE

Questions 172-175 refer to the following advertisement.

Leave Your Water Needs to AQUALEN Inc.!

Aqualen Inc. is the number one provider of filtered water coolers to businesses in Sydney, Brisbane and Melbourne.

How does Aqualen work?
A filtered water cooler unit which is connected directly to the city water line will be installed in your office. This means no bottled water or water delivery service is needed. Your staff will appreciate not having to waste their time moving bottles or going out to get more when they run out. It also saves space as you don't need to store gallons of bottled water. And, of course, the best part is that it costs less!

Who uses Aqualen?
30 businesses ranked among *Biznow Magazine's* "100 Top Companies in Australia" use Aqualen. It is simply the smarter way to get water.

What's more, from June this year, we are also bringing water solutions to households in the service areas! Now you can enjoy clean, safe water in your home as well as in your office.

If you would like to get a free quote or make an order, please visit our offices, or contact us at 555-8978 or 555-9928 for mobile users, or e-mail us at customerservice@aqualen.com.
* We are working hard to update our Web site at the moment. Please use the above contact methods until our inquiry form is back online.

172. What is indicated about Aqualen Inc.?

(A) It is ranked among 100 top national companies.
(B) It has a broad range of filtered water cooler products.
(C) It is a local leading provider of filtered water coolers.
(D) It has invented a new filtration technology.

173. What will customers NOT save on by choosing Aqualen Inc.'s products?

(A) Delivery charges
(B) Storage space
(C) Water fees
(D) Time and trouble

174. According to the advertisement, what will happen this year?

(A) A new branch office will open.
(B) The customer base will be expanded.
(C) Water prices will be lowered.
(D) User manuals will be distributed.

175. What is the contact method currently unavailable for customers?

(A) Calling to a representative
(B) E-mailing to customer services
(C) Visiting an office
(D) Inquiring online

GO ON TO THE NEXT PAGE

Questions 176-180 refer to the following article.

Chef Paul's Voted Best Restaurant in Sydney

According to a survey conducted by Restaurant Guide, Chef Paul's was named the best restaurant in Sydney. More than 40% of those surveyed replied that Chef Paul's was their favorite.

Overlooking the Sydney Harbor, Chef Paul's, run by owner-chef Paul Durand, serves original French-Chinese fusion cuisine. The Chinese ingredients add a taste of the East to what would otherwise be a traditional French course. Each tastefully delightful dish is pleasant to the eyes as well. Durand has personally traveled to every corner in China looking for tableware that now defines the modern Asian style of Chef Paul's.

More than the food, however, is the impeccable service at Chef Paul's which many claim to be "outstanding." All the waiters are courteous without being pretentious and each table is served with perfect timing. Naturally, the view of the harbor at night helps.

Paul Durand, who is French, was born and raised in Hong Kong where his father was stationed as a diplomat. His understanding of the Chinese and their food culture is said to have been cultivated at this time.

When told of his restaurant being named the best in Sydney, he replied modestly, "We are just doing what is expected of us — serving good food in a good atmosphere."

176. Where is Chef Paul's located?

(A) Downtown
(B) In the business district
(C) In the bay area
(D) In the airport

177. Where did Paul Durand buy the dishware used at the restaurant?

(A) In Japan
(B) In Australia
(C) In China
(D) In France

178. What is mentioned about Paul Durand's family?

(A) They run a small restaurant.
(B) They enjoy making a voyage.
(C) They financially supported the opening of his restaurant.
(D) They experienced living abroad.

179. When did Durand cultivate his understanding of Chinese food?

(A) During his childhood
(B) During his apprenticeship
(C) During his travels
(D) During his work as assistant chef

180. The word "courteous" in paragraph 3, line 4, is closest in meaning to

(A) polite
(B) sympathetic
(C) excellent
(D) anxious

GO ON TO THE NEXT PAGE

Questions 181-185 refer to the following advertisement and e-mail.

SHORTMAN DEPOT
MOVING SALE! EVERYTHING MUST GO!!!
SATURDAY, OCTOBER 17th, 8 A.M. - 9 P.M.
Section G21-G24, STATE FAIR GROUNDS, SHORTMAN, TX

Section	
G21	Trading Room
G22	Desks
G23	Chairs & Couches
G24	Appliances

Looking to furnish your office? We've got some of the finest office furniture in the country, all at low prices!

Desks: We offer both large and small desks and tables in a variety of styles in metal, hardwood, and composite with natural wood finishes. Starting at $220.
Chairs & Couches: Shortman is the biggest supplier of leather office chairs, massage chairs, and couches in all of Texas! We've got plenty of deals for you. Order four leather office chairs and receive a fifth free of charge! Prices start at $150 per chair.
Appliances: Looking for refrigerators, microwaves, flat-screen TVs, and stereo systems? Shortman has it all. Our used refrigerators start at $580. We have the biggest inventory of used flat-screen TVs in the country, starting at $780. Come check out our custom-made stereo systems, too! We can redesign them for your office, home or car.

To participate in this event, you must sign up at reception, where you will be asked to pay a $15 entrance fee.

To:	Jeff Peterson, Shortman Depot
From:	Michael Grandyman
Subject:	Moving Sale Pre-Order
Date:	October 15

Thank you very much for last week. I like your idea of the trading room as I can expect another good deal to be signed.
As I mentioned on the phone, I am representing several buyers in the area who are interested in your goods on sale. Consequently, on their behalf, I have a few more

questions to ask prior to the event.

First, which flat screen TVs do you offer, LCD or plasma? Do you have both of them?

Second, what sizes of used refrigerators do you have? I want to know because one buyer is interested in purchasing several of them if they fit in his office space. So, could you send me details on them along with pictures?

Third, how many leather office chairs do you have in stock? If you only have less than 15, could you suggest other kinds? I would like to purchase a chair that costs less than $250.

I look forward to hearing from you at your earliest convenience.

181. In the advertisement, what area of business is being advertised?

(A) An interior designer
(B) An office supplies store
(C) An appliance repair service
(D) A homemade furniture shop

182. What product does Shortman Depot stock the most of in the United States?

(A) Office chairs
(B) Used-flat-screen TVs
(C) Hardwood desks
(D) Used refrigerators

183. Why is Michael Grandyman writing this e-mail?

(A) To arrange for delivery of goods to his customers
(B) To ask about goods for his clients
(C) To complain about several goods he purchased
(D) To sell desks, couches and refrigerators

184. What does Michael ask about the TV sets?

(A) Production areas
(B) Years of manufacture
(C) Sizes of TV screens
(D) Types of TV displays

185. Which section will Grandyman NOT likely enter?

(A) G21
(B) G22
(C) G23
(D) G24

GO ON TO THE NEXT PAGE

Questions 186-190 refer to the following letter and flyer.

November 5

Mr. Chris Taylor
Taylor's Deli

Dear Mr. Taylor,

 Thank you very much for your generous donation to our 3rd Annual Holiday Bingo Event. Your $50 gift voucher was won by a lady who, it turns out, often shops at your store!
 This is our 3rd year since we first began to organize this event. This time, we were able to raise $230,987 (up 30% from last year), thanks to all the generous donations made by everyone in the community.
 The idea for the Holiday Bingo Event was first born when several of us were discussing how we would be spending our holidays. The discussion eventually led to how there are still many unfortunate people in the world who are deprived of the basics in life and if there is anything we can do to help them.
 The proceeds go to a different charity every year. On this occasion, we have chosen a charity that provides food and medication to people, especially children, living in refugee camps in Africa.
 We have enclosed a flyer of a photograph exhibition at the First Bank Center and two invitations for the previous day of the opening. The photographs feature children of the world. All of them are endearing, but there are some that just break your heart. This is why we continue our charity work.
 We hope that you will continue to support our cause.
 Once again, we would like to express our appreciation for your generosity.

Sincerely,

Patricia Walker

Committee Chairman
Enclosure

Photograph Exhibition
Children of the World

Date: November 25 to December 3
Venue: First Bank Center, 1st Floor
Admission Fee:

Adults $10

Children (12-18 years old) $3

(under 12) free of charge

A child being hugged by her mother.

A child intensely watching an ant carrying food twice its size.

These endearing yet heart-breaking photographs remind us of a child's need for love, security and protection.

Three photographers have traveled across the world to take these pictures. They have put together this exhibition to raise money for children living in poverty.

186. What did Mr. Taylor contribute to the bingo event?

(A) $50 in cash
(B) Items from his shop
(C) A gift certificate for his shop
(D) A gift basket

187. Where do the proceeds of the event go?

(A) To the local community
(B) To a holiday event
(C) To three photographers
(D) To a charity organization

188. What is enclosed in the letter?

(A) A pamphlet of the charity organization
(B) A document explaining the plight of African refugees
(C) A leaflet and two invitation tickets to a display
(D) An accounting report of the bingo event

189. Who organized this exhibition?

(A) Three photographers
(B) The organizing committee of the bingo event
(C) The local community
(D) First Bank Center

190. When will Mr. Taylor see the exhibition for free?

(A) On November 24
(B) On November 25
(C) On December 2
(D) On December 3

GO ON TO THE NEXT PAGE

Questions 191-195 refer to the following memo and letter.

MEMO

From: Daisy Sparks, Manager
To: All Buchow Hotel Employees
Date: Monday, June 5
Re: Renovations and Checks Agenda

The following renovations and checks will be performed on hotel assets this week. Please note that respective facilities will be closed on the day of renovations or checks. The renovations and checks are performed in order to ensure our guests will continue to enjoy a safe, comfortable stay at our hotel. However, these may cause some inconvenience, so please be extra attentive to guests' needs.

Date	Description
June 6	The main elevators will be checked for safety.
June 7	The conference room will be re-carpeted.
June 8	Four new computers will be set up in the business center.
June 9	Equipment in the hotel fitness center will be inspected.

June 21

Ms. Daisy Sparks
The Buchow Hotel
267 Nelson Blvd, Montrose
MN 52873

Dear Ms. Sparks,

My name is Ed Banks and I have stayed at the Buchow Hotel on several occasions. I have always favored the hotel for the genuine helpfulness of its employees and its deluxe atmosphere. Although I am happy to say that the former has not changed, I have noticed a significant decline in the latter.

The last time I stayed at the hotel, I noticed that the lobby furniture looked like it was in need of some cleaning. The guest room was pleasant as usual, but the brand named shampoo and conditioner have been replaced with cheap, generic ones. Also, I ordered a bacon sandwich to my room at night, which arrived an hour later, cold.

Finally, I was looking forward to working out when I returned to the hotel after attending a business conference, but the fitness facility was closed without any prior notice.

As a concerned customer, I hope my opinions here will benefit the future operation of your hotel.

Kind regards,

Ed Banks

Ed Banks

191. What is the purpose of the memo?

(A) To call an employee meeting
(B) To inform of a change in management
(C) To announce a maintenance schedule
(D) To schedule a safety inspection

192. In the memo, the word "assets" in paragraph 1, line 1, is closest in meaning to

(A) property
(B) rooms
(C) services
(D) administration

193. Why was the letter written?

(A) To report a safety concern
(B) To complain about construction noise
(C) To offer a customer opinion
(D) To demand a refund

194. What was Mr. Banks satisfied with?

(A) Hotel personnel
(B) Conference room
(C) Bathroom amenities
(D) In-room dining

195. On which day did Mr. Banks most likely stay at the hotel?

(A) June 6
(B) June 7
(C) June 8
(D) June 9

GO ON TO THE NEXT PAGE

Questions 196-200 refer to the following notice and e-mail.

ISSUER: HR Department of IIMG Inc. Headquarters, Chicago
DATE ISSUED: JUNE 1
TO THE STAFF

A MANAGERIAL POSITION VACANCY FOR A SUPPLY CHAIN DIVISION IN LOS ANGELES

Our Los Angeles branch is currently seeking a supply chain director due to the planned expansion of its service providing areas. The position will start September 1.

The job holder will be responsible for overseeing overall distribution operations on the West Coast. In addition, she/he will be principally accountable for consumer affairs both with current and prospective clients, and quarterly assessments. The successful candidate will meet the following requirements:

- Minimum of five service years in distribution, logistics, merchandising and other related business fields
- Professional leadership experience and team-building skills
- Consent from your spouse, children, and/or other family members to move to Los Angeles, if an applicant lives with her/his family (accommodation will be provided in the first month)
- Preferably hold a master's degree in business administration

APPLICATION:
Interested individuals are encouraged to send an e-mail by June 28 with a brief self-introduction to Ms. Rachel Harper, Manager of Human Resources, at rachharper@hr.iimg.com. Ms. Harper and Mr. Chris McCartney, LA Branch Manager, will do a one-time interview with each applicant at our headquarters between July 3 and 5. A fixed interview schedule will be determined.

FROM:	Ryu Xin Chu < xincryu@sp.iimg.com >
SUBJECT:	Applying for the SCM post in LA
DATE:	June 24
TO:	Ms. Rachel Harper < rachharper@hr.iimg.com >

Dear Ms. Harper,

I am Ryu Xin Chu, Deputy Manager of the Merchandising Department. I am contacting you because I am quite interested in the LA position on June 1.

Since graduating from the McMillan School of Business with an MBA, I have worked for IIMG for the last seven years. In the first three years, I was stationed in the Supply Chain Division, where I worked on projects to maintain the competitiveness of our services in the Mid-West. My role as chief negotiator in the project proved to be beneficial to regional sales over that period. As for the last four years, I have worked in the Merchandising Department, where I have devoted myself to leading the team toward more cost-effective advertisement plans. My decision to install new promotion methods has successfully increased the number of new customers over the last four years.

I can assure you that my family is supportive of my desire to take on a new challenge. In addition, my husband and children are willing to move to Los Angeles since they are originally from Southern California.

I look forward to your reply.

Sincerely,

Ryu Xin Chu

196. What is the main topic of the notice?

(A) Relocation of the headquarters
(B) Study abroad programs for employees
(C) Evaluation interviews
(D) In-house staff recruitment

197. In the notice, the word "prospective" in paragraph 2, line 3, is closest in meaning to

(A) credentials
(B) potential
(C) confidential
(D) essential

198. According to the notice, what is NOT suggested about the interview?

(A) Questions to be asked
(B) Interviewers
(C) Number of times
(D) Location

199. For which responsibility does Ms. Ryu Xin Chu most likely have the greatest confidence?

(A) Information collection
(B) External affairs
(C) Producing electronic documents
(D) Organizing outgoing mail

200. What is true about Ms. Ryu Xin Chu?

(A) She used to work in the LA branch.
(B) She cannot live with her family in LA.
(C) She meets all the requirements.
(D) She comes recommended by her supervisor.

Stop! This is the end of the test. If you finish before time is called, you may go back to Parts 5, 6, and 7 check your work.

READING TEST

READING TEST

In the Reading test, you will be asked to demonstrate how well you comprehend written English. The Reading test is comprised of three parts and directions are given for each part. The entire test will last 75 minutes. Within the time allowed, you should answer as many questions as you can. You must mark your answers on the separate answer sheet provided. Do not write your answers in the test book.

PART 5

Directions: A word or phrase is missing in the following sentences. For each sentence, four answer choices are given below. Select the best answer to fill in the blank. You must mark your answer on the answer sheet.

101. Christine has finished ------- paychecks for all employees.

(A) preparing
(B) to prepare
(C) prepare
(D) prepared

102. Technical support is available ------- a 24-hour basis for all registered users.

(A) from
(B) for
(C) on
(D) in

103. The property ------- by the real estate agent is fairly close to what we had in mind.

(A) will show
(B) shown
(C) shows
(D) showing

104. Many ------- sales techniques, particularly Internet advertising, were introduced in the training session.

(A) usage
(B) useful
(C) use
(D) usefully

66

105. Joanne Stanley dedicated herself ------- helping the company launch a new business.

(A) for
(B) on
(C) to
(D) of

106. Jack patiently explained to new employees how spyware -------, because he knew it would take time to understand.

(A) works
(B) to work
(C) be worked
(D) working

107. The protection of ------- heritage is regarded as one of the most important tasks of this community.

(A) historical
(B) historically
(C) histories
(D) history

108. The two parties have ------- reached an agreement on the diplomatic policy submitted to a committee a year ago.

(A) finalized
(B) finally
(C) final
(D) finality

109. An R&D project of new product lineups is in ------- in order to expand to foreign markets.

(A) short
(B) progress
(C) return
(D) tune

110. After interviewing all the applicants, we will determine ------- ones to hire.

(A) whose
(B) when
(C) which
(D) what

111. Jupiter Group has set a new target for ------- in energy use, including electricity.

(A) reduce
(B) reduced
(C) reduction
(D) reducing

112. This program was designed to help our athletes be better prepared both physically ------- mentally.

(A) so
(B) and
(C) or
(D) but

GO ON TO THE NEXT PAGE

113. An annual maximum of two months' sick leave is paid in ------- with current company rules and regulations.

    (A) accordance
    (B) accord
    (C) accordingly
    (D) accorded

114. ------- half of the employees at Murata Trading Co. can speak two different languages.

    (A) Much
    (B) Every
    (C) Almost
    (D) Most

115. HQ Organic Corp. has ------- high standards in environmental sanitation in order to insure the safety of their food products.

    (A) restricted
    (B) abandoned
    (C) remained
    (D) maintained

116. The author points out that ------- of the news articles distributed on websites are not based on fact.

    (A) one
    (B) each
    (C) every
    (D) some

117. Please note that discount rates ------- in this pamphlet do not include tax and are subject to change.

    (A) listed
    (B) list
    (C) listing
    (D) to list

118. Please keep in mind that parking violations in this particular area are ------- penalized.

    (A) cautiously
    (B) severely
    (C) necessarily
    (D) accurately

119. You must turn off any electronic devices and refrain ------- using mobile phones while you are in a hospital.

    (A) of
    (B) in
    (C) from
    (D) to

120. The labor union ------- up against a new labor law that would make it harder to keep a job.

    (A) rising
    (B) were risen
    (C) raised
    (D) rose

121. ------- who want to use the company car must make a reservation at least a week in advance.

(A) They
(B) Those
(C) These
(D) That

122. The program offered at Bomona College teaches sales representatives various ways to streamline ------- marketing plans for maximum benefit.

(A) themselves
(B) they
(C) them
(D) their

123. The guest speaker for today's investment seminar is expected to arrive at the hall at ------- 9:00 A.M.

(A) recently
(B) newly
(C) approximately
(D) properly

124. The workshop includes a free, one-hour private consultation to answer any questions a ------- may have.

(A) participation
(B) participates
(C) participating
(D) participant

125. Our economist, Mike James, is going to summarize the expected ------- of devaluing the Chinese yuan.

(A) effective
(B) effectively
(C) effects
(D) to effect

126. If you need some technical assistance, you can contact us by phone or e-mail, ------- you prefer.

(A) however
(B) where
(C) whoever
(D) whichever

127. Signs have been ------- stating that the beaches are closed because of the strong winds.

(A) performed
(B) practiced
(C) proceeded
(D) posted

128. ------- a clerical error, the ordered items were delivered to the wrong address.

(A) Since
(B) As
(C) Whereas
(D) Because of

GO ON TO THE NEXT PAGE

129. Tucker & Benson is accused of breaching its ------- to protect shareholder rights.

(A) reputation
(B) ambition
(C) transition
(D) obligation

130. Ms. Atkinson is tied ------- preparing for the autumn exhibition, so Ms. Johnson will be in charge of the store for a while.

(A) in
(B) back
(C) up
(D) on

131. Any employees who have worked at the company for more than three years are ------- to apply for the assistant manager position at the Newport Branch.

(A) eligible
(B) manageable
(C) affordable
(D) accessible

132. The board was not ------- the management team had the right plan to get the company out of financial trouble.

(A) convincing
(B) conviction
(C) convinced
(D) convincible

133. The sales figures for the ------- computer from Oregon Computing are skyrocketing as a result of having more functions than previous models.

(A) latest
(B) later
(C) late
(D) lately

134. Nick Hilton got promoted for his ------- ideas for the company's new product which will be marketed in Singapore.

(A) creativity
(B) creative
(C) creatively
(D) create

135. EZ Net's main shopping menu is temporarily unavailable ------- system maintenance.

(A) as for
(B) in case
(C) as well
(D) due to

136. At least 50 companies were affected to some ------- by the bankruptcy of TJ Electronics.

(A) presence
(B) extent
(C) aspect
(D) width

137. The Lighton Hotel is famous for its courteous service and many critics say that it is ------- one of the greatest hotels in the region.

(A) define
(B) definition
(C) definitely
(D) definite

138. Mr. Anderson was the head of his own small, yet successful Internet start-up company ------- he turned twenty-five years old.

(A) whether
(B) whereas
(C) by the time
(D) in the end

139. Details of the partnership agreement ------- need to be carefully reviewed, but both parties hope to sign a contract by the end of the month.

(A) once
(B) still
(C) ever
(D) even

140. ------- the support of the Pinage Art Association and the local government, the exposition on 19th century paintings would not have succeeded.

(A) Without
(B) Despite
(C) Unless
(D) Otherwise

GO ON TO THE NEXT PAGE

PART 6

Directions: A word or phrase is missing in sentences in the texts. For each sentence, four answer choices are given below. Select the best answer to fill in the blank. You must mark your answer on the answer sheet.

Questions 141-143 refer to the following memo.

BUSHBY, GERARD & DWYER INTER-OFFICE MEMO
Date: August 11
Subject: Air Conditioning Repair
To: All Employees and Staff

As some of you may have noticed, the air conditioning has not been working properly in our main office ------ last weekend.
      141. (A) before
           (B) since
           (C) by
           (D) after

Temperatures in the office rose to a maximum of 39 degrees Celsius, which is not healthy or conducive to work. Due to the extreme heat, the main office of BUSHBY, GERARD & DWYER will close temporarily for repairs. The main office will re-open early next week.

------ it re-opens, we would like all employees and staff to work in rotation at the
142. (A) Although
     (B) Instead
     (C) Until
     (D) Since

branch office.
Shifts are divided into morning and afternoon, so that each person ------ half a day.
                    143. (A) works
                         (B) has worked
                         (C) was working
                         (D) will work

Questions 144-146 refer to the following notice.

Notice to All Employees

We will be offering a new health insurance policy beginning September 1. There are various options including vision and dental plans for you to consider. On July 12, Ms. Martha Akers will be here for the day to advise ------- seeking consultation

144. (A) the one
(B) who
(C) anyone
(D) that

about new plans.
To make an appointment with Ms. Akers, send an e-mail to MAkers@omnihealth.biz with 3 ------- for appointment times.

145. (A) prefers
(B) preferable
(C) preferences
(D) preferably

Ms. Akers will see employees for 15 minutes from 8:30 A.M. to 4:30 P.M. (unavailable during lunch break 12:30 P.M.-1:30 P.M.). Please cc your supervisor in all correspondence and Ms. Akers will use the "reply all" function to make sure that you are ------- from work at that time.

146. (A) excuse
(B) to excuse
(C) excusing
(D) excused

GO ON TO THE NEXT PAGE

Questions 147-149 refer to the following e-mail.

To: Mark Stuart
From: Jonathan Woods
Subject: Incorrect Numbers in Master Chemicals' Order

I have just received a call from Mr. Pitt regarding an inaccurate order quantity for plastic bottles. The correct amount is 100,000 pieces, not 10,000 and they are ------- that the complete amount be delivered as originally scheduled.

147. (A) demanding
(B) decreasing
(C) canceling
(D) increasing

Master Chemicals has been one of our most valued clients and we are entirely ------- here. I urge you to talk with the production line manager immediately to

148. (A) at fault
(B) hopeful
(C) with success
(D) on schedule

fulfill this order on time. Please report to me on the changes in production schedule, so Mr. Pitt can be updated on the situation shortly.
-------, remember that such a fundamental error only lowers our corporate value.

149. (A) Otherwise
(B) Therefore
(C) However
(D) Meanwhile

From now on, I hope you will take the necessary measures to ensure this kind of error never happens again.

Questions 150-152 refer to the following article.

Gourmet Stores to Open in U.K.

Gourmet Stores announced plans to open its stores in the U.K. early next year.
------- its spokesperson, the company will start with 3 outlets in London and

150. (A) Accorded by
 (B) Accorded to
 (C) Accordingly
 (D) According to

gradually increase the number to 50 within 3 years.
------- 15 years ago, Gourmet Stores has been successful for providing fresh and

151. (A) Regulated
 (B) Announced
 (C) Enforced
 (D) Founded

exotic produce from around the world. It currently has 100 stores in 20 major U.S. cities. This will be the first time for the company to expand its business abroad. While the franchise is well-known among the American upper class, it is relatively unknown elsewhere.
Through its first international operation the company aims to provide goods that are not easily ------- at local supermarkets.

152. (A) charged
 (B) applicable
 (C) obtainable
 (D) ready

GO ON TO THE NEXT PAGE

PART 7

Directions: In this part, you are asked to answer questions based on a variety of texts, such as notices, e-mails, memos, and articles. Select the best answer for each question and mark your answer on the answer sheet.

Questions 153-154 refer to the following advertisement.

Fisher's Country Club Golf Camp for Adults!

Want to learn how to play golf?
Want to improve your game?
Want to work on your swing?
You can do all this and more at our Golf Camp!

Our professional golf instructors will teach you everything you need to know about the game at our fabulous facilities: an 18-hole championship course, a 300-yard driving range, a putting green, and a large short-game area.

Our camps range from a minimum of 2-days to one week. At the beginning of each camp, your swing will be videotaped to identify the weak areas you will work on improving during your stay. There will also be daily lessons on the short game and, in the afternoons, a lesson round at our championship course.

And that's not all we have to offer. Our accommodation is one of the best in the area. Our lavishly appointed rooms, luxurious spa, fitness center, swimming pool, and three restaurants attract not only golfers but their partners, friends and spouses who just want to relax.

Contact our camp office today for more information.

153. What is suggested about Golf Camp?

(A) It offers a one-day trial camp.
(B) It extends instruction from professional tennis players.
(C) It assists in correcting swings with audiovisuals.
(D) It provides rental gear for activities.

154. What is NOT indicated about the accommodation offered?

(A) Luxurious furnishings
(B) Several cafeterias
(C) Souvenir shops
(D) Gymnasium facilities

Questions 155-156 refer to the following e-mail.

From:	Rosenberg Hotel
To:	Mr. J. Simmons
Subject:	Room Reservation
Date:	Thursday, February 16

Dear Mr. Simmons,

We are happy to confirm your reservation as follows.
Name: Mr. & Mrs. John Simmons
Room reserved: 1 Twin with a garden view
No. of nights: 4
Check-in: November 18
Check-out: November 22

To guarantee this reservation, the hotel will charge a one-night deposit fee plus tax to the credit card number you have provided. For our cancellation policies, please refer to our Web site.
We offer complimentary shuttle service to and from the airport. Should you require this, please let us know your flight number and arrival time and we will be happy to pick you up from the arrivals area.
If there is anything else we can be of service with, please let us know.
We look forward to welcoming you to the Rosenberg Hotel.

Sincerely,

John Patterson
Reservation Manager

155. Why was the e-mail sent to Mr. J. Simmons?

(A) To verify the booking request
(B) To inquire about an arrival time
(C) To notify him of the cancellation policy
(D) To publicize the hotel brand

156. How will the Rosenberg Hotel secure the room?

(A) By asking for responses from guests with reservations
(B) By giving warnings about cancellations in advance
(C) By charging prepayment to credit accounts
(D) By requesting credit card numbers from guests

GO ON TO THE NEXT PAGE

Questions 157-158 refer to the following invitation.

The Law Firm of Black & Crawford

Cordially Invites You
To a Surprise Birthday Party
For the Firm's Founding Father
The Honorable Julius Black

When: October 3rd, 6:30-10 P.M. (buffet dinner at 7:30)

Where: Oxdale Country Club

Dress: Black Tie

Mr. Black founded the firm in 1957 at the age of 26 and continues to be an active member of counsel, advising blue-chip companies and the philanthropic organization, Children with Dreams. Mr. Black is scheduled to arrive at 6:45, and, after a toast led by Mr. Black's son (and partner) Howard, cocktails will be served promptly from 7 p.m. Spouses and children are welcome to join us for dinner. Mr. Black's family has asked that instead of gifts, donations be made to the following philanthropic organization: Children with Dreams.

157. What is the main purpose of the party?

(A) To commemorate the 50th anniversary of the firm
(B) To honor Julius' retiring father
(C) To celebrate the firm founder's birthday
(D) To welcome Howard's entrance into the firm

158. What is indicated about the party?

(A) Donating to a benevolent group is recommended.
(B) Dress code should be business casual.
(C) Guests are expected to bring gifts.
(D) Guests can bring friends.

Questions 159-160 refer to the following coupon.

Guadix Airport Parking
729 Pine Street

Park for up to 31 days for only **$99.99**!*

Complimentary 24 hour shuttle bus service to terminals
Luggage assistance
Surveillance cameras installed on premises

*Valid for one trip only. No Frequent Parker Points with this coupon.

159. For whom is the coupon intended?

(A) Frequent customers
(B) Long-term service users
(C) Tourist groups
(D) Airport workers

160. What does the parking lot NOT offer?

(A) Free airport rides
(B) Security cameras
(C) Porter services
(D) Security patrol

GO ON TO THE NEXT PAGE

Questions 161-163 refer to the following press release.

Arlington Mall will soon gain three new tenants.

Wildbane is the number one sports gear and equipment store in Canada. It will open its first shop in the U.S. on the upper floor next to North Hammer in April.

Littleton, a children's clothing retailer, will occupy the 2,600 square feet of space across from Morgan Electronics on the upper floor in May. The same month, customers can also start enjoying a taste of Italy at Giorgio's Trattoria. The restaurant will be located at the south end of the lower floor.

The new tenants will offer goods and services at special low prices for the first week after opening, so we urge customers to take advantage of this opportunity.

161. What is mentioned about the Arlington Mall?

(A) It will add a second floor.
(B) It will expand the food court.
(C) It will extend business hours.
(D) It will enhance the line-up of stores.

162. What is NOT indicated in the press release?

(A) Wildbane is a popular shop in Canada.
(B) Littleton sells garments for kids.
(C) Morgan Electronics is located on the lower floor.
(D) Giorgio's Trattoria offers Italian cuisine.

163. According to the press release, when will the sale take place?

(A) In autumn
(B) In winter
(C) In spring
(D) In summer

GO ON TO THE NEXT PAGE

Questions 164-166 refer to the following notice.

Notice

To: All residents of 54 Brown Street Apartment
From: Jackson Waterworks Co., Ltd.
Date: April 12

The water supply to the building will be shut off due to necessary plumbing repair work scheduled on the following day and time:

Date: May 15
Time: 2 P.M. for approximately 3 hours

Please make sure water taps in your home are turned off during this time period to avoid overflow when the service is reinstated.
If you have any questions, please call 555-7839.

We apologize for the inconvenience.

164. What is the purpose of the notice?

(A) To report a water leakage
(B) To caution about a power outage
(C) To inform of a service disruption
(D) To announce a wall work

165. What is suggested about the repair work?

(A) It will be done along with road construction.
(B) It will be rescheduled in case of rain.
(C) It will be carried out by several contractors.
(D) It will be finished by the end of the day.

166. What are the residents asked to do?

(A) Turn off faucets
(B) Leave their residence
(C) Save sufficient water
(D) Switch off electricity

GO ON TO THE NEXT PAGE

Questions 167-170 refer to the following information.

The Top 3 Weekly Best Sellers
The three bestselling books in the first week of June at our store

Places	Titles	Authors	Prices	Last Week
1	The Autumn Leaves	Stephan Brownstone	$28.00	3
2	Classic Fairy Tales Volume 1		$25.00	10
3	The Art of Italian Cooking	Luciana Russo	$35.00	2

The Autumn Leaves
By Stephan Brownstone
Hardcover: 389 pages
$28.00
The Autumn Leaves, a heartbreaking story about a relationship between a mother and a daughter dreaming of becoming a music star, is Stephan Brownstone's debut novel. Brownstone, known as the author of several non-fiction books on family issues, has now expanded into the world of fiction. It seems his past meticulous research on families with different backgrounds has provided the foundation for this novel.

Classic Fairy Tales Volume 1
Hardcover: 70 pages
$25.00
Classic Fairy Tales Volume 1 contains ten of the most loved stories from around the world. The book has been edited to be read aloud, and its quaint illustrations will entice the reader to immerse oneself in the story. Volume 2 will be on sale next spring.

The Art of Italian Cooking
By Luciana Russo
Hardcover: 150 pages
$35.00
Learn how to cook authentic Italian food. *The Art of Italian Cooking* is sure to please everyone regardless of their cooking experience. For first-time cooks, each basic recipe comes with step-by-step photographs. For veteran cooks, Russo has prepared original and tasty variations of basic recipes for you to try. This is definitely a cookbook you will want to keep in the kitchen.

167. Who most likely published this information?

(A) A publisher
(B) A library
(C) A bookstore
(D) A schoolteacher

168. What is Stephan Brownstone famous for?

(A) His interviews with famous families of the world
(B) His TV documentaries on Family problems
(C) His research on social behavior
(D) His non-fiction works on family matters

169. What is true about *Classic Fairy Tales Volume 1*?

(A) It raised its rank more than any other book.
(B) It is a work of renowned authors.
(C) It covers numerous eccentric photographs.
(D) It is the most expensive book on the list.

170. What did Luciana Russo prepare to satisfy experienced cooks?

(A) Numerous variations of food
(B) Recipes from famous Italian restaurants
(C) Advice on using new cooking gadgets
(D) Information on organic farms

GO ON TO THE NEXT PAGE

Questions 171-175 refer to the following announcement.

September 20

Voluntarily Recall of Maxi Food Processor (Model# TSN 590 to TSN 650)

Maxi Kitchen Appliances, through internal testing, detected that the joint parts supporting the processor's rotating blades do not consistently work. No injury nor harm has been reported regarding the product. The Maxi Kitchen Appliances headquarters has issued a recall of 10,000 Maxi Food Processors (Model# TSN 590 to TSN 650) from markets, taking consumer safety seriously. The recall has been reported to the Consumer Safety Committee of the Government, and now free product replacement is being arranged. We sincerely apologize for any inconvenience this might have caused.

Hazard:
The internal electrical component can overheat and ignite, posing a potential fire hazard.

Type of Products: Maxi Food Processor (Model# TSN 590 to TSN 650)
The 10,000 recalled Maxi Food Processors had been sold and distributed through television infomercials and the company's Web site from January 15 to August 13. The units should have serial numbers, starting from TSN 590 to TSN 650. To check the serial number on a unit, please see the back left side of product, next to the electrical cord.

What to do:
If the serial number on a unit is between TSN 590 to TSN 650, please stop using the product immediately. Customers are asked to return a faulty unit to the store it was purchased at and ensure they receive a certificate of returned item. Customers may send it for a full refund or a replacement product of a similar value. Please send the document to the following address:
Attention: Recall Model# TSN 590
Maxi Kitchen Appliances
1123 Baker St.
Christchurch 2020

Contact Details:
For further information or any questions, please do not hesitate to speak to a representative from Quality Control Department at 1-888-555-6255 or visit our website at http://service.MaxiKitchen.co.nz. Customer service on this recall will be available from September 20 to December 20.

Maxi Kitchen Appliances

171. Who most likely issued the announcement?

(A) A consumer electronics retailer
(B) A newspaper publisher
(C) A manufacturer
(D) A trading company

172. Why are Maxi Food Processors being recalled?

(A) The safety lock can fail.
(B) The unit is a fire risk.
(C) The blades may come loose gradually.
(D) The switch can malfunction.

173. The word "representative" in paragraph 5, line 1, is closest in meaning to

(A) secretary
(B) executive
(C) clerk
(D) supervisor

174. What is NOT indicated in the announcement?

(A) Production facilities
(B) Consumer support period
(C) Recalled product quantity
(D) Causes of harm

175. How can consumers receive compensation?

(A) By mailing the verification of return to the company
(B) By completing the online registration for reimbursement
(C) By visiting stores and getting a refund there
(D) By making a phone call to the public office

GO ON TO THE NEXT PAGE

Questions 176-180 refer to the following memo.

MEMO

From: Valerie Sanchez, HR
To: All ICE Electronics employees
Date: October 20
Subject: End of Act Green Marathon on Oct. 30

As of October 30, the Act Green Marathon will end its half century-long history. We'd like to thank all ICE employees for participating in the Act Green Marathon during this period of time.

The idea of the Act Green Marathon has developed so as to raise public awareness to save the planet. To achieve the goal, membership has offered points to every green choice, such as taking public transportation instead of driving a car, shopping with reusable bags, and so forth. As each member makes her/his commitment and the cumulative points count up, the company has donated to philanthropic organizations around the world. As a result of the members' collective efforts, we have contributed to providing vaccinations to children in poverty, protecting endangered species, and saving rain forests. Now, our primary objective has been accomplished. As a global company, however, we will continue our efforts to promote energy-conserving actions in our neighborhoods with the launch of our Eco team project. For those who are interested in the new eco-friendly weekly activities, please join the ICE Eco team. The ICE Eco team meets every Saturday morning to plant trees and manage flower gardens in business districts, chiefly in Springton Park. For more details, please contact Andy at extension 7829.

176. What is the purpose of the memo?

(A) To announce the date of the city marathon
(B) To notify of renewed company activity
(C) To encourage workers to exercise daily
(D) To invite people to a charity event

177. How can ICE employees collect points?

(A) By conserving energy
(B) By selling ICE products
(C) By working as a volunteer
(D) By showing leadership

178. What is mentioned about the accomplishment of the Act Green Marathon?

(A) It raised money for charity.
(B) It made employees healthier.
(C) It improved the company's image.
(D) It resulted in worldwide races and events.

179. What is indicated about ICE?

(A) It is an organizer of sporting events.
(B) It was founded 50 years ago.
(C) It is an international company.
(D) It is shutting down its business.

180. What is true about the ICE Eco team?

(A) They meet biweekly.
(B) They grow vegetables.
(C) They operate locally.
(D) They clean a park.

GO ON TO THE NEXT PAGE

Questions 181-185 refer to the following e-mails.

To:	Evan Garfield <egarfield@clarksville.ll.com>
From:	Drew at Customer Service <drew@speedycards.biz>
Subject:	Speedy Online Business Cards Confirmation Order 22401
Date:	October 22

Dear Mr. Garfield,

Thank you for your order. Your card will be shipped to you in the next 48 hours.

Order #: 22401
Shipping Condition: In process, ready for delivery
Sample: Please see below.

> **Evan the Clown** *"Birthday Parties in Your Way!"*
> Balloons and Fun for the Kid in All of Us
> Evan Garfield
> 510-555-8354
> egarfield@clarksville.ll.com
> www.evandown.com

Caution:
In order to keep the color on the cards from fading, we suggest you store the cards away from direct sunlight. A few months on a desk that gets direct and daily sunlight can cause the cards to fade considerably.

Again, thank you for your order.

To:	Drew at Customer Service <drew@speedycards.biz>
From:	Evan Garfield <egarfield@clarksville.ll.com>
Subject:	Problems regarding Speedy Online Business Cards
Date:	November 2

Dear Drew,

I want to call your attention to a few problems with order number 22401.
First of all, I can only imagine that someone retyped my website address as the cards say www.evandown.com instead of www.evanclown.com. I realize that a "c" and an "l" right next to one another might look like a "d," but I assumed you copied the text electronically. The wrong URL for my homepage makes the cards unusable.

I'm also afraid to say that I have two other issues. You mentioned there might be a color quality variation, but in my case, the color for the first 50 cards was vibrant and clear, but then the next 450 were already quite faded from the moment they were delivered despite never being exposed to sunlight. Moreover, the confirmation e-mail said my shipment was scheduled soon after, but the cards did not arrive until Nov. 1. I am very disappointed with your service and your product's overall quality. Please replace my cards with the correct URL and stable color quality in a prompt manner. Thank you.

Evan Garfield

181. Why was the e-mail sent to Mr. Garfield?

(A) To consult about the design of his card
(B) To advertise entertainment at a party
(C) To deliver a message from children
(D) To inform him that his order was being properly processed

182. According to the confirmation e-mail, when are orders usually sent out?

(A) On the day of purchase
(B) In a couple of hours
(C) Within two days
(D) A week later

183. What does Mr. Garfield say about the color?

(A) It didn't match what he had requested.
(B) It was faded from the beginning.
(C) It should be a lighter shade.
(D) It was vivid on every single item.

184. When does Mr. Garfield say his cards were delivered?

(A) Within 48 hours of confirmation
(B) Four days from confirmation
(C) Within a week of confirmation
(D) About ten days after confirmation

185. What is NOT mentioned in the second e-mail?

(A) Delay of delivery
(B) Additional 50 more cards ordered
(C) Descriptions of the correct web address
(D) Request for replacement

GO ON TO THE NEXT PAGE

Questions 186-190 refer to the following e-mails.

To:	Scott Parsons, K&G Design Associates
From:	Andy Itoh, Knight Owl Internet Cafe
Subject:	Remodeling Plan
Date:	December 9

Dear Mr. Parsons,

Many thanks for coming by last week. Here is our preliminary renovation plan. We really value your expertise, so could you give us some advice on it? Any suggestions you can make will be greatly appreciated.

Regarding our private single rooms on the first floor, we're considering installing hardwood floors if it costs less than $800 per room. If you find any other type of material that is inexpensive, please let me know.

Another major renovation targets private couple's rooms on the second and third floor. We are planning to double the number from five to ten. In all couple's rooms, we would like to have private bathrooms installed. Our budget to renovate couple's rooms is $3,000 per room.

Finally, we would like to renew the service sections. Our snack services should be upgraded for high-end users. We would like you to refurbish our snack lounge in the lobby and fit out a new drink counter on the second floor within a budget of $2,000 each. It is also important to equip bathrooms next to these sections for the same amount.

Again, thank you very much for your time and help.

Andy

To:	Andy Itoh, Knight Owl Internet Cafe
From:	Scott Parsons, K&G Design Associates
Subject:	Re: Remodeling Plan
Date:	December 14

Dear Mr. Itoh,

On close examination of your remodeling plan, we have sorted out what can be done.

For changes, I recommend you take into account the following.
Firstly, I don't think we will be able to install hardwood flooring within your budget. Instead, I suggest an alternative material: Hardwood-surfaced plastic material. It is

easily maintained and cleaned, costing $400 per room.

Secondly, I agree with the remodeling ideas for your couple's rooms. However, you might want to reconsider how many rooms you want to add.

The last thing we can suggest concerns the drink counter. We can offer you a lower price if you choose to place it in the area next to the snack lounge. In sum, it will cost $1,800 in addition to the cost of the snack lounge. However, you can save $200.

We look forward to hearing whether you are interested in our proposal.

Best regards,

Scott

186. Why did Mr. Itoh write the e-mail?

(A) To consult on a remodeling
(B) To suggest an innovative room design
(C) To charge for extra services
(D) To offer Internet services

187. In the first e-mail, the word "install" in paragraph 2, line 1, is closest in meaning to

(A) input
(B) convert
(C) place
(D) remove

188. What most likely will be remodeled as it is planned?

(A) Renewal of flooring material
(B) Private rooms with new flooring
(C) Drink counters on the second floor
(D) Lavatories for paired customers

189. What does Mr. Parsons say about hardwood flooring?

(A) It is easy to clean.
(B) It is too expensive.
(C) It is made from plastic.
(D) It is a substitution.

190. Where will the new drink counter most likely be installed?

(A) In the restaurant
(B) On the second floor
(C) On the third floor
(D) In the lobby

GO ON TO THE NEXT PAGE

Questions 191-195 refer to the following notice and list.

NOTICE

To the residents of Arbor View Apartments:

As of the first week of next month, a new policy for the collection of recyclables will be started in this apartment complex. Please refer to the following guidelines. Building management will distribute boxes to each apartment later this week. Boxes must be emptied directly into the large containers in the alley behind the apartment building by 6 A.M. on the day of pickup. Items do not have to be separated on Mondays, as the recycling company that comes on Mondays will take care of that. Unfortunately, the companies that handle recycling on the other days will not separate items, so please put your recyclables into the appropriate containers on those days. All containers will be labeled. Please consider saving items now according to the enclosed list.

Electronics can be put out for recycling the last week of each month at no cost. However, in order to keep the alley from getting blocked, please do not put your electronics out until the night before pickup. See the list for details.

Please contact building management with questions: 555-8688.

RECYCLING	
Monday	Plastics: water bottles, household cleaner bottles, yogurt cups, butter containers, etc. Please be sure to secure the lids tightly on these bottles and containers. The labels can remain on. Note that Styrofoam cannot be recycled.
Tuesday	Glass: clear and colored glass bottles, containers, and jars. Metal lids and labels can remain on, though containers must be empty. No light bulbs, ceramics, or Pyrex.
Wednesday	Paper: newspapers, magazines, wrapping paper, telephone books, cereal boxes, cardboard, etc. Staples are acceptable. No tissue paper, candy wrappers, paper cups, shredded paper, or used paper plates.

Thursday	Electronics: TVs, refrigerators, DVD players, etc.
Friday	Cans: pop cans, soup cans, coffee cans, etc. All cans must be empty. Labels can remain on. No aerosol cans or aluminum foil.

Recycling company phone numbers

Plastics Redone: 555-9063
Glass Works: 555-0021
Recycled Paper: 555-8214
Metal Disposal: 555-3679
Electronic Recycling: 555-1132

191. What is the purpose of the notice?

(A) To inform residents of a meeting
(B) To announce the launching of new rules
(C) To solicit volunteers among residents
(D) To promote a new garbage company

192. The word "keep" in the notice, paragraph 2, line 2, is closest in meaning to

(A) oppose
(B) prevent
(C) cancel
(D) remove

193. When in the month will electronics be picked up free of charge?

(A) The last Friday
(B) The first Thursday
(C) The last Thursday
(D) The third Wednesday

194. According to the list, what are residents required to do?

(A) Shred their magazines
(B) Remove the labels from their cans
(C) Take the staples out of papers
(D) Put the lids on plastic bottles

195. Which days can residents most likely recycle flyers?

(A) On Tuesdays
(B) On Wednesdays
(C) On Thursdays
(D) On Fridays

GO ON TO THE NEXT PAGE

Questions 196-200 refer to the following notice and e-mail.

The 20th Anniversary Sale

Tom & Tailor is celebrating its 20th anniversary this coming Wednesday. Our clothing line has been widely popular among the executives of various well-known companies and everyday folks alike. We would like to take a moment to truly appreciate the patronage of our customers. THANK YOU!!

During this month, as a token of appreciation, we would like to offer our customers 10% off our price tag. Only this week, if you shop before 5 P.M., you can get an additional 10% discount on every item in our store. Please come and take advantage of this special occasion.

Our policy stands to serve customers of any shapes and sizes, and we continue to do so. The best part of our business is interacting with you, so we can find out what you are looking for. Our highly trained tailor is more than happy to assist you. Please do not hesitate to contact us at tom@tailor.com if you have any questions.

We are all looking forward to serving old and new customers alike to celebrate our 20th anniversary together!!

To:	Tom & Tailor service<ttservice@tailor.com>
From:	James White<james@coolmail.com>
Date:	September 21
Subject:	10% discount

To whom it may concern :

Last week, I bought two well-designed business shirts. In sorting out all my receipts, I realized I didn't receive the full discount for the shirts purchased on Wednesday around 4 o'clock.

I'm surprised to find mistakes with this purchase. As I will visit your store tomorrow, I hope this matter will be resolved immediately.

James White

196. What is the main purpose of this notice?

(A) To let customers know the great deal is over
(B) To invite people to a special occasion
(C) To greet new customers
(D) To explain available sizes at a store

197. According to the notice, which does the store value the most?

(A) Carrying the latest fashion
(B) Interacting with customers
(C) Training professional tailors
(D) Serving more new clients

198. Who is Mr. White?

(A) A regular customer
(B) A well-experienced tailor
(C) A new neighbor
(D) An executive

199. Why is Mr. White visiting Tom & Tailor?

(A) To respond to the advisement
(B) To clarify the opening hours of the store
(C) To order extra shirts
(D) To get a refund for the difference

200. What is the discount rate Mr. White should have received?

(A) 20%
(B) 10%
(C) 30%
(D) 15%

Stop! This is the end of the test. If you finish before time is called, you may go back to Parts 5, 6, and 7 check your work.

READING TEST

In the Reading test, you will be asked to demonstrate how well you comprehend written English. The Reading test is comprised of three parts and directions are given for each part. The entire test will last 75 minutes. Within the time allowed, you should answer as many questions as you can. You must mark your answers on the separate answer sheet provided. Do not write your answers in the test book.

PART 5

Directions: A word or phrase is missing in the following sentences. For each sentence, four answer choices are given below. Select the best answer to fill in the blank. You must mark your answer on the answer sheet.

101. Professor Fontaine of Tucker University ------- one of our external auditors since last February.

    (A) was
    (B) has been
    (C) is
    (D) will be

102. The pictures must be chosen ------- tomorrow morning so that they can be included in our press release.

    (A) until
    (B) for
    (C) in
    (D) by

103. Anyone ------- in the position should contact Ms.Lee Monday through Friday between 10:00 A.M. and 4:00 P.M.

    (A) interest
    (B) interesting
    (C) interested
    (D) to interest

104. Sales representatives are encouraged to ------- up with new ideas about advertising strategies.

    (A) raise
    (B) go
    (C) come
    (D) think

105. Ken Automotive Supplies has been a client of ------- for over 20 years in the South American region.

(A) we
(B) our
(C) ours
(D) us

106. A ten percent discount and free delivery service is offered ------- for customers with a membership card.

(A) exclude
(B) exclusion
(C) exclusive
(D) exclusively

107. Mr. Chen was extremely ------- to receive a job offer from a well-known beverage company in New York.

(A) happier
(B) happiest
(C) happily
(D) happy

108. Please be reminded that MSG Corporation ------- the contents of the service in the coming year.

(A) discontinue
(B) to discontinue
(C) have discontinued
(D) will discontinue

109. The Korean restaurant is closed ------- further notice due to building repairs.

(A) by
(B) next
(C) until
(D) to

110. To show our appreciation to our ------- customers, we're offering free tickets to a popular comedy show held downtown.

(A) value
(B) valuate
(C) valuing
(D) valued

111. One of the growing concerns for people who are worried about the earth is the ------- of our air and water.

(A) quality
(B) quantity
(C) quest
(D) questionnaire

112. A group of consumers criticized the government for being indifferent ------- public opinion.

(A) to
(B) for
(C) from
(D) with

GO ON TO THE NEXT PAGE

113. With the appearance of a competing company, it has become ------- important for BWU Corporation to expand its business to different fields.

   (A) increase
   (B) increasingly
   (C) increasing
   (D) increased

114. Any person ------- income falls below the poverty line qualifies for this program.

   (A) whom
   (B) whose
   (C) who
   (D) whoever

115. This new technology enabled us to ------- an e-payment system which best fits your business needs.

   (A) be delivered
   (B) delivered
   (C) delivering
   (D) deliver

116. Please make sure the format of the new edition is ------- with the first edition.

   (A) consistently
   (B) consistent
   (C) consistence
   (D) consist

117. The city council announced that the reform of its health services would take ------- the following fiscal year.

   (A) place
   (B) occasion
   (C) hold
   (D) event

118. The Siam Palace Resort & Club Pattaya is ------- for its excellent location combined with the tranquility of a private beach.

   (A) renown
   (B) renewal
   (C) renowned
   (D) renovated

119. Financial projections show that if the market ------- to decline, the retail division will find itself with a negative cash flow.

   (A) continued
   (B) continuing
   (C) continual
   (D) continues

120. ------- people would prefer to work in the communities where they live, but this is not always possible.

   (A) Many of
   (B) Much of
   (C) Most
   (D) Almost

121. Richmond Corporation's new warehouse is comparatively large among ------- of other companies nearby.

(A) those
(B) what
(C) who
(D) whom

122. The neighbors formed a community organization ------- protect their families from increasing incidents of crime.

(A) now
(B) so that
(C) in order to
(D) which

123. ------ candidates are required to write a mandatory essay for the interview scheduled next Wednesday.

(A) Potential
(B) Potentially
(C) Potentiality
(D) Potentiate

124. Because the massage services in the Sunshine Spa are very popular on weekends, you need to consider ------- a space in advance.

(A) reserved
(B) reserves
(C) reserving
(D) reserve

125. The chairperson of the board of directors declared she does not ------- to seek another term, though she will remain on the board.

(A) attend
(B) intend
(C) predict
(D) concur

126. By State Law, you need a ------- in order to purchase contact lenses.

(A) definition
(B) prescription
(C) conception
(D) motivation

127. ------- an effort as to overhaul vocational training programs does not seem to be sufficient.

(A) So
(B) Much
(C) Same
(D) Such

128. The ------- price tag on the project is expected to range somewhere between 2.5 and 3 million dollars.

(A) estimating
(B) estimate
(C) estimation
(D) estimated

GO ON TO THE NEXT PAGE

129. The certification demonstrates that Gutierrez Dairy meets the highest social ------- environmental standards in the industry.

(A) but
(B) toward
(C) and
(D) such

130. Mr. White was awarded the company's Best Salesperson of the Year for three ------- years.

(A) entire
(B) precise
(C) consecutive
(D) restless

131. Jackie looked ------- when she finally realized that nobody was paying attention to her opinion.

(A) embarrass
(B) embarrassing
(C) to be embarrassed
(D) embarrassed

132. We believe that the new lineup of our AF digital camera series will ------- catch everyone's attention.

(A) patiently
(B) gratefully
(C) definitely
(D) deliberately

133. Cape Clothing Store will have to undergo drastic downsizing due to a long-term economic -------.

(A) downturn
(B) growth
(C) market
(D) scale

134. Known as a skilled technician, Mason Ford has no ------- of accounting.

(A) confidence
(B) knowledge
(C) expectation
(D) evidence

135. Jens Technology Group, Inc. announced today its ------- into Southeast Asian markets.

(A) expand
(B) expandable
(C) expansively
(D) expansion

136. Workers need to comply ------- the safety regulations and report to the factory manager any defects they find in the machine.

(A) for
(B) to
(C) along
(D) with

137. Travelers can easily book ------- at the cheapest rate by using a rate comparison tool on Web sites.

(A) rewards
(B) contents
(C) accommodations
(D) destinations

138. A typhoon ------- by strong winds is likely to arrive in Okinawa by tomorrow morning.

(A) accompanied
(B) to accompany
(C) accompanying
(D) will accompany

139. Always at the forefront of health-consciousness, California has become the first state to ------- ban trans fats in restaurants.

(A) complete
(B) completed
(C) completely
(D) be completed

140. ------- being knowledgeable about the latest industry trends, it is important to treat our customers fairly and honestly.

(A) Otherwise
(B) Along with
(C) Wherever
(D) As a result

GO ON TO THE NEXT PAGE

PART 6

Directions: A word or phrase is missing in sentences in the texts. For each sentence, four answer choices are given below. Select the best answer to fill in the blank. You must mark your answer on the answer sheet.

Questions 141-143 refer to the following e-mail.

To: Zack Anderson
From: Karen Milestone
Subject: Our Apologies

Dear Mr. Anderson,

I am writing on behalf of Pro-Fast Delivery Systems, Inc., to apologize for the mix-up ------- resulted in your packages being delivered late.
  141. (A) which
      (B) so that
      (C) being
      (D) when

As a long-time valued customer, you probably know that we at Pro-Fast endeavor to deliver all packages on schedule, on or ------- the estimated delivery date.
                      142. (A) during
                            (B) after
                            (C) before
                            (D) while

Unfortunately, due to intense storms caused by the hurricane, there was a delay in delivering your packages. As a result, please accept this $30 printable voucher as a ------- of our apology and goodwill.
  143. (A) mark
      (B) choice
      (C) reason
      (D) token

Questions 144-146 refer to the following notice.

Our New Hours and Dinner Menu.

Green Thumb Gourmet is proud to announce its new dinner menu. A ------- of

144. (A) various
(B) variety
(C) varied
(D) variable

cooked-from-scratch dishes are served from 5:00 P.M. to 8:00 P.M. To name a few from the menu, there is the Four Cheese Lasagna, the Sag Tofu Indian Curry and the Lebanese Stuffed Vegetables. -------, we will continue to serve our original

145. (A) However
(B) If
(C) Moreover
(D) While

organic salad and soup to everyone who orders their meal.
In addition, we will remain open during the late afternoon, so we can offer our hot takeouts to those ------- a late lunch or an early dinner. Our new hours are 10:30

146. (A) desire
(B) to desire
(C) desiring
(D) desired

A.M. to 8:00 P.M.

Green Thumb Gourmet
439 E. Moss St
555-9600

GO ON TO THE NEXT PAGE

Questions 147-149 refer to the following letter.

To our customers,

Thank you for using Natural Equipment products.
This is to inform you there has been a change in our maintenance personnel. James Brandon, who has been servicing your units for the past five years, will be transferred to our Atlanta branch, ------- September 1.

    147. (A) ever since
         (B) effective
         (C) in
         (D) always on

Brad Wayne will be replacing him. Since the beginning of his service, Brad has been a dedicated ------- who makes sure your units continue to operate

    148. (A) swimmer
         (B) teacher
         (C) professional
         (D) driver

smoothly. Please be assured this change will not affect our services in any way. If you have any further questions, please ------- to call our office at 555-5545.

    149. (A) hope
         (B) do not
         (C) expect
         (D) feel free

We hope to continue providing you with the quality service for which we are known.

Sincerely,

Adam Schultz
General Manager
Maintenance Division

Questions 150-152 refer to the following memo.

Subject: Company Retreat

All staff

In our history, this year has been our best -------. This is all thanks to your hard

150. (A) throughout
(B) else
(C) after
(D) yet

work.
I have always had ------- in our head chef Hiroaki Takagi, and I am proud of the

151. (A) confidence
(B) confidential
(C) confident
(D) confided

service quality of our staff. I am also pleased that Natalie Borden has newly joined us as our Banquet Service manager.
Customers have been responding positively to our improved selection of food and beverages. I cannot think of any better way ------- your effort than a three-day

152. (A) repaying
(B) repayment
(C) to repay
(D) repaid

vacation in Miami, Florida.
Needless to say, travel expenses and accommodation will be covered by the company. I hope all of you will participate and celebrate our success together.

With my appreciation,
Jean Bedeau, Owner Chef

GO ON TO THE NEXT PAGE

PART 7

Directions: In this part, you are asked to answer questions based on a variety of texts, such as notices, e-mails, memos, and articles. Select the best answer for each question and mark your answer on the answer sheet.

Questions 153-154 refer to the following advertisement.

Guinevere's Incredible Edible Gardens

Come to Guinevere's for all your organic food gardening needs. We specialize in developing your garden from seed to food for your table. We school you in the French-intensive method of gardening, first used in the tight city quarters of Paris. Crops are planted close together to save water, which encourages roots to grow deep, while discouraging weeds and bringing high yields. We help you design the best organic edible garden for your needs and then assist you in constructing and maintaining it, deterring pests, and harvesting it. We can test the quality of your soil and recommend plant food and organic fertilizers. We have plans for every group and hobby: Cook's Paradise Gardens; Kids' Gardens, Zesty & Spicy Gardens, etc.

153. What is being advertised?
 (A) Organic catering
 (B) French lessons
 (C) Garden tours
 (D) Gardening services

154. Which is NOT a service mentioned in the advertisement?
 (A) Waste removal
 (B) Pest control
 (C) Construction
 (D) Soil diagnostics

Questions 155-156 refer to the following e-mail.

To:	rcrawford@pr.nextcellular.com
From:	catehodgeson@tech.nextcellular.com
Subject:	Recall of product
Date:	May 7

Dear Ron,

This is Cate from the Technologies Department. As you know by now we have to recall over 100,000 NT Quasar cellular phones because of a problem with overheating batteries. This is not only an economic and technical setback for our company but also a public relations issue. This recall will affect thousands of mobile phone distributors and electronics stores throughout the country. We need to assure retailers and our customers that safety is our number one concern and that we have a well-coordinated plan for collecting faulty batteries and replacing them with new ones. Once we have worked out the technical aspects of the recall, I will be in direct contact with you.

Cate Hodgeson
Director of Technology

155. What is the e-mail about?

(A) Planning a new cell phone launch
(B) Planning to ask for the return of products
(C) Asking a retailer to carry a product
(D) Apologizing to customers

156. What is wrong with the product?

(A) It is not being marketed properly.
(B) Its screen is faulty.
(C) It is too expensive.
(D) Its battery is not safe to use.

GO ON TO THE NEXT PAGE

Questions 157-158 refer to the following memo.

Memo

From: Linda Perry, Personnel Director
To: All staff
Date: Monday, August 25
Subject: Monthly staff meeting

Due to Labor Day on the first Monday next month, we would like to inform all staff that our usual monthly meeting in September will be postponed until the second Monday at 9 o'clock.

The agenda will be slightly different. Yes, this is the time of year when we will present the most productive department with an award. Last year it was the sales team that obtained the invitation to the dinner at a five-star hotel.

Our CEO will also make a presentation on the current business situation in our industry and what it means for our company.

Well done to all staff for your efforts over the last 6 months.

157. What is the main purpose of the memo?

(A) To announce a change in schedule
(B) To recognize an employee
(C) To hold an emergent meeting
(D) To invite a company excursion

158. What information is NOT included in the memo?

(A) The day of the next staff meeting
(B) The topic of the CEO's presentation
(C) The department to be commended
(D) The expression of gratitude to the staff

Questions 159-160 refer to the following letter.

Westfield Housing Loans
88 Jasper Ave.
Bluebell, Ohio
213-555-7623

June 30

Dear Mr. North,

Thank you for applying for a loan with Westfield Housing Loans. We appreciate your business and would like to help you. However, it has come to our attention that the loan documentation you sent in is missing a few pages. The only information we have received so far is your application and employment history. We need a list of your previous addresses and a signed statement personally allowing us to look at your credit records. I have included these forms with this letter. Once we have all the required information, the process of approving a loan will take 2-3 weeks. After that time, we will notify you by mail of the amount you are qualified to borrow.

If you have any questions about the documents or the approval process, please contact our customer service department at 800-555-0902 or visit our website at www.westfieldhousing.org.

Sincerely,

Jody Brown, Loan Officer

159. What is the purpose of this letter?

(A) To advertise a loan
(B) To request some more documents
(C) To send more information to Mr. North
(D) To explain how long a process takes

160. Why is a signature needed?

(A) To record previous addresses
(B) To pay off a loan
(C) To view a job record
(D) To inquire about credit history

GO ON TO THE NEXT PAGE

Questions 161-163 refer to the following advertisement.

House Repair, The Home Repair Service
No job is too small for us!

From cleaning exhaust fans to installing shelves, if you require help around your home, call House Repair now.

We can fix, install, clean and remodel - jobs that perhaps you can do but don't have time for. Our professional service people are trained to tackle all kinds of home-related problems and are equipped with the tools to handle them.

Just give us a call. Our office is open 24 hours a day, 7 days a week. Tell us your problem and we can give you a rough estimate on the phone. Your home problems can usually be fixed in one visit!

161. Who will most likely be calling House Repair?

(A) Building janitors
(B) Home owners
(C) Architectural design offices
(D) Cleaning companies

162. What is true about House Repair?

(A) They will accept all trivial requests.
(B) They provide cheap and quick repairs.
(C) They will send courteous staff.
(D) They will charge extra for estimates.

163. What is indicated about the service for regular home problems?

(A) Repairs will end in one hour.
(B) Problems will be repaired in one visit.
(C) It will take two days to diagnose.
(D) Reservation should be made a week before.

Questions 164-166 refer to the following information.

Lakeland Shore Charity Art Auction Welcomes Clive Tavares

The 13th annual Lakeland Shore Charity Art Auction will be held February 11th at 6 P.M.

Location:
LS Art Gallery on East Torrance between Pine and 21st Street.

Special Guest:
Clive Tavares, Sculptor

6:00 P.M.	Opening Ceremony
6:30 P.M.	Remarks by Clive Tavares
7:00 P.M.	Auction Begins
10:00 P.M.	Closing Ceremony

Mr. Tavares has been kind enough to donate his four most recent bronze pieces to the auction: *The Hand*, *Mother & Child*, *Roses*, and his latest art piece, *Breakfast*. The bidding for each of these works will begin at $7,000. Over five hundred other artworks including paintings by Salle, Roth and Freilicher will be presented for auction. Admission is free for Lakeland Shore Art Museum members (non-members, $10). All auction items are provided by Lakeland Shore Art Museum in collaboration with The International Earthquake Relief Fund.

164. How often is the Lakeland Shore Charity Art Auction held?

(A) Once a year
(B) Twice a year
(C) Every other year
(D) Every four years

165. Which is the most recent work of Mr. Tavares?

(A) *The Hand*
(B) *Roses*
(C) *Breakfast*
(D) *Mother & Child*

166. What is mentioned about the auction?

(A) The collection adds up to 7,000.
(B) Entrance fees are equally charged.
(C) An artist makes a speech.
(D) One institution provides all the items.

Questions 167-170 refer to the following letter.

Pacific Airlines
Your choice to fly

May 9

Ms. Sarah Watson
53 Oak Street,
Pittsburgh, PA

Dear Ms. Watson,

Welcome to Pacific Airlines' Frequent Flyer Program!

Our program is the only one where you are awarded bonus miles when you travel again with Pacific Airlines within ten days of your last flight (restrictions apply). Furthermore, register your whole family so you can share awarded miles. You can also earn miles on the ground every time you use the Pacific Airlines' credit card.

The more miles you fly, the more free services you get as well. You will start out at bronze level, which is followed by silver and gold. At gold level (more than 100,000 flying miles in one calendar year), you are entitled to free use of airport lounges, two upgraded tickets and a one night free stay for two at a designated hotel.

Our Frequent Flyer Program has also made it easier for you to redeem awards. Just log on to our Web site and make your reservation. Don't want to travel? You can also choose to exchange your miles for gift certificates that can be used at several nationwide retail outlets.

We have enclosed a booklet on our Frequent Flyer Program. Inside, you will find everything you need to know about it.

Your Pacific Airlines' credit card will be sent to you via registered mail within two weeks.
We hope to see you soon on one of Pacific Airlines' flights!

Sincerely,

Edward Paine
President and Chief Executive Officer

167. What is the main purpose of this letter?

(A) To thank Ms. Watson for joining the Frequent Flyer Program
(B) To respond to Ms. Watson's inquiry
(C) To explain how to redeem awards
(D) To explain their program's benefits compared to competitors

168. How can miles add up without flying?

(A) By registering family members
(B) By using the Pacific Airlines' credit card
(C) By using gift certificates
(D) By shopping at certain retail outlets

169. What are customers advised to do in order to use miles accumulated?

(A) Mail an application form
(B) Visit the airline office
(C) Call the Awards Desk
(D) Go to the Web site

170. What is most likely written in the enclosed booklet?

(A) Corporate profile and financial information
(B) Credit card details
(C) How to apply for the program
(D) Details of the program

GO ON TO THE NEXT PAGE

Questions 171-175 refer to the following brochure.

Chemical Engineering B.S./M.S. in Petroleum Technology

The unique five-year degree program here at Dinmore University is a combined Bachelor and Master of Science in Chemical Engineering. Because of the significant role oil and gas continue to play in the global energy market, the need for people trained in this field has increased. Accessing and preserving these valuable resources require technological advances and the participation of many different scientific fields. Chemical Engineering graduates can seek jobs with a variety of fuel and energy companies.

The first three years are much the same as other chemical engineering programs with some options for special courses and seminars. Beginning in the fourth year, the areas of study cover advanced topics, such as the production of oil and gas from reservoirs. Students continue to study advanced chemical engineering at this time. There is also a course on practical matters that deals with issues resulting from the development of new products in the field of fossil fuel energy. Students start their individual research projects which are concluded in the fifth year.

Throughout the final year, students finish their research projects and work on specialized energy topics. At this time, everyone in the program takes a course called "Technology in the Oil Industry." Upon graduation, Dinmore students have a high success rate in finding key positions in companies in the oil and gas production industry.

To apply online go to: www.Petrotech.Dinmore.edu

171. What is the main topic of this brochure?

(A) Methods of procuring oil and gas from reservoirs
(B) Ways of using new fossil fuel products
(C) Features of a chemical engineering program
(D) All scientific fields that support the oil industry

172. What does the brochure say about the initial three years of the program?

(A) They are very specialized in petroleum technology.
(B) They are similar to other chemical engineering programs.
(C) They offer students job-seeking opportunities.
(D) They change depending upon what is happening in the oil industry.

173. What is indicated about students working on their research?

(A) Their areas of study are limited to practical matters.
(B) They finish their projects in two years.
(C) Their funding is provided from affiliated corporations.
(D) They conduct experiments in a small group.

174. The word "positions" in paragraph 3, line 4, is closest in meaning to

(A) poses
(B) points
(C) locations
(D) jobs

175. What is suggested about Dinmore graduates?

(A) They start up industry-university collaboration projects.
(B) They succeed in finding good positions in some industries.
(C) They are in need of support from career counselors.
(D) They are hired by the university as faculty.

GO ON TO THE NEXT PAGE

Questions 176-180 refer to the following article.

Local Tech Innovator Awarded for Community Achievement

To locals, Ernie Samson will always be the passionate kid who grew up in a working class neighborhood of Gregston. To the rest of the city, he is best known as this year's winner of the E. Lawrence Community Service award for his work helping to start computer science programs in some of our city's poorest schools. Ernie, whose mother is from Mexico, is the first Latino descendant to receive the award.

Since graduating from college, Ernie and his tech company have contributed over a million dollars to help provide equipment and instructors to disadvantaged high schools for courses in programming, website design, and graphic design. Ernie doesn't just donate money to courses and send others to do the work, but actually volunteers once a week to teach a course on how to start and run a tech business. His company also chooses the best students from these schools to work part-time at his company after school or during vacation. Starting next year, Ernie's company will offer college scholarships to the top computer science students.

Ernie believes it's important to get kids interested in technology at an early age. He attributes his success in the tech business to his ninth grade computer science teacher, Mr. Dan Paulson. Mr. Paulson not only encouraged Ernie to learn about computers, but even gave him a used computer so he could make computer programs at home after school.

176. Where did Mr. Samson grow up?

(A) In the inner city
(B) In a working class area
(C) In an affluent suburb
(D) In a foreign country

177. Why has Mr. Samson and his company contributed a large sum of money?

(A) To recruit the top-ranked students at schools
(B) To offer internship programs to young adults
(C) To improve the learning conditions in the city
(D) To advertise their new programs

178. What did Mr. Samson receive?

(A) A scholarship to college
(B) A job promotion
(C) A computer science degree
(D) Recognition for service

179. What does Mr. Samson do once a week?

(A) Attends computer science classes
(B) Teaches a business class
(C) Prepares to start a new program
(D) Chooses a new intern

180. The word, "attributes" in paragraph 3, line 3, is closest in meaning to

(A) credits
(B) measures
(C) achieves
(D) celebrates

GO ON TO THE NEXT PAGE

Questions 181-185 refer to the following notice and article.

Call for Entries
The Fourth Annual Hopton Film Festival
We are looking for new talent!

Hopton Film Festival is now accepting original film works. The winners from each category will be awarded 1,000 dollars and a silver trophy of recognition. The winning films will be presented at the Hopton Film Festival in March, where participants will get a chance to meet top directors and screenwriters.

We invite entries for the following categories:

Categories	Description
Main Category	All film types not specified in other categories
Animation Category	Animated films
Short-film Category	Films less than 7 minutes long
Youth Category	Films created by persons under the age of eighteen

Fees and Deadlines
Entry Fee: $55
Deadline: September 18 (All materials must be postmarked by the deadline date.)

For printable entry forms and other details of the Fourth Annual Hopton Film Festival, please visit our website at www.hoptonfestival.com.

Film Festival Winner *"Flying Wings"*
by Tobias Payne

Among the winners of this year's Hopton Film Festival is *"Flying Wings"* by Danny Evans. Unlike most other contestants, Evans had no prior experience in creating films until now.
"I didn't expect to win, so I was really surprised. Now I am grateful to my parents for their words of encouragement," Evans commented.
"Flying Wings" is about a fictional character called Mauli Jones who quits his

job as a high-paid financial analyst to travel the world. Mauli visits exotic countries where he tries local delicacies and makes amazing new friends. Although just 6-minutes long, "*Flying Wings*" is a well-structured film with a touch of humor. We cannot wait to see more from Evans.

181. What is indicated in the notice?

(A) The applicants will fill in the online entry forms.
(B) The judges will be people from the entertainment sector.
(C) The winners will receive prize money and an award.
(D) The organizers are hoping to discover talented actors.

182. In the notice, the word "presented" in paragraph 1, line 3, is closest in meaning to

(A) endorsed
(B) shown
(C) rolled
(D) produced

183. According to the article, what is unique about Mr.Evans?

(A) He experienced studying abroad.
(B) He quit his job to shoot a film.
(C) He borrowed money from his parents.
(D) He had never made a film before.

184. What most likely is the topic of *Flying Wings*?

(A) Traveling on a budget
(B) Getting a pilot's license
(C) Discovering new cultures
(D) Working overseas

185. Which category did Mr. Evans enter?

(A) Main
(B) Animation
(C) Short-film
(D) Youth

GO ON TO THE NEXT PAGE

Questions 186-190 refer to the following itinerary and e-mail.

Dear Keith,
This is our itinerary.
Please contact me any time for questions or changes.
Thank you very much,
Bob Cassidy

J.D. WATKINS SECURITIES CORP.
OFFICIAL VISIT TO EAST ASIA

SCHEDULE
September 3 – 6 (4 days and 2 nights)

DAY1: September 3
11:15 A.M.   Departure, San Francisco
(September 4)
3:15 P.M.   Arrival, Tokyo
6:00 P.M.   Check-in, New Tokyo Oriental Hotel
              Dinner

DAY2: September 5
              Breakfast at Terrace Restaurant
Presentations
9:00 A.M. - 10:30 A.M.
              • Allen Keefer Associates: "The Current State of Arbitrage"
              • Vanderburg Consulting: "Investing in Japanese Real Estate"
10:40 A.M. - noon
              • Honda Securities:"How Oil Imports Affect Japanese Markets"
              • Law Firm of Takizawa & Murphy: "Recruiting Bi-Lingual Attorneys"
1:00 P.M.   Check-out
              Lunch

1:30 P.M. - 5:30 P.M.
              Stock Market tours with members of Honda Securities
7:00 P.M.   Departure, Tokyo
              Dinner on airplane
10:15 P.M.   Arrival, Hong Kong
11:00 P.M.   Check-in, Hong Kong Grand Dragon Hotel

DAY3: September 6
              Breakfast at Aqua Azure
Presentations:
9:00 A.M. - 10:30 A.M.
              • South China Securities:"Chinese Investment in Foreign Markets"
10:40 A.M. - noon
              • Grover Wu Consulting: "Chinese Hot Stock Tips"
              • Jackson Cole Investment Banking: "British Banking in East Asia"

1:00 P.M.   Check-out
              Lunch
2:50 P.M.   Departure, Hong Kong
11:50 A.M.   Arrival, San Francisco

To:	Bob Cassidy
From:	Keith Woodridge
Subject:	A few modifications on the itinerary
Date:	August 26

Dear Bob,

I am sending you this e-mail to let you know some changes to our itinerary. Tyrone Taylor gave me a call to bring some good and bad news.

First, the bad news: South China Securities and Grover Wu Consulting have both pulled out of the conference due to the recent financial crisis. This means we'll have only one session in Hong Kong.

Now the good news: Our regular customer, Mr. Billy Lo of Mansfield & Lo is offering an expedition to the Hong Kong Stock Exchange on September 7. It's a wonderful opportunity, isn't it? I think we should take him up on it. Please write back as to whether it will conflict with your schedule by the end of this month. If not, I will reschedule the return date to accept his offer.

Regardless of the changes, I must say we have arranged the most exciting business trip in my career.

Best Regards,

Keith

186. What is the main topic of the itinerary?

(A) A private tour to East Asia
(B) A conference schedule
(C) A business trip plan
(D) An international trade negotiation

187. In the itinerary, the word "SECURITIES" in line 6, is closest in meaning to

(A) savings
(B) safety
(C) stocks
(D) defense

188. In the e-mail, what is implied about the itinerary?

(A) Some parties' withdrawal from the schedule
(B) Closing a mutual contract by the end of month
(C) Changes in the careers fair venue
(D) A one-day tour to Asian street markets

189. Why does Mr. Woodridge ask for a reply?

(A) He wants to decide the arrival date in San Francisco.
(B) He needs to introduce a new client in Hong Kong.
(C) He ought to contact the presenters in China.
(D) He has to arrange another business trip to Tokyo.

190. Which presentation in Hong Kong is held as scheduled?

(A) The Current State of Arbitrage
(B) Chinese Hot Stock Tips
(C) Recruiting Bi-Lingual Attorneys
(D) British Banking in East Asia

GO ON TO THE NEXT PAGE

Questions 191-195 refer to the following memo and schedule.

Memo

From: Bob Tyler <General Affairs Department>
To: Steve Briggs <Compliance Department>
Subject: 'Company Employee Handbook' revisions
Date: Feb. 6

Dear Steve,

Following the amendments to the privacy law passed this week, we need to review and make necessary changes to the 'Company Employee Handbook.'

Our corporate lawyers will soon be sending us a simplified breakdown of what exactly the new law expects from private limited companies. Briefly, the revisions must involve staff training programs targeted at the IT, Accounting, and Administration departments and other staff members who have a chance to handle client data. Under the current circumstances, we are initially required to carry out a new risk management exercise.

I have attached my first draft of the schedule. Please look it over and get back to me if there is a problem. If everything is OK, please let me know. I will arrange for the managers to meet and reserve the venues while you continue with the exercise and implement the new compliance program. As there remain undecided agendas on the schedule, I'm counting on you to handle these.

Schedule (Feb.6 Draft)

Date	Details
June 2	Meeting with all departments and staff to inform them what will be happening and why the training program is being launched.
June 3	**IT** (All day) : not yet fixed
June 4	**Accounting** (AM) : On the subjects of a) filing cabinet and b) procedures of document disposal **Reception** (PM) : On the subjects of a) check on visitors and b) appropriate registration

June 5	**Administration** (AM) : not yet fixed
	Sales (PM) : On the subjects of a) tips on using mobile devices and b) a proper procedure for taking out data from the office
June 6	**Customer Service** (AM) : not yet fixed
June 9	Collection of reports from each department
June 12	Submit the summary of results and proposals to me

191. What is the main purpose of the memo?

(A) To inform the deadline
(B) To request Mr. Briggs to work
(C) To call an urgent meeting
(D) To introduce an article

192. Why will the Company Employee Handbook be changed?

(A) To incorporate the incoming legal changes
(B) To reflect new management policies
(C) To make the modifications in design and format
(D) To raise the employees' motivation

193. In the memo, the word "implement" in paragraph 3, line 3, is closest in meaning to

(A) announce
(B) execute
(C) choose
(D) explain

194. What is NOT indicated on the schedule?

(A) Attendees are required to file a report.
(B) The situation will be explained on the first day.
(C) Each department has its own subjects.
(D) An achievement test will be conducted.

195. What will Mr. Briggs probably do?

(A) Search for a convention center
(B) Issue revised company guidelines
(C) Select topics for some sessions
(D) Rearrange the schedule for lecturers

GO ON TO THE NEXT PAGE

Questions 196-200 refer to the following e-mails.

To:	Amanda Cole
From:	Johnathan Parks
Subject:	The press release for our new product
Date:	April 14

Good evening Amanda,

On June 1, we will release UX200, a new air conditioner. Prior to that, we are planning to hold a press release to introduce and advertise the newly available product to the public. Consequently, I was wondering if you could help us set it up.

The press release is planned for a date between Monday, May 16 and Friday, May 20. We would like to hold it in the vicinity of FN Consumer Electronics headquarters. The location needs to have enough room for approximately 90 reporters and 30 to 40 cameras. If you have trouble finding a venue that complies with our wishes, let me know and I will discuss alternative options with our manager.

If you require more information or have any questions, please e-mail me. Thank you in advance for your help.

Johnathan Parks
Deputy Manager
Business Administration Department

To:	Johnathan Parks
From:	Amanda Cole
Subject:	Re: The press release for our new product
Date:	April 15

Good afternoon John,

Thank you for your e-mail yesterday regarding the press release preparation for our new product. I am writing to confirm the place, date, and time with you and ask a few questions on the matter.

I have contacted the locations that meet your requirements and discovered that the Edmond Hill Building has an opening in Event Hall A on Wednesday, May 18. The hall has a seating capacity of 150, so I think it should be enough. I have already reserved it from 10

A.M., so if you prefer a different time, please e-mail me as soon as possible.

Could you also tell me if you are planning to use a video projector? If so, do you prefer us to deal with it? Regarding any devices you may need, we can also arrange for them if you inform us of the number needed. It would be most helpful if you could reply to these questions by Monday, April 25.

Again, thank you very much for your cooperation.

Amanda Cole
Publicity Department

196. Why did Mr. Parks send an e-mail to Ms. Cole?

(A) To give details of a new product release
(B) To announce the press release schedule
(C) To request arrangements for an upcoming event
(D) To discuss an advertising plan

197. What is NOT suggested about the press release?

(A) A new household appliance will be presented.
(B) The hall has already been booked.
(C) The starting time can be rearranged.
(D) Investors are the main audience.

198. What new information is indicated in the second e-mail?

(A) The preferable dates
(B) The rental fee amount
(C) The number of attendants
(D) The hours to hold the event

199. In the second e-mail, the word "meet" in paragraph 2, line 1, is closest in meaning to

(A) answer
(B) satisfy
(C) gather
(D) see

200. What is indicated about the Edmond Hill Building?

(A) It only holds 100 people.
(B) It opens after 11 A.M.
(C) It is close to the headquarters.
(D) It is a historical building.

Stop! This is the end of the test. If you finish before time is called, you may go back to Parts 5, 6, and 7 check your work.

READING TEST

In the Reading test, you will be asked to demonstrate how well you comprehend written English. The Reading test is comprised of three parts and directions are given for each part. The entire test will last 75 minutes. Within the time allowed, you should answer as many questions as you can. You must mark your answers on the separate answer sheet provided. Do not write your answers in the test book.

PART 5

Directions: A word or phrase is missing in the following sentences. For each sentence, four answer choices are given below. Select the best answer to fill in the blank. You must mark your answer on the answer sheet.

101. If you are eligible ------- Medicare, please fill in this form.

    (A) to
    (B) for
    (C) of
    (D) about

102. The island of Sun ------- for its beautiful scenery, historical heritage, and natural hot springs.

    (A) has known
    (B) will know
    (C) is known
    (D) knowing

103. Beverage industry giant Gordon Sax ------- a pilot shop of its coffee chain in downtown Bangkok next week.

    (A) opened
    (B) to open
    (C) is going to open
    (D) to be opening

104. The Music Scholarship Competition is held every year for all high school seniors ------- are going to college.

    (A) which
    (B) whose
    (C) who
    (D) they

105. Mr. Brook has suggested ------- help from the consultants to put together a revolutionary marketing plan.

(A) getting
(B) gotten
(C) to get
(D) get

106. All employees are expected to make a ------- to superior customer service.

(A) commitment
(B) commit
(C) committing
(D) committed

107. Due to ------- maintenance of the air conditioning, smoking in this building will be temporarily prohibited.

(A) regular
(B) regularize
(C) regularly
(D) regularity

108. Unfortunately, the product ------- did not meet our standards of quality.

(A) itself
(B) yourself
(C) themselves
(D) himself

109. Initially, MG Electronics was planning to sell its new product only during the summer, but increased production ------- it sold well.

(A) regarding
(B) before
(C) despite
(D) when

110. A timetable released by the construction company shows even more ------- in a project that started years ago.

(A) to delay
(B) delaying
(C) delays
(D) delayed

111. Purchased items can be returned to FS Interiors free of ------- if it is within two weeks of purchase.

(A) payment
(B) fee
(C) fair
(D) charge

112. Professor Wilson of Carlton University was awarded $100,000 for ------- contributions to the study of the human genome.

(A) legitimate
(B) actual
(C) extraordinary
(D) tentative

GO ON TO THE NEXT PAGE

113. Mr. Kean, the president of Dubmen Company, was introduced to the audience ------- after the screening of the corporate promotion movie.

(A) shorter
(B) shortened
(C) shortly
(D) shortness

114. The new cellular phone is designed to meet the most ------- requirements of our clients.

(A) independent
(B) extinct
(C) demanding
(D) intensive

115. The football game was delayed 4 hours ------- account of heavy snow.

(A) for
(B) in
(C) on
(D) by

116. Of the ------- candidates who had applied for the position, only three were left for the final interview.

(A) much
(B) most
(C) more
(D) many

117. A social-media venture eventually recorded its greatest profits for the last quarter and ------- its competitors.

(A) to surpass
(B) surpassing
(C) was surpassed
(D) surpassed

118. It took ------- amount of effort on my part before Mr. Taylor finally agreed to let the project continue.

(A) an enormous
(B) a conservative
(C) a heavy
(D) a stable

119. Mr. Bennet got promoted to vice president not because of his age ------- because of his outstanding achievements.

(A) so
(B) or
(C) and
(D) but

120. The Andersons tried to ------- eating fast food, so they always brought healthy snacks with them when they traveled.

(A) avoid
(B) actualize
(C) attract
(D) accept

121. Please allow one week from the time of submission of your application for -------.

(A) approve
(B) approval
(C) approved
(D) approver

122. Thunderstorms are ------- likely to occur in the Midwestern states today as a cold front blows through the entire region.

(A) most
(B) few
(C) many
(D) some

123. Ms. Clooney updated the company's Web site by ------- because the person in charge was out of town on vacation.

(A) themselves
(B) himself
(C) itself
(D) herself

124. Ndjamena Coffee Trade Inc. has specialized ------- Ethiopian beans for decades and successfully led the market with its refined products.

(A) in
(B) at
(C) upon
(D) on

125. In order to ------- a group study room in the library, you need to follow the instructions in the student's guidebook.

(A) appoint
(B) contact
(C) reserve
(D) reply

126. Divlin Museum takes pride in its position as the most popular museum for three ------- years.

(A) success
(B) successful
(C) successive
(D) succeeding

127. BPI Group recently went ------- a massive reorganization after billions of dollars were wasted.

(A) through
(B) over
(C) around
(D) behind

128. We would like to remind you that this year's career fair will be ------- at The Mount Royal Hotel instead of The King Edward Hotel.

(A) holding
(B) holds
(C) held
(D) hold

GO ON TO THE NEXT PAGE

129. ------- we get booked up quickly during the summer holiday season, we strongly recommend you make a reservation early.

(A) If
(B) After
(C) When
(D) As

130. J&K Inc. and SGM Group plan to hold ------- negotiations on all the outstanding issues.

(A) intensive
(B) impressive
(C) instructive
(D) expensive

131. After having intervened in the FX market, the authorities are now considering ------- options to deal with the current account deficit.

(A) either
(B) another
(C) every
(D) other

132. The Faculty of Medicine in Duxton University got a ------- to the *Dental Journal*.

(A) description
(B) subscription
(C) legislation
(D) comprehension

133. YN Textile Company was established ------- recently and has been developing very fast in the last few years.

(A) relatively
(B) relative
(C) related
(D) relation

134. I'd appreciate it if you checked the content of the ------- document files I forwarded to you this morning.

(A) attached
(B) attach
(C) attaching
(D) to attach

135. The Consumer Confidence Index is still well below the historical average ------- income and job security have significantly improved.

(A) even though
(B) as a result of
(C) because of
(D) according to

136. We must ensure we meet the ------- by sharing workloads, or we will lose our credibility since competition is becoming fierce.

(A) deadline
(B) distribution
(C) proposal
(D) cancellation

137. ------, Michael has been recognized for his high skills and has become a section chief in just a year of service in the company.

(A) Amazed
(B) Amazing
(C) Amazingly
(D) Amazement

138. A new taxation law that passed Congress this spring will come into ------ next September.

(A) influence
(B) effect
(C) outcome
(D) result

139. Alamo Footwear offers the ------ selection of brand name shoes, boots and sandals in the U.K.

(A) widely
(B) widest
(C) wider
(D) more widely

140. In most instances, ------ a country begins to open its market to free trade, social and political freedoms soon follow.

(A) only
(B) once
(C) first
(D) soon

GO ON TO THE NEXT PAGE

PART 6

Directions: A word or phrase is missing in sentences in the texts. For each sentence, four answer choices are given below. Select the best answer to fill in the blank. You must mark your answer on the answer sheet.

Questions 141-143 refer to the following e-mail.

To: david@freshcakedesign.org
From: hallenguyen@cybertree.net
Subject: Modeling for your brand

Dear David,

I'm Halle Nguyen, a freelance model. I saw an article about your brand in the online design and fashion magazine *Up & Up* and am interested in modeling for you. Your clothes, ------- the T-shirts, are creative and cute and I think my look would

141. (A) especially
(B) naturally
(C) relatively
(D) regularly

------- well with your designs.
142. (A) stop
(B) get
(C) go
(D) run

I have five years of experience and ------- last November was a regular model for
143. (A) by
(B) until
(C) for
(D) in

the lifestyle magazine *Color/Life*. Attached are several photos of me, including pictures of a photo spread I did for July cover of *Color/Life*. I look forward to hearing from you.

Sincerely,
Halle

Questions 144-146 refer to the following notice.

Come Join Us at Our Annual Company Picnic

The season for the Annual Company Picnic is here!

When: Sept. 30 (Sat.) 11:00 A.M.-3:00 P.M.
Where: Ridgestone Park

This year, the Picnic Organizing Committee (that's us!) has specially invited Misty, the Magician to join us. She ------- a performance as well as making animal

144. (A) had given
(B) will be giving
(C) has been given
(D) was giving

balloons for the kids. We also have a variety of fun games and sports -------: face

145. (A) right up
(B) lined up
(C) brought up
(D) heads up

painting, tag football, mini-soccer, raffles and more!
For gourmet food lovers, Sawyer's is catering this year and the menu will include their famous Mexican tacos.
So ------- your family and friends for a day of fun! Reservations are necessary.

146. (A) carry out
(B) pick up
(C) bring along
(D) depend on

Sign up with Kathy at the Administrative Division by Sept. 5.

GO ON TO THE NEXT PAGE

Questions 147-149 refer to the following e-mail.

To: Brian Fuller
From: John Monroe
Date: June 30
Subject: Property in Buena Park

Dear Brian,

I am interested in the property at 5 Oak Avenue in Buena Park, advertised on renthow.org. According to the website, it will be available ------- August 31 and I

      147. (A) starting
           (B) start
           (C) to start
           (D) started

am hoping to move in September 14.
I'd be happy to see the property ------- my business trip to Buena Park shortly in

      148. (A) during
           (B) along
           (C) within
           (D) while

July.
I will be there from July 1 to July 5. Please let me know your schedule for showing the house during my stay.
Also, please ------- me a rental application as well, so I will have everything ready if

      149. (A) have
           (B) get
           (C) take
           (D) send

I do decide to rent.

Sincerely,
John Monroe

Questions 150-152 refer to the following article.

Original Wear to Develop New Women's Brand

Original Wear has just announced its plans ------- a new brand for women. The

150. (A) develop
(B) developed
(C) will develop
(D) to develop

brand will target the low-end market and will be sold exclusively at Drayton retail outlets next spring.
Items include apparel, footwear and bags. The company will unveil the ------- of its

151. (A) requirement
(B) summary
(C) celebration
(D) productivity

plans to work closely with Drayton before the details are disclosed next month. Sales of this brand ------- to grow continuously. Original Wear will take advantage

152. (A) are expected
(B) expect
(C) expected
(D) have expected

of the marketing potential of Drayton, especially anticipating a chance to tap into a part of the market others haven't.

GO ON TO THE NEXT PAGE

PART 7

Directions: In this part, you are asked to answer questions based on a variety of texts, such as notices, e-mails, memos, and articles. Select the best answer for each question and mark your answer on the answer sheet.

Questions 153-154 refer to the following Web page.

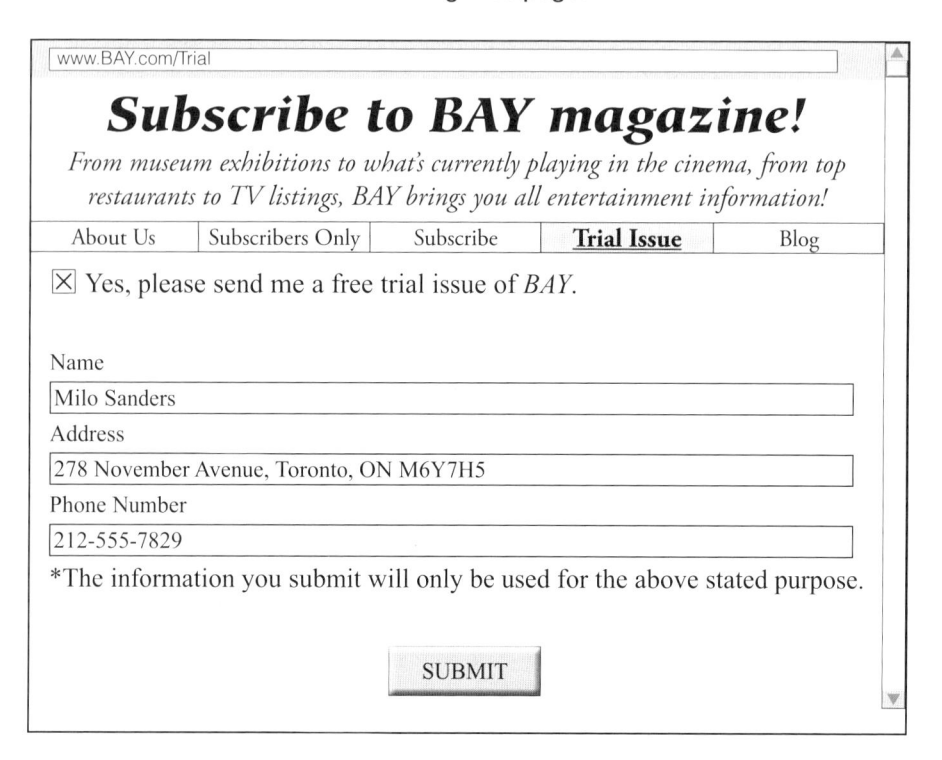

www.BAY.com/Trial

Subscribe to BAY magazine!

From museum exhibitions to what's currently playing in the cinema, from top restaurants to TV listings, BAY brings you all entertainment information!

| About Us | Subscribers Only | Subscribe | **Trial Issue** | Blog |

☒ Yes, please send me a free trial issue of *BAY*.

Name
Milo Sanders

Address
278 November Avenue, Toronto, ON M6Y7H5

Phone Number
212-555-7829

*The information you submit will only be used for the above stated purpose.

SUBMIT

153. What kind of topic does *BAY* magazine most likely cover?

(A) Business
(B) Technology
(C) Entertainment
(D) Fashion

154. What is implied about Mr. Sanders?

(A) He has started a subscription to *BAY*.
(B) He will get a free copy by mail.
(C) He will send an e-mail to the publisher.
(D) He has agreed to receive advertisements.

Questions 155-156 refer to the following e-mail.

To:	All first year employees
From:	Training Department
Subject:	Sales training
Date:	September 4

First year sales representatives will be required to attend an all-day sales training next Friday. The purpose of the training is to show you practical techniques to attract customers, get your message across, and to increase your chances of closing deals with them.

The training will consist of two sessions. A lecture in the morning introduces speaking methods. In the afternoon, a hands-on sales workshop features Patty Clark, our vice president of Sales, who had engaged in door-to-door sales for fifteen years. She will share her experiences and knowledge with new colleagues.

Please meet in the large conference room on the 2nd floor at 9:30 next Friday.

Sincerely,

Rachel Sanchez
Director, Training Department

155. What is the main purpose of the event?

(A) To introduce new technologies
(B) To instruct newcomers in sales methods
(C) To spread business strategies
(D) To renew contracts with customers

156. What is mentioned about Ms. Clark?

(A) She previously worked for another company.
(B) She has been training sales people for fifteen years.
(C) She had been selling products for a long time.
(D) She developed the company's sales methods.

GO ON TO THE NEXT PAGE

Questions 157-158 refer to the following letter.

Fairbanks Department Store
609 Stratton Street
Baltimore, MD 24242
August 30

To all our valued customers,

Thank you for shopping at Fairbanks Department Store.

This is to inform you that our flagship store will be reopening on October 1 after a lengthy refurbishment.

Our store on Stratton Street will expand its selling space to 500,000 sq. ft., making it our largest store. Each floor has been redesigned to ease your shopping, fitted with wider aisles and comfortable fitting rooms. The centerpiece of our flagship is a nursery with childcare professionals. This facility aims to support family-shopping leisure and will open on the children's floor.

With five new international brands mutually celebrating the opening, we will bring clothes from the world's fashion centers - London, Paris, Milan, and Tokyo - into our store.

Special events are lined up for the opening week and an invitation is forthcoming in days to come.

We hope our new store will give you more shopping pleasure than you can imagine.

Sincerely,

Robert Trent
CEO of Fairbanks Department Store

157. What is the main purpose of this letter?

(A) To invite guests to an opening ceremony
(B) To announce a temporal move to a different address
(C) To advertise worldwide clothing brands
(D) To attract customers to a reopened store

158. How can Fairbanks Department Store support family customers shopping?

(A) By providing sizeable and comfortable fitting rooms
(B) By providing childcare workers for babysitting services
(C) By resizing shopping space for more goods
(D) By contracting to produce clothes for different generations

Questions 159-160 refer to the following information.

WORLD-RENOWNED CHEF TO LEAD COOKING CLASS
Kulawy Brings a Touch of Spice To North Dallas

Mr. Ranjit Kulawy, 72-year-old owner of famous restaurants, such as Taj Mahal, Madras East, and Curry Palace will be holding a cooking class on February 19 at the North Dallas Community Center. The class is open to the public. Mr. Kulawy's class will focus on Indian cuisine, in particular curry, nan, and tandoori chicken. Mr. Kulawy will teach participants the essentials of making three different types of curry: spinach, bean (dal), and vegetable (tomato base). A resident of San Antonio and a strict vegetarian, Mr. Kulawy began cooking in his native Mumbai at the age of nine. He has worked at restaurants around the world and owned over a hundred restaurants, in cities such as Paris, London, Berlin, Moscow, Cairo, Tokyo, Beijing, Los Angeles, Houston, Mexico City, and Rio de Janeiro.

159. According to the information, what kind of event takes place on February 19?

(A) A table manners course
(B) A travel orientation
(C) A spice trade fair
(D) A culinary lesson

160. Where does Mr. Kulawy live?

(A) San Antonio
(B) Houston
(C) Dallas
(D) Mumbai

GO ON TO THE NEXT PAGE

Questions 161-163 refer to the following memo.

MEMO

From: Rickey Sanchez, HR
To: All Ostox employees
Date: October 12
Re: Food Drive

We are organizing a food drive next week! The theme of the food drive is "Fall Bounty" and the collected foods and goods will be donated to World Without Hunger (WWH), the local food bank. John Wiley, the head of WWH, has informed us that they are especially in need of canned vegetables and soup, printer paper, and dish soap.
We need a few people to set up a banner and a collection box for donations in every department by next Monday. Please contact Melanie in the Payroll Department if you are willing to help prepare for the event.

161. What is the main topic of the memo?

(A) An all-staff meeting
(B) A welfare activity
(C) A cooking event
(D) A new company rule

162. Who is John Wiley?

(A) A manager of a HR department
(B) A head of an organization
(C) A clerk at a local bank
(D) An owner of a grocery store

163. What is NOT requested by World Without Hunger?

(A) Housekeeping items
(B) Stationery
(C) Used clothing
(D) Preserved foods

GO ON TO THE NEXT PAGE

Questions 164-166 refer to the following notice.

Prima Trading Co.
Prima Tower
520 10th Avenue
New York,
NY 10018

Attention Prima Supermarket Customers!

We are introducing our Loyalty Card for use in all our 310 stores. Take advantage now and receive DOUBLE POINTS for a limited period on every one of our products.

This is a limited offer and will end in 6 weeks. Please complete the form if you agree to the privacy statement as detailed in the accompanying leaflet. The 'Terms and Conditions' is also included. Please sign and mail it back to us in the attached envelope for the premium membership.

☑ Please send me the Prima Loyalty Card.
☑ I have read and agreed to the privacy statement and the Terms and Conditions.

Name: Jenny Miller
Address: 1355 Oak Tree Road, Washington, 98109
Tel: 555-3111

Signature: *Jenny Miller*

164. What is NOT mentioned in the notice?

(A) Number of stores accepting the card
(B) Design of the loyalty card
(C) Promotion period
(D) Extra points per purchase

165. What does Prima Trading Co. ask customers to do?

(A) Send back a signed form
(B) Check its website for promotional codes
(C) Renew membership
(D) Write down current points

166. What is implied about Jenny Miller?

(A) She is sending a complaint.
(B) She is signing up for the program.
(C) She is redeeming bonus points.
(D) She is getting novelties.

GO ON TO THE NEXT PAGE

Questions 167-170 refer to the following e-mail.

From: Taisia Kaminski [Kaminski@archives-mg.com]
To: Louie Bombarger [Director@mg.com]
Subject: Corporate Archives
Date: January 31

Dear Louie,

In the last couple of weeks, the Archives Department has been receiving an unusually high volume of requests. As you can see from the data sheet I have attached, on some days we get as much as seventy requests per day. Our department simply does not have enough personnel to handle these.

I have been talking to Jiro Zhao in the IT Department, and he thinks he can come up with a program which lets the public access the archive files through the Internet. Since at the moment all the information materials are mailed physically instead of electronically, this kind of program will benefit both the public and staff in terms of time and effort. Also, it will significantly cut the cost of postage used to send out material.

I'd like to discuss this issue in more detail at our meeting on Thursday if there are no other pressing concerns.

Thanks,

Taisia Kaminski
Assistant Manager,
Archives Department

167. Why did Ms. Kaminski send the e-mail to Mr. Bombarger?

(A) To report a recent problem
(B) To describe an equipment malfunction
(C) To address an issue of the IT Department
(D) To complain about employee behavior

168. What is mentioned about the Archives Department?

(A) It lacks funding.
(B) It is understaffed.
(C) It has safety concerns.
(D) It is overcrowded.

169. Who most likely is Jiro Zhao?

(A) A public servant
(B) A computer programmer
(C) A delivery person
(D) An administrative assistant

170. What will be the main advantage of the suggested solution?

(A) The public won't have to send requests for archive material by mail.
(B) The company will make money by charging the public.
(C) The Archives Department will have doubled staff.
(D) It will take only one day to physically send requested materials.

GO ON TO THE NEXT PAGE

Questions 171-175 refer to the following memo.

MEMORANDUM - LAW OFFICES OF STEVENS & DOUGLASS
From: Management
To: All Attorneys and Staff

Due to certain changes in our health insurance coverage this year, the firm would like to announce a new employee fitness incentive.

As you may know, last year, as a result of reviewing the premium, we switched health insurance providers from Ball State (who provided us with insurance for over twenty years) to Gotham Life & Equity.

Gotham Life & Equity has announced a 25% rate cut for companies in which 75% or more of the employees join physical fitness clubs and engage in regular exercise for a minimum of 30 minutes per day, three days per week. Our biggest competitor, Steele & Wiggins, has already enrolled 80% of their employees in the plan.

With this in mind, we would like to offer all members of the firm and staff half-price memberships at Silver's Gym. Silver's Gym is conveniently located on the fifteenth floor of our building. It operates in convenient hours as well, opening at 5:30 A.M. and closing at 11:30 P. M. seven days a week. Silver's Gym has personal trainers, professional weight-lifting and aerobics facilities, as well as a sauna and a 25 meter indoor swimming pool.

171. What is the purpose of the memorandum?

(A) To encourage employees to exercise more
(B) To publicize an effective working policy
(C) To announce the merger with Steele & Wiggins
(D) To introduce the firm's newest client

172. Why did the firm switch health insurance providers?

(A) It introduced a new system.
(B) It failed to reach a long-term agreement.
(C) It merged with a conflicting insurance company.
(D) It reconsidered payment for insurance.

173. What is mentioned as an added benefit of the employee fitness program?

(A) Reduction in yearly electric bills
(B) Deducted premiums for implementation
(C) Lowered rates for regular health checkups
(D) Continuous increases in work-efficiency

174. In the memorandum, the word "competitor" in paragraph 3, line 4, is closest in meaning to

(A) entrepreneur
(B) interest
(C) rival
(D) administrator

175. What is NOT mentioned as a feature of Silver's Gym?

(A) Favorable opening hours
(B) Various course activities
(C) Accessible location
(D) Fully equipped facilities

GO ON TO THE NEXT PAGE

Questions 176-180 refer to the following advertisement.

Harrison's Vacation Ownership Program

Experience a luxurious vacation with first-class accommodation every year with Harrison's timeshare ownership system. Harrison's has over 30 five-star resorts around the world, and now, they are yours to enjoy. From the pristine beaches of the Bahamas to exotic destinations in Asia, you can travel around the world to your "own" home.

With Harrison's Vacation Ownership, you will have access to gorgeous 2- or 3-bedroom villas with beautiful living and dining rooms, fully equipped kitchens and 2-3 bathrooms with oversize tubs/showers. Most villas come with a scenic balcony, large enough for a family barbecue. A 2-bedroom villa will comfortably house 6-8 persons. Forget cramped hotel rooms. You and your family can now enjoy a dream vacation with plenty of space, while being pampered with high-quality service. Naturally, you will have access to all hotel facilities and services within each resort.

With timeshare, you will be prepaying for your future vacations. So, you will receive constant rates, irrespective of any changes in room rates in the future. Timeshares start at a minimum of one week each at two exciting destinations of your choice.

For more information, visit our Web site or call 1-800-555-8888.

176. What is the main purpose of this advertisement?

(A) To draw readers to relaxing spas
(B) To propose a long stay vacation to readers
(C) To promote outdoor lodges on the beach
(D) To guide readers in housing renovation

177. According to the advertisement, what is Harrison's?

(A) A hospitality enterprise
(B) A charter flight service
(C) A real estate agent
(D) A film production company

178. What is indicated about the accommodation?

(A) A luxurious twin room at a hotel resort
(B) A comfortable apartment near the city center
(C) A first-class condominium
(D) A multiple-room villa

179. What is NOT true about the Harrison's Vacation Ownership Program?

(A) It targets families and large groups.
(B) It is a package deal of hotels and meals.
(C) It requires payment in advance.
(D) It offers rooms in many destinations.

180. What does the advertisement say about the advantages of timeshare?

(A) Flexible check-out time
(B) Flat room rates any time
(C) Extra bonus points every stay
(D) No cancellation fees

GO ON TO THE NEXT PAGE

Questions 181-185 refer to the following itinerary and e-mail.

Itinerary for Mr. Michael Corwin
Vice President, I-Electronics

Welcome back to Hong Kong, Mike! We all are waiting for your official visit to our newest factory. Please see the itinerary that follows. Your entire schedule is arranged, including dinner in Tokyo. For more details on our Japanese connections, you may contact Ms. Nami Uchida, Personnel Department Chief, I-Electronics Tokyo.
If you would like to make any changes, please feel free to contact me.
(t_huang@iehongkong.com)

Mon:
    7:00 P.M. Arrive, Hong Kong International Airport (HKIA)
                Shuttle service to New Pearl Hotel

Tues:
    9:15 A.M. Visit Factory at Kwun Tong Industrial Centre.
                Ms. Fang, Factory Manager, will guide you around the facilities.
    4:00 P.M. Mr. Liu, Vice President I-Electronics Hong Kong, will welcome you in the lounge.
                A briefing with us at our Kowloon office followed by an evening banquet (location to be determined).

Wed:
    7:15 A.M. Morning Shuttle back to HKIA
                Flight to Tokyo
    11:20 A.M. Arrive, New Tokyo International Airport (Narita)
                Shuttle service to Shinjuku Central Hotel
    3:00 P.M. Visit I-Electronics Tokyo
                Ms. Nami Uchida, Personnel Department Chief
                She will meet you in the lobby and brief you on prospective clients.
    6:00 P.M. Dinner at Shabu Matsumoto
                With clients from Horikoshi Metals

Thurs:
                Free Time

Fri:
    4:00 P.M. Shuttle back to Narita Airport
                Flight to L.A.

Prepared by Thomas Huang
Secretary, I-Electronics Hong Kong

TO:	Thomas Huang <t_huang@iehongkong.com>
FROM:	Michael Corwin <m_corwin@ieamerica.com>
SUBJECT:	Itinerary
Date:	June 8

Dear Thomas,

Thank you for the schedule you sent. It seems perfect, except for a few modifications I may ask you to make. By the way, thanks to your introduction, I could speak with Ms. Uchida. Now, my arrangements in Tokyo are also all set.

We would like to be in Hong Kong Sunday evening and take time for sightseeing Monday. I hope you remember I am traveling with my wife, Karen. Although she will not be there on business, you should know she is also working for I-Electronics. I would greatly appreciate it if Karen could also join the banquet so you can get to know each other.

On another note, my cell phone should now be able to accept calls internationally. I can be reached at +1-310-555-0987.

I look forward to seeing you at the meeting.

Kind regards,

Michael

181. Why will Mr. Corwin visit Hong Kong?

   (A) To perform a yearly audit
   (B) To negotiate a project launching
   (C) To look around the latest plant
   (D) To discuss restructuring worldwide operations

182. Where will the banquet take place?

   (A) At New Pearl Hotel
   (B) At Mr. Liu's home
   (C) At Shabu Matsumoto
   (D) Undecided

183. According to the e-mail, what will change in the itinerary?

   (A) The attendee
   (B) The arrival date
   (C) Contact information
   (D) The return date

184. What is suggested about Mr. and Mrs. Corwin?

   (A) They want to participate in the factory tour.
   (B) They would like to attend the company meeting.
   (C) They want to socialize at the dinner party.
   (D) They need guides in Hong Kong.

185. On what day does Mr. Corwin say he will see Mr. Huang?

   (A) Sunday
   (B) Monday
   (C) Tuesday
   (D) Wednesday

GO ON TO THE NEXT PAGE

Questions 186-190 refer to the following letters.

June 25
Frank Richardson, M.D.
Ophthalmologist
Florentine General Hospital

Dear Dr. Richardson,

We would like to invite you to deliver a speech as the guest speaker at our health seminar in September. This will be held on Friday, September 15 from 1 P.M. to 3 P.M. in the Rose Ballroom at the Merlton Hotel. The event is expected to have a large turnout, more than 100 people.

First Sports is one of the largest fitness centers in Minnesota and certified as an approved physical therapy and rehabilitation provider. More than 500 people register as active members. As part of our mission to promote a healthy life-style, we host a health seminar once a month.

As the next one focuses on "Laser Eye Surgery," Dr. David Hudson recommended contacting you. He has also informed us of your extensive experience in laser eye surgery. We would like to conclude the gathering with an hour-long talk by you on this topic. While we usually select themes in advance, this particular issue is of current concern to our customers, many of whom, have expressed interest in the treatment. Recent reports on some well-known athletes who have undergone this procedure may perhaps draw everyone's attention to it.

In closing, we would be honored and pleased if you would be willing to be our speaker for the September event. If there is a conflict with your schedule, please let us know. We will make every effort to rearrange things within the stated time period.

We look forward to your reply.

Respectfully,

Stuart Harris
Event Coordinator
First Sports Co.

July 2
Stuart Harris
Event Coordinator
First Sports Co.

Dear Mr. Harris,

Thank you for your letter dated June 25.

I have heard of your health seminars from Dr. Hudson, and would be honored to talk about laser eye surgery.

On September 15, however, I need to fly to New York in the late afternoon, and have to leave the venue by 2:30 P.M. at the latest. I hope you would not mind my inflexible schedule.

Please call me on my cell phone at the following number so we may discuss the details: 054-555-2999.

Sincerely,

Frank Richardson, M.D.
Ophthalmologist

---

186. How often does First Sports organize health seminars?

(A) Weekly
(B) Monthly
(C) Annually
(D) Quarterly

187. Who usually chooses the subjects for the health seminars?

(A) Customers
(B) Event Organizers
(C) The general public
(D) Doctors

188. What does Mr. Harris think caused the increased interest in laser eye surgery?

(A) Broad insurance coverage, including the surgery
(B) Recent approval by a government body
(C) Increases in the number of qualified ophthalmologists
(D) Reports on famous sports players having the operation

189. Why does Dr. Richardson write to Mr. Harris?

(A) To arrange the schedule
(B) To change the topic of the seminar
(C) To negotiate the fee
(D) To recommend another expert in the field

190. What is suggested about Dr. Richardson's speech?

(A) It will be rescheduled to the morning.
(B) It will be held in a different location.
(C) It will be rearranged for a different day.
(D) It will be brought forward to the first half.

GO ON TO THE NEXT PAGE

Questions 191-195 refer to the following e-mail and advertisement.

To:	habrams@lotmail.com
From:	jgoldberg@tornioTA.com
Date:	October 12
Subject:	Re: Job Application

Dear Hafiza Abrams,

I'm responding to your e-mail inquiring about a contract worker. I am attaching an advertisement posted in the *Ontario Daily* this morning. Since you are looking for a position that provides flexible working hours, I thought some of the jobs here may be of interest to you.

I can see from your résumé that you have previously worked as a waitress at Max Café. I advise you to elaborate on this experience in your cover letter. If you need help writing your application, please call me at 555-8966 and we can arrange a time to meet.

Sincerely,
Joanna Goldberg
Tornio Temp Agency

El Vita Glass Museum

The following positions are currently available at El Vita Glass Museum:

<Museum>
Tour Guide
- Duties include providing guests with an extensive tour of the museum. On-site training will be provided. Must be fluent in English and Spanish. Other language skills are a plus.

<Museum Restaurant & Cafeteria>
Banquet Server
- Responsible for cleaning tables and serving guests. Various schedules are available, but may include weekends and holidays.

Prep Cook
- Must be able to follow written recipes and produce high-quality cold and warm dishes. More than 3 years of work experience required. Work hours are weekdays 11 A.M. to 9 P.M.

<Museum Gift Shop>
Sales Representative
- Responsible for handling money transactions and delivering product information to guests. Must have excellent communication skills. Knowledge of glass products is a plus. Various work shifts are available.

All employees receive free access to the Museum during open hours, as well as a discount at the Museum Gift Shop.

To apply, please send your résumé with salary requirements to:
Human Resources, El Vita Museum, 243 Triton Square,
Ottawa, Ontario K7T 5A6
or e-mail to: hr@elvita.org

191. Why did Ms. Goldberg send the e-mail?

(A) To respond to an application
(B) To apply for a part-time job
(C) To advertise an open position
(D) To help Ms. Abrams find employment

192. What does Ms. Abrams put stress on in her job search?

(A) Location
(B) Salary
(C) Job contents
(D) Hours on duty

193. What is mentioned in the advertisement?

(A) Applicants should call the Museum directly.
(B) All employees can receive complimentary food.
(C) Some staff may need to work on weekends.
(D) The institution provides external training programs.

194. According to the advertisement, what is required for the Tour Guide position?

(A) Linguistic proficiency
(B) Academic degrees
(C) Work experience
(D) Culinary skills

195. Which job will probably best suit Ms. Abrams?

(A) Tour Guide
(B) Banquet Server
(C) Prep Cook
(D) Sales Representative

GO ON TO THE NEXT PAGE

Questions 196-200 refer to the following article and e-mail.

City Hall Hardly Endures Weathering Damage

Costa Rosa, VI (June 15)— On May 25, the city council gathered for its preliminary meeting to discuss preservation plans. The accountants estimated the cost to be 2,500,000 dollars, more than a quarter of the yearly budget. Council members found it unrealistic for the city to cover the costs itself.

Local scholars held a series of conferences on the cultural and historical values of the building. Phillip Warhol, an archivist, emphasized the history of Clairville City Hall. His voice represents the tone of discussion among scholars, which focuses on the cultural monument as a symbol.

In the meantime, little attention has been drawn towards the redevelopment of the building and its neighboring district. Rachel Gordon, a pedestrian, who advocates the redevelopment plan, claimed, "Many other cities in the nation have successfully attracted sports teams, entertainment businesses, and, of course, fashion boutiques."

On June 14, the mayor summoned town residents to a series of meetings on the issue commencing June 26. All locals are welcome and eligible to attend the gatherings and are encouraged to speak out. For discussion topics or questions, please send an e-mail to mayor_30@costarosa.vi. Mayor Heath will reply.

FROM:	Robert Kendrick
TO:	Elizabeth Heath
SUBJECT:	Expert's Participation in Town Meetings
DATE:	June 18

Dear Ms. Heath,

My name is Robert Kendrick and I work at the Costa Rosa Art Museum as a painting specialist. For your information our museum has organized a workshop on the preservation of historical sites the past few days. As a result, I'd like to introduce you to a professional who has examined cost-efficient approaches in conservation, in the hope this will shed a light on the current Clairville City Hall issues.

Ms. Ming Wei Wang, who participated in the workshop, is known for her experience in preservation techniques applied to both Western and Eastern heritages. She is quite willing to discuss the city hall conservation plans. Hang Seng conservation, one of her projects in Vietnam, is appreciated for its quality of work within a tight budget. However, she does not meet the needs reported in the paper.

Thus, I would like to ask if she could share her expertise with us by attending the gatherings. If needed, her references can be provided. In any case, I'd appreciate it if you could reply me as soon as possible due to time constraints.

Sincerely,

Robert Kendrick

196. According to the article, what is the city's problem with its city hall?

 (A) Strong protests against preservation
 (B) Remodeling city's monuments
 (C) Financial limitations to its budget
 (D) Delays in construction

197. Who most likely is Phillip Warhol?

 (A) A council member
 (B) An architect
 (C) A representative of Costa Rosa
 (D) A historian

198. In the article, the word "neighboring" in paragraph 3, line 3, is closest in meaning to

 (A) traditional
 (B) expansive
 (C) adjacent
 (D) subordinate

199. What is the purpose of the e-mail?

 (A) To solicit support for the museum workshop
 (B) To undertake construction work
 (C) To promote new books written by experts
 (D) To introduce an excellent authority in the field

200. What is indicated about Ms. Ming Wei Wang?

 (A) She does not reside in Costa Rosa.
 (B) Her projects are highly regarded by Mayor Heath.
 (C) She needs to work on the site in Vietnam.
 (D) Her conservation plan was voted down by the council.

Stop! This is the end of the test. If you finish before time is called, you may go back to Parts 5, 6, and 7 check your work.